Modernization and Postmodernization

Modernization and Postmodernization

CULTURAL, ECONOMIC, AND

POLITICAL CHANGE IN 43 SOCIETIES

RONALD INGLEHART

PRINCETON UNIVERSITY PRESS

PRINCETON, NEW JERSEY

Library of Congress Cataloging-in-Publication Data

Inglehart, Ronald.
Modernization and postmodernization : cultural, economic, and
political change in 43 societies / Ronald Inglehart.
p. cm.
Includes bibliographical references (p.   ) and index.
ISBN 0-691-01181-8 (cloth : alk. paper). — ISBN 0-691-01180-X (pbk. : alk. paper)
1. Progress—Cross-cultural studies.   2. Political development—
Cross-cultural studies.   3. Economic development—Cross-cultural
studies.   4. Social change—Cross-cultural studies.   I. Title.
HM101.I554   1997
303.44—dc21   96-53839   CIP

This book has been composed in Times Roman expanded 5%

Princeton University Press books are printed on acid-free paper and meet the guidelines for
permanence and durability of the Committee on Production Guidelines for Book
Longevity of the Council on Library Resources

http:// pup.princeton.edu

Printed in the United States of America

1   2   3   4   5   6   7   8   9   10

2   3   4   5   6   7   8   9   10
(pbk)

THIS BOOK IS DEDICATED WITH LOVE TO

MY WIFE, MARITA, AND MY CHILDREN,

ELIZABETH, RACHEL, RONALD, AND MARITA

CONTENTS

ACKNOWLEDGMENTS

THIS BOOK WAS MADE POSSIBLE by the combined efforts of more than 80 principal investigators who carried out the World Values surveys in 43 societies. The author expresses his deep gratitude to Rasa Alishauskiene, Vladimir Andreyenkov, Soo Young Auh, David Barker, Miguel Basanez, Elena Bashkirova, Marek Boguszak, Pi-chao Chen, Marita Carballo de Cilley, Eric da Costa, Juan Diez Nicolas, Karel Dobbelaere, Mattei Dogan, Javier Elzo, Ustun Erguder, Yilmaz Esmer, Blanka Filipcova, Michael Fogarty, Luis de Franca, Christian Friesl, Yuji Fukuda, Ivan Gabal, Alec Gallup, George Gallup, Renzo Gubert, Peter Gundelach, Loek Halman, Elemer Hankiss, Stephen Harding, Gordon Heald, Felix Heunks, Carlos Huneeus, Kenji Iijima, J. C. Jesumo, Fridrik Jonsson, Ersin Kalaycioglu, Jan Kerkhofs, Hans-Dieter Klingemann, Renate Koecher, Marta Lagos, Max Larsen, Ola Listhaug, Jin-yun Liu, Nicolae Lotreanu, Leila Lotti, V. P. Madhok, Robert Manchin, Carlos Eduardo Meirelles Matheus, Anna Melich, Ruud de Moor, Neil Nevitte, Elisabeth Noelle-Neumann, Stefan Olafsson, Francisco Andres Orizo, R. C. Pandit, Juhani Pehkonen, Thorleif Petterson, Jacques-Rene Rabier, Andrei Raichev, Vladimir Rak, Helene Riffault, Ole Riis, Andrus Saar, Renata Siemienska, Kancho Stoichev, Kareem Tejumola, Noel Timms, Mikk Titma, Niko Tos, Jorge Vala, Andrei Vardomatski, Christine Woessner, Jiang Xingrong, Vladimir Yadov, Seiko Yamazaki, Catalin Zamfir, Brigita Zepa, Xiang Zongde, and Paul Zulehner. The World Values surveys build on the 1981 European Values Systems Survey directed by Jan Kerkhofs, Ruud de Moor, Juan Linz, Elisabeth Noelle-Neumann, Jacques-Rene Rabier, and Helene Riffault. Thanks are also due to Karlheinz Reif and Anna Melich of the Commission of the European Union, who directed the Euro-Barometer surveys which constitute another major data source. Finally, I would like to acknowledge the contributions made by my colleagues in the two-wave Political Action study, Samuel Barnes, Dieter Fuchs, Jacques Hagenaars, Felix Heunks, M. Kent Jennings, Max Kaase, Hans-Dieter Klingemann, Jacques Thomasson, and Jan Van Deth.

Chapter 5 builds on a long-term collaboration with Paul Abramson; a much more detailed analysis of the shift toward Postmaterialist values appears in our jointly authored book, *Value Change in Global Perspective* (1995). Chapters 6 and 7 draw on collaborative work with James Granato, David Leblang, and Sue Ellis. I wish to express my deep appreciation to Abramson, Ellis, Granato, and Leblang, who are co-authors of these chapters. This book benefited from criticism and suggestions from David Appel, Sylvia Evers, Judy Federbush and Marita Inglehart, and from extensive discussions with Kazufumi Manabe, with whom I am exploring Japanese political culture.

I am also indebted to a number of people who have written criticism of my work: their efforts stimulated me to rethink various aspects of social change, to carry out new analyses, and sometimes even to change my mind. I appreciate the contributions of Thomas Baldino, Ferdinand Boeltken, Wilhelm Buerklin, Harold Clarke, Russell Dalton, Raymond Duch, Nitish Dutt, Scott Flanagan, James Gibson, Nan Dirk de Graaf, Thomas Herz, Nobutaka Ike, Wolfgang Jagodzinski, Max Kaase, Helmut Klages, Markus Klein, Oddbjorn Knutsen, William Lafferty, Alan Marsh, Sidney Milkis, Edward Muller, Rafaella Nardi, Achim Russ, James Savage, Elinor Scarbrough, Mitchell Seligson, Michaell Taylor, Jacques Thomassen, Thomas Trump, Jan Van Deth, and others who provided stimulation and ideas through scholarly debate.

Data from both the World Values surveys and the Euro-Barometer surveys are available from the ICPSR survey data archive at the University of Michigan. The processing and documentation of these surveys was made possible by a National Science Foundation grant to the author, SES 91–22433. Thanks are due to Julio Borquez, Georgia Aktan, Alejandro Moreno, and Bettina Schroeder for skillful and effective research assistance, and to Judith Ottmar for outstanding secretarial and administrative assistance.

Modernization and Postmodernization

INTRODUCTION

CHANGING VALUES AND CHANGING SOCIETIES

DEEP-ROOTED CHANGES in mass worldviews are reshaping economic, political, and social life. This book examines changes in political and economic goals, religious norms, and family values, and it explores how these changes affect economic growth rates, political party strategies, and the prospects for democratic institutions.

Throughout advanced industrial society, freedom of expression and political participation are becoming increasingly important to a growing share of the public. The literature on democratic theory suggests that mass participation, interpersonal trust, tolerance of minority groups, and free speech are important to the consolidation and stability of democracy. But until recently it has not been possible to analyze the linkages between individual-level attitudes such as these and the persistence of democratic institutions at the societal level: most of the research on political culture has been limited to democratic societies, with a small number of cases and little or no time series data. Reliable cross-level analysis requires data from a large number of societies that vary across the full economic and political spectrum. This book draws on a unique database, the World Values surveys, which opens up new possibilities for analyzing how peoples' worldviews influence the world.

These surveys cover a broader range of variation than has ever before been available for analyzing the impact of mass publics on political and social life. They provide data from 43 societies representing 70 percent of the world's population and covering the full range of variation, from societies with per capita incomes as low as $300 per year to societies with per capita incomes 100 times that high, and from long-established democracies with market economies to authoritarian states and ex-socialist states. The 1990 wave of this survey was carried out in Argentina, Austria, Belarus, Belgium, Brazil, Bulgaria, Canada, Chile, China, Czechoslovakia, Denmark, Estonia, Finland, France, Germany (with separate samples in the East and West regions), Great Britain, Hungary, Iceland, India, Ireland, Northern Ireland, Italy, Japan, South Korea, Latvia, Lithuania, Mexico, greater Moscow, the Netherlands, Nigeria, Norway, Poland, Portugal, Russia, Romania, Slovenia, South Africa, Spain, Sweden, Switzerland, Turkey, and the United States. The 1981 surveys provide time series data for 22 of these societies, enabling us to analyze the changes in values and attitudes that took place from 1981 to 1990. Figure 0.1 shows the countries covered in these surveys. We also analyze data from the Euro-Barometer surveys, carried out annually in all member countries of the European Union from 1970 to the 1990s; this provides a longer and more detailed time series with which to analyze change.

The World Values survey measures mass attitudes in a sufficiently large number of countries so that it is possible to carry out statistically significant analyses of cross-level linkages, such as those between political culture and democratic institutions. We find remarkably strong linkages between macro-level characteristics such as stable democracy, and micro-level characteristics, such as trust, tolerance, Postmaterialist values, and subjective well-being among individuals. Many other important societal-level variables—ranging from divorce rates to the emergence of environmentalist movements—also show strong cross-level linkages with underlying values and attitudes. One could argue that cultural changes are caused by societal changes, or that cultural changes are contributing to societal changes, or that the influences are reciprocal; but these data make it clear that mass belief systems and global change are intimately related.

The World Values surveys explore the hypothesis that mass belief systems are changing in ways that have important economic, political, and social consequences. We do not assume either economic or cultural determinism: our findings suggest that the relationships between values, economics, and politics are reciprocal, and the exact nature of the linkages in given cases is an empirical question, rather than something to be decided a priori.

The design of these surveys was influenced by various theories, including a theory of intergenerational value change (Inglehart, 1971, 1977, 1990). They explore the hypothesis that, as a result of the rapid economic development and the expansion of the welfare state that followed World War II, the formative experiences of the younger birth cohorts in most industrial societies differed from those of older cohorts in fundamental ways that were leading them to develop different value priorities. Throughout most of history, the threat of severe economic deprivation or even starvation has been a crucial concern for most people. But the historically unprecedented degree of economic security experienced by the postwar generation in most industrial societies was leading to a gradual shift from "Materialist" values (emphasizing economic and physical security above all) toward "Postmaterialist" priorities (emphasizing self-expression and the quality of life). Evidence of intergenerational value change began to be gathered cross-nationally in 1970; a long time series has now been built up with which to test these hypotheses.

This theory has been controversial: during the past 20 years, scores of critiques of various aspects of the theory have been published in this country and abroad. Much of the research on value change has been designed to disprove the thesis of a Postmaterialist shift or to propose alternative explanations of why this shift is occurring.

Some of the conceptualization underlying this debate is outdated: evidence from the World Values surveys indicates that the shift toward Materialist/Postmaterialist values is only one component of a much broader cultural shift. About 40 of the variables included in these surveys seem to be involved in this shift. These variables tap a variety of orientations from religious outlook to sexual norms; but they all display large generational differences, are strongly correlated with Postmaterialist values, and in most societies moved in a predictable direction from 1981 to 1990. We use the label "Postmodernization" to describe this pervasive change in worldviews. The shift from Materialist to Postmaterialist values is by far the best documented component of this broader cultural change, but it is not necessarily the most important one: changing gender roles and changes in attitudes toward gays and lesbians have been even more dramatic.

The evidence accumulated so far indicates that pervasive changes are taking place in basic values of the publics of industrialized and industrializing societies throughout the world. Moreover, these changes seem to be linked with intergenerational population replacement processes, which means that they are gradual but have a good deal of long-term momentum.

This book argues that economic development, cultural change, and political change go together in coherent and even, to some extent, predictable patterns. This is a controversial claim. It implies that some trajectories of socioeconomic change are more likely than others—and consequently, that certain changes are foreseeable. Once a society has embarked on industrialization, for example, a whole syndrome of related changes, from mass mobilization to diminishing differences in gender roles, are likely to occur.

This, of course, is the central claim of Modernization theory; it was proposed by Marx and has been debated for well over a century. Although any simplistic version of this claim has long since been exploded, we *do* endorse the idea that some scenarios of social change are far more probable than others—and we will present a good deal of empirical evidence supporting this proposition. The World Values surveys reveal coherent cultural patterns that are closely linked with economic development.

At the same time, it seems clear to us that Modernization is not linear. In advanced industrial societies, the prevailing direction of development has changed in the last quarter century, and the change in what is happening is so fundamental that it seems appropriate to describe it as "Postmodernization" rather than "Modernization."

Modernization is, above all, a process that increases the economic and political capabilities of a society: it increases economic capabilities through industrialization, and political capabilities through bureaucratization. Modernization is widely attractive because it enables a society to move from being poor, to being rich. Accordingly, the core process of Modernization is industrialization; economic growth becomes the dominant societal goal, and achievement motivation becomes the dominant individual-level goal. The transition from preindustrial society to industrial society is characterized by "the pervasive rationalization of all spheres of society" (as Weber put it), bringing a shift from Traditional, usually religious values, to Rational-Legal values in economic, political, and social life.

But Modernization is not the final stage of history. The rise of advanced industrial society leads to another fundamentally different shift in basic values—one that de-emphasizes the instrumental rationality that characterized industrial society. Postmodern values become prevalent, bringing a variety of societal changes, from equal rights for women to democratic political institutions and the decline of state socialist regimes. The emergence of this Postmodern value syndrome is described in the following chapters.

This book demonstrates that there are powerful linkages between belief systems and political and socioeconomic variables such as democracy or economic growth rates. It also demonstrates coherent and to some extent predictable patterns of change in values and belief systems. These changes in worldviews reflect changes in the economic and political environment, but they take place with a generational time lag and have considerable autonomy and momentum of their own. Major cultural changes are occurring. They have global implications that are too important to ignore.

Value Systems: The Subjective Aspect of Politics and Economics

MODERNIZATION AND POSTMODERNIZATION

Economic, cultural, and political change go together in coherent patterns that are changing the world in predictable ways.

This has been the central claim of Modernization theory, from Karl Marx to Max Weber to Daniel Bell. The claim has given rise to heated debate during the last two centuries. This book presents evidence that this claim is largely correct: though we cannot predict exactly what will happen in a given society at a given time, some major trends are predictable in broad outline. When given processes of change are set in motion, certain characteristics are likely to emerge in the long run.

The idea that social and economic change go together on coherent trajectories has been attractive but controversial ever since it was proposed by Marx. It is intellectually exciting because it not only helps *explain* economic, social, and political change, but may even provide a certain degree of predictability. So far, most efforts at prediction in human affairs have been exercises in hubris; it is common knowledge that many of Marx's predictions were wrong. Human behavior is so complex and influenced by such a wide range of factors, operating on so many levels, that any claim to provide precise, unqualified predictions is likely to go unfulfilled.

We do not make such promises: one cannot foretell the precise course of social change. Nevertheless, certain syndromes of economic, political, and cultural changes go together in coherent trajectories, with some trajectories being more probable than others. In the long term, across many societies, once given processes are set in motion, certain important changes are likely to happen. Industrialization, for example, tends to bring increasing urbanization, growing occupational specialization, and higher levels of formal education in any society that undertakes it (Lerner, 1958; Deutsch, 1964). These are core elements of a trajectory that is generally called "Modernization."

This trajectory also tends to bring less obvious but equally important long-term consequences, such as rising levels of mass political participation. Thus, although we cannot predict the actions of specific leaders in given countries, we *can* say that (at this point in history) mass input to politics is likelier to play a decisive role in Sweden or Japan than in Albania or Burma. And we can even specify, with far better than random success, what issues are likely to be most salient in the politics of the respective types of societies.

The Modernization trajectory is linked with a wide range of other cultural changes. As we will see, certain cultural values are conducive to the economic accumulation and investment that make industrialization possible, and the sharply contrasting gender roles that characterize all preindustrial societies almost inevitably give way to increasingly similar gender roles in advanced industrial society.

But social change is not linear. Although a specific Modernization syndrome of changes becomes probable when societies move from an agrarian mode to an industrial mode, no trend goes on in the same direction forever. It eventually reaches a point of diminishing returns. Modernization is no exception. In the past few decades, advanced industrial societies have reached an inflection point and begun moving on a new trajectory that might be called "Postmodernization."

With Postmodernization, a new worldview is gradually replacing the outlook that has dominated industrializing societies since the Industrial Revolution. It reflects a shift in what people want out of life. It is transforming basic norms governing politics, work, religion, family, and sexual behavior. Thus, the process of economic development leads to two successive trajectories, Modernization and Postmodernization. Both of them are strongly linked with economic development, but Postmodernization represents a later stage of development that is linked with very different beliefs from those that characterize Modernization. These belief systems are not mere consequences of economic or social changes, but shape socioeconomic conditions and are shaped by them, in reciprocal fashion.

Modernization Theory: The Linkages between
Culture, Economics, and Politics

The study of Modernization played a major role in social science in the late 1950s and early 1960s. Severely criticized subsequently, since the 1970s the Modernization concept has been widely considered discredited. As Pye (1990) has argued, it may be time to reexamine it. This chapter does so, presenting new empirical evidence and proposing a modified view of how Modernization works.

The central claim of Modernization theory is that industrialization is linked with specific processes of sociopolitical change that apply widely: though preindustrial societies vary immensely, one can meaningfully speak of a model of "modern" or "industrial" society toward which all societies tend to move if they commit themselves to industrialization. Economic development is linked with a syndrome of changes that includes not only industrialization, but also urbanization, mass education, occupational specialization, bureaucratization, and communications development, which in turn are linked with still broader cultural, social, and political changes.

One reason why Modernization theory aroused such great interest was its promise of predictive power: it implied that once a society entered the trajectory of industrialization, certain types of cultural and political change were likely to take place, ranging from lower birth rates to greater penetration by government, higher life expectancies, increased mass political participation, and perhaps even democracy. Some critics caricatured Modernization theory as implying that economic development would easily and automatically produce liberal democracies, and they dismissed this outlook as naive ethnocentrism. In fact, most Modernization theorists made more qualified prognoses than this, but if we drop the gratuitous assumption that Modernization is easy and automatic, even this claim does not seem totally implausible today.

Modernization theory has been developing for over a century. A wide variety of social theorists have argued that technological and economic changes are linked with coherent and predictable patterns of cultural and political change. But there has been continuing debate over the causal linkages: does economic change cause cultural and political change, or does it work in the opposite direction?

Marx emphasized economic determinism, arguing that a society's technological level shapes its economic system, which in turn determines its cultural and political characteristics: given the technological level of the windmill, a society will be based on subsistence agriculture, with a mass of impoverished peasants dominated by a landed aristocracy; the steam engine brings an industrial society in which the bourgeoisie becomes the dominant elite, exploiting and repressing an urban proletariat.

Weber, on the other hand, emphasized the impact of culture: it was not just an epiphenomenon of the economic system, but an important causal factor in itself; culture can shape economic behavior, as well as being shaped by it. Thus, the emergence of the Protestant Ethic facilitated the rise of capitalism, which contributed to both the Industrial Revolution and the Democratic Revolution: this view held that belief systems influence economic and political life, as well as being influenced by them.

Some of Marx's successors shifted the emphasis from economic determinism (which suggests that the revolutionary Utopia will come spontaneously) toward greater emphasis on the impact of ideology and culture. Thus Lenin argued that by itself, the working class would never develop sufficient class consciousness for a successful revolution; they needed to be led by an ideologically aware vanguard of professional revolutionaries.

Mao emphasized the power of revolutionary thinking even more strongly. Breaking with Marxist orthodoxy, he held that China need not wait for the processes of urbanization and industrialization to transform it; if an ideologically committed cadre could instill sufficient enthusiasm among the Chinese masses, a communist revolution could succeed even in an agrarian society. Mao's faith in the power of ideological fervor to triumph over material obstacles seemed justified by the Chinese communist victory in 1949 over forces with vastly superior financial resources and manpower. On the other hand, the fact that ideological determinism has limits was demonstrated by the disastrous failure of the Great Leap Forward in 1959: to develop a complex society, it seems, one needs experts with specialized knowledge, as well as right-thinking masses. When building a drainage system or constructing a steel mill, there are ways that work and ways that do not work, regardless of one's ideological perspective.

While conceding an important role to cultural factors, recent Modernization theorists such as Bell (1973) viewed changes in the structure of the workforce as the leading cause of cultural change. For Bell, the crucial milestone in the coming of "Postindustrial society" is reached when a majority of the workforce is in the tertiary sector of the economy, producing neither raw materials, nor manufactured goods, but services. This leads to a massive expansion of formal education, driven by the need for an increasingly skilled and specialized workforce. Other writers such as Lerner (1958) and Inkeles and Smith (1974) emphasized the importance of formal education as the main factor shaping a "modern" worldview.

Does Modernization lead to democracy? In the late 1950s, Khrushchev's reforms gave rise to hopes that the communist bloc might be on the brink of democratizing. The emergence of scores of newly independent postcolonial nations in the 1960s intensified these hopes. But optimism collapsed after the communist elite drove Khrushchev from power in 1964, the Soviet world settled down into a seemingly permanent authoritarian regime under Brezhnev, and authoritarian regimes took over in most postcolonial nations. Rostow (1961) had argued that economic development was inherently conducive to democratization, but by the 1970s most social scientists were skeptical of the idea. Authoritarian regimes seemed to be a permanent feature of the world—even (or perhaps especially) in those communist states that had achieved impressive economic growth. Industrialization could give rise to either democracy or dictatorship.

We propose a revised view of Modernization theory. We agree with the Modernization theorists on their most central point: that economic development, cultural change, and political change are linked in coherent and even, to some extent, predictable patterns. Some trajectories of change are more probable than others because certain configurations of values and beliefs, and political and economic institutions, are mutually supportive—while others are not. Thus, if one knows one component of a society, one can predict what other components will be present with far better than random success.

But while we follow Marx, Weber, and their successors in believing that change tends to take predictable rather than random trajectories, we differ from most Modernization theorists on four essential points:

1. Change is not linear. It does not move in one continuous direction until the end of history. Instead, it eventually reaches points of diminishing returns and has begun to move in a fundamentally new direction during the past few decades.

2. Previous versions of Modernization theory were deterministic, with the Marxist version tending toward economic determinism and the Weberian version sometimes tending toward cultural determinism. We believe that the relationships between economics and culture and politics are mutually support-

ive, as are the various systems of a biological organism. It would be senseless to ask whether the behavior of the human body is "really" determined by the muscular system, the circulatory system, the nervous system, or the respiratory system: each plays an essential role, and all activity ceases if any of them breaks down. Similarly, political systems and economic systems require a supportive cultural system—otherwise they would need to rely on naked coercion, which almost never endures for long. Conversely, a cultural system that was incompatible with its economic system would be unlikely to endure. Economic determinism, cultural determinism, and political determinism are *all* oversimplified: the causal linkages tend to be reciprocal. Unless these systems are mutually supportive, they are unlikely to survive.

3. We reject the ethnocentric perspective of those who equated Modernization with "Westernization": At one point in history, Modernization *was* concentrated in the West; today it is evident that the process is global, and that in some ways East Asia is now leading the process of Modernization. In keeping with this outlook, we propose a modified interpretation of Weber's (1904–5) thesis concerning the role of the Protestant Ethic in economic development. Weber was correct in viewing the rise of Protestantism as a crucial event in the Modernization of Europe. However, its impact was not unique to Protestantism but was mainly due to the fact that its acquisitive rationality supplanted a set of religious norms that are common to most preindustrial societies and that inhibit economic achievement. Protestantism was uniquely Western, but acquisitive rationality is not. Although industrialization occurred first in the West, the rise of the West was only one version of Modernization.

4. Democracy is not inherent in the Modernization phase, as some Modernization theorists suggested. There are alternative outcomes, with fascism and communism being the most prominent alternatives as Moore (1966) has pointed out. But democracy *does* become increasingly likely as societies move beyond the Modernization phase into Postmodernization. In the Postmodern phase, a distinctive syndrome of changes occur that make democracy increasingly likely—to the point where it eventually becomes costly to avoid.

We have stated four ways in which our view—which might be termed Postmodernization theory—differs from Modernization theory. Let us provide more detail on these points. Chapter 3 will present empirical evidence that supports the central claim underlying both Modernization theory and Postmodernization theory: that technological and economic changes tend to be linked with specific types of cultural, political, and social change. In other words, history tends to move in coherent and to some extent predictable patterns.

Socioeconomic Change Is Not Linear

The prevailing direction of development has changed in the last quarter century, and this shift is so distinctive that, rather than continuing to use the term "Modernization," we prefer to speak of "Postmodernization." The term "Postmodern" has been used with scores of different meanings, some of which are associated with a cultural relativism so extreme that it approaches cultural determinism: it asserts that culture shapes human experience almost entirely, unlimited by any external reality. Nevertheless, the term conveys an important insight, suggesting that the process known as Modernization is no longer at the cutting edge, and that social change is now moving in a fundamentally different direction. Moreover, the literature on Postmodernism suggests some of the specific attributes of this new direction: it is a move away from the emphasis on economic efficiency, bureaucratic authority, and scientific rationality that characterized Modernization, toward a more human society with more room for individual autonomy, diversity, and self-expression.

Unfortunately, the word "Postmodern" has become loaded with so many meanings that it is in danger of conveying everything and nothing. In architecture, the term has a clear meaning, designating a style of architecture that departs strikingly from the bare functionalism of "modern" architecture, which had become sterile and aesthetically repelling. The first glass box was a stunning tour de force, but by the one-hundredth box, the novelty had worn thin. Postmodern architecture reintroduced a human scale, with touches of adornment and references to the past, but incorporating new technology. In a similar vein, we suggest that Postmodern society is moving away from the standardized functionalism and the enthusiasm for science and economic growth that dominated industrial society during an era of scarcity—giving more weight to aesthetic and human considerations and incorporating elements of the past into a new context.

Neither Cultural Determinism Nor Economic Determinism

We disagree with the cultural determinism that is sometimes linked with the concept of Postmodernism. Postmodern writers are certainly correct in thinking that everyone perceives reality through some kind of cultural filter. Moreover, these cultural factors are steadily becoming a more *important* component of experience as we move from societies of scarcity, in which economic necessity limits one's behavior rather narrowly, to a world in which human will increasingly prevails over the external environment, allowing broader room for individual choice: this is a major reason why the Postmodern perspective has become increasingly credible.

But we reject the notion that cultural construction is the *only* factor shaping human experience. There is an objective reality out there too, and it applies to social relations as well as to natural science. External reality is crucial when it comes to the ultimate political resource, violence: when you shoot someone, that person dies regardless of whether he or she believes in ballistics or bullets. Similarly, though an architect has considerable scope for choice and imagination, if one forgets objective engineering principles, the building may collapse. Partly for this reason, architecture has preserved a healthy respect for reality. Similarly again, among physicists and astronomers, cultural biases play a minimal role. Despite some nonscientists' garbled references to the Heisenberg uncertainty principle, there is a worldwide consensus among natural scientists that they are studying a reality that exists independently of their preconceptions;[1] a theory eventually triumphs or is rejected depending on how well it models and predicts that reality—even if it violates people's long-standing beliefs.

The fact that some Postmodern writers' grasp of the physical sciences is a bit shaky was demonstrated rather strikingly in 1996, when Alan Sokal, a physicist irked with Postmodernist claims that objective reality had dissolved in the physical sciences, submitted an article to *Social Text*, one of this school's leading reviews. His article, entitled "Transgressing the Boundaries: Toward a Transformative Hermeneutics of Quantam Gravity," began: "There are many natural scientists, and especially physicists, who . . . cling to the dogma . . . that there exists an external world, whose properties are independent of any individual human being. . . . It has thus become increasingly apparent that physical 'reality,' no less than social 'reality,' is at bottom a social and linguistic construct; that scientific 'knowledge,' far from being objective, reflects and encodes the dominant ideologies and power relations of the culture that produced it" (Sokal, 1996: 217–18).

Though the text that followed was full of nonsense, this viewpoint was all too congenial to many Poststructuralists. Sokol went on to solemnly proclaim a long series of palpable absurdities about physical reality, including claims that the force of gravity and pi were socially constructed.

According to the *New York Times* account, this article was reviewed by a half dozen members of the review's editorial board, none of whom seemed to realize that the piece was a broad self-parody; they caught on shortly after the article was published, when the author himself revealed that it was a hoax.

This is not the first time that an august body has taken pi to be a social construct. In the nineteenth century, the Indiana state legislature passed a resolution officially declaring that pi would henceforth be a round 4.0, instead of the

---

[1] The Heisenberg principle is often misread as indicating that the laws of physics do not really govern the universe, which is fundamentally disorderly and unpredictable. At the ultimate level of smallness, the universe *is* probabilistic, not deterministic. Thus, the behavior of individual photons is unpredictable. But large numbers of photons behave in ways that are indistinguishable from being deterministic; and since human beings normally only deal with enormous numbers of photons, the behavior of light can be predicted very accurately by deterministic physical laws.

Other laws of physics are also slight oversimplifications of reality. For example, though the laws of gases say otherwise, it is conceivable that all of the air molecules in the reader's vicinity could suddenly rush to the far end of the room and remain there until you died a horrible death. The reader need not worry. This is technically possible, but the probability is so overwhelmingly low that it would not be expected to occur even once during the entire lifetime of the universe (or even in many lifetimes of the universe). At the microlevel, the universe is probabilistic; this is a very significant fact. But it is extremely misleading to leap from this fact to the conclusion that Newton and Avogadro had it all wrong, and that the universe is disorderly and your brain could spontaneously explode at any moment. Technically, it could. But it's not likely to happen until long after the sun and the stars have all disappeared from the sky.

inconvenient 3.1416; but this may be the first time that the proposition has been accepted by a panel of Ph.D.'s.

Despite this bit of entrapment, Postmodern thinkers are making a valid and profoundly important point in emphasizing that everyone's perception of reality is shaped by his or her subjective values and preconceptions. Moreover, these factors help shape even natural scientists' perceptions of reality—though not quite to the extent that some Postmodernists seem to think it does.

As Kuhn (1962) pointed out, objective tests alone do not immediately cause an entire scientific paradigm to be rejected; as inconsistent observations accumulate, the dominant paradigm may increasingly be called into question and new explanations proposed, but the new paradigm generally comes to be accepted through intergenerational replacement of scientists, more than through conversion of the older scientists. This reflects the fact that the cognitive structures of the older generation are organized around the old paradigm; it is far easier for the new generation to integrate their thinking according to the new paradigm than it is for the older generation, which would have to dismantle elaborate cognitive structures of inconsistent previous learning. At any given time, natural science reflects a cross-cultural consensus depending, ultimately, on how well given interpretations model and predict an external reality. The fine arts are at the opposite extreme. Aesthetic preferences largely *are* a matter of cultural predispositions.

Social phenomena fall between these extremes. Human behavior is heavily influenced by the culture in which one has been socialized. But objective factors set limits too, a recent example being the collapse and abandonment of state-run economies from Czechoslovakia to China: in running an economy, there are ways that work and ways that do not work.

Nevertheless, the term "Postmodern" is potentially useful: it implies that social change has moved beyond the instrumental rationality that was central to Modernization and is now taking a fundamentally different direction. This book does not discuss in any detail the various writers who have been labeled Postmodern: it is not about them. It deals with a set of empirical changes that are taking place among mass publics and will examine some specific ways in which the direction of social change has shifted. They include the fact that, while Modernization was not necessarily linked with democratization, Postmodernization *does* seem to be inherently conducive to the emergence of democratic political institutions.

Functional Analysis and Predictable Syndromes of Change

Economic, cultural, and political change go together in coherent patterns. The two most influential proponents of Modernization theory, Marx and Weber, agreed on this point. They disagreed profoundly on *why* economic, cultural, and political changes go together. For Marx and his disciples, they are linked because economic and technological change determines political and cultural changes. For Weber and his disciples, they are linked because culture shapes economic and political life.

Both Marx and Weber had major insights. We believe that economics shapes culture and politics—*and* vice versa. The causal linkages tend to be reciprocal. Political, economic, and cultural changes go together because societies without mutually supportive political, economic, and cultural systems are unlikely to survive for long: in the long run, the respective components either adapt to each other or the system flounders. And systems do indeed flounder: most of the societies that have ever existed are now extinct.

A culture is a system of attitudes, values, and knowledge that is widely shared within a society and is transmitted from generation to generation. While human nature is biologically innate and universal, culture is learned and varies from one society to another. The more central and early learned aspects of culture are resistant to change, both because it requires a massive effort to change central elements of an adult's cognitive organization, and because abandoning one's most central beliefs produces uncertainty and anxiety. In the face of enduring shifts in socioeconomic conditions, even central parts of culture may be transformed, but they are more likely to change through intergenerational population replacement than by the conversion of already socialized adults.

By culture, we refer to the *subjective* aspect of a society's institutions: the beliefs, values, knowledge, and skills that have been *internalized* by the people of a given society, complementing their external systems of coercion and exchange. This is a narrower definition of culture than is generally used in anthropology, because our purpose here is empirical analysis. We will examine the degree to which internal cultural orientations and external social institutions are linked empirically, rather than simply assume that they are. Building everything into one's definition of culture would make the concept useless for this type of analysis.

Any stable economic or political system has a compatible and supportive cultural system which legitimates that system. The people of that society have internalized a set of rules and norms. If they had not, the rulers could only get their subjects to comply with their rules by external coercion, which is costly and insecure. Moreover, to be effective in legitimating the system, cultures set limits to elite as well as mass behavior—shaping the political and economic systems, as well as being shaped by them. The process is not teleological, but it operates as if it were: societies with legitimate authority systems are more likely to survive than those without them.

Like Axelrod (1984), we find the evolutionary perspective a useful way to analyze how cultures and institutions develop: certain characteristics survive and spread because they have functional advantages in a given environment. Elster (1982) argues that functionalist interpretations of institutions are fundamentally flawed because they anthropomorphize institutions, postulating a purpose without a purposive actor—a view that has become widely accepted. But this criticism actually only applies to a crude and naive type of functionalist interpretation. Biologists today regularly use functionalist interpretations, especially when dealing with evolution. For example, plants are said to have developed bright flowers and nectar in order to attract bees so that the bees will fertilize them. Other plants are said to have developed poisonous leaves to discourage animals and insects from eating them. The newly hatched cuckoo chick pushes the other eggs out of the nest so that the parent birds will devote all their efforts to nourishing the cuckoo. And mammals living in the far North have developed white fur in order to be less visible against the snow.

Although they use this interpretation, neither biologists nor social scientists accept the crude teleological assumptions that Elster attributes to functional analysis. This mode of explanation is not used because biologists think that flowers or newly hatched cuckoos are consciously planning ahead or because they believe that evolution is guided by an anthropomorphic force. They use it because it is the most direct and parsimonious way to discuss the interaction between random mutations and natural selection that causes most mutations to die out—except for those with some functional advantage that enhances the organism's chances for survival. The mutations do not occur in order to serve some function; but they survive and spread because they do. A similar principle applies to functional interpretations of society. Dawkins (1989) argues convincingly that cultural traits or "memes" that function relatively well in a given environment replicate and spread for the same basic reason as do genes: they confer a survival advantage. Axelrod (1984) has demonstrated that certain strategies of conflict or cooperation function better than others and eventually drive out competing strategies.

Among the numerous types of societies that ever existed, the great majority have disappeared and the process is still going on. At the start of the twentieth century, absolute monarchy was the most widespread form of government. Today it has dwindled to a handful of surviving cases. Fascism spread rapidly in the 1920s and 1930s, and then all but disappeared in the 1940s, with a few loosely fascistic regimes surviving until the 1970s. The most recent case of mass extinction among societies has been the sudden collapse of communist regimes, which until recently controlled one-third of the world's population. Authoritarian state-run economies proved to be unworkable and uncompetitive in a high-technology environment. Although many of the ex-communist societies are still run by ex-communist elites, even the hard-liners among them are unlikely to return to the Stalinist model: it is a type of society that eventually proved to be dysfunctional.

Political institutions are also shaped by processes of natural selection. Some institutions survive for long periods, but most do not: three-quarters of the national constitutions now in effect were written since 1965. And even the surviving institutions undergo mutations. Thus, legislatures no longer initiate much legislation in most societies, but they do fill a legitimating function. Legislatures themselves do not possess a conscious will to serve a legitimating function—but the fact that they fill this function is a major reason why they survive and spread. A great many new constitutions have been written in the past decade, and virtually all of them give prominent roles to legislatures. This reflects a widespread awareness that in the contemporary world those political systems that have legislatures are more likely to enjoy legitimacy and to survive and flourish than are those without them.

Is the Modernization Concept Ethnocentric?

A standard criticism of Modernization theories is that they are either ethnocentric or teleological or both. Some of the early Modernization literature *did* simplistically equate Modernization with becoming (1) morally superior and (2) like the West. The flaws in this perspective are pretty obvious. Few people would attribute moral superiority to Western society today, and it is evident that East Asia is now at the cutting edge of Modernization in many respects.

But there is nothing ethnocentric in the concept that social change tends to take coherent, broadly predictable trajectories. In a given economic and technological environment, certain trajectories *are* more probable than others: it is clear that in the course of history, numerous patterns of social organization have been tried and discarded, while other patterns eventually became dominant. At the dawn of recorded history, a wide variety of hunting and gathering societies existed, but the invention of agriculture led to their almost total disappearance. They were displaced because agriculture has functional advantages over hunting and gathering. An account of the displacement of hunting-gathering societies by farming societies in precolonial Africa attributes this shift to an interaction between economic, biological, and cultural factors:

> Farming and herding yield far more calories per acre than does hunting wild animals or gathering wild plants. As a result, population densities of farmers and herders are typically at least 10 times those of hunter-gatherers. That's not to say that farmers are happier, healthier or in any way superior to hunter-gatherers. They are, however, more numerous. And that alone is enough to allow them to kill or displace hunter-gatherers.
>
> In addition, human diseases such as smallpox and measles developed from diseases plaguing domestic animals. The farmers eventually became resistant to those diseases, but hunter-gatherers do not have the opportunity. So when hunter-gatherers first come into contact with farmers, they tend to die in droves from the farmers' diseases.
>
> Finally, only in a farming society—with its stored food surpluses and concentrated villages—do people have the chance to specialize, to become full-time metalworkers, soldiers, kings and bureaucrats. Hence the farmers, and not the hunter-gatherers, are the ones who develop swords and guns, standing armies and political organization. Add that to their sheer numbers and their germs and it is easy to see how the farmers in Africa were able to push the hunter-gatherers aside. (Diamond, 1993)

Although a few hunting and gathering societies still survive today, they comprise less than one one-thousandth of the human population. After supplanting them, agricultural societies were dominant for many centuries, until the industrial revolution finally gave rise to a fundamentally new pattern of society. The transition to industrial society is far from complete, but today almost every society on earth has at least begun to industrialize, and it seems likely that within the next century, most of humanity will live in predominantly urban industrialized societies.

This does not mean that all societies will be identical. Industrial societies have a wide variety of cultures and institutions. But their common characteristics are also striking: virtually without exception, they are characterized by high degrees of urbanization, industrialization, occupational specialization, the use of science and technology, bureaucratization, reliance on legal-rational authority, relatively high levels of social mobility and emphasis on achieved rather than ascribed social status, high levels of formal education, diminishing sex role specialization, high standards of material well-being, and much higher life expectancies than were ever achieved in agrarian or hunting and gathering societies. Hunting and agriculture will not disappear from the earth—but they will no longer be the predominant way of life. They will shape the worldview of a small minority of the population (and even the remaining hunters and farmers will have their lives transformed by the fact that they live in a predominantly urban industrial world).

It is neither ethnocentric nor teleological to assert that hunting and gathering societies gave way to agricultural societies. It is a simple historical fact. It *would* be ethnocentric to assert that the people living in one type of society are inherently wiser, nobler, or morally superior to those living in another—but that gratuitous claim has nothing to do with the logic of the effort to discern which type of society is most likely to survive and spread in a given economic and technological environment. The people of industrial society are not more admirable than those of agrarian society, nor does history have an anthropomorphic preference for the former; but it *is* clear that a majority of the world's population once shifted from hunting and gathering into the agrarian mode— and are now moving into the industrial mode. They have done so because in a given technological and economic environment, certain forms of society have functional advantages over others. Moreover, modern industrial society is not the end of history. The process of cultural evolution is still going on. This book will explore the cultural changes that go with both Modernization and Postmodernization.

For many years, it has been alleged that cultural interpretations of society are inherently conservative. This is a half-truth. The Marxist Left did indeed view emphasis on cultural factors as reactionary, but more recently the Postmodern Left has strongly emphasized the crucial role played by subjective perceptions and cultural values. From this perspective, recognizing the decisive influence of cultural factors is considered a prerequisite to social progress.

Nevertheless, there is some truth in the idea that culture *itself* tends to be a conservative influence. The cultural approach argues that (1) people's responses to their situation are shaped by subjective orientations that vary cross-culturally and within subcultures, and (2) these variations in subjective orientations reflect differences in one's socialization experiences, with early learning conditioning later learning, making the former more difficult to undo. Consequently, action does not simply reflect external situations. Enduring differences in cultural learning also play an essential part in shaping what people do and think.

These postulates of the cultural approach have important implications for social change. Cultural theory implies that a culture *cannot* be changed overnight. One may change the rulers and the laws, but to change basic aspects of the underlying culture generally takes many years. Even then, the long-run effects of revolutionary transformation are likely to diverge widely from revolutionary visions and to retain important elements of the old pattern of society. Furthermore, when basic cultural change does occur, it will take place more readily among younger groups (where it does not need to overcome the resistance of inconsistent early learning) than among older ones, resulting in intergenerational differences. An awareness of the inertia linked with cultural factors may be dismaying to those who would like to believe they have a quick fix for deep-rooted social problems. But this awareness is essential to any realistic strategy of social change, and therefore is likely to produce policies that are more effective in the long run, than a perspective which simply denies that cultural factors are important. An awareness of the fact that deep-rooted values are not easily changed is essential to any realistic and effective program for social change.

The Marxist Left saw cultural factors as opiates of the people—forms of false consciousness that could only distract the attention of the masses from the real problems, which were economic. They found it attractive to believe that the proper indoctrination could speedily wash away all previous orientations: if the right elite, guided by the one true ideology, could take power and enforce the right programs, all social problems could be quickly solved.

Unfortunately, Marxist programs designed to bring swift and massive change to entire societies overlooked the reality of cultural persistence. When these programs did not correspond to the deep-rooted values and habits of the peoples on whom they were targeted, they could be implemented only through massive coercion. The most ambitious programs of rapid social change required enormous coercion and failed nevertheless: Stalin's Forced Collectivization and Great Purges and Mao's Great Leap Forward and Great Cultural Revolution not only failed to create a New Soviet Man, or a new Chinese culture, but led to enormous human suffering and ultimately were immensely counterproductive.

The Postmodern Left tends toward the other extreme, sometimes presenting culture as virtually supreme. There are no objective limits or standards: everything is determined by one's cultural perspective—to such an extent that any reference to objective reality is viewed as almost reactionary.

Both of these extremes distort the role of culture. This book presents empirical evidence that culture *is* a crucial part of reality. But it is only part of it.

CHANGE IS NOT LINEAR: POSTMODERNIZATION

Another way in which early versions of Modernization theory were deficient lay in the fact that they presented a linear view of social change: the future, everywhere, would simply be more of the same. Marx's tendency to do this is particularly well known, but he had plenty of company. With the advantages of a longer time perspective, it has become evident that such linear projections are far too simple. Although industrial society has become widespread (as Marx correctly predicted), it is not the end of the road. This book presents evidence that, beyond a certain threshold, social change takes a fundamental change in direction. In the past few decades, advanced industrial societies have moved through an inflection point, from the Modernization phase into a Postmodernization phase.

This book does not examine the intellectual history of Postmodern thought and will refer to Postmodern writers only in passing. It is, instead, an empirical analysis of how a Postmodern worldview is spreading among mass publics: as it will demonstrate, a Postmodern cultural shift is taking place that manifests many of the key characteristics discussed by Postmodern thinkers. This book will not discuss how Postmodern thought developed among these writers; but we *will* examine the reasons why they have become widely influential. No one has fully explained *why* Postmodern culture has emerged: a vast amount has been written about it, but the explanation has been almost entirely at the level of the intellectual history and permeation of Postmodernism. This is an important aspect of Postmodernism, but it is not an adequate explanation of why popular culture today is strikingly different from what it was a generation or two ago. Should we assume that the masses have been profoundly influenced by the writings of Foucault and Derrida? They may have had some (largely indirect) impact. But the change is mainly due to the fact that the first-hand life experience of mass publics in recent decades has been profoundly different from that of earlier generations. Deep-rooted changes in mass worldviews have taken place that enabled Postmodern ideas to find a receptive audience. This is why a Postmodern worldview that would almost certainly have been generally rejected a generation earlier has gained widespread acceptance in the last few decades.

It is not easy to give a brief account of Postmodern thought: there are several different versions of Postmodernism, and multiple readings of given authors. The literature is complex, contradictory, full of hyperbole, and sometimes reads like gibberish. *Question*: What is the difference between the Mafia and a deconstructionist? *Answer*: A deconstructionist makes you an offer you can't understand.

Ambiguity is a central component of Postmodern worldviews, and some writers seem to consider it a virtue. This is unfortunate because, underlying the ambiguous rhetoric, a real and important phenomenon is emerging. Another key tenet of Postmodernism is incredulity toward all metanarratives: all ideologies, religions, and other overarching explanations including natural science (and Postmodernism itself) cannot be believed. There is no external standard against which theories can be tested.

This perspective is carried to an extreme by Lyotard (1979) who depicts natural science as having dissolved into a relativism characterized by abrupt ruptures and sudden unforeseen changes of direction. His interpretation, which has had wide influence, implies that science, like normative thought, is no longer oriented by any external reality. Baudrillard (1983) also tends toward this extreme, implying that there is no objective reality out there.[2] This picture of science is one that few natural scientists would recognize. It is true, as Kuhn (1962) pointed out, that the development of knowledge is partly a social enterprise in which, when paradigm shifts occur, there is a temporary breakdown of the prevailing theoretical consensus. Kuhn's finding concerning the structure of scientific revolutions is frequently misinterpreted to mean that science itself is culture-bound. This is not the case: as we have noted, when a paradigm shift occurs, the split in acceptance is mainly along generational lines, based on different degrees of commitment to prior learning. The fact that science has a hermeneutic aspect does not mean that Indian or Chinese scientists are rejecting an interpretation that is accepted by French or German scientists. Instead, what occurs is an intergenerational culture lag.

But even these historic paradigm shifts involve much less discontinuity than Lyotard seems to imagine. Thus, Einstein's astonishing and paradigm-shifting breakthrough did *not* cause the previous body of scientific knowledge to be discarded. Newtonian physics continued (and continues) to function quite adequately: it simply became a special case within a broader Einsteinian framework. Many decades later, Newtonian calculations were used to take people safely to and from the moon: Einstein's limits become significant only under far more extreme conditions than are normally experienced on earth, or even in lunar voyages.

The way for Einstein's revolution was prepared by a series of findings that were inconsistent with the implications of Newtonian physics. Einstein developed a new theory that resolved these inconsistencies and generated a number of precise predictions that were then confirmed by a series of empirical tests that left little room for doubt that Einstein was right. These findings (with some delay) gave rise to a new theoretical consensus that gained acceptance from Buenos Aires to Tokyo.

Today, we seem to be on the brink of a new paradigm shift in physics—but it is unlikely to consign previous research to oblivion. Instead, the work of both Newton and Einstein will continue to apply, though within a still broader the-

---

[2] Thus, in 1991 Baudrillard asserted with characteristic hyperbole that the Gulf War did not take place: it was all a media event (Baudrillard, cited in Lyon, 1994: 52). But whether or not the war took place was not simply a question of one's cultural perspective: thousands of corpses testified to the fact that it was a reality. From the opposite end of the ideological spectrum, German revisionist historians have argued that the Holocaust did not really take place—it is just a case of the victors writing history. In this case, millions of corpses constitute a fact that goes beyond questions of interpretation.

oretical framework. The emerging Grand Unified Theory is designed to integrate all of the laws of physics into one coherent theory that will account for everything that has happened in the physical world from the birth of the universe to the present moment. Far from disintegrating into discontinuous and mutually incomprehensible islands of short-lived insights, natural science seems to be moving toward a mega-metanarrative. This is precisely the opposite of what Lyotard's followers seem to believe.

Nevertheless, stripped of its hyperbolic extremes, the literature on Postmodernity is dealing with a very real and important phenomenon: the world (or, at least, large parts of it) has moved onto a different trajectory from the one it had been following since the industrial revolution. And this new trajectory corresponds, in many respects, to what Postmodern observers claim is happening. Although there still is an external reality out there, culture does indeed have a tremendous influence on how reality is perceived. Moreover, the relative importance of culture seems to be increasing. On this new Postmodern trajectory, economic rationality determines human behavior less narrowly than before: the realm of the possible has expanded, and cultural factors are becoming more important. An empirically demonstrable cultural shift is taking place. The great religious and ideological metanarratives are losing their authority among the masses. The uniformity and hierarchy that shaped modernity are giving way to an increasing acceptance of diversity. And the increasing dominance of instrumental rationality that characterized Modernization is giving way to a greater emphasis on value rationality and quality of life concerns.

As this book will demonstrate with empirical evidence, a Postmodern shift in mass values and attitudes actually *is* taking place. This is why the ideas of Postmodern writers have found a receptive audience in recent decades. Although our analysis of empirical evidence cannot solve Postmodernity's normative questions, it does enable us to identify where the Postmodern shift is occurring and how fast it is moving, and it helps explain why it is taking place.

Has the entire world suddenly turned Postmodern, as some writers seem to assume? The empirical answer is No. Instead, some societies (such as Nigeria) are starting to modernize; others (such as China) are now modernizing very rapidly; still others (such as South Korea), seem to be reaching a turning point where they may be about to begin Postmodernization; and still others, such as Britain, Germany, and the United States, are well into the Postmodernization process—but even they do not lead the world in this respect. As we will see, the evidence indicates that the Nordic countries and the Netherlands are now the most Postmodern societies on earth.

This book will not merely chart the progress of Postmodernization; we will propose a theoretical explanation of *why* it is taking place. Before doing so, let us try to categorize Postmodernist thought: to a large extent, the changes that are occurring among mass publics correspond to these ideas. But how true this is depends on what version of Postmodernism one has in mind.

One could start by dividing Postmodern thought into three broad schools:

1. Postmodernism is the rejection of modernity: that is, of rationality, authority, technology, and science. Within this school, there is a widespread tendency to equate rationality, authority, technology, and science with Westernization. From this perspective, Postmodernism is considered to be the rejection of Westernization.

2. Postmodernism is the revalorization of tradition. Since Modernization drastically devalued tradition, its demise opens the way for this revalorization.

3. Postmodernism is the rise of *new* values and lifestyles, with greater tolerance for ethnic, cultural, and sexual diversity and individual choice concerning the kind of life one wants to lead.

These three versions of Postmodernism all capture important elements of what is taking place; though they are not incompatible, they emphasize different things.

Let us start with the rejection of modernity. Modernization offers great rewards, but imposes huge costs. It dismantles a traditional world in which the meaning of life is clear; warm, personal communal ties give way to an impersonal competitive society geared to individual achievement. Industrialization vastly increases human productivity; but (especially before labor unions and working-class political parties bring countervailing pressures to bear against capitalism) it gives rise to inhuman working conditions. Marx criticized not only the ruthless economic exploitation of early capitalism, but also the tremendous psychological costs of industrialization.

Decades later, Weber saw the rationalization of society as an inexorable aspect of Modernization; though it facilitated economic growth and public order, ever-increasing rationalization was disenchanting the world, forcing humanity into a painfully narrow iron cage of bureaucracy and mass production. What Weber deplored was the ubiquitous penetration of *instrumental* rationality: the rationality of immediate means was driving out the rationality of ultimate ends. Subsequently, Heidegger (1946, 1949) and Horkheimer and Adorno (1947) carried the critique of modernity farther, arguing that the instrumental rationality of industrialization had, ironically, undermined any absolute moral standards and given rise to new forms of irrationality and repression, culminating in the horrors of Hitler and Stalin. Instrumental rationality had virtually banished value rationality.

Today, this trend is beginning to reverse itself: instrumental rationality gained an exaggerated predominance during the rise of industrialization, but today, for reasons we will discuss in this book, a growing segment of society is concluding that the price is too high. Rationality, science, technology, and authority are here to stay; but their relative priority and their authority among mass publics are declining.

Within this first version of Postmodernism, there is a widespread tendency to confound rationality, authority, technology, and science with Westernization. Some of the (now outmoded) Modernization literature also equated Modernization with Westernization. If Postmodernism is the rejection of modernity, it would logically follow that Postmodernism is the rejection of

Westernization. This perspective is found in the work of Lyotard and Derrida, who tend to equate modernization with Western imperialism.

Western imperialism was an important phenomenon: it was brutally imposed on the rest of the world, it deserved to be rejected, and it deserves the scorn with which Postmodern writers treat it. But equating Modernization with Westernization is not a useful way to proceed. It emphasizes superficial and accidental aspects of Modernization and ignores the core process. Wearing Western clothing was not crucial; industrialization was. Moreover, it is inaccurate to equate modern imperialism with Westernization. In the number of people it subjugated, the Japanese empire was the second largest colonial empire in history and was fully as oppressive as any Western empire.

The essential core of Modernization is a syndrome of changes closely linked with industrialization: this syndrome includes urbanization, the application of science and technology, rapidly increasing occupational specialization, rising bureaucratization, and rising educational levels. It also includes one more thing, which was the motivating force behind the whole process: industrialization was a way to get rich.

By getting rich, one could dispel hunger, acquire military strength, and obtain a number of other desirable things, including a much longer life expectancy than was possible in preindustrial society. Adopting a life strategy aimed at getting rich becomes compellingly attractive from the perspective of low-income societies, once it has been demonstrated that it can be done. Furthermore, as we will show in this chapter, economic development actually seems to be conducive to subjective well-being (though only up to a certain point in history). In short, industrialization and the Modernization syndrome that goes with it were an attractive package. It carries a high cost, and from the viewpoint of advanced industrial society these costs may seem excessive. But from the perspective of most preindustrial societies, it seemed worth the price.

This constitutes another crucial difference between Modernization and Westernization: Western imperialism was imposed on non-Western societies, which almost universally rejected it when they were free to do so. By contrast, the goal of Modernization (that is, the industrialization syndrome) has now been adopted by almost every society on earth—and non-Western societies show no sign of wishing to abandon it. Quite the contrary, it is being pursued today with far more enthusiasm in the non-Western world than in the West. The Postmodern critique of Modernization comes overwhelmingly from within *Western* societies.

By the 1960s, the tendency to equate Modernization with Westernization had been abandoned by most Modernization theorists. And even if one goes by obvious external indicators, this concept has been outdated since at least 1980, when Japan became the world's leading automobile producer—outdoing the United States at Fordism itself. During the ensuing decade, Japan also attained the highest GNP per capita of any major nation, leading the world in attaining the fruits, as well as the tools, of Modernization. Historically, the Industrial Revolution occurred first in the West. But there is nothing uniquely

Western about technology and industrialization, or even bureaucratic rationality. Mathematics came to Europe from India and Egypt. China was the technologically most advanced society in the world for most of the past 2,000 years, losing its technological lead only in the seventeenth century (and it is not inconceivable that the nation will regain it). Similarly, another key aspect of modernity—bureaucracy—originated in China. The idea that rationality and technology are Western inventions is simply a myth. In the modern era, Westerners raised them to unprecedented levels and applied them to production to an unprecedented degree, but they are part of the human heritage, not something uniquely European. Today, East Asian and Southeast Asian societies are achieving the world's highest rates of economic growth and are at the cutting edge of Modernization in numerous other respects. Japan has become the world leader in various aspects of modernity, from consumer electronics to human life expectancy. And in recent years a growing flow of Western experts have made the pilgrimage to Japan to study the secrets of Japanese management, just as the Japanese earlier made the reverse voyage to learn industrialization from the West.

Another perspective views Postmodernism as the revalorization of tradition. This reverses one of the most prominent trends associated with Modernization. In the early modern era, the astonishing achievements of science and industry gave rise to a myth of Progress and radically discredited tradition. "New" became virtually synonymous with "good." But more recently, the instrumental rationality of modernity has lost its prestige. This has not only opened the way for tradition to regain status, but created a need for a new legitimating myth. In the Postmodern worldview, tradition once again has positive value—especially non-Western traditions. But the revalorization of tradition is sharply selective. Despite their ubiquitous presence in the traditional societies of both the Western and non-Western world, the norm that "Women's place is in the home" and the stern prohibition of extramarital sex are not among the aspects of premodern tradition that Postmodern writers admire.

The rise of new values and lifestyles is a profoundly important aspect of what is taking place today, throughout advanced industrial society. Derrida (1979, 1981) emphasizes this aspect of Postmodernity. Although Postmodernization *does* involve a downgrading of modernity and a revalorization of tradition, the emergence of a new culture is even more crucial, in our view. The best documented example of the rise of new values is the intergenerational shift from Materialist to Postmaterialist value priorities that seems to be taking place throughout advanced industrial society (Inglehart, 1971, 1977, 1990); but the rise of new values and lifestyles is taking place across many other aspects of life, from sexual orientation to religion.

Critical Theory

Apart from the Postmodern thinkers, Habermas (1984, 1987) has developed the most influential recent philosophical critique of modernity. Habermas differs from the Postmodern school on a number of points. One major disagreement is that, while Postmodernism tends to depict Modernization as a basically bad choice and rejects it, Habermas argues that while it imposed high costs, it also brought major benefits. Modernization is an unfinished project; we should build on it rather than reject it. Although we think that the process of change has taken a fundamentally new Postmodern turn, we agree with Habermas on this point. Industrialization provided more than just noisy, polluting automobiles and mindless television sitcoms. It provided two things that would be considered valuable from almost any cultural perspective: (1) greatly enhanced chances for survival, as measured by human life expectancy, and (2) higher levels of subjective well-being. Empirical evidence will be presented below in support of these assertions.

Another major disagreement centers on the fact that Postmodern thinkers conclude that there is no longer any basis by which universal moral standards could be validated: both God and Marx are dead. Habermas has not given up: he argues that moral norms may be merely social conventions, but if they are, it is imperative to develop rules for arriving at universally acceptable conventions. In a new version of the social contract, Habermas argues that a rational basis for collective life can be achieved only when social relations are organized so that the validity of every norm depends on a consensus arrived at in communication free from domination. Against the Postmodern position that moral rules are simply myths created by the ruling elite to justify the social order they control, Habermas argues that it *is* possible to reach a moral consensus that is not simply dominated by the ruling elites. Here again, we think he is right, and this debate raises a crucial question: Are cultural norms simply tools of the ruling elite? In order to answer this question, let us examine the relationship between authority and culture.

Authority and Culture

Marx defined ideology as false consciousness—that is, a consciousness shaped by power-holders to justify their right to rule (and to exploit), and to make it seem inevitable. The insight that culture is closely linked with power is important. It would be naive to believe that culture is neutral: in virtually every society, it legitimates the established social order—partly because the dominant elite try to shape it to help perpetuate their rule.

One of the leading themes in the literature on Postmodernism is the claim that culture is used to legitimate political authority; Foucault is a prominent advocate of this view. An extreme version of this position would hold that every reality is a politically constructed system of myths, and the key task of the social critic is to deconstruct these myths, which are simply a means to justify privilege and exploitation.

Without a doubt, culture serves to legitimate the social order. From an elite perspective, this may even be the most important thing it does. But it certainly is not the *only* thing it does. Culture integrates society in terms of common goals, satisfies intellectual and aesthetic needs, and finally—no insignificant point—also places some restraints on elites.

The extreme position, that mass belief systems are completely dominated by elite interests, assumes a degree of mass manipulability that is simply unrealistic. Recent historical developments illustrate this point. Thus, after 70 years of controlling the Soviet Union's educational systems, public discussion, the mass media, churches, and all other channels of communication to an historically unprecedented extent, the Soviet elite ultimately was not able to shape the worldviews of their people to conform to their goals: toward the end, not even the Soviet elite really believed the official ideology.

Western advanced industrial societies are also changing—whether their elites like it or not. A modern worldview that was once firmly established has gradually given way to Postmodern values that emphasize human autonomy and diversity instead of the hierarchy and conformity that are central to modernity. In both cases, a major factor leading to basic cultural change was the fact that the life experience of a new generation gave rise to new perceptions of reality. For the reality of one's firsthand experience ultimately intrudes. The official truth, propagated by the dominant elite, usually has a great deal of influence. But the firsthand life experience of ordinary people *also* counts—and ultimately may have even greater credibility than the official truth. How do established worldviews begin to crumble?

WHY IS THE POSTMODERN SHIFT OCCURRING?

The shift toward Postmodern values is not the first time that a major cultural shift has occurred. The transition from agrarian society to industrial society was facilitated by a shift from a worldview shaped by a steady-state economy. This worldview discouraged social mobility and emphasized tradition, inherited status, and communal obligations, backed up by absolute religious norms; it gave way to a worldview that encouraged economic achievement, individualism, and innovation, with increasingly secular social norms. Today, some of these trends linked with the transition from "Traditional" to "Modern" society have reached their limits in advanced industrial society, where change is taking a new direction.

This change of direction reflects the principle of diminishing marginal utility. Industrialization and Modernization required breaking the cultural constraints on accumulation that are found in any steady-state economy. In Western European history, this was achieved by the rise of the Protestant Ethic, which (though it had a long intellectual history) was like a random mutation from a functional perspective. If it had occurred two centuries earlier it might have died out. In the environment of its time, it found a niche: technological developments were making rapid economic growth possible, and the Calvinist worldview complemented these developments beautifully, forming a cultural-economic syndrome that led to the rise of capitalism and eventually to the industrial revolution. Once this had occurred, economic accumulation (for individuals) and economic growth (for societies) became the top priorities for an increasing part of the world's population; they are still the central goals for much of humanity. But eventually, diminishing returns from economic growth lead to a Postmodern shift that in some ways constitutes the decline of the Protestant Ethic.

Advanced industrial societies are now changing their sociopolitical trajectories in two fundamental respects:

1. Value systems. Increasing emphasis on individual economic achievement was one of the crucial changes that made Modernization possible. This shift toward Materialistic priorities entailed a de-emphasis on communal obligations and an acceptance of social mobility: increasingly, social status became something that an individual could achieve, rather than something into which one was born. Economic growth came to be equated with progress and was seen as the hallmark of a successful society.

In Postmodern society this emphasis on economic achievement as the top priority is now giving way to an increasing emphasis on the quality of life. In a major part of the world, the disciplined, self-denying, and achievement-oriented norms of industrial society are giving way to an increasingly broad latitude for individual choice of lifestyles and individual self-expression. The shift from "Materialist" values, emphasizing economic and physical security, to "Postmaterialist" values, emphasizing individual self-expression and quality of life concerns, is the most amply documented aspect of this change; but it is only one component of a much broader syndrome of cultural change.

2. Institutional structure. We are also reaching limits to the development of the hierarchical bureaucratic organizations that helped create modern society. The bureaucratic state, the disciplined, oligarchical political party, the mass-production assembly line, the old-line labor union, and the hierarchical corporation all played enormously important roles in mobilizing and organizing the energies of masses of people; they made the industrial revolution and the modern state possible. But they have come to a turning point for two reasons: first, they are reaching limits in their functional effectiveness; and second, they are reaching limits in their mass acceptability. Let us consider both factors.

Functional Limits to the Expansion of the Bureaucratic State

The rise and fall of the Soviet Union illustrates the limits of the centralized, hierarchical state. In its early decades, the USSR was remarkably efficient in mobilizing masses of relatively unskilled workers and vast quantities of raw materials to build the world's largest steel mill and the world's largest hydroelectric dam, and to attain one of the fastest rates of economic growth in the world. Although Stalin starved and murdered millions of Soviet citizens, the economic and military achievements of the Soviet state were so impressive that they convinced many people throughout the world that this type of society was the irresistible wave of the future. Soviet economic growth was remarkable in the 1950s, was still impressive in the 1960s, tapered off in the 1970s, and stagnated in the 1980s. Partly, this happened because a hypertrophied bureaucracy paralyzed adaptation and innovation. Bureaucracy is inherently deadening to innovation, and this problem became acute once the Soviet Union had moved past the stage of simply importing already proven technology from the West and was attempting to innovate in competition with the West and Japan. But the problem was not only the failure of central economic planning to cope with an increasingly complex and rapidly changing society. It also reflected a collapse of motivation and morale. Absenteeism rose to massive proportions, alcoholism became a tremendous problem, and confidence in government eroded until finally the entire economic and political system collapsed. Although the Soviet example is the most striking case, similar manifestations of the diminishing effectiveness of hierarchical, centralized bureaucratic institutions can be seen throughout industrial society. State-run economies are giving way to market forces; old-line political parties and labor unions are in decline; and bureaucratic corporations are losing ground to more loosely organized and participatory types of organization.

These organizational and motivational changes are intimately related. One reason for the decline of the classic bureaucratic institutions of industrial society is the fact that they are inherently less effective in high-technology societies with highly specialized workforces than they were in the earlier stages of industrial society. But another reason for their decline is the fact that they also became less *acceptable* to the publics of Postmodern society than they were earlier, because of changes in these people's values.

The mass production assembly line broke down manufacturing into simple standardized routines that were repeated endlessly. This was marvelously effective in turning out masses of relatively simple, standardized products. But a price was paid for the increased productivity that resulted: the workers became cogs in huge centrally coordinated machines. Marx, Weber, and others were concerned with the alienation and depersonalization of industrial society that made one's work uninteresting, dehumanizing, devoid of meaning. In societies of scarcity, people were willing to accept these costs, for the sake of economic gains. In affluent societies, they are less willing to do so.

Modern bureaucracy makes a similar tradeoff involving loss of individual identity and autonomy for the sake of increased productivity; this enables it to process thousands or millions of people, using standardized routines. It, too, is inherently depersonalizing: in a rational bureaucracy, individuals are reduced to interchangeable roles. Bureaucracy strips away spontaneity, personal likes and dislikes, individual self-expression and creativity. Nevertheless it was an effective tool for coordinating the efforts of hundreds or even millions of individuals, in the large organizations of modern society.

But its effectiveness and its acceptability are eroding. Postmodern values give a higher priority to self-expression than to economic effectiveness: people are becoming less willing to accept the human costs of bureaucracy and of rigid social norms. As this book will demonstrate, Postmodern society is characterized by the decline of hierarchical institutions and rigid social norms, and by the expansion of the realm of individual choice and mass participation.

Up to the middle of the twentieth century, "Modernization" was an unambiguous term. It referred to urbanization, industrialization, secularization, bureaucratization, and a culture based on bureaucratization—a culture that requires a shift from ascriptive status to achieved status, from diffuse to specific forms of authority, from personalistic obligations to impersonal roles, and from particularistic to universalistic rules. In some areas this Modernization process is still going on. But elsewhere, trends that were central to the Modernization process have undergone a fundamental change of direction.

For example, one of the most striking phenomena of the past two hundred years was the rapidly expanding scope of government. Industrial societies became increasingly centralized, hierarchical, and bureaucratized. Until recently, highly centralized state-run economies and societies like the Soviet Union seemed to be the logical end point of Modernization. One might view this trend as profoundly progressive, with the Marxists, or deplore it as threatening to human liberty, with Schumpeter (1947) and Orwell (1949)—but the growth of government seemed inexorable. At the start of the twentieth century, government spending in most societies consumed from 4 to 10 percent of gross domestic product. By 1980, it ranged from 33 to 60 percent of a much bigger output in Western societies, and 70 to 80 percent in some socialist societies. Increasing government ownership and control of the economy seemed to be the wave of the future.

It was not. During the 1980s, further expansion of the state reached a point of diminishing returns, both functionally and in terms of mass acceptance. It first ran into growing political opposition in the West and then collapsed in the Eastern bloc.

The mass production assembly line and the mass production bureaucracy were the two key organizational instruments of industrial society, and in the early phase of Modernization they had a high payoff—enabling factories to produce millions of units and governments to process millions of individuals through standardized routines. But the trend toward bureaucratization, centralization, and government ownership and control has reversed itself. Modern economies lose their effectiveness when the public sphere becomes overwhelmingly large. And public confidence in hierarchical institutions is eroding throughout advanced industrial society.

Cultural Changes Leading to Postmodernization

An equally basic change in the direction of change has been a shift in the predominant norms and motivations underlying human behavior. Virtually all agrarian societies were characterized by value systems that stigmatized social mobility. This was inevitable, given their steady-state economies. The main source of wealth was land, which is in fixed supply: the only way to become rich was by seizing someone else's land—which probably required killing the owner. Such internal violence was threatening to the survival of any society and was repressed by norms that emphasized acceptance of the status into which one was born and stigmatized the ambitious and the arriviste. At the same time, traditional societies emphasized duties of sharing and charity— which helped compensate the poor for the absence of social mobility, but further undermined the legitimacy of economic accumulation.

The rise of a Materialistic value system that not only tolerated economic accumulation but encouraged it as something laudable and heroic was a key cultural change that opened the way for capitalism and industrialization. Weber (1904–5) examined this process in *The Protestant Ethic and the Spirit of Capitalism*, but his work can be seen as a case study of a more general phenomenon. Today the functional equivalent of the Protestant Ethic is operating most vigorously in East Asia and is fading away in Protestant Europe, as technological development and cultural change have become global phenomena.

Precisely because they attained high levels of economic security, the populations of the first nations to industrialize have gradually come to emphasize Postmaterialist values, giving higher priority to the quality of life than to economic growth. This shift has been taking place throughout advanced industrial society during the past few decades, as we will see in chapter 4. With this has come a shift from the politics of class conflict, to political conflict based on such issues as environmental protection and the status of women and sexual minorities. Marxist ideology, based on economic determinism, was an immensely influential guide for interpreting the transition from agrarian to "modern" or industrial society. It is outmoded for the analysis of "Postmodern" society.

To clarify what we mean by this term, let us examine the specific changes that are linked with Postmodern values. Some of these trends differ radically from those of Modernization.

The Origins of Postmodern Values: Existential Security

A new worldview is gradually replacing one that has dominated Western society since the Industrial Revolution. The consequences of this transformation are still taking shape, and elements of the older culture are still widespread, but the major features of the new pattern can be discerned.

This shift in worldview and motivations springs from the fact that there is a fundamental difference between growing up with an awareness that survival is precarious, and growing up with the feeling that one's survival can be taken for granted.

The urge to survive is common to all creatures, and normally survival is precarious. This reflects a basic ecological principle: the population of any organism tends to rise to meet the available food supply; it is then held constant by starvation, disease, or predators. Throughout most of history, this principle has governed the lives of all organisms, including humanity. Until very recently, the survival of most human beings was precarious.

Eventually, culture began to soften the competition for survival among humans. Although the ways in which this was done varied enormously from one society to another, virtually all traditional societies established cultural norms that limited the use of violence and repressed aspirations for social mobility. On one hand, they emphasized sharing and charity among those who were relatively well-off, stigmatizing accumulation as greed; and on the other hand, they justified acceptance of the existing social order by the poor. And cultural norms limiting reproduction softened the ruthless competition for survival that overpopulation brought.

A few centuries ago, cultural changes in Protestant Europe led to the reversal of the traditional stigma against economic accumulation, and a Materialistic worldview began to spread. Using new technology and organizational techniques, production began to outpace population growth. Nevertheless, well into the twentieth century, severe economic scarcity still prevailed widely: the Marxist view that people and history were motivated primarily by the struggle for economic goods was a fairly accurate first approximation of the driving force underlying the modernizing phase of industrial society.

The economic miracles and the welfare states that emerged after World War II gave rise to a new stage of history, and ultimately laid the way for the rise of Postmodern values. Fundamental changes in formative experiences have given rise to a distinct value system among a growing segment of those raised in advanced industrial societies during the years since World War II. The postwar birth cohorts in these societies grew up under conditions profoundly unlike those that shaped previous generations. They differed in two respects: first, the postwar economic miracles produced levels of prosperity that were literally unprecedented in human history. Real per capita income in most industrial societies rose to levels several times as high as had ever been experienced before the war, and in some cases (such as Japan) to levels 20 or 30 times higher than ever before. The economic pie became much bigger; this alone would tend to encourage a greater sense of economic security.

But the impact of unprecedented prosperity interacted with a second factor: the emergence of the modern welfare state. A sense of existential security, not absolute wealth, is the crucial variable, and the welfare state reinforced economic growth in producing a sense of security. The pie was much bigger than ever before, and it was distributed more evenly and more reliably than before. For the first time in history, a large share of the masses grew up with the feeling that survival could be taken for granted.

This led to a process of intergenerational value change that is gradually transforming the politics and cultural norms of advanced industrial societies. The best documented aspect of this process is the shift from giving top priority to economic and physical security, to giving top priority to self-expression and the quality of life. This shift from Materialist to Postmaterialist priorities has been measured annually since 1970 in surveys carried out in a number of Western societies. A massive body of evidence is now available, and it demonstrates that an intergenerational shift has been taking place in the predicted direction. This shift from Materialist to Postmaterialist value priorities has brought new political issues to the center of the stage and provided much of the impetus for new political movements.

More recent research indicates that the rise of Postmaterialism itself is only one aspect of a still broader process of cultural change that is reshaping the political outlook, religious orientations, gender roles, and sexual mores of advanced industrial society (Inglehart, 1990). These changes are related to a common concern: the need for a sense of security that religion and absolute cultural norms have traditionally provided. In advanced industrial societies during the decades since World War II, the emergence of unprecedentedly high levels of prosperity, together with the relatively high levels of social security provided by the welfare state, have contributed to a decline in the prevailing sense of vulnerability. For the general public, one's fate is no longer so heavily influenced by unpredictable forces as it was in agrarian and early industrial society. This has been conducive to the spread of Postmodern orientations that place less emphasis on traditional cultural norms—especially those norms that limit individual self-expression.

THE THEORY OF INTERGENERATIONAL VALUE CHANGE

Let us reexamine the theory of intergenerational value change in light of recent findings. Our theory is based on two key hypotheses (Inglehart, 1977):

1. *A Scarcity Hypothesis.* An individual's priorities reflect the socioeconomic environment: one places the greatest subjective value on those things that are in relatively short supply.

2. *A Socialization Hypothesis.* The relationship between socioeconomic environment and value priorities is not one of immediate adjustment: a substantial time lag is involved because, to a large extent, one's basic values reflect the conditions that prevailed during one's preadult years.

The scarcity hypothesis is similar to the principle of diminishing marginal utility in economic theory. The complementary concept of a need hierarchy (Maslow, 1954) helped shape the survey items used to measure value priorities. In its simplest form, the idea of a need hierarchy would probably command almost universal assent. The fact that unmet physiological needs take priority over social, intellectual, or aesthetic needs has been demonstrated all too often in human history: starving people will go to almost any length to obtain food. The rank ordering of human needs varies as we move beyond those needs directly related to survival; Maslow's need hierarchy does not hold up in detail. But there does seem to be a basic distinction between the "material" needs for physiological sustenance and safety, and nonphysiological needs such as those for esteem, self-expression, and aesthetic satisfaction.

The recent economic history of advanced industrial societies has significant implications in light of the scarcity hypothesis. For these societies are a striking exception to the prevailing historical pattern: they still contain poor people, but most of their population does *not* live under conditions of hunger and economic insecurity. This has led to a gradual shift in which needs for belonging, esteem, and intellectual and aesthetic satisfaction became more prominent. Other things being equal, we would expect prolonged periods of high prosperity to encourage the spread of Postmaterialist values; economic decline would have the opposite effect.

But it is not quite that simple: there is no one-to-one relationship between economic level and the prevalence of Postmaterialist values, for these values reflect one's *subjective* sense of security, not one's economic level per se. While rich individuals and nationalities tend to feel more secure than poor ones, these feelings are also influenced by the cultural setting and social welfare institutions in which one is raised. Thus, the scarcity hypothesis must be interpreted in connection with the socialization hypothesis.

One of the most pervasive concepts in social science is the notion of a basic human personality structure that tends to crystallize by the time an individual reaches adulthood, with relatively little change thereafter. This concept permeates the literature from Plato through Freud and extends to the findings of contemporary survey research. Early socialization seems to carry greater weight than later socialization.

This, of course, does not imply that no change occurs during adult years. In individual cases, dramatic behavioral shifts are known to occur, and the process of human development never comes to a complete stop (Erikson, 1982; Levinson et al., 1979; Brim and Kagan, 1980). Nevertheless, human development seems to be far more rapid during the preadult years than afterward, and the great bulk of the evidence points to the conclusion that the statistical likelihood of basic personality change declines sharply after one reaches adulthood (Block, 1981; Costa and McCrae, 1980; Jennings and Niemi, 1981; Jennings and Markus, 1984).

Taken together, these two hypotheses generate a clear set of predictions concerning value change. First, while the scarcity hypothesis implies that prosperity is conducive to the spread of Postmaterialist and Postmodern values, the socialization hypothesis implies that neither an individual's values nor those of a society as a whole are likely to change overnight. Instead, fundamental value change takes place gradually; largely it occurs as a younger generation replaces an older one in the adult population of a society.

Consequently, after a period of sharply rising economic and physical security, one would expect to find substantial differences between the value priorities of older and younger groups: they would have been shaped by different experiences in their formative years. But there would be a sizable time lag between economic changes and their political effects. Ten or 15 years after an era of prosperity began, the age cohorts that had spent their formative years in prosperity would begin to enter the electorate. A decade or so might pass before these groups began to occupy positions of power and influence in their society; another decade or so would pass before they reached the level of top decision makers. But their influence would become important long before this final stage. Postmaterialists are more highly educated, more articulate, and politically more active than Materialists. Consequently, their political impact tends to outweigh that of the Materialists.

The socialization hypothesis complements the scarcity hypothesis. It helps account for apparently deviant behavior: on one hand, the miser who experienced poverty in early years and relentlessly continues piling up wealth long after attaining material security; and on the other hand, the saint who remains true to the higher-order goals instilled by his or her culture, even in the face of severe deprivation. In both instances, an explanation for the seemingly deviant behavior of such individuals lies in their early socialization.

The unprecedented economic and physical security of the postwar era has led to an intergenerational shift from Materialist to Postmaterialist values. The young emphasize Postmaterialist goals to a far greater extent than do the old, and cohort analysis indicates that this reflects generational change rather than aging effects. At the time of our first surveys, in 1970–71, Materialists held an overwhelming numerical preponderance over Postmaterialists, outnumbering them by nearly four to one. By 1990, the balance had shifted dramatically, to a point where Materialists outnumbered Postmaterialists by only four to three. Projections based on population replacement suggest that by the year 2000 Materialists and Postmaterialists will be about equally numerous in many Western countries (Abramson and Inglehart, 1992).

Postmaterialists are not non-Materialists, still less are they anti-Materialists. The term *"Post-*materialist" denotes a set of goals that are emphasized *after* people have attained material security, and *because* they have attained material security. Thus, the collapse of security would lead to a gradual shift back toward Materialist priorities. The emergence of Postmaterialism does not reflect a reversal of polarities, but a change of *priorities*: Postmaterialists do not place a negative value on economic and physical security—they value it positively, like everyone else; but unlike Materialists, they give even higher priority to self-expression and the quality of life.

Thus, Inglehart (1977: 179–261) found that an emerging emphasis on quality of life issues was being superimposed on the older, class-based cleavages of industrial society. Although social class voting was declining, it had by no means disappeared (and was unlikely to do so). But while the old class-based polarization over ownership and control of the means of production had once dominated politics, it was increasingly sharing the stage with new Postmaterialist issues. Both industrial and preindustrial cleavages persisted, beside cross-cutting new issues.

The shift from Materialist to Postmaterialist priorities is a core element of the Postmodernization process. In early industrial society, emphasis on economic achievement rose to unprecedented levels. While traditional societies stigmatized social mobility and individual economic accumulation, modern industrial societies provided a positive evaluation of economic achievement. The Captain of Industry became a cultural hero, and the nineteenth-century U.S. Supreme Court interpreted "the pursuit of happiness" to mean "freedom to accumulate property." The core societal goal of the Modernization process was economic growth. This made a good deal of sense. Early industrializing nations had only recently acquired the technological means to cope with chronic scarcity. In such societies, where malnutrition is the main cause of death, economic achievement is an overwhelmingly important part of the pursuit of happiness. The transition from preindustrial society to advanced industrial society brings a change from a life expectancy of 35 or 40 years, to one of 75 or 80 years. This is a huge improvement.

As the possibility of starvation receded from being a major concern to an almost insignificant prospect for most people, prevailing values gradually changed. Economic security is still something that everyone wants, but it is no longer a synonym for happiness. Increasingly, the publics of advanced industrial societies have come to emphasize quality of life concerns, sometimes giving environmental protection priority over economic growth. Thus, emphasis on economic achievement rises sharply with the Modernization process, but then levels off as Postmodernization occurs. Societies in which Postmaterialists are most numerous have lower growth rates than those in which Materialists are overwhelmingly predominant—but the former tend to have higher levels of subjective well-being. Postmodernization brings declining emphasis not only on economic growth itself, but also on the scientific and technological developments that make it possible; emphasis shifts from coping with survival, to maximizing subjective well-being.

The Risk Society

Ironically, as survival has become unprecedentedly secure, the peoples of advanced industrial societies have become increasingly sensitive to risk. Indeed, one of the most influential critics of postmodern society characterizes it as Risk Society (Beck, 1992). According to this diagnosis, the distributional conflicts over "goods" (such as property, income, and jobs) that characterized industrial society have given way to distributional conflicts over "bads," such as the risks of nuclear technology, genetic research, and the threat to the environment. With industrialization, the religious certainties of feudal society were eroded, but they gave rise to an increasing degree of existential security; with the rise of Postmodern society, the risks of life have become incalculable and increasingly escape the control mechanisms of society. In this updated version of the doctrine of late capitalism, the ecological crisis takes over the role previously played by the legitimation crisis of late capitalism.

It is ironic that in societies where human life expectancy has risen by 20 years during the last century, concerns about risk have become central political issues. It is ironic, but logical: for it is precisely *because* the risk of starvation has receded almost to the vanishing point that people have been able to redirect their concerns from pervasive daily uncertainty concerning survival to more remote concerns such as the ecological crisis. The very success of the welfare states of advanced industrial society in providing an unprecedented degree of existential insecurity has given rise to the expectation that the state can and should ensure everyone against all uncertainties. As Samuelson has put it,

> The reason for this paradox is entitlement: a postwar word and concept. By entitlement, I mean more than the catalogue of well-known government benefits (Social Security being the most prominent) or various modern "rights" (such as the "right" of those in wheelchairs to public ramps). Entitlement expresses a modern conviction, a broader sensibility, that defines Americans' attitudes toward social conditions, national institutions and even the world. Increasingly, we have come to believe that certain things are (or ought to be) guaranteed to us. We feel entitled. Among other things, we expect secure jobs, rising living standards, enlightened corporations, generous government, high-quality health care, racial harmony, a clean environment, safe cities, satisfying work, and personal fulfillment. (Samuelson, 1995: 4)

What Samuelson attributes to American society holds true of other Postmodern societies. As long as people were overwhelmingly engaged in coping with survival, more remote concerns had little salience. But the attainment of existential security does not bring Nirvana. Postmodern society has brought increasing attention to quality of life problems, and far more demanding standards for societal performance. As a net result, people probably worry as much as ever, but they worry about different things: there are profound differences in the behavior and worldviews of people who feel insecure about their personal survival and people who worry about global warming.

Stress, Coping Stategies, and Belief Systems

Far-reaching though it is, the rise of Postmaterialist values is only one aspect of a still broader process of cultural change that is reshaping orientations toward authority, religion, politics, gender roles, and sexual norms among the publics of advanced industrial society. What is driving this broad shift from survival values toward well-being values? This question is illuminated by recent research in social psychology on the relationships between stress, coping strategies, and belief systems.

People who feel that their survival is threatened react with stress; this stimulates efforts to cope with the threat. But high levels of stress can become dysfunctional and even life-threatening. One's belief system mediates the response to new or threatening situations, helping the individual deal with stress and shaping the strategy used to cope with the threat. If one *has* a belief system that provides a sense of predictability and control, it reduces stress to a level conducive to coping behavior (Rotter, 1966). In the absence of such a belief system, people experience a sense of helplessness, leading to withdrawal instead of coping behavior; these withdrawal responses may take the form of depression, fatalism, resignation, or alcohol or drug abuse (M. Inglehart, 1991).

Virtually all of the world's major cultures have belief systems which provide reassurance that, even though the individual alone cannot understand or predict what lies ahead, it is in the hands of a benevolent higher power. One's future may be unpredictable, but this higher power will ensure that things work out. Both religion and secular ideologies provide assurance that the universe is not random, but follows a plan which guarantees that (in this world or the next) everything will turn out well. This belief reduces stress, enabling one to shut out anxiety and focus on some immediate coping strategy. Without such a belief system, extreme stress is likely to produce withdrawal reactions.

Religion is the dominant influence on the belief systems of most preindustrial societies. In religious worldviews, the higher power is an omniscient and benevolent God. Stress is reduced by a system of absolute rules that govern many aspects of life and maximize predictability. In secular societies, the state or a strong political leader fills the role of the higher power. Under conditions of great unpredictability, people have a powerful need to see authority as not only strong, but also benevolent—even in the face of evidence to the contrary.

Communist ideology provided a functional equivalent to religion, furnishing an explanation of how the universe functioned and where history was going. Although many of Marx's predictions eventually turned out to be wrong, the ideology provided a sense of predictability and reassured people that infallible leaders were in charge.

The Authoritarian Reflex

In societies undergoing an historical crisis, a phenomenon has been observed that might be called the Authoritarian Reflex. Rapid change leads to severe insecurity, giving rise to a powerful need for predictability. Under these circumstances, the Authoritarian Reflex takes two forms:

1. Fundamentalist or nativist reactions. This phenomenon frequently occurs in preindustrial societies when they are confronted with rapid political and economic change through contact with industrialized societies; and it is often found among the more traditional and less secure strata in industrial societies, especially during times of stress. In both cases, the reaction to change takes the form of a rejection of the new, and a compulsive insistence on the infallibility of old, familiar cultural patterns.

2. Adulation of strong secular leaders. In secularized societies, severe insecurity brings a readiness to defer to strong secular leaders, in hopes that superior men of iron will can lead their people to safety. This phenomenon frequently occurs in response to military defeat or economic or political collapse.

Thus, disintegrating societies often give rise to authoritarian and xenophobic reactions. Pogroms broke out in the declining years of Czarist Russia, and after its collapse power was seized by rulers who were even more ruthlessly authoritarian than the czars. Similarly, the Great Depression of the 1930s helped bring Hitler to power in Germany and contributed to the rise of fascistic dictators in a number of other countries, from Spain to Hungary to Japan.

Massive insecurity is conducive not only to a need for strong authority figures to protect one from threatening forces, but also to xenophobia (Tajfel,

1978; Tajfel and Turner, 1979; Hamilton, 1981; Jackson and Inglehart, 1996). Frighteningly rapid change breeds an intolerance of cultural change, and of different ethnic groups. Thus, in the United States during the late nineteenth and early twentieth centuries, when the price of cotton went down, lynchings of Blacks went up in the South. This was a reaction to insecurity, not a cognitive response to the belief that Blacks were manipulating the price of cotton: the lynchers were aware that Blacks had little influence on the cotton market (Beck, Massey, and Tolnay, 1989). Similarly, the Great Depression of the 1930s gave rise to the twin phenomena of Hitler and anti-Semitism—and ultimately, to the Holocaust. There was nothing inevitable in this horror story. It occurred in a society that previously had been more tolerant toward Jews than had Russia or France and had one of the most socially integrated Jewish communities in Europe. It reflected traumatic insecurity caused by military defeat and political and economic collapse, rather than anything uniquely German. In a hauntingly parallel phenomenon, the collapse of the economic and political systems of what used to be the Soviet Union and Yugoslavia has given rise to ultranationalism and "ethnic cleansing."

Postmodernism: Declining Emphasis on Political, Economic,
and Scientific Authority

All societies depend on some legitimating formula for authority: unless their leaders' decisions are seen as legitimate, they rest solely on coercion. A central component of Modernization was the shift from religious authority to rational-bureaucratic authority, justified by claims that the governing institutions were conducive to the general good.

A major component of the Postmodern shift is a shift away from *both* religious and bureaucratic authority, bringing declining emphasis on all kinds of authority. For deference to authority has high costs: the individual's personal goals must be subordinated to those of a broader entity. But under conditions of insecurity, people are more than willing to do so. Under threat of invasion, internal disorder, or economic collapse, people eagerly seek strong authority figures who can protect them.

Conversely, conditions of prosperity and security are conducive to pluralism in general and democracy in particular. This helps explain a long-established finding: rich societies are much likelier to be democratic than poor ones. This finding was pointed out by Lipset (1960) and has been confirmed most recently by Burkhart and Lewis-Beck (1994). The reasons why this is true are complex (we will examine them in chapter 5); but one factor is that the authoritarian reflex is strongest under conditions of insecurity.

Until recently, insecurity was a central part of the human condition. Only recently have societies emerged in which most of the population did *not* feel insecure concerning survival. Thus, both premodern agrarian society and modern industrial society were shaped by survival values. But the Postmodern shift has brought a broad de-emphasis on all forms of authority.

Changing Religious Orientations, Gender Roles, and Sexual Norms

The rise of Postmodernism is the reverse of the Authoritarian Reflex: Postmaterialist values characterize the most *secure* segment of advanced industrial society. Postmaterialist values developed in the environment of the historically unprecedented economic growth and the welfare states that emerged after World War II. And they are a core element of a Postmodern shift that is reshaping the political outlook, religious orientations, gender roles, and sexual norms of advanced industrial society. Two factors contribute to the decline of traditional political, religious, social, and sexual norms in advanced industrial societies.

The first is that an increasing sense of security brings a diminishing need for absolute rules. Individuals under high stress have a need for rigid, predictable rules. They need to be sure of what is going to happen because they are in danger—their margin for error is slender and they need maximum predictability. Postmaterialists embody the opposite outlook: raised under conditions of relative security, they can tolerate more ambiguity; they are less likely to need the security of absolute rigid rules that religious sanctions provide. The psychological costs of deviating from whatever norms one grew up with are harder to bear if a person is under stress than if a person feels secure. Taking one's world apart and putting it together again is extremely stressful. But Postmaterialists—people with relatively high levels of security—can more readily accept deviation from familiar patterns than can people who feel anxiety concerning their basic existential needs. Consequently, Postmaterialists accept cultural change more readily than others.

The second reason is that societal and religious norms usually have a function. Such basic norms as "Thou shalt not kill" (the Judeo-Christian version of a virtually universal social norm) serve an important societal function. Restricting violence to narrow, predictable channels is crucial to a society's viability. Without such norms, a society would tear itself apart.

Many religious norms such as "Thou shalt not commit adultery" or "Honor thy father and mother" are linked with maintaining the family unit. Various versions of these norms are also found in virtually every society on earth because they serve crucial functions. But in advanced industrial society, some of these functions have dwindled.

The role of the family has become less crucial than it once was. Although the family was once the key economic unit, in advanced industrial society one's working life overwhelmingly takes place outside the home. Similarly, education now takes place mainly outside the family. Furthermore, the welfare state has taken over responsibility for survival. Formerly, whether children lived or died depended on whether their parents provided for them, and the parents' survival depended on their children when they reached old age. Today, though the family is still important, it is no longer a life or death relationship; its role has largely been taken over by the welfare state. The new generation can survive if the family breaks up—or even if neither parent is around. One-parent families and childless old people have vastly better chances for survival under contemporary conditions than ever before. As long as it threatens the survival of children, society is apt to view divorce as absolutely wrong: it undermines the long-term viability of society itself. Today, the functional basis of this norm and other norms reinforcing the two-parent family has eroded: does that mean that society changes its values? No—at least, not immediately.

Cultural norms are usually internalized very firmly at an early age, and backed up by prerational sanctions. People's opposition to divorce does not simply reflect an individual's rational calculation that "the family is an important social unit, so I should stay married." Instead, divorce tends to be made a question of good and evil, through absolute norms. Norms that constrain people's behavior even when they strongly want to do something else are norms that have been taught as absolute rules, and inculcated so that their consciences torture them if these norms are violated. Such societal norms have a great deal of momentum. The mere fact that the function of a given cultural pattern has weakened or disappeared does not mean that the norm immediately disappears. But it opens the way for that norm to weaken gradually, especially if those norms conflict with strong impulses to the contrary.

Norms supporting the two-parent heterosexual family are weakening for a variety of reasons, ranging from the rise of the welfare state to the drastic decline of infant mortality rates, which means that a couple no longer needs to produce four or five children in order for the population to reproduce itself. Experimentation and testing of the old rules takes place; gradually, new forms of behavior emerge that deviate from traditional norms, and the groups most likely to accept these new forms of behavior are the young more than the old, and the relatively secure, more than the insecure.

The Postmodern shift involves an intergenerational change in a wide variety of basic social norms, from cultural norms linked with ensuring survival of the species, to norms linked with the pursuit of individual well-being. For example, Postmaterialists and the young are markedly more tolerant of homosexuality than are Materialists and the old. This is part of a pervasive pattern. Postmaterialists have been shaped by security during their formative years and are far more permissive than Materialists in their attitudes toward abortion, divorce, extramarital affairs, prostitution, and euthanasia. Materialists, conversely, are likely to adhere to the traditional societal norms that favored childbearing, but only within the traditional two-parent family—and that heavily stigmatized any sexual activity outside that setting.

Traditional gender role norms from East Asia to the Islamic world to Western society discouraged women from taking jobs outside the home. Virtually all preindustrial societies emphasized childbearing and childrearing as the central goal of any woman, her most important function in life, and her greatest source of satisfaction. In recent years, this perspective has been increasingly called into question, as growing numbers of women postpone having children or forego them completely in order to devote themselves to careers outside the home.

EXISTENTIAL SECURITY AND THE RISE OF POSTMODERN VALUES

Throughout advanced industrial society, there is evidence of a long-term shift away from traditional religious and cultural norms. This decline of traditional norms is closely linked with the shift from Materialist toward Postmaterialist values. In terms of face content, this is not obvious: none of the survey items used to measure Materialist/Postmaterialist values makes any reference whatever to religion or to sexual or gender norms. Nevertheless, all of these values are components of a broad cultural change linked with the transition from industrial to postindustrial society. The shift to Postmaterialism and the decline of traditional religious and sexual norms go together because they share a common cause: the unprecedented levels of existential security attained in contemporary advanced industrial society that grows out of the economic miracles (both Western and Asian) of the past several decades, and the rise of the welfare state.

In the highly uncertain world of subsistence societies, the need for absolute standards and a sense that an infallible higher power will ensure that things ultimately turn out well filled a major psychological need. One of the key functions of religion has been to provide a sense of certainty in an insecure environment. Not only economic insecurity gives rise to this need: the old saying that "there are no atheists in foxholes" reflects the fact that physical danger also leads to a need for belief in a higher power. But in the absence of war, prosperity and the welfare state have produced an unprecedented sense of security concerning one's survival. This has diminished the need for the reassurance that religion traditionally provided.

These same factors have weakened the functional basis of a pervasive set of norms linked with the fact that, throughout most of history, the traditional two-parent family was crucial to the survival of children, and thus, of society. These norms ranged from disapproval of divorce, abortion, and homosexuality, to negative attitudes toward careers outside the home for married women. As we will see, it is precisely in the most advanced welfare states that mass adherence to traditional religious and family norms has declined most rapidly. This is no coincidence. These factors are also changing another major aspect of people's worldviews: respect for authority is declining throughout advanced industrial society.

The difference between feeling secure or insecure about survival is so basic that it has led to a wide-ranging but coherent syndrome of changes, from the "survival" values that characterized agrarian and early industrial society, to the "well-being" values that characterize advanced industrial society.

The difference between whether one views survival as uncertain, or assumes that it can be taken for granted, is central in shaping people's life strategies, giving rise to very distinct worldviews. Throughout most of history, in both agrarian and early industrial society, survival has been uncertain for the great majority of the population; consequently, they have emphasized survival values. Postmodern values grow out of the unprecedented mass prosperity of advanced industrial societies in which, for the first time in history, large segments of the public take survival for granted. These contrasting value systems have ramifications that extend across politics, economics, sexual and family norms, and religion, as table 1.1 illustrates.

The shift from modern to Postmodern values is eroding many of the key institutions of industrial society, through the following changes:

1. In the political realm, the rise of Postmodern values brings declining respect for authority, and growing emphasis on participation and self-expression. These two trends are conducive to democratization (in authoritarian societies) and to more participatory, issue-oriented democracy (in already democratic societies). But they are making the position of governing elites more difficult.

Respect for authority is eroding. And the long-term trend toward increased mass participation is not only continuing, but has taken on a new character. In large-scale agrarian societies, political participation was limited to a narrow minority. In industrial society, the masses were mobilized by disciplined elite-led political parties. This was a major advance for democratization, and it resulted in unprecedented numbers of people taking part in politics by voting—but mass participation rarely went much beyond this level. In Postmodern society the emphasis is shifting from voting, to more active and issue-specific forms of mass participation. Mass loyalties to long-established hierarchical political parties are eroding; no longer content to be disciplined troops, the pub-

TABLE 1.1
Security and Insecurity: Two Contrasting Value Systems

Survival Is Seen as	
Insecure	*Secure*
1. Politics	
Need for strong leaders	De-emphasis on political authority
Order	Self-expression, participation
Xenophobia/fundamentalism	Exotic/new are stimulating
2. Economics	
Priority to economic growth	Quality of life = top priority
Achievement motivation	Subjective well-being
Individual vs. state ownership	Diminishing authority of both private and state ownership
3. Sexual/Family Norms	
Maximize reproduction—but only in two-parent heterosexual family	Individual sexual gratification Individual self-expression
4. Religion	
Emphasis on higher power	Diminishing religious authority
Absolute rules	Flexible rules, situational ethics
Emphasis on predictability	Emphasis on meaning and purpose of life

lic has become increasingly autonomous and elite-challenging. Consequently, though voter turnout is stagnant or declining, people are participating in politics in increasingly active and more issue-specific ways. Moreover, a growing segment of the population is coming to value freedom of expression and political participation as things that are good in themselves, rather than simply as a possible means to attain economic security.

But these changes have had a traumatic impact on the old-line political machines of industrial society, which are in disarray almost everywhere. Throughout the history of industrial society, the scope of state activities had been growing rapidly; it seemed to be a law of nature that government control of economy and society would continue to expand. That trend has now reached a set of natural limits—both for functional reasons and because of eroding public trust in government and a growing resistance to government intrusion. The people of each society tend to assume that this erosion of confidence is due to factors unique to their own country; in reality, it is taking place throughout advanced industrial society.

Xenophobia thrives under conditions of rapid change and insecurity. Today, this is especially evident in what used to be Yugoslavia and the Soviet Union, and ethnic hatred has not disappeared even in more secure industrial societies. But xenophobia is less widespread in secure societies than in insecure ones; and in long-term perspective, the more secure societies seem to be moving toward increasing acceptance of diversity. Finally, Postmodern politics are distinguished by a shift from the class-based political conflict that characterized industrial society, to increasing emphasis on cultural and quality of life issues.

2. In the economic realm, existential security leads to increasing emphasis on subjective well-being and quality of life concerns; for many people, these become higher priorities than economic growth. The core goals of Modernization, economic growth, and economic achievement are still positively valued, but their relative importance is declining.

There is also a gradual shift in what motivates people to work: emphasis shifts from maximizing one's income and job security toward a growing insistence on interesting and meaningful work. Along with this comes a twofold shift in the relationship between owners and managers. On one hand, we find a growing emphasis on more collegial and participatory styles of management. But at the same time, there is a reversal of the tendency to look to government for solutions to such problems and a growing acceptance of capitalism and market principles. Both trends are linked with a growing rejection of hierarchical authority patterns and rising emphasis on individual autonomy. Ever since the era of laissez-faire capitalism, people have almost automatically turned to government to offset the power of private business. Today, there is a widespread feeling that the growth of government is becoming functionally ineffective and a threat to individual autonomy.

3. In the realm of sexual behavior, reproduction, and the family, there is a continued trend away from the rigid norms that were a functional necessity in

agrarian society. In these societies, traditional methods of contraception were unreliable, and children born outside a family with a male breadwinner were likely to starve; sexual abstinence except in marriage was a key means of population control. The development of effective birth control technology, together with prosperity and the welfare state, have eroded the functional basis of traditional norms in this area; there is a general shift toward greater flexibility for individual choice in sexual behavior, and a dramatic increase in the acceptance of homosexuality. This not only continues some of the trends associated with modernity, but breaks through to new levels. Gays and lesbians have come out of the closet, and unmarried parenthood is a normal part of prime time television.

4. In the realm of ultimate values, we also find both continuity and striking change. One of the key trends associated with Modernization was secularization. This trend has continued, where established religious institutions are concerned: the publics of most advanced industrial societies show both declining confidence in churches and falling rates of church attendance and are placing less emphasis on organized religion. This does not mean that spiritual concerns are vanishing, however: for we also find a consistent cross-national tendency for people to spend *more* time thinking about the meaning and purpose of life. The dominance of instrumental rationality is giving way to growing concern for ultimate ends.

These trends reflect the unprecedented security that has developed in Postmodern society. Economic accumulation for the sake of economic security was the central goal of industrial society. Ironically, their attainment set in motion a process of gradual cultural change that has made these goals less central—and is now bringing a rejection of the hierarchical institutions that helped attain them.

PREDICTING CULTURAL CHANGE

The theory of value change generates a number of clear predictions. Table 1.1 outlines a set of qualitative shifts linked with growing existential security. This table shows what *kinds* of values we would expect to become more widespread as Postmodernization takes place. But the theory is not limited to qualitative predictions concerning the general direction of cultural change. It also generates a set of quantitative predictions concerning where and how fast these changes should occur. The scarcity hypothesis postulates that a sense of existential security is conducive to Postmodern values. This gives rise to the following predictions:

1. In cross-national perspective, Postmodern values will be most widespread in the richest and most secure societies; the publics of impoverished societies will place more emphasis on survival values.

2. Within any given society, Postmodern values will be most widespread

among the more secure strata: the wealthier and better educated will be most likely to hold a whole range of security values, including Postmaterialism; the less secure strata will emphasize survival priorities.

3. Short-term fluctuations will follow the implications of the scarcity hypothesis: prosperity will enhance the tendency to emphasize well-being values; economic downturn, civil disorder, or war will lead people to emphasize survival values.

4. Long-term changes will also reflect the scarcity hypothesis. In societies that have experienced high levels of security for several decades, we should find a long-term shift from survival values toward well-being values. This is not a universal trend that sweeps the entire world, like the popularization of pop culture fostered by the global mass media. Instead, the shift toward well-being values is occurring mainly in those societies that have attained such a high level of prosperity and safety that a substantial share of the population takes survival for granted; it is not found in societies that have not experienced rising prosperity. On the other hand, it is *not* a uniquely Western phenomenon: it should appear in any society that *has* experienced the transition to high mass security.

The socialization hypothesis postulates that neither an individual's values nor those of a society as a whole will change overnight. In connection with the scarcity hypothesis, this generates three additional predictions:

5. In societies that have experienced a long period of rising economic and physical security, we will find substantial differences between the value priorities of older and younger groups: the young will be much likelier to emphasize well-being values than the old. This reflects the fact that the young experienced greater security during their formative years than did the old. Fundamental value change takes place mainly as younger birth cohorts replace older ones in a given society.

6. These intergenerational value differences should be reasonably stable over time: though immediate conditions of security or insecurity will produce short-term fluctuations, the underlying differences between younger and older birth cohorts should persist over long periods of time. The young will not take on the values of the old as they age, as would happen if the intergenerational differences reflected life-cycle effects; instead, after two or three decades have passed, the younger cohorts should still show the distinctive values that characterized them at the start of the period.

7. In cross-national perspective, large amounts of intergenerational *change* will be found in those countries that have experienced relatively high rates of economic *growth*: if differences between the values of young and old were a normal feature of the human life cycle, they would be found everywhere. But if, as our theory implies, this process of value change is driven by historical changes in the degree of security experienced during one's preadult years, then the age differences found in a given society will reflect that society's economic history: the difference between the values of young and old will be largest in countries like Western Germany or South Korea that experienced the greatest

increases in prosperity during the past 40 years; and conversely, the difference between the values of young and old will be small or nonexistent in such countries as Nigeria and India, which experienced relatively little increase in per capita income from 1950 to 1990.

Thus, high *levels* of prosperity should be conducive to high *levels* of Postmaterialism and other Postmodern values; high rates of economic *growth* should produce relatively rapid rates of value *change* and relatively large intergenerational *differences*.

8. Finally, the theory of intergenerational value change not only yields predictions about what kinds of values should be emerging and where, but even predicts how much value change should be observed in a given period of time. Since the change is based on intergenerational population replacement, if one knows the distribution of values across birth cohorts in a given nation and the sizes of the cohorts, one can estimate how much change will be produced in a given time span, as a result of intergenerational population replacement. With the four-item Materialist/Postmaterialist values battery, for example, population replacement should produce a shift toward Postmaterialism of approximately one point per year on the Materialist-Postmaterialist percentage difference index (Abramson and Inglehart, 1992).

Authoritarianism and the Postmodern Shift

We have just described a syndrome of cultural changes through which people are shifting from one belief system to another. Under conditions of insecurity people seek strong authority; this is part of a worldview that also embraces ethnocentrism, traditional gender roles, and traditional religious norms.

This is not the first time that such a configuration of orientations has been observed. Several decades ago, Adorno et al. (1950) demonstrated that orientations toward authority, aggression toward outgroups, and a high degree of adherence to social conventions go together in a syndrome that they called *The Authoritarian Personality*. This work was controversial, evoking numerous critiques on both theoretical and methodological grounds. Despite massive criticism, this thesis generated an immense body of research that has survived and evolved over the years, with particularly significant recent contributions being made by Altemeyer (1981, 1988).

From the outset of our research, the Authoritarian Personality thesis seemed potentially relevant to the rise of Materialist/Postmaterialist values that are at the core of Postmodern values. A standardized set of authoritarianism items was used in a cross-national exploration of nationalism and internationalism. The results were disappointing: dimensional analysis showed that the authoritarianism items did not cluster together as they theoretically should (Inglehart, 1970).

Subsequent pilot tests gave similar results. Authoritarianism items showed relatively weak relationships with each other; some were closely related to the Materialist/Postmaterialist dimension, but others tapped quite different dimensions. Authoritarianism, as originally operationalized, has a poor empirical fit with Materialism/Postmaterialism.

The theoretical basis of authoritarianism is not necessarily incompatible with that of Materialism/Postmaterialism, but there are important differences in focus. The initial concept of authoritarianism emphasizes the psychodynamics of harsh discipline in early childrearing, rather than influences from the broader economic and political environment. On the other hand, Hyman and Sheatsley (1954), in their critique of the original study, argue a cognitive explanation: certain respondents, especially those from a lower socioeconomic level, may show an authoritarian-type response because this is a more or less accurate reflection of the conditions governing their adult lives; Altemeyer also endorses this interpretation. Our own interpretation of the genesis of Materialist/Postmaterialist values contains elements of both positions. It emphasizes the importance of early experiences, but links them with one's formative experiences as a whole, and not just parental discipline.

The original authoritarianism hypothesis does not predict either the age-group differences or the social class differences that are strikingly evident in our data. Quite the contrary, studies of authoritarianism have found that children tend to be *more* authoritarian than adults. It would not be impossible to reinterpret the *Authoritarian Personality* hypothesis in such a way as to explain the age and class differences. One might argue that childrearing practices vary according to social class and have changed over time. But if one did so, one would then need to seek an explanation of *why* they vary and *why* they have changed. Quite probably, one would eventually trace this explanation to the economic and political changes on which we rest our own interpretation.

Another important distinction between authoritarianism and Materialist/Postmaterialist values lies in the way they are measured: authoritarianism reflects *levels* of support for given positions; Materialist/Postmaterialist values deal with *priorities*—that is, the relative *rank* of various goals. This distinction is crucial, and will be discussed at some length in chapter 3. Our theory implies that an intergenerational change in *priorities* is taking place—and *not* that people no longer value economic security. Nevertheless, the two streams of research agree on one major point: orientations toward authority are related to a broad range of other orientations, forming the core of a coherent worldview.

Changing Mass Values: Testing Our Predictions

We now have a large body of empirical evidence on cultural change, from surveys carried out in more than 40 societies over the past 25 years. Using these data, this book will test these predictions. Chapter 4 focuses on the relatively detailed and abundant body of data concerning the Materialist/Postmaterialist value shift; chapters 8 and 9 examine the evidence of a much broader process of cultural change involving religious, civic, sexual, and economic norms as well as Materialist/Postmaterialist values.

The following chapters examine survey data from societies containing 70

percent of the world's population. For 21 of these societies, we have time series data from the World Values surveys carried out in 1981 and 1990. For several societies, we also have detailed time series data on value changes from
1970 to 1994. The evidence from these surveys indicates that advanced industrial societies are moving on a common trajectory. To a striking degree, societies in Western Europe, North America, Latin America, Eastern Europe, and
East Asia are undergoing similar cultural changes in politics, economics, sex
and gender norms, and religion. Although they have widely varying cultural
traditions and start from very different levels, they are generally moving in the
same direction.

Do the values linked with secure survival actually move in the predicted direction from 1981 to 1990? As we will see below, on the whole our predictions
hold up very well when tested against data from the 21 nations surveyed in
both 1981 and 1990. About 40 variables were strongly correlated with existential security. These variables move in the predicted direction in most countries for which data are available. Moreover our predictions hold up best in
those countries that experienced relatively prosperous circumstances; they fail
to apply in those countries that experienced economic decline and political upheaval—precisely as the theory implies.

These findings suggest that social science can sometimes have predictive
power: when we are dealing with relatively enduring aspects of the outlook of
given birth cohorts, we can anticipate that change will tend to move in a specific direction, as intergenerational population replacement occurs. Other factors such as the rise and fall of the economic cycle or war and peace will also
shape the outlook of a given society at a given time. But in the long run, across
many societies, such situational factors tend to cancel each other out: the influence of intergenerational population replacement, on the other hand, tends
to work in a specific direction for many decades, and its cumulative impact can
be great.

This study was motivated by the belief that mass belief systems have important economic, political, and social consequences. Although it has long
been believed that given cultural patterns tend to go with given economic and
political systems, this belief has rested mainly on impressionistic evidence: it
has been difficult to demonstrate empirically because, until recently, cross-culturally comparable measures of beliefs and values have not been available on
a global scale. Empirical evidence from 43 societies demonstrates that cultural
patterns are, indeed, linked with important economic and political variables—
and that the cross-level linkages are astonishingly strong.

Chapter 5 examines the causal linkages between culture and democracy in
greater detail; chapter 6 focuses on the linkages between culture and economic
growth. In both cases, the evidence suggests that culture is not just a dependent variable, but has an important impact on both democracy and economic
growth.

The evidence we will examine makes it clear that—as both Marx and Weber
argued—belief systems, economics, and politics *are* intimately related. Their

linkages seem to reflect neither a simple Marxian causality (with economics driving culture and politics) nor a simple Weberian causality (with culture driving economics and politics), but reciprocal causal relationships. Cultural, economic, and political systems tend to be mutually supportive in any society that survives for long. They help shape each other, and they are changing the world in ways that are to some extent predictable.

Individual-Level Change and Societal-Level Change

THE NEXT SEVERAL CHAPTERS examine the linkages between individual-level value change and changes at the societal level. This chapter investigates how economic development brings changes in human life strategies—and then examines the ways in which cultural changes can give rise to legal and institutional changes. Chapter 5 will analyze how belief systems influence the emergence of democratic institutions, chapter 6 examines the impact of values on economic growth, and chapter 7 examines their impact on political cleavages.

In analyzing the linkages between belief systems and societal variables, the first question one is likely to ask is, Do the values and attitudes of individuals affect their behavior? If they *do not*, then changes in these values and attitudes could scarcely have any impact on the society as a whole. And it has often been claimed that people's attitudes have no impact on their behavior.

DO ATTITUDES SHAPE BEHAVIOR?

In the 1930s, an American social scientist reported that, in response to a written inquiry, most of the restaurant owners whom he contacted said they would not serve Chinese customers; but when he appeared at these same restaurants with a young Chinese couple, almost all of them actually did so (LaPiere, 1934). He concluded that attitudes were irrelevant to actual behavior. This finding was so counterintuitive and so interesting that it was widely cited for several decades. And as recently as the 1960s, a review of empirical studies concluded that attitudes were generally "unrelated or only slightly related to overt behaviors" (Wicker, 1969: 65).

A more recent review of 88 attitude-behavior studies comes to a very different conclusion: Kraus (1995) finds that attitudes significantly and substantially predict future behavior. Furthermore, the most important factor associated with high attitude-behavior correlations was whether the research design used the same level of specificity in the attitudinal and behavioral measures—as Fishbein and Ajzen (1975) had suggested 20 years earlier. Not surprisingly, broad global attitudes do not necessarily predict specific behaviors. For example, one's answer to the question "Are you a liberal or a conservative?" is not nearly as good a predictor of voting behavior, as is one's voting intention. And the question "Do you believe in God?" does not predict church attendance as well as the question "Do you think it's important to go to church?" Belief in God is a more global attitude than is emphasis on church attendance. On the other hand, global attitudes *are* relatively good at predicting global patterns of behavior. In short, low levels of attitude-behavior consistency are largely a measurement problem.

The situation in which behavior occurs *does* influence one's behavior. It is even possible to contrive situations in which the underlying attitude is completely irrelevant to the behavior being measured: for example, regardless of their attitudes, no one votes for environmentalist parties in countries where no such parties exist. It is equally true, however, that if people give low priority to environmental protection (as was generally the case until a few decades ago), there is little support for environmentalist movements or parties, even if they *do* exist. As criminologists discovered long ago, both the motive and the opportunity must be present for behavior to take place. In appropriately designed studies, one generally *does* find significant and substantial linkages between attitudes and behavior.

Furthermore, it is important to distinguish between central and strongly held attitudes, and peripheral and fleeting ones. In the early 1930s, when the classic LaPiere study was carried out, there were very few Chinese in most parts of the United States. Some respondents may have responded to LaPiere's hypothetical question on the basis of vague and rarely examined stereotypes of coolie laborers. When confronted with a well-dressed young couple accompanied by a college professor, they served them without hesitation.

But at precisely the same time, attitudes toward African Americans were highly salient and strongly held in most parts of the United States If exactly the same experiment had been held in 1934 using Blacks instead of Chinese as the test case, it seems likely that a large proportion of the restaurant owners would have said that they would not serve Blacks—and then proceeded to *do* exactly what they had said. To anyone who recalls the lunch counter sit-ins and the protracted desegregation struggles of the 1960s, it is evident that attitudes and behavior were all too consistent (and all too racist) where African Americans were concerned. During the first half of this century even more than today, a large proportion of the American people had negative attitudes toward Blacks *and* went to great lengths to exclude them from all aspects of their lives.

In short, attitudes do not determine behavior in any one-to-one fashion. One must also take situational factors into account. But the same is true of situations: by themselves, they do not determine what happens. Behavior requires both motive and opportunity.

CULTURE AND COERCION: TWO ASPECTS OF POLITICAL AUTHORITY

Value systems play an important role in any society. They provide the cultural basis for loyalty to given economic and political systems. And value systems interact with external economic and political factors in shaping social change. One cannot understand social change without taking it into account.

Culture has a crucial relationship to political authority. Culture is not just a random collection of the values, beliefs, and skills of the people in a given society. It constitutes a survival strategy. In any society that has survived for long, the cultural system is likely to have a mutually supportive relationship with the economic and political systems (see Bell, 1976). As Eckstein (1961, 1988) argues in his theory of stable democracy, a society's authority patterns and its political system must be congruent, for democracy to survive over the long term. Almond and Verba (1963) make a similar argument in *The Civic Culture*. Though they approach the question from a very different perspective, Marx and various Postmodernist thinkers also make essentially the same claim: a society's belief system tends to justify its social order, legitimating a given elite's right to rule. This is a crucial function.

A government is a decision-making system for a society. And the people in that society comply with their government's decisions either (1) because of external coercion, or (2) because they have internalized a set of norms that justifies compliance. All societies depend on some mixture of the two, though there are crucial differences in the *degree* to which given societies depend on coercion or on enculturated legitimacy. This is the crucial difference between unstable dictatorships and stable democracies. This balance between culture and coercion is so central to politics that Weber (1925) defined the political realm in terms of the *legitimate* use of *violence*, emphasizing the complementary roles of the two factors. As figure 2.1 indicates, legitimacy and violence (or culture and coercion) are at opposite poles of the political spectrum.

Any sociopolitical system that endures for long is supported by an underlying moral order. A warlord or military dictator can stay in power for a limited time through naked repression, but doing so is risky. It is costly to keep a soldier on every corner, enforcing government edicts at bayonet point; it is costly to maintain a massive repressive apparatus; and it is costly to buy loyalty that is not culturally internalized, but maintained only by external payoffs. Ultimately, the society's entire economic surplus may be diverted into maintaining the loyalty of the military elite. Moreover, the absence of culturally based loyalties means that the dictator is dependent on some kind of Praetorian Guard to stay in power, and therefore chronically vulnerable to a coup. Number one in the power structure lives in perpetual fear of number two.

Any elite that aspires to hold power for long will seek to legitimate itself—usually by conforming to established cultural norms, but sometimes by trying to reshape these norms so as to justify its right to rule. Conformity is much easier and less coercive than reshaping the culture; but when a truly revolutionary elite seizes power, it may attempt to reshape the cultural system to conform with its new ideology. This is a huge undertaking that generally requires the coercive capabilities of a totalitarian state. In the real world, all regimes rely on coercion to some extent, but it is far cheaper and safer to rely on inter-

CULTURE  **COERCION**

Figure 2.1. Legitimacy and violence in politics.
The continuum from internalized controls to external coercion.

nalized values and norms than to depend on naked force in order to get people to comply with one's policies. While newly established totalitarian regimes tend to be located near the pole labeled "coercion" on figure 2.1, democracies enjoying widespread legitimacy are located near the pole labeled "culture."

One of the most important functions of culture is its role in legitimating the society's political and economic systems. Indeed, Wilson (1992) goes so far as to define political culture as "a dominant ideology justifying compliance with a society's institutional system." This *is* one of political culture's most important functions, but not the only thing it does: in a democracy, for example, it may also legitimate dissent, through such norms as "the loyal opposition." In most systems, culture also has norms that place limits and obligations on elite behavior—and by doing so in the long run help legitimate the elites' right to rule.

Any political system that endures for long is virtually certain to be supported by an appropriate moral order, which shapes the political and the economic systems as well as being shaped by them. In preindustrial societies the moral order usually takes the form of a religion.

This moral order shapes all aspects of life, not just politics. It integrates the society through injunctions against internal violence (some variation of "Thou shalt not kill" is a basic principle in any society), and by instilling norms protecting private property (such as "Thou shalt not steal")—but balancing them with norms of charity and sharing that soften the struggle for survival.

These norms perform crucial functions in traditional societies. In order to be compelling enough to bring compliance even in the face of strong temptations to disobey, these norms are inculcated as absolute values, usually as rules that reflect the divine will. This is workable in relatively unchanging agrarian societies, but absolute values are inherently rigid and difficult to adjust to a rapidly changing environment. Breaking down at least some components of traditional value systems was necessary in order for Modernization to occur. This is one reason why the Protestant Reformation was so important in modernizing Western Europe, and why similar challenges to traditional values have been crucial elsewhere. In China, for example, key norms of the Confucian system (those stigmatizing manual work and mercantile and technological work as incompatible with the role of the refined scholar-bureaucrat) had to be broken down through successive waves of reform (first liberal and then Maoist) before modern economic development could take place. Similarly, the traditional virtue of unreservedly helping one's relatives and fellow villagers must be reined in: it becomes a major vice—nepotism—in a modern bureaucratic society.

The Balance between Culture and Coercion

Throughout history most regimes have been initiated by conquest, and as recently as 1970, most of the world's societies were governed by military dictatorships. Even after the recent global wave of democratization, the military still threaten to play a crucial role in politics, from Latin America to the former Soviet Union to Africa, if the new democratic regimes flounder. It is often asked, "Why do the military so often take over?" One might better ask, "Why doesn't the military *always* take power?" Control of the means of coercion is central to politics; it is only when cultural norms are strongly enough entrenched to prevent domination by force of arms that any *other* type of regime emerges. Without a strongly internalized cultural system, rule by the military is the simplest solution: in politics, clubs are trumps.

The question, then, is "How do you *prevent* the military from taking over?" The answer is, by instilling cultural norms that support other types of authority. It is especially important to instill these norms among the military elite. In a monarchy, these norms emphasize unquestioning obedience and loyalty to the king or queen. In the United States, they emphasize fidelity to the constitutional chain of command, with the president as commander-in-chief. And in Marxist regimes, the ideological taboo on "Bonapartism" played a crucial role: the founder of the Red Army, Leon Trotsky, accepted it even though it cost him political power and ultimately his life. These norms amount to a quasi-religious commandment, "Thou Shalt Not Carry Out a Military Coup."

Since coercion and culture are simply different aspects of political power, the elite most likely to dominate any society (after the military) is the priesthood or the other ideologues who provide the authoritative interpretation of the society's cultural norms. In ancient Egypt and Sumeria, Medieval Europe and the Aztec empire, the priesthood was dominant or ruled on equal terms with military elites; in Soviet Russia and Maoist China, Marxist ideologues played a dominant role. And in legalistic societies, lawyers rule: as the authoritative interpreters of American society's legitimating myth, lawyers are the functional equivalent of the priesthood.

Culture is the subjective component of a society's equipment for coping with its environment: the values, attitudes, beliefs, skills, knowledge of its people. Economic, political, and other external factors are equally important, but they are not decisive by themselves. When dealing with human beings, there is a continual interaction between subjective and objective factors—between culture and environment. What goes on inside people's heads is as important as what goes on outside them. Although it usually changes slowly, culture does change through interaction with the environment (as processed through subjective cultural filters).

Culture does not simply consist of the myths propagated to justify those in power (though this is always an important component). It reflects the entire historical heritage and life experiences of a given people. Some Postmodern theorists collapse the continuum from culture to coercion, making culture simply a disguised form of coercion. We reject this position. With Habermas, we believe that uncoerced communication is also possible—and that this possibility expands in advanced industrial society.

Changing Values and Changing Family Patterns

Postmodern values reflect the assumption that survival can be taken for granted, which leads to a growing emphasis on self-expression. In preindustrial society, the two-parent family was crucial to the survival of children; in advanced industrial societies, growing numbers of people have come to see the family as an optional aspect of one's lifestyle. Postmodern values place top priority on self-fulfillment through careers, rather than childbearing. Nevertheless, they are relatively permissive toward single parenthood, because they tend to take the economic viability of the single mother for granted.

This changing cultural outlook among individuals is reflected in changes at the societal level. Starting in the mid-1960s, birth rates declined throughout advanced industrial societies. Meanwhile, divorce rates, abortion rates, and illegitimate births rose sharply. By 1990, fertility rates were below the population replacement level in almost all advanced industrial societies. Such demographic phenomena are complex, involving economic, political, and other factors, but it seems clear that cultural change has played a significant role in this shift (see Lesthaeghe and Meekers, 1986).

Although birth rates fell, the proportion of births that took place outside of marriage *rose* tremendously, tripling in the United States and increasing by 250 percent from 1960 to 1990 in the European Union as a whole. Here, too, it appears that cultural factors play a major role.

Finally, divorce rates rose in almost all advanced industrial societies but one—the Republic of Ireland, where divorce remained illegal until 1995. In Italy and Spain, it became legal only recently. For Western Europe as a whole, however, the divorce rate more than quadrupled from 1960 to 1990. Aggregate statistical data support the interpretation that norms linked with religion and the inviolability of the family have been growing weaker.

Here, as with any major social change, the causes can be interpreted on more than one level. One could argue, for example, that the dramatic decline in birth rates is due to advances in contraceptive technology. There is no question that developments in contraceptive technology played an important instrumental role—but effective birth control techniques have existed for many decades. Nevertheless, in the 1950s birth rates rose to levels far above those of previous years; and the decline that is now so dramatically apparent set in after 1965. The emergence of below-replacement-level birth rates reflects a combination of two things: 1. The availability of effective birth control technology, and 2. The fact that people choose to use it. The fact that people increasingly choose to have children later in life or not at all seems to reflect a gradual change in underlying norms. Both the technology and the fact that people choose to use it are essential, and to ask which one was the real cause is to pose false alternatives.

Similarly, one might argue that the recent surge in divorces in Italy and Spain is the result of legal changes: divorce used to be illegal, but is no longer. This interpretation is perfectly true, but superficial. If one probes deeper, the first question that arises is "*Why* did divorce become legal in these countries?" Divorce had been illegal for centuries because it violated deeply held religious norms in those cultures. This still was true in the Republic of Ireland until 1995: a majority of the public had voted against legalizing divorce as recently as 1987. But, as our data suggest, these norms have gradually been weakening over time. Public support for legalizing divorce became increasingly widespread and articulate in Italy and Spain, until the laws themselves were changed in the 1970s. And by 1995, even the Irish finally accepted divorce in a national referendum. One consequence was a sudden surge of divorces in these countries immediately after the laws were changed. Although this *behavioral* change was sudden and lumpy, it reflected a long process of incremental value change.

Some writers have interpreted the lumpiness of the behavioral symptoms of cultural change as meaning that no long-term decline in traditional norms is taking place. For example, Hout and Greeley (1987) point out that in the United States church attendance among Protestants has not declined in recent decades; and, while it fell sharply among Catholics from 1968 to 1975, it has not declined subsequently. They conclude that the lack of a steady downward trend contradicts the secularization thesis.

This argument is not compelling: church attendance rates provide only a very rough indicator of underlying cultural changes. More important, this argument assumes that there must be a one-to-one relationship between the pace of attitudinal changes and their behavioral consequences. Since they operate on different levels, with behavioral patterns often more subject to institutional and situational constraints, this is not necessarily the case. The sudden decline in Catholic church attendance, for example, may have been precipitated by the strong opposition to artificial birth control that Pope Paul VI voiced in 1968. But the public's negative reaction to papal authority also reflected the fact that a majority of American Catholics had come to *disagree* with the church's long-standing position on birth control by that point in time—a change that had taken place gradually, over a long period of time.

The rise of the Greens in West Germany provides another illustration of the disparity between the incremental pace of cultural change and the sudden emergence of its behavioral symptoms. In 1983 the Greens suddenly achieved worldwide prominence when they won enough votes to enter the West German parliament for the first time, bringing a fundamental change in the equilibrium of West German politics. But this abrupt breakthrough reflected a gradual intergenerational rise of mass support for environmentalist policies. Institutional barriers, such as the fact that a party must win at least 5 percent of the vote to gain seats in the Bundestag, made the party's breakthrough to prominence sudden and dramatic. But its rise reflected long-term processes of incremental change. If one focuses only on the immediate causes, a society's electoral rules appear to be the decisive factor: the Greens had little visibility until they surmounted the 5 percent threshold; and in societies without proportional representation, such as the United States and Great Britain, ecology parties may never play an important role. But even in these countries, a rising concern for environmental protection has transformed the agendas of existing parties. In most societies, the activists of Green parties are mainly Postmaterialists, and it seems unlikely that Green parties or environmentalist movements would have emerged without the cultural changes that gave rise to a Postmaterialist worldview.

In the United States, there has recently been a renewed emphasis on religious issues, including a heated antiabortion movement and a campaign to allow prayer in public schools. This has been interpreted as a manifestation of a swing to the Right on cultural issues.

This interpretation seems to be mistaken. Our evidence points to a pervasive tendency toward secularization. Clearly, the pro-prayer and Right to Life movements *do* have devoted partisans. But their revival of religious issues reflects a reaction among a gradually dwindling traditionalist sector, rather than a surge toward cultural conservatism among the population at large. Glenn (1987) has examined long-term trends in American survey data on this subject. He finds only a moderate overall decline in church membership, but a substantial decline in endorsement of traditional Christian beliefs. For example, the share of the American public who considered religion very important in their lives declined from 75 percent in the 1950s to 56 percent in the 1980s. This book will present additional evidence from many countries, indicating that for the past several decades adherence to traditional cultural norms has been in retreat. The societal-level consequences of this retreat have become manifest in rising rates of divorce and abortion—and in institutional changes that have made them easier to obtain. The intensity with which religious issues have been raised in recent years reflects their adherents' alarmed and passionate conviction that some of their most basic values are rapidly eroding—and not the growth of mass support for traditional religion.

Institutional determinists (e.g., Skocpol, 1982, Jackman and Miller, 1996) argue that institutions are exogenous while culture is endogenous—in other words, that institutions always shape attitudes and beliefs, never the other way around. This attempt to solve an empirical question by definitional fiat is begging the question. And historical evidence indicates that the assumption that institutions are always exogenous is simplistic. It works both ways: sometimes institutions shape cultural values, and sometimes culture shapes institutions.

Switzerland, for example, has a federal structure with extreme decentralization of authority and a seven-person council instead of one individual as prime minister. If one knows Swiss history, it is obvious that its ethnic diversity gave rise to these institutions, and not the other way around (they are a means of avoiding the appearance that one ethnic group dominates the others). Belgium, India, and Canada have somewhat similar institutions for similar reasons. To anyone familiar with these societies, the claim that the institutions gave rise to the culture would seem preposterous. Historically, the ethnic diversity preceded the federal structure and other institutions that help these societies cope with diversity. In a variety of ways, from Spain to Canada to India, it is clear that culture often shapes institutions, as well as the other way around.

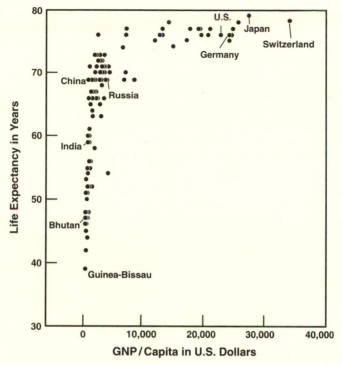

Figure 2.2. Life expectancy by economic development level.
Mean life expectancy at birth, by GNP per capita in 124 countries.
Source: Data from World Bank, *World Development Report, 1993.*

THE SOCIETAL ROOTS OF THE POSTMODERN SHIFT: DIMINISHING MARGINAL RETURNS FROM ECONOMIC DEVELOPMENT

Although culture can shape economic and political life, it is equally true that major socioeconomic changes reshape culture. The shift from Modernization to Postmodernization reflects the diminishing marginal utility of economic determinism: economic factors tend to play a decisive role under conditions of economic scarcity, but as scarcity diminishes, other factors shape society to an increasing degree. Thus, through processes of random mutation and natural selection, culture adapts to a given environment. Chapter 4 examines how this process works at the individual level, through intergenerational population replacement. Here, let us briefly examine it at the societal level.

Figure 2.2 illustrates the diminishing impact of economic development on human life expectancy. As it demonstrates, life expectancy is closely linked to a nation's level of economic development, especially at the low end of the economic continuum. The people of poor nations have relatively short average life spans. Guinea-Bissau falls at the low end of the spectrum on both income and life expectancy, with a per capita gross national product of $180 and a life expectancy of 39 years. Just above this level is a cluster of nations having per capita GNPs of less than $300 and life expectancies of about 45 years. Next comes a group of societies with GNPs of $1,000 to $3,000 and life expectancies of 60 to 75 years. At the high end of the spectrum are Japan and Switzerland, with per capita GNPs of $28,000 and $33,000, respectively, and life expectancies of 79 and 78 years, respectively—twice that of Guinea-Bissau. A cross-national relationship like this does not always reflect developmental change, but in this case it does: historical evidence demonstrates that life expectancies have indeed risen as economic development took place.

The curve rises steeply with relatively modest increases in wealth, until it reaches about $3,000 per capita. Thereafter, the curve levels off. Economic factors become less decisive, and lifestyle factors more so. Among the poorer nations in figure 2.2, GNP per capita explains 51 percent of the variance in life expectancy; among the richer half it accounts for only 15 percent. There is still a good deal of cross-national variation, but longevity becomes less and less a question of adequate nutrition and sanitary facilities, and more and more a question of cholesterol intake, tobacco and alcohol consumption, exercise, levels of stress, and environmental pollution. Increasingly, life expectancy is determined by lifestyle and behavioral patterns, rather than by economics.

Some striking recent cultural phenomena could be interpreted as a rational response to this shift from economic factors to lifestyle factors as the main determinants of survival. For example, a generation ago, Americans were notorious for their unwillingness to walk even short distances. Some people jokingly claimed that the next generation would be born with wheels instead of legs. It did not work out that way. Quite the contrary, two decades later jogging and emphasis on physical fitness became widespread. There has also been a growing concern for avoiding cholesterol and food additives, an increasingly successful movement to reduce environmental pollution and to ban smoking in public places, and a growing interest in less stressful lifestyles—all of which reflect a spreading awareness that, today, longevity has more to do with lifestyle than with sheer income.

The leveling off of the curve does not simply reflect ceiling effects. In 1975 only a few nations had male life expectancies above 70 years, but in the ensuing years life expectancies in most nations went up by several years. By 1990, female life expectancy in Switzerland and Japan had risen above 80 years, and this almost certainly does not represent the ultimate biological ceiling. In advanced industrial society, the most rapidly growing demographic segment is the group 100 years of age and over. Most developed nations still have considerable room for improvement—but changes in life expectancy are no longer as closely tied to economic development as they were when starvation was the leading cause of death. Thus male life expectancy in the former Soviet Union declined sharply during the 1970s and 1980s and continued to fall after the collapse of the USSR. In large part, this seems to reflect cultural-historical factors, such as rising alcoholism rates and psychological stress. By contrast, East

Asian countries have long been overachievers in life expectancies. China, North Korea, South Korea, Taiwan, Hong Kong, and Japan (now the world leader in life expectancy) all have historically shown higher life expectancies than their economic level would predict. The nations of the former Soviet Union have shown the opposite tendency: for decades, nearly all of them have shown lower life expectancies than their economic level would predict. Recent changes have accentuated these tendencies to the point where—although Russia's GNP/capita is still much higher than China's—China now shows a higher life expectancy than Russia. The reasons are complex, but they seem to have a significant cultural component, with a tradition of alcohol abuse having a negative impact on the life expectancy of Russian males, while the low-cholesterol diet traditionally prevalent in East Asia may have a positive effect on life expectancies in that region.

As our diminishing returns hypothesis implies, a logarithmic transformation of GNP per capita shows a much better fit with life expectancy than does a linear model. Figure 2.2 shows untransformed GNP per capita in order to demonstrate the diminishing impact of economic gains. Similar patterns of diminishing returns from economic development are found with numerous other social indicators. Caloric intake, literacy rates, the number of physicians per capita, and other objective indicators all rise steeply at the low end of the scale, but level off among advanced industrial societies (Hirsch [1976], in *Social Limits to Growth*, makes a loosely related point, arguing that development brings no gain in *positional* goods). In short, a narrow focus on economic achievement has a tremendous payoff in the early stages of industrialization: the instrumental rationality associated with Modernization had high rewards. But when a society reaches a fairly high level of industrialization (at a per capita GNP of $6,000 to $7,000 in 1990 dollars) it reaches a point of diminishing returns.

This pattern of diminishing marginal returns from economic development is not limited to objective aspects of life, such as caloric intake and life expectancy. New evidence from the 1990 World Values Survey indicates that this applies to subjective well-being too. Figure 2.3 demonstrates this point. It is based on the responses of 43 publics to questions concerning their happiness and satisfaction with their lives as a whole—questions that have been shown to be excellent indicators of overall subjective well-being, and relatively stable cultural characteristics (Andrews and Withey, 1976; Inglehart, 1990, ch. 7).

As one might expect, subjective well-being rises with rising levels of economic development: the people of rich and secure societies such as Sweden are happier and more satisfied with their lives as a whole than are those living in societies where disease and starvation are widespread, such as India. The overall relationship has impressive strength ($r = .74$). But here again, we find a marked leveling off above a certain threshold. This effect is so pronounced that earlier studies, carried out mainly in rich societies, concluded that there was no cross-national relationship between economic development and subjective well-being. Above a threshold of about $6,000 (in 1991 dollars), there

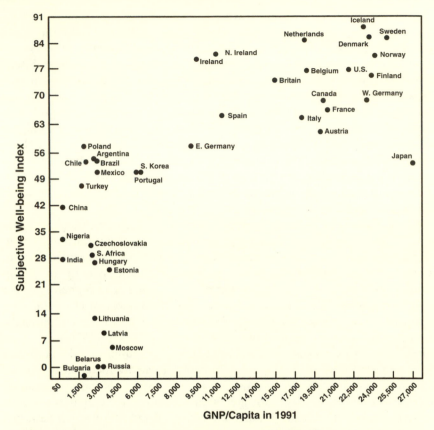

Figure 2.3. Economic development and subjective well-being.
N = 40, r = .74, p < .00001. *Source*: subjective well-being data from 1990–91 World Values Survey; GNP/capita data from World Bank, *World Development Report, 1993. Note*: The subjective well-being index reflects the average between the percentage of the public in each country who (1) describe themselves as "Very happy" or "happy," minus the percentage who describe themselves as "not very happy" or "unhappy," and (2) the percentage placing themselves in the 7–10 range, minus the percentage placing themselves in the 1–4 range, on a 10-point scale on which "1" indicates that the person is strongly dissatisfied with his or her life as a whole, and "10" indicates that the person is highly satisfied with his or her life as a whole.

is virtually no relationship between wealth and subjective well-being. Thus, the Irish show a higher level of subjective well-being than do the Western Germans, though the latter are more than twice as rich; and the South Koreans show subjective well-being levels as high as the Japanese, although the Japanese are more than four times as rich.

Our interpretation here is more speculative than it was with the relationship between economic development and life expectancy. We know for certain that numerous objective indicators (from calories consumed per person to telephones per capita and automobiles per capita to human life expectancy) follow a curve of diminishing returns: ample historical data demonstrate that as given societies underwent economic development, all of these things increased sharply at first, but then reached a point of diminishing returns, with further economic growth producing only modest increases. But we simply do not have this kind of historical information concerning the relationship between economic development and subjective well-being: subjective well-being only began to be measured a few decades ago, and until recently it was measured only in a handful of rich Western societies. The 1990 World Values Survey was the first study to measure it in representative national samples of a majority of the world's population.

One possible interpretation of figure 2.3 would be that the pattern has nothing to do with economic development: one might argue that for some reason (perhaps cultural or climatic or geographic), Nigeria, India, and Russia may have *always* ranked low on subjective well-being, while Sweden, Denmark, and the Netherlands have always had high levels of well-being, for reasons having nothing to do with economic development.

We cannot disprove this interpretation, but it seems extremely unlikely. The relationship between economic development level and subjective well-being is remarkably strong and is significant at the .00001 level: it could scarcely have resulted from sheer chance. Furthermore, the linkage between economic level and subjective well-being manifests itself not only at the cross-national level but also within given societies: as common sense might lead one to expect, people with high incomes tend to have higher levels of subjective well-being than do those with low incomes. Moreover, Eastern and Western Germany provide a sort of controlled experiment, in which nationality and culture are held constant, but in Eastern Germany, per capita income is much lower than in Western Germany: as our interpretation implies, the Western Germans show substantially higher levels of subjective well-being than do the Eastern Germans. Moreover, this same comparison helps explain why the impact of economic development eventually levels off: in terms of what they consider important, economic factors (such as income) rank much higher among Eastern Germans than among Western Germans; and conversely, noneconomic aspects of life (such as leisure time) are considered much more important by the Western Germans than by the Eastern Germans (Staatistisches Bundesamt, 1994: 441).

The interpretation that prosperity and security are conducive to subjective well-being is further supported by the extremely low levels of well-being shown by the former Soviet societies. Here again, one might attribute this finding to something inherent in Slavic (and Baltic) culture, or to something inherent in the Soviet type of socialism. But a much more obvious interpretation would see it as linked with the disintegration of the economic, political, and social fabric of these societies that was taking place when these surveys were carried out in 1990. In the 1981 World Values Survey, a sample from the Tambov region of Russia showed relatively low levels of subjective well-being; but the levels found here are lower than any ever registered before, either in the Tambov region of Russia or in any other country. We should note that these phenomenally low levels of subjective well-being manifested themselves *before* the political disintegration of the Soviet Union in December 1991: they were a leading indicator of deep-rooted demoralization and dissatisfaction among the masses, and not simply a response to political collapse. Our interpretation is that the Soviet successor states are experiencing a profound malaise that could have dramatic consequences.

Until we have a longer time series, it will not be possible to conclusively prove or disprove our interpretation that economic growth is conducive to increased subjective well-being, but eventually reaches a point of diminishing returns. But this interpretation is supported by the fact that, among prosperous European Union societies, subjective well-being has been roughly constant since 1973: as figure 6.4 indicates, subjective well-being has risen slightly in some of these societies (e.g., Western Germany) and fallen slightly in others (especially, Belgium), but there is no clear overall trend. Within wealthy societies, the correlation between income and subjective well-being is relatively weak. In societies where a higher income may make the difference between survival and starvation, a good income is a pretty good first approximation of what well-being really means. But in rich societies, income differences have a surprisingly small impact on subjective well-being: the rich are slightly happier and more satisfied than the poor, but only to a modest extent (Andrews and Withey, 1976; Campbell, Converse, and Rodgers, 1976; Inglehart, 1990).

The overall evidence supports the thesis of diminishing marginal utility from economic gains. As figure 2.3 suggests, the transition from a society of scarcity to a society of security brings a dramatic increase in subjective well-being. But (at roughly the economic level of Ireland in 1990) we find a threshold at which economic growth no longer seems to increase subjective well-being significantly. This may be linked with the fact that at this level starvation is no longer a real concern for most people. Survival begins to be taken for granted. Significant numbers of Postmaterialists begin to emerge, and for them further economic gains no longer produce an increase in subjective well-being. Indeed, if further economic growth brings deterioration in the nonmaterial quality of life, it may actually lead to *lower* levels of subjective well-being. Beyond this level, economic development no longer seems to bring rising subjective well-being. The stage is set for the Postmodern shift to begin.

From a rational actor's perspective, one would expect economic development to eventually bring a shift in survival strategies. Figure 2.4 suggests how this works. At low levels of economic development, even modest economic gains bring a high return in terms of caloric intake, clothing, shelter, medical care, and ultimately in life expectancy itself. For individuals to give top priority to maximizing economic gains, and for a society to give top priority to economic growth, is a highly effective survival strategy. But once a society has reached a certain threshold of development—at about the level where the Soviet Union was before its collapse, or where Portugal or South Korea are today—one reaches a point at which further economic growth brings only min-

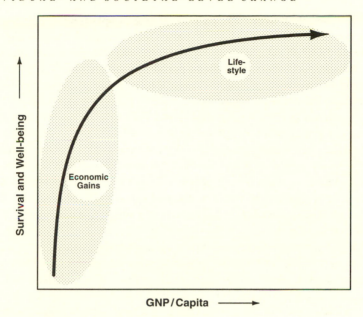

Figure 2.4. Economic development leads to a shift in survival strategies.

imal gains in both life expectancy and in subjective well-being. There is still a good deal of cross-national variation, but from this point on, noneconomic aspects of life become increasingly important influences on how long, and how well, people live. Beyond this point, a rational strategy would be to place increasing emphasis on quality of life concerns, rather than to continue the inflexible pursuit of economic growth as if it were a good in itself. Instrumental rationality begins to give way to value rationality.

Normally, culture changes slowly; but it does eventually respond to a changing environment. Changes in the socioeconomic environment help reshape individual-level beliefs, attitudes, and values through their impact on the life experience of individuals. Cultures do not change overnight. Once they have matured, people tend to retain whatever worldview they have learned. Consequently, the impact of major changes in the environment tends to be most significant on those generations that spent their formative years under the new conditions.

The best documented case of this phenomenon is the shift from Materialist to Postmaterialist values in Western societies during the last few decades. This intergenerational cultural shift is one of the few cases in which we can follow a gradual cultural shift based on intergenerational population replacement, through times of prosperity and times of recession, and under widely varying conditions in different societies. Comparable data are available for few if any other cultural variables, but there is no reason to assume that this pattern does not apply to changes in other basic values.

Culture is resistant to change, partly because people tend to believe whatever their society's institutions teach them. But one's worldview is also influenced by one's firsthand experience—and if the two are in conflict, one's firsthand experience may have even greater credibility than what one is told. This is one reason why political systems, even totalitarian ones, have limited ability to reshape their culture. People are sensitive to those aspects of reality that directly affect them. This was crucial in the shift toward Postmodern values. The younger birth cohorts in advanced industrial societies perceived, during their formative years, that survival was *not* precarious and that they could take it more or less for granted. This experience was profoundly different from the conditions that have shaped most people's lives throughout most of history. It led to pervasive changes in worldviews. For these birth cohorts, maximizing their economic gains no longer maximized their subjective well-being as it had for earlier generations.

People did not consciously set out to change their worldviews. New outlooks and new modes of behavior, like random mutations, arose for a variety of reasons—and some of them spread. Even within a given birth cohort, many continued to accept the established norms of industrial society; but others took on new orientations and transmitted them to some of their peers through social learning processes. Change has been uneven. But the new lifestyles have spread gradually—and in the last analysis, they have done so because they represent more effective ways to maximize survival and subjective well-being under new conditions. At a much earlier stage of history, new norms linked with the rise of modern society (such as the Protestant Ethic) gradually spread in somewhat similar fashion. We lack detailed information on how this took place, but it seems to have occurred more slowly than the rise of Postmodern values, which in some ways represents its reversal. In both cases, culture was gradually reshaped by changes in the socioeconomic environment; and these cultural changes eventually produced feedback that helped reshape political and economic life.

Postmodernization is a shift in survival strategies. It moves from maximizing economic growth to maximizing survival and well-being through lifestyle changes. Once industrialization had become possible, Modernization focused on rapid economic growth as the best way of maximizing survival and well-being. But no strategy is optimal for all times. Modernization was dramatically successful in raising life expectancies, but it has begun to produce diminishing returns in advanced industrial societies. Emphasizing competition, it reduces the risk of starvation, but increases psychological stress. With the transition from Modernization to Postmodernization, the trajectory of change has shifted from maximizing economic growth to maximizing the quality of life.

CHAPTER 3

Modernization and Postmodernization in 43 Societies

INTRODUCTION

As we have seen, Modernization theory falls into two main schools: (1) a Marxist version, which claims that economics, politics, and culture are closely linked because economic development determines the political and cultural characteristics of a society, and (2) a Weberian version, which claims that culture shapes economic and political life. Despite an enduring debate between the two schools, they agree on one crucial point: that socioeconomic change follows coherent and relatively predictable patterns. This means that key social, political, and economic characteristics are not randomly related; they tend to be closely linked so that by knowing one such trait, one can predict the presence of other key traits with much better than random success.

Cultural relativists, on the other hand, claimed that it would be ethnocentric not to believe that all cultures are equally conducive to economic development and democracy. And dependency theorists viewed a given society's culture as irrelevant to economic development and democracy, which were determined by the forces of global capitalism. Both of these views imply that the relationships between culture and economics and politics are more or less random.

This chapter presents a broad overview of a huge body of data from more than 40 societies. It demonstrates that, far from being randomly related, specific cultural, economic, and political variables are closely correlated. Although this chapter does not attempt to demonstrate whether causality flows in the Marxist or the Weberian direction, the linkages we find indicate that at least one version of Modernization theory was right. Subsequent chapters will probe more deeply into the causal linkages.

Although we find strong support for the central claim of Modernization theory, we disagree with it on several narrower points—above all, the notion that socioeconomic change is linear. Instead, we find evidence that a major change of direction occurs when societies reach an advanced level of industrial development. The Modernization phase involves the familiar syndrome of industrialization, occupational specialization, bureaucratization, centralization, rising educational levels, and beliefs and values that support high rates of economic growth; but among advanced industrial societies, a second syndrome of cultural and institutional changes emerges in which economic growth becomes less central, and there is rising emphasis on the quality of life and democratic political institutions.

CROSS-SECTIONAL EVIDENCE OF CHANGE OVER TIME

This chapter will undertake something that verges on heresy: we will examine hypotheses about changes over time in the light of cross-sectional evidence. This procedure has been criticized (quite appropriately) in the past: taken by itself, cross-sectional evidence is an uncertain indicator of change. There is no substitute for time series data if one hopes to draw firm conclusions about social change. In keeping with this idea, much of this book is devoted to analyzing time series data concerning sociocultural change.

Nevertheless, we are convinced that the World Values surveys can usefully supplement the available time series evidence, providing additional insight on patterns of cultural change. Global cross-national data are needed because the available survey data on this topic are largely drawn from advanced industrial societies and limited to the past few decades. The World Values survey provides a much broader range of variation than has ever before been available, bringing together data from 43 nations throughout the world, covering the full range of economic and political variation.

If we had survey data covering the entire period from the early nineteenth century to the present we could analyze the interplay between changing cultural values and economic and political Modernization over many decades. We could then determine which came first, cultural change or economic or political change. But such data are not available. The analysis of cross-sectional data offers the nearest substitute. Examining the orientations of people in poor societies gives some sense of what prevailing mass orientations in today's rich democracies may have been like when these countries were poor and predemocratic.

Conversely, comparing the worldviews of rich and poor countries provides some idea of how the outlook of the publics of poorer countries may change if their societies become industrialized and economically secure. We do not view these changes as deterministic: economic and technological changes interact with political, cultural, and other variables. The cultural heritage of a given society may facilitate or retard Modernization; and determined leaders can repress or accelerate social change. Nevertheless, as we will demonstrate, it is possible to identify a specific syndrome of cultural values and beliefs that is likely to be present, if urbanization, industrialization, higher education, and other components of Modernization become widespread.

Inkeles and Smith (1974) suggested that this should be true, but their conclusion was based on a comparison of the belief systems of those working within the "modern" and premodern sectors of six developing societies, and it did not compare societies at various levels of development. This analysis, for the first time, demonstrates the existence of fundamentally different worldviews between the publics of preindustrial and industrial societies, confirming Inkeles and Smith's insight. But our analysis goes a step farther: it also analyzes the cultural differences between societies of scarcity (both preindustrial and early industrial) and economically affluent "Postmodern" societies.

MODERNIZATION AND POSTMODERNIZATION
IN CROSS-SECTIONAL PERSPECTIVE

The concepts of both Modernization and Postmodernization are based on two key assumptions:

1. Various cultural elements tend to go together in coherent patterns. For example, do societies that place relatively strong emphasis on religion also tend to favor large families (or respect for authority or other distinctive attitudes)? If each culture goes its own way, elements such as these would be uncorrelated, and one would find no consistent patterns of constraint.

2. Coherent cultural patterns exist, *and* they are linked with economic and technological development. For example, industrialization was accompanied by secularization in Western history. But some observers argue that, since some Islamic countries such as Iran and Libya have grown rich without secularization, there is no linkage between economic development and secularization. This argument ignores the fact that Modernization is not just the possession of large oil deposits: it is a syndrome of cultural, economic, and technological changes closely linked with industrialization—a syndrome that Iran and Libya have not experienced, and which *does* tend to be linked with secularization.

Together, these two postulates imply that some patterns are more probable than others—and hence, that development is to some extent predictable. *Is* economic development linked with coherent cultural patterns, distinct from those found in less developed societies? If so, then cross-national surveys should reveal clear patterns, with one syndrome of orientations being found in economically developed societies, and another syndrome being found in less developed societies. If such patterns are found, the evidence would support Modernization theory. Furthermore, it would imply that sociopolitical change has an element of predictability.

Do coherent cultural patterns exist, and are they linked with levels of economic development? To answer this question, we will analyze the World Values survey data on key values and beliefs among representative national samples of publics around the world. This survey was designed to test the hypothesis that economic development leads to specific changes in mass values and belief systems—which in turn produce feedback, leading to changes in the economic and political systems of these societies. We do not assume that *all* elements of culture will change, leading to a uniform global culture: we see no reason to expect that the Chinese will stop using chopsticks in the foreseeable future, or that Brazilians will learn to polka. But certain cultural and political changes *do* seem to be logically linked with the dynamics of a core syndrome of Modernization, involving urbanization, industrialization, economic development, occupational specialization, and the spread of mass literacy.

Change is not linear in any system subject to feedback. This complicates our analysis. If the process of economic-cultural-political change moved smoothly in one continuous direction, a cross section of the world's societies would show a simple developmental progression of cultural changes as one moved from the least developed to the economically most developed societies. Analogously, a cross section of the earth's surface sometimes reveals neatly ordered geological layers, with the oldest stratum of rock lowest and the newer strata located above the older ones. But reality is not this simple: social change produces feedback, which eventually changes the direction of change. Thus, we are likely to find patterns similar to those produced by tectonic upheavals, in which identifiable geological layers are shifted and juxtaposed with other strata. The result is not chaos, but neither is it a simple layering from oldest to newest strata.

We suggest that we will find the residue of two major waves of change (along with many lesser ones) mirrored in the World Values survey's cross section of the world's cultures: the distribution of these cultural traits reflects the processes of Modernization and Postmodernization, respectively.

The literature on Modernization focuses on the first of these two processes. It argues (correctly, we believe) that a broad syndrome of changes has been linked with modern economic development. These changes include urbanization, industrialization, occupational specialization, mass formal education, development of mass media, secularization, individuation, the rise of entrepreneurs and entrepreneurial motivations, bureaucratization, the mass production assembly line, and the emergence of the modern state. The material core of this process is industrialization; and though the industrial revolution originated in the West, this process is not inherently Western and should not be confused with Westernization. Although there are arguments about what the "real" driving force is behind this syndrome, there is widespread agreement that these changes include technological, economic, cultural, and political components.

RELIGION AND ECONOMIC GROWTH

We propose a modified interpretation of Weber's thesis concerning the role of the Protestant Ethic in economic development. Weber was correct in arguing that the rise of Protestantism was a crucial event in modernizing Europe. But this was not due to factors unique to Protestantism—it has been argued that everything Weber ascribed to Puritanism might equally well be ascribed to Judaism (Sombart, 1913). European Judaism had an outlook that was in some ways modern, but it could not transform Europe because it held a marginal position there. The crucial impact of Protestantism was due to the fact that it supplanted a set of religious norms that are common to most preindustrial societies, and which inhibit economic achievement; and it replaced them with norms favorable to economic achievement.

Because they experience little or no economic growth, preindustrial economies are zero-sum systems: upward social mobility can only come at someone else's expense. In any preindustrial society that has endured for some time, the cultural system is likely to have adapted accordingly: social status is hereditary rather than achieved, and the culture encourages people to accept their social position in this life, emphasizing that meek acceptance and denial of worldly aspirations will be rewarded in the next life. Aspirations toward social mobility are sternly repressed. Such value systems help to maintain social solidarity and discourage economic accumulation in a variety of ways, ranging from norms of sharing and charity, to the norms of noblesse oblige, to the potlatch and similar institutions in which one attains prestige by recklessly giving away one's worldly goods.

For Weber, the central element in the rise of modernity was the movement away from traditional religious authority to secular rational-legal authority: a shift from ascriptive status to impersonal, achievement-based roles, and a shift of power from society to state. Traditional value systems must be shattered in order for modern economic development to take place. In a society undergoing rapid economic expansion, social mobility is acceptable, even a virtue. But in hunting and gathering or agrarian societies, the main basis of production—land—is a fixed quantity, and social mobility can only occur if an individual or group seizes the lands of another. To preserve social peace, virtually all traditional cultures discourage upward social mobility and the accumulation of wealth. They help to integrate society by providing a rationale that legitimates the established social order, in which social status is hereditary; but these cultures also inculcate norms of sharing, charity, and other obligations that help mitigate the harshness of a subsistence economy.

The Confucian system was an exception in one important respect. Although (like virtually all traditional cultures) it inculcated the duty to be satisfied with one's station in life and to respect authority, it did permit social mobility based on individual achievement, through the Confucian examination system. Moreover, it did not justify meek acceptance of one's lot in this world, by stressing the infinitely greater rewards that this would bring in the next world. It was based on a secular worldview: if one were to rise, one would do so in this world or not at all.

On the whole, however, the traditional value systems of agrarian society (China included) are adapted to maintaining a stable balance in unchanging societies. Accordingly, they tend to discourage social change in general and accumulative entrepreneurial motivation in particular, which is stigmatized and relegated to pariah groups if tolerated at all. Economic accumulation is characterized as ignoble greed. To facilitate the economic accumulation needed to launch industrialization, these cultural inhibitions must be relaxed.

In Western society, the Protestant Reformation helped break the grip of the medieval Christian worldview on a significant part of Europe. It did not do this by itself. The emergence of scientific inquiry had already begun to undermine this worldview. But Weber's emphasis on the role of Protestantism captures an important part of reality. Prior to the Reformation, Southern Europe was economically more advanced than Northern Europe. During the three centuries after the Reformation, capitalism emerged—mainly in Protestant countries, and among the Protestant minorities in Catholic countries. Within this cultural context, economic accumulation was no longer despised. Quite the contrary, it was highly respected because it was taken as evidence of divine favor: those whom God had chosen, he made rich.

Protestant Europe manifested a subsequent economic dynamism that was extraordinary, moving it far ahead of Catholic Europe. Shifting trade patterns, declining food production in Southern Europe, and other factors also contributed to this shift, but the evidence suggests that cultural factors played a major role. Throughout the first 150 years of the Industrial Revolution, industrial development took place almost entirely within the Protestant regions of Europe, and the Protestant portions of the New World. This began to change only during the second half of the twentieth century, when those regions that had been most strongly influenced by the Protestant Ethic—and had become economically secure—began to deemphasize economic growth. As we will argue, they did so precisely *because* they had become economically secure. At the same time, an entrepreneurial outlook had emerged in Catholic Europe and (even more strikingly) in East Asia, both of which are now showing higher rates of economic growth than Protestant Europe. The concept of the Protestant Ethic is outdated if we take it to mean something that can only exist in Protestant countries. But Weber's more general concept that culture influences economic growth is a crucial insight.

MODERNIZATION: THE SHIFT FROM RELIGIOUS AUTHORITY TO STATE AUTHORITY

Secularization is inherently linked with Modernization. This holds true despite frequent assertions that a rapid growth of fundamentalist religion is taking place throughout the world. This interpretation reflects a misconception of what is happening, generalizing from two very different phenomena. The apparent rise of religious fundamentalism reflects two disparate elements:

1. Advanced industrial societies in North America, Western Europe, and East Asia, traditional forms of religion have been, *and still are*, declining, as we will demonstrate. During the past 40 years, church attendance rates have been falling and adherence to traditional norms concerning divorce, abortion, suicide, single parenthood, and homosexuality have been eroding—and continue to erode. Resurgent fundamentalist activism has indeed been dramatic: gay bashing and the bombing of abortion centers have received widespread coverage in the mass media, encouraging the perception that these actions have a rapidly growing constituency. They do not. Instead, precisely because fundamentalists correctly perceive that many of their central norms are rapidly eroding, they have been galvanized into unprecedented activism. But this reflects the rearguard action of a dwindling segment of the population, not the wave of the future.

2. Islamic fundamentalism, on the other hand, does have a growing mass constituency. But it is growing in societies that have *not* modernized: though

some of these societies are rich, they have not become rich by moving along the Modernization trajectory of industrialization, occupational specialization, rising educational levels, and so on, but simply by virtue of the fact that they have large oil revenues. Even without modernizing, it is possible to become rich if one possesses large petroleum reserves that can be sold to industrialized countries, enabling traditional elites to buy the external trappings of Modernization.

The possession of this wealth is important: it has enabled oil-rich fundamentalist regimes to obtain such things as automobiles, air conditioning, modern medical treatment for elites, and, above all, modern weapons: without them, the fundamentalist regimes would be perceived as militarily weak and technologically backward—and their mass appeal and prospects for survival would be far weaker.

Modernization involves more than the shift away from cultural traditions (usually based on religious norms) that emphasize ascribed status and sharing, toward placing a positive value on achievement and accumulation. For Weber, the key to Modernization was the shift from a religion-oriented worldview to a rational-legal worldview. There were two key components of Modernization.

1. *Secularization.* Weber emphasized the *cognitive* roots of secularization. For him, the rise of the scientific worldview was the crucial factor that led to the decline of the sacred/prerational elements of religious faith. We suggest that, more recently, the rise of a sense of *security* among mass publics of advanced welfare states has been an equally important factor in the decline of traditional religious orientations. This difference in emphasis has important implications. The cognitive interpretation implies that secularization is inevitable: scientific knowledge can diffuse across national boundaries rapidly, and its spread is more or less irreversible. By contrast, the rise of a sense of security among mass publics takes place only after a society has successfully industrialized; and it can be reversed to some extent by rapid change or economic decline. Thus although scientific knowledge has been permeating throughout the world for many decades, religious fanaticism continues to flourish in societies that are still in the early stages of industrialization; and fundamentalist movements continue to emerge among the less secure strata of even the most advanced industrial societies, especially during times of stress.

2. *Bureaucratization.* The process of secularization paved the way for another key component of Modernization, Bureaucratization, the rise of "rational" organizations, based on rules designed to move efficiently toward explicit goals, and with recruitment based on impersonal goal-oriented achievement standards. A prerequisiite for bureaucratization was the erosion of the belief systems supporting ascriptive traditional authority and zero-sum economies; and their replacement by achievement-oriented, rational, and scientifically oriented belief systems that supported the authority of large, centralized bureaucratic states geared to facilitating economic growth. The core of cultural Modernization was the shift from traditional (usually religious) authority to rational-legal authority.

Along with this went a shift of prestige and socioeconomic functions away from the key institutions of traditional society—the family and the church—to the state, and a shift in economic activity from the small family enterprise to mass production that was state-regulated or even state-owned. Globally, it was a shift of prestige and power from society to state.

During the modernizing phase of history, it seemed (to Marxists and non-Marxists alike) that the direction of social evolution was toward the increasing subordination of the individual to a Leviathan state having superhuman powers. The state would become an omnipotent and benevolent entity, replacing God in a secular world. And for most of the nineteenth and twentieth centuries, the dominant trend (the wave of the future, as it was sometimes called) was a shift from societal authority toward state authority, manifested in the apparently inexorable growth of the economic, political, and social role of government. Even non-Marxist thinkers such as Schumpeter (1947) reluctantly considered the triumph of socialism to be inevitable. And until recently, even such mainstream figures as Lindblom (1977) thought that the only question was whether socialism would triumph over capitalism, or whether capitalism and socialism would continue to coexist. The possibility that socialism might give way to capitalism was not even entertained.

THE POSTMODERN SHIFT

The socialist leviathan-state *was* the logical culmination of the Modernization process, but it did not turn out to be the wave of the future. Instead, the expansion of the bureaucratic state eventually approached a set of natural limits, and change began to move in a new direction. Figure 3.1 illustrates what happened. From the Industrial Revolution until well into the second half of the twentieth century, industrial society underwent Modernization. This process transformed political and cultural systems from traditional regimes legitimated by religious belief systems to rational-legal states legitimated by their claim to maximize the welfare of their people through scientific expertise. It was a transfer of authority from family and religious institutions to political institutions.

Within the last 25 years, a major change in the direction of change has occurred that might be called the Postmodern shift. Its origins are rooted in the economic miracles that occurred first in Western Europe and North America, and later in East Asia and now in Southeast Asia. Coupled with the safety net of the modern welfare state, this has produced unprecedentedly high levels of economic security, giving rise to a cultural feedback that is having a major impact on both the economic and political systems of advanced industrial societies. This new trajectory shifts authority away from *both* religion and the state to the individual, with an increasing focus on individual concerns such as friends and leisure. Postmodernization deemphasizes all kinds of authority,

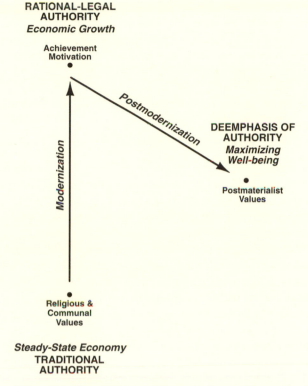

Figure 3.1. The shift from Modernization to Postmodernization: changing emphasis on key aspects of life.

whether religious or secular, allowing much wider range for individual autonomy in the pursuit of individual subjective well-being.

The core function of culture in traditional society was to maintain social cohesion and stability in a steady-state economy. Norms of sharing were crucial to survival in an environment where there was no social security bureau and no unemployment benefits: in bad times, one's survival depended on how strongly the norms of sharing were inculcated.

The importance of these norms is almost certain to be underestimated by anyone brought up in an individualistic society. In relatively traditional societies such as Nigeria, even today people feel a strong obligation to help take care of not only their immediate family, but their brothers, sisters, cousins, nieces, nephews, and old friends and neighbors. These norms are highly functional in traditional societies: they enable people to survive who would otherwise starve. In industrial societies, this sense of obligation has eroded almost to the point of extinction.

The core project of Modernization is economic growth, and the means to attain it is through industrialization—the systematic application of technology

TABLE 3.1
Traditional, Modern, and Postmodern Society: Societal Goals and Individual Values

	Traditional	*Modern*	*Postmodern*
Core Societal Project	Survival in a steady-state economy	Maximize economic growth	Maximize subjective well-being
Individual Value	Traditional religious and communal norms	Achievement motivation	Postmaterialist and Postmodern values
Authority System	Traditional authority	Rational-legal authority	De-emphasis of *both* legal and religious authority

to maximize the output of tangible things, such as wheat, textiles, coal, steel, and tractors.

In Postmodernization, the core project is to maximize individual well-being, which is increasingly dependent on subjective factors. Human behavior shifts from being dominated by the economic imperatives of providing food, clothing, and shelter toward the pursuit of quality of life concerns.

Even economic behavior becomes less a matter of meeting the survival needs and becomes increasingly oriented toward attaining subjective well-being. Economic growth continues, but output consists less and less of tangible things that contribute directly to survival, and more and more of intangibles whose value is subjective. The Postmodernization writers are on target in emphasizing the increasingly subjective nature of life experience in advanced industrial society.

For example, government has become an enormous sector, now employing a larger proportion of the U.S. workforce than does industrial manufacturing. Government services are intangible, and their value is highly subjective—people even disagree about whether their value is positive or negative. Computer software, education, research, entertainment, and tourism have all become major industries. Unlike food, clothing, and shelter, their products are intangible and their value is largely subjective. Computer software, microchips, and entertainment have become three of the United States' largest exports, but the value of the film or silicon or disk on which they are stored is negligible. A successful motion picture or computer program may be worth hundreds of millions of dollars; another film or program that costs just as much to produce may be virtually valueless. Ideas and innovation are the crucial component—and their value is whatever people feel it is worth. With psychotherapy and tourism, this is equally true: they have become major economic activities, and their value lies almost entirely in their contribution to subjective well-being.

Table 3.1 compares the societal goals and individual value systems underlying traditional, modern, and postmodern society. As it indicates, the core societal goal of traditional society is survival under the conditions of a steady-state economy, in which social mobility is a zero-sum game. During the

Modernization phase, by contrast, the core societal project is maximizing economic growth—and, in both capitalist and socialist societies, it tends to be carried out by ruthlessly extracting the necessary capital from an impoverished populace, regardless of the costs to the environment and quality of life. In Postmodern society, by contrast, the top priority shifts from maximizing economic growth to maximizing subjective well-being.

From Survival Values to Well-being Values

Individual-level value systems reflect the core societal project of the three respective types of societies. Traditional societies vary enormously, but virtually all of them emphasize individual conformity to societal norms limiting violence, sexual behavior, and economic accumulation; and encouraging acceptance of the existing economic and social order. These norms are usually codified and legitimated within a religious framework. Perhaps the most central individual-level change linked with Modernization is the rise of achievement motivation; but the broad shift toward instrumental rationality weakens all traditional norms.

During the Modernization era, there was a consensus throughout industrial society that economic growth was not only a good thing, but virtually the ultimate good: though Marxists and capitalists disagreed sharply about how the fruits of production should be distributed, both sides shared an implicit consensus that economic growth was desirable. This consensus was unquestioned because it seemed self-evident. Economic growth and scientific discoveries constituted Progress: they were good almost by definition.

During the Cold War there was a similar shared sentiment that the question of whether East or West was the better society would be decided by which one achieved the most economic growth. And during the first half of the Cold War, the Eastern bloc seemed to be winning by the test that really counted: high growth rates. In 1972 Meadows et al.'s *The Limits to Growth* called this consensus into question, arguing that economic growth was *not* desirable and should be brought to a stop before it was too late. Shortly afterward, Schumacher's (1973) *Small Is Beautiful* questioned another key principle of the Modernization era: the tendency to equate Biggest with Best—a tendency that was widespread, but especially strong in the socialist bloc, where bigness and centralization were elevated almost to the rank of moral virtues. Both of these critiques reflected the emergence of well-being values, a core element of Postmodernism.

From Achievement Motivation to Postmaterialist Motivation

In the Postmodern shift, values that played a key role in the emergence of industrial society—economic achievement motivation, economic growth, economic rationality—have faded in salience. At the societal level, there is a radical shift from the priorities of early industrialization, and a growing tendency for emphasis on economic growth to become subordinate to concern for its impact on the environment. At the individual level, maximizing economic gains is gradually fading from top priority: self-expression and the desire for meaningful work are becoming even more crucial for a growing segment of the population. And the motivations for work are changing, from an emphasis on maximizing income as the top priority, toward increasing emphasis on the quality of the work experience. There is even some willingness to accept ascriptive criteria rather than achievement criteria for recruitment, if it is justified by social goals.

Scarcity has prevailed throughout most of history: it follows from the ecological principle that population normally rises to meet the available food supply and is then held in check by starvation, disease, and war. The result has been chronic scarcity, with the possibility of starvation shaping the daily awareness and life strategies of most people. Both traditional and modern societies were shaped by scarcity, but industrial society developed the belief that scarcity could be alleviated by individual achievement and economic growth, a radical change in outlook.

The root *cause* of the Postmodern value shift has been the gradual withering away of value systems that emerged under conditions of scarcity, and the spread of security values among a growing segment of the publics of these societies. This, in turn, grows out of the unprecedentedly high levels of subjective well-being that characterize the publics of advanced industrial society, as compared with those of earlier societies. In advanced industrial societies, most people take survival for granted. Precisely *because* they take it for granted, they are not aware of how profoundly this supposition shapes their worldviews.

Starvation is no longer a real concern for most of the people in high-technology societies, where production has been increasing much faster than the rate of population growth. These societies have attained unprecedentedly high life expectancies and unprecedentedly high levels of subjective well-being. One consequence of this fact is the rise of Postmaterialist values, but this is only one component of a broader cultural shift. The emergence and spread of Postmaterialist values is only the tip of the iceberg—one component of a much broader syndrome of cultural changes that we term Postmodernization. There are several additional important components.

GROWING EMPHASIS ON INDIVIDUAL FREEDOM
AND REJECTION OF BUREAUCRATIC AUTHORITY

The shift from traditional society to industrial society brought a shift from traditional authority to rational bureaucratic authority. In most societies, this simply substituted political authority for religious authority. But in Postmodern society, authority, centralization, and bigness are all under growing suspicion. They have reached a point of diminishing effectiveness; and they have reached a point of diminishing acceptability.

Every stable culture is linked with a congruent authority system. But the Postmodern shift is a move away from *both* traditional authority and state authority. It reflects a declining emphasis on authority in general—regardless of whether it is legitimated by societal or state formulae. This leads to declining confidence in hierarchical institutions. Today, political leaders throughout the industrialized world are experiencing some of the lowest levels of support ever recorded. This is not simply because they are less competent than previous leaders. It reflects a systematic decline in mass support for established political institutions, and a shift of focus toward individual concerns.

Because Postmaterialists view self-expression and political participation as things that are valuable in themselves, the Postmodern phase of development is inherently conducive to democratization. There is nothing easy or automatic about this tendency. Determined authoritarian elites can repress it almost indefinitely, though at growing cost to the morale and cooperativeness of their subjects. Similarly, the institutional structure and cultural heritage of a given society can facilitate or retard this tendency, as can external pressures and other macropolitical factors. But as economic development takes place, mass input to the political process becomes increasingly widespread and effective. Economic development leads mass publics to place growing emphasis on participatory values.

In addition to the changes in core societal goals, individual values, and authority systems outlined in table 3.1, the Postmodern shift has two other aspects.

First, as Postmodern philosophers argue, an essential attribute of postmodernity is a diminishing faith in science, technology, and rationality. One of the core components of Modernization was a growing faith in the power of science and rational analysis to solve virtually all problems. At the elite level (especially among Postmodern writers) Postmodernization is linked with a diminishing faith in rationality and a diminishing confidence that science and technology will help solve humanity's problems. This change in worldview has advanced farthest in the economically and technologically most advanced societies. And insofar as industrial society's culture of instrumental rationality is identified with the West, Postmodernity is linked with a rejection of the West. But for mass publics, Postmodernity has *also* brought a rejection of the Soviet model, which was even more hierarchical and instrumentally oriented than the Western version of industrial society.

Initially, Postmodernism focused on discontent with the dehumanizing aspects of modernity as manifested in the *West*. Many of the most prominent Postmodernist thinkers even considered themselves Marxists (and some still do). But it was inevitable that Postmodernization would eventually lead to the rejection of hierarchical, bureaucratic, centralized big government in the socialist world as well, where it was most extreme. This contributed to an unexpected development: the collapse of socialism. State socialism failed because (1) it no longer functioned well, in advanced industrial society—though it *had* functioned relatively well during the Modernization era, and (2) because it was no longer acceptable. The declining effectiveness and accept-ability of massive, centralized bureaucratic authority contributed to the col-lapse of state socialism, as did the fact that Postmodernization brings an in-herent tendency toward democratization, linked with its growing emphasis on individual autonomy.

ELEMENTS OF CONTINUITY BETWEEN MODERNIZATION AND POSTMODERNIZATION

Postmodernization continues some of the trends that were launched by Mod-ernization, particularly the processes of specialization, secularization, and in-dividuation. The growing complexity of advanced industrial society results in increasing specialization in all areas of life. But the processes of seculariza-tion and individuation have taken on a new character.

Secularization

Weber attributed the decline of religious belief largely to the rise of the scien-tific worldview, which gradually replaced the sacred/mystical prerational ele-ments of religious faith. Although the scientific worldview has lost its glamor, secularization continues—but for a new reason: the emergence of a sense of security among the economically more advanced societies diminishes the need for the reassurance that has traditionally been provided by absolute belief sys-tems, which purport to provide certainty and the assurance of salvation, if not in this world at least in the next.

It would be a major mistake to equate either Modernization or Postmodern-ization with the decline of religion. Modernization does require the disman-tling of some core aspects of traditional religion—in particular, it abolishes tra-ditional tendencies to equate the old with the good, and the rigid rejection of social mobility and individual economic achievement. But—significantly—in the Protestant Ethic thesis, Weber argued that this was accomplished by hav-ing one type of religion replace another. The Marxist route to modernity achieved this by replacing traditional religion with a secular ideology that ini-tially inspired widespread Utopian hopes and expectations of a new sort of Judgment Day that would come with the revolution. As it lost its ability to in-spire such hopes, Marxism began to crumble.

In some form or other, spiritual concerns will always be a part of the human condition. This remains true after the shift from Modernization to Postmod-ernization. A core element in Postmodernization is the decline of instrumental rationality (equating economic growth with the good) to value rationality, seeking human happiness itself, rather than the economic means to that end. Although Postmodernism goes with a continuing decline in traditional reli-gious beliefs, it is linked with a *growing* concern for the meaning and purpose of life.

Individuation

With industrialization, the erosion of religious social controls opened up a broader space for individual autonomy, but this space was largely taken up by growing obligations to the state. The Postmodern shift away from *both* religious and state authority continues this long-standing shift toward individuation, but in a much stronger form. Increasingly, individual rights and entitlements take priority over any other obligation.

Globally, there is a great deal of cross-national variation in degrees of Modernization: even today, only a minority of the world's population live in industrialized societies. An even smaller proportion of humanity live in the rich and secure advanced industrial societies in which Postmodern value systems have taken root.

Consequently, we would expect to find two main dimensions of cross-cultural variation across the 43 societies we are about to analyze. During the past two centuries, the two most pervasive and important processes that have shaped them have been (1) Modernization and (2) Postmodernization. Accordingly, we would expect the world's societies to vary according to the degree to which they have been transformed by these two processes. Furthermore, a given society's position on these two dimensions should be closely linked with its level of economic and technological development: societies that are only beginning to industrialize should manifest relatively traditional belief systems; those that are now in the stage of rapid industrialization should manifest value systems keyed to maximizing economic growth; and societies that had already attained high levels of existential security some time ago should have undergone an intergenerational value shift toward Postmodern values that give priority to subjective well-being over economic growth.

MODERNIZATION AND POSTMODERNIZATION DIMENSIONS:
EMPIRICAL FINDINGS

We have outlined the patterns of cross-cultural variation we expect to find, and why. Now let us examine cross-cultural variation empirically, as reflected in survey data from 43 societies. Our first question is whether the various religious, social, economic, and political components of given cultures are randomly related, or whether they go together, with certain coherent combinations being more probable than others. Figure 3.2 shows the results of a principal components factor analysis of the data from representative national surveys in the 43 societies included in the 1990–91 World Values Survey. The responses to each of the variables used here are boiled down to a mean score for each country; using the society as the unit of analysis, we can examine cross-cultural variation in a wide range of norms and values.

Figure 3.2 sums up an immense amount of information. It presents an overview of findings from the World Values surveys, showing the relationships

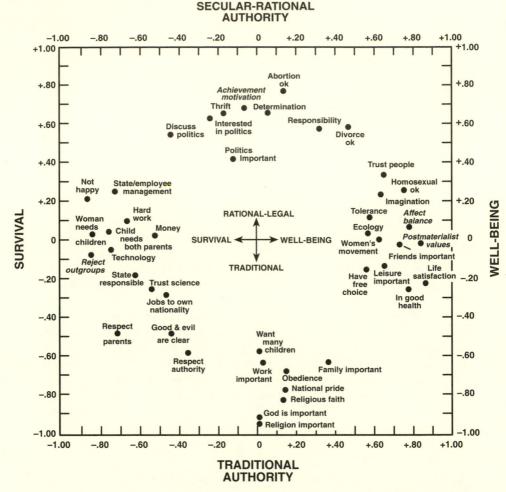

Figure 3.2. Variation in the values emphasized by different societies: traditional authority vs. rational-legal authority and scarcity values vs. Postmodern values. *Source*: 1990–93 World Values Survey. This figure shows the first and second principal components emerging from a factor analysis of data from representative national surveys of 43 societies, aggregated to the national level. The scales on the margins show each item's loadings on the two respective dimensions. The items in italics (e.g., "reject outgroups") are multi-item indicators.

between scores of items. Subsequent chapters will probe more deeply into the causal relationships between key variables and examine changes over time. This figure is based on the responses given by nearly 60,000 respondents in 43 societies. We do not provide the full text of each question used here. A short phrase (such as "Abortion OK") is used to convey the gist of each item on figure 3.2; for the full text, see Appendix 2. The 43 variables used here reflect a much larger number of questions: some of them are based on responses to whole batteries of questions. "Affect balance," for example, sums up each respondent's answers to the 10 questions in the Bradburn Affect Balance Scale; "Postmaterialist Values" sums up the responses to a series of questions through which each respondent ranks a set of 12 basic goals; and "Achievement Motivation" sums up responses to four items concerning important values for a child to learn; "Reject outgroups" also sums up the responses to several questions.

Furthermore, these variables were chosen to reflect a considerably larger number of related items that show similar patterns. "God is important," for example, taps a cluster of more than 30 items that measure the extent to which religion is, or is not, an important part of the respondent's life. Similarly, "Life satisfaction," "Affect balance," and "Not happy" reflect a larger cluster of items that tap subjective well-being. To avoid redundancy, and to limit figure 3.2 to a readable size, we have only included the most sensitive indicators of each cluster. Figure 3.2 depicts the structure underlying responses to more than 100 questions dealing with many aspects of life in 43 societies, providing a global overview of basic cultural patterns.

Figure 3.2 shows the relationships between scores of variables covering a wide variety of topics ranging from religion to politics to sexual norms to attitudes toward science. These diverse orientations tend to go together in coherent patterns. For example, certain societies place relatively heavy emphasis on religion: the people of these societies also show high levels of national pride, prefer to have relatively large families, would like to see more respect for authority, tend to rank relatively low on achievement motivation and political interest, oppose divorce, and have a number of other distinctive cultural orientations. The people of other societies consistently fall toward the opposite end of the spectrum on all of these orientations, giving rise to a vertical dimension that reflects Traditional versus Secular-Rational orientations.

Figure 3.2 greatly simplifies a complex reality—in a sense, it is a one-page summary of the entire 1990 World Values Survey. It is, of course, an oversimplification. The present author has written two books on Postmaterialist values alone, and in this analysis, these values serve as only one indicator of a much broader Survival–well-being dimension. Nevertheless—to a surprising degree—reality fits this simplified model: over half of the cross-national variance among these variables can be explained by two dimensions that reflect the Modernization and Postmodernization processes, respectively.

Our first major finding is that there is a great deal of constraint among cultural systems. The pattern found here is anything but random. The first two dimensions that emerge from the principal components factor analysis depicted in figure 3.2 account for fully 51 percent of the cross-national variation among these variables. Additional dimensions explain relatively small amounts of variance. Moreover, these two main dimensions are robust, showing little change when we drop given items, even high-loading ones. The vertical axis reflects the polarization between Traditional authority and Secular-Rational authority; the horizontal axis depicts the polarization between a cluster of items labeled Survival Values and another cluster labeled Well-being Values.

The scales on the borders of figure 3.2 indicate each item's loadings on these two dimensions.

Just two dimensions account for over half of the cross-national variance among these items: this also means that about half of the variance in these values and orientations is *not* explained by the Modernization and Postmodernization dimensions. It is important to keep this in mind. Historical change cannot be entirely reduced to universal processes: to a great extent, each society works out its history in its own unique fashion, influenced by the culture, leaders, institutions, climate, geography, situation-specific events, and other unique elements that make up its own distinctive heritage. General explanatory factors can never account for everything in cross-cultural research. Just as each individual is unique, each society is unique (and each historical moment is unique). Thus, while we find the metaphor of evolution useful in describing how social change works, we do not equate evolution with determinism. Certain strategies for coping with a given environment are far more probable than others: such a strategy represents a mutually supportive combination of economic, technological, political, and cultural factors, and one that is likely to survive—while other, almost limitless, dysfunctional combinations prove abortive. But social change also involves less systematic factors that make each society unique.

Brilliant and instructive books have been written about the ways in which given societies differ from others. This book focuses on the general themes underlying the cross-national pattern, not because we are uninterested in the unique aspects of given societies—few things are more fascinating—but because the common themes are *also* interesting, and because any book that undertakes to deal with more than 40 societies almost inevitably *must* focus on what is common, rather than on what is unique. The evidence examined here indicates that common underlying themes *do* exist: it suggests that roughly half of the cross-national variance in these values and attitudes can be accounted for by the processes of Modernization and Postmodernization, while the remaining half of the variation reflects factors that are more or less nation-specific.

Religion plays a much more important role in some societies than in others. In Nigeria, fully 85 percent of the population said that religion is "very important" in their lives; in South Africa, the figure was 66 percent; in Turkey, 61 percent; in both Poland and the United States, 53 percent; in Italy, the figure was only 34 percent; in Great Britain, France, and Germany, the figures were 16, 14, and 13 percent, respectively; in Russia, it was 12 percent; in Denmark, 9 percent; in Japan, it was 6 percent; and in China, 1 percent.

"Do societies that place relatively strong emphasis on religion also tend to favor large families?" The answer is an unequivocal "Yes," as the proximity of "Religion important" and "Want many children" near the bottom of figure 3.2 suggests: the correlation between these two items is $r = .51$ (significant at the .001 level). Moreover, societies characterized by an emphasis on religion also tend to place relatively strong emphasis on work, as the proximity between "Work important" and "Religion important" suggests ($r = .62$, significant at the .0000 level). The emphasis here is on *having* work, for the sake of survival; in economically more developed societies, people place much greater emphasis on work as a source of personal *satisfaction*. Relatively traditional societies also tend to stress "Obedience" as an important quality to teach a child (r = .58), and to view the family as relatively important ("Family important," r = .56). And, as one would expect, those societies in which the public considers "Religion important" also tend to be those in which the public believe that "God is important," and to say that religious faith is an important quality to teach a child ("Religious faith"): these are almost 1:1 relationships (r = .95 and .87, respectively). These last two linkages are obvious; the others, though intuitively plausible, are not. All of these items have high loadings on the vertical dimension, labeled "Traditional Authority" vs. "Secular-Rational Authority."

Societies that place relatively strong emphasis on religion are characterized by very distinctive norms concerning sexual behavior, childrearing, the role of women, and fertility rates; they have distinctive attitudes toward divorce, abortion, and homosexuality; they also place relatively strong emphasis on deference to authority; and they have distinctive norms concerning economic achievement and distinctive motivations for work.

It is not particularly surprising that societies in which religion is relatively important have distinctive norms concerning abortion, childbearing, and the role of women. But these differences also extend to areas in which the connection is far from obvious. For example, societies in which religion is important are characterized by much higher levels of national pride than those in which it is not, as figure 3.3 demonstrates. Here, the horizontal axis shows the percentage in each society who say that God plays an important role in their lives. The people of societies that rank high on this variable show much higher levels of national pride than do those that rank low. China is a deviant case, with a high level of national pride despite being overwhelmingly secular, and West Germany deviates in the opposite direction, showing a lower level of national pride than its level of religiosity would predict. But the overall linkage is remarkably strong and significant at the .0000 level (see figure 3.3).

As these findings suggest, high levels of constraint exist between various cultural attributes. For example, if we know that a society ranks high on national pride, we can pretty accurately predict its position on childrearing practices, religiosity, and a number of other important attributes. But the pattern extends even farther. Societies that emphasize the importance of religion tend to attach low importance to politics, as the locations of "Religion important" and "Politics important" (far apart from each other on the vertical dimension) suggests: the correlation between the two is −0.39. And these same societies tend to place *low* emphasis on "Thrift" and "Determination" as important qualities to teach a child (r = −.57 and −.59, respectively). As we will see in a more detailed analysis in chapter 5, emphasis on these values is part of an Achievement Motivation syndrome that is strongly linked with the economic growth rates of given societies.

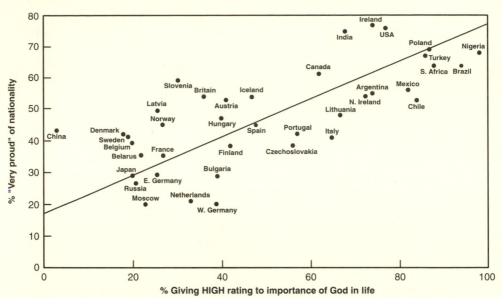

Figure 3.3. Coherent values patterns on the traditional vs. secular-rational authority dimension: the linkage between religiosity and national pride.

Horizontal dimension shows percentage ranking importance of God in their lives as relatively high (i.e., scores of 7–10 on a 10-point scale ranging from "not at all important" [1] to "very important" [10]). r = .71, significant at .0000 level.

COHERENT VALUE PATTERNS: THE POSTMODERNIZATION DIMENSION

In the Postmodernization phase of development, emphasis shifts from maximizing economic gains to maximizing subjective well-being. This gives rise to another major dimension of cross-cultural variation, on which a wide range of orientations are structured. So far, we have been discussing items with high loadings on the second principal component, labeled "Traditional Authority" vs. "Rational-Legal Authority." This dimension reflects the Modernization process, in which authority moves away from a traditional (usually religious) basis, toward increasing emphasis on impersonal bureaucratic authority. This is an important dimension, accounting for 21 percent of the variance among these 47 variables. But it is overshadowed by the first principal component, which accounts for 30 percent of the total variance. This dimension taps "Survival Values" versus "Well-being Values." A very sensitive indicator of this dimension is "Postmaterialist Values" (located near the right-hand pole of the horizontal axis on figure 3.2). This is a central element in a much broader cultural configuration.

Societies with large numbers of Postmaterialists tend to be characterized by a relatively strong sense of subjective well-being. Their publics tend to express high levels of satisfaction with their lives as a whole ("Postmaterialist Values" has a .68 correlation with "Life satisfaction"). Moreover, they report relatively high levels of positive affect (saying that within the past few days they felt interested in something, or proud, or pleased about having accomplished something) rather than negative affect (reporting that they were restless, or felt lonely, or upset because someone criticized them), which produces high scores on the Bradburn "Affect balance" scale. Furthermore, the publics of societies with high levels of Postmaterialism are likely to rate themselves as "In good health," (r = .58) and are *not* likely to describe themselves as "Not happy" (the correlation with "Postmaterialist Values" is −.71).

Subjective well-being is a condition, not a value, and is not correlated with Postmaterialism at the individual level. But high levels of subjective well-being are a key element in the cultural syndrome called Postmodernism. When a society attains high levels of economic security and subjective well-being, it is conducive to Postmaterialist values; but further economic development does not necessarily bring increased subjective well-being.

The linkage between Postmaterialism and subjective well-being is a cultural syndrome, not an individual-level ideology. It reflects the fact that societies with high levels of economic development not only have relatively high levels of *objective* need satisfaction (being relatively well-nourished, in good health, and having relatively high life expectancies); but their publics also experience relatively high levels of *subjective* security and well-being, which leads to an intergenerational shift toward Postmaterialist values. This cultural syndrome has gone largely unnoticed in previous Modernization literature, but manifests itself clearly when one has survey data covering a sufficiently broad range of countries.

At the individual level, however, Postmaterialists do *not* report relatively high levels of subjective well-being. Far from being a paradox, this is central to their nature: Postmaterialists have experienced relatively high levels of economic security throughout their formative years. They develop Postmaterialist priorities precisely because further economic gains do *not* produce additional subjective well-being: they take economic security for granted and go on to emphasize other (nonmaterial) goals. Moreover, they have relatively demanding standards for these other aspects of life—to such an extent that they often manifest *lower* levels of overall life satisfaction than do Materialists in the same society.

This leads to another finding that at first seems paradoxical. Generally, within any given society, the rich show higher levels of subjective well-being than the poor, as common sense might suggest. But Postmaterialists are an exception: they are richer (and have better education, more prestigious occupations, etc.) than most people—but they do *not* rank higher on subjective well-being than other people. This is significant. It reflects the fact that, as given nations become advanced industrial societies, they reach a point of diminishing marginal utility at which maximizing economic gains (for the individual) or economic growth (for the society) no longer results in higher levels of subjective well-being (we noted this phenomenon in chapter 2). From this perspective, it is perfectly rational to cease making economic efficiency and economic growth top priorities, and give increasing emphasis to quality of life concerns.

This cultural syndrome is pervasive and lies at the heart of Postmodernization. The publics of societies with high proportions of Postmaterialists do *not* emphasize "Hard work" as one of the most important qualities to teach a child (reflected in a loading of -0.67 on the Scarcity-Security dimension); instead, they emphasize "Tolerance" and "Imagination." Similarly, their publics do not view more emphasis on "Money" as a desirable change.

The polarization between survival values and well-being values extends to family values as well. The publics of societies with high proportions of Postmaterialists tend to reject the proposition that "A woman needs children" to be fulfilled, and disagree that "A child needs both parents," in a home with both a father and a mother, to grow up happily. There is a growing emphasis on self-realization for women, linked with a shift of emphasis from the role of mother to emphasis on careers.

"Respect parents" and "Respect authority" show strong loadings on both dimensions in figure 3.2. Their loadings indicate that *both* the Modernization process and the Postmodernization process are linked with declining respect for authority. And "Good and Evil are clear" has a negative relationship with both the shift from traditional authority to rational-legal authority and the shift from survival values to well-being values. A growing moral relativism is linked with both Modernization and Postmodernization. In traditional societies, moral rules are absolute truths, revealed by God. At the opposite extreme, in Postmodern society, absolute standards dissolve, giving way to an increasing sense of ambiguity.

We have argued that these two dimensions reflect the Modernization process and the Postmodernization process, respectively. And the fit is generally good. For example, the rise of Achievement Motivation is strongly linked with the vertical (Modernization) dimension. Moreover, the rankings of the global domains of life fit the expected configuration: as we move up the vertical dimension we see a shift in emphasis from family and religion (as indicated by "Family important" and "Religion important") toward increasing emphasis on the state ("Politics important"). Then, as we move from left to right on the horizontal dimension, we move away from emphasis on *both* traditional authority and state authority, toward increasing emphasis on individual concerns: "Leisure important" and "Friends important" show loadings of .66 and .72, respectively, on the Postmodernization dimension.

An emphasis on science and technology was a core element of modernity. But the publics of societies with high proportions of Postmaterialists (at the Postmodern end of the continuum) tend to have little confidence that scientific advances will help, rather than harm, humanity ("Trust science" has a negative correlation with "Postmaterialist values" that is significant at the .001 level); similarly, they tend to doubt that more emphasis on "Technology" would be a good thing. Conversely, these same societies have relatively high levels of support for the "Ecology" movement. The fact that societies shaped by security tend to reject science and technology is a major departure from the basic thrust of Modernization—another reason why this dimension reflects change in a *Post*-modern direction.

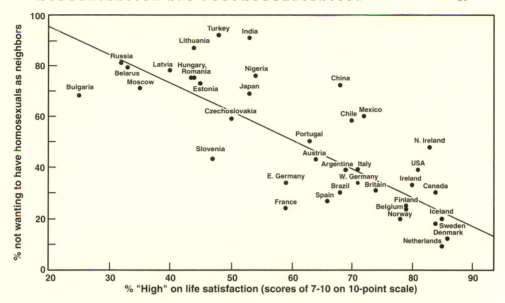

Figure 3.4. Coherent values patterns on the survival vs. well-being dimension: the linkage between life satisfaction and rejection of homosexuals as neighbors (part of the "Reject outgroups" cluster).

r = −.75, significant at .0000 level.

Societies influenced by Postmodern or well-being values tend to be markedly more tolerant than are those characterized by survival values. These societies emphasize "Tolerance" as an important quality to teach a child. Similarly, their publics are less likely to "Reject outgroups," saying that they would not like to have foreigners, people with AIDS, or homosexuals as neighbors; and they are relatively likely to feel that homosexuality is acceptable ("Homosexual OK"). Both of these correlations with "Postmaterialist values" are significant at the .001 level. Moreover, societies with relatively high levels of subjective well-being rank relatively low on intolerance of outgroups, as figure 3.4 illustrates.

The outgroup dealt with here is homosexuals, but the same pattern applies to rejection of other outgroups. In Russia and Belarus, where subjective well-being was extremely low in 1990, fully 80 percent of the public said they would not like to have homosexuals as neighbors. In such societies as Denmark or the Netherlands, where overall life satisfaction was much higher, only about 10 percent of the public were unwilling to have homosexuals as neighbors. Numerous other orientations are closely related to whether a society has high or low levels of subjective well-being.

Security is conducive to tolerance and conversely, insecurity is conducive to xenophobia. The narrower one's margin for survival is, the more likely one is to fear that strangers are threatening. This is especially true if the strangers speak a foreign language or hold different values and therefore seem incomprehensible and unpredictable.

In an agrarian or hunting and gathering society in which the land supply is just sufficient to feed the existing population, the arrival of a foreign group poses a direct threat to survival: in such a situation, xenophobia is realistic and almost certain to arise. In a technologically advanced society with a growing economy, foreigners may be tolerated or even welcomed. They do not pose a threat to survival and may even enhance the standard of living. But in times of economic or political crisis, even advanced industrial societies are prone to xenophobia, as the rise of fascism during the Great Depression demonstrated, and as recent events in Western Europe and the United States continue to demonstrate. But the severity of xenophobia tends to be proportionate to the degree of insecurity; hence, ethnic conflict is far more severe in Eastern Europe, where the economic systems and political systems have collapsed, than in Western Europe: far more people have been killed in ethnic conflicts in Eastern Europe, by several orders of magnitude.

No culture is immune to xenophobia, but it tends to be most intense where insecurity is most severe. Conversely, at the individual level, Postmaterialists—those who have grown up under conditions of relative economic and physical security—tend to be relatively tolerant of people with different ethnicity or sexual orientations. Similarly, they are relatively supportive of the "Women's movement." The rise of security values seems conducive to increasing tolerance of diversity, an essential component of democracy.

An environment of security and subjective well-being seems to foster not only tolerance, but a whole cluster of traits that are conducive to democracy. For example, well-being values are linked with high levels of interpersonal trust (as reflected in the .66 loading of "Trust people" on this dimension). Moreover, a participant public is an essential component of democracy—and one of the defining characteristics of Postmaterialist values is the fact that they give a high priority to self-expression and participation in decision making at all levels, including the political. Postmaterialism constitutes a central component of Postmodern values. Are these values linked with stable democracy? As we will see shortly, the answer is Yes.

In addition to its emphasis on science and technology, another key characteristic of Modernization was its tendency to bureaucratize all aspects of life, with the biggest bureaucracy of all resulting from the seemingly inexorable growth of government. But Postmodern values are linked with *declining* support for big government: believing that the state (rather than the individual) should take more responsibility to ensure that everyone is provided for ("State responsible") is linked with survival values, and not with well-being values; the same is true of support for "State/employee management" rather than owner management. Support for big government was a central component of Modernization. It does *not* go with Postmodern values, which is another indication that Postmodernization reflects a fundamental change of direction.

The analysis presented here is not the only possible way to slice the data. If one applies varimax rotation to the factors, one gets a somewhat different solution. Similarly, one can generate a three-dimensional or six-dimensional or even a 30-dimensional solution. Doing so produces a far more complicated result that might superficially seem more scholarly. But if one is looking for the *simplest* possible configuration, a reasonable approach is to use principal components analysis and focus on the first dimensions. Figure 3.2 is what emerges then—a structure that sums up a surprisingly wide range of phenomena in just two dimensions that capture over half of the total cross-national variance in this array of orientations. Additional dimensions exist, but they explain relatively small amounts of additional variance. The reality is that cross-cultural variation is surprisingly orderly and can be interpreted with a relatively parsimonious model.

Another critique of this approach would be to point that it is based on the assumption that our questions have comparable meaning to people from 43 widely varying societies, who were interviewed in 31 different languages. Our questionnaire was, of course, designed with this in mind: building on extensive previous cross-national survey research and extensive pilot testing, with input from social scientists on five continents, it was designed to ask questions that *do* have a shared meaning across many cultures. If we had asked questions about nation-specific issues, the cross-cultural comparability would have broken down. In France, for example, a recent hot political issue (linked with Islamic immigration) was the question whether or not girls should be allowed to wear scarves over their heads in school. This question would have had totally different meanings (or would have seemed meaningless) in other societies. On the other hand, a question about whether religion is important in one's life *is* meaningful in virtually every society on earth, including those in which most people say it is not. The same is true of questions about respect for authority, or about how many children one would like to have, or whether or not one is satisfied with one's life as a whole.

Moreover, the cross-national placement of societies underlying this configuration of worldviews is astonishingly coherent. As we will see below, societies that show similar cultural orientations in our surveys fall into compact and theoretically meaningful clusters. Working independently and without knowledge of each other's findings, the World Values survey investigators in the five Nordic countries came up with relatively similar results. So did our colleagues in Nigeria and South Africa, and so did those in the four Latin American countries and in Eastern Europe. The evidence suggests that the World Values survey group was generally successful in framing cross-nationally meaningful questions. If these items had idiosyncratic meanings in each society, we would not have attained such a parsimonious and coherent structure. Instead, the orientations that went together in one society would be unrelated in other societies, and it would take 15 or 20 dimensions to explain half of the variance.

WHERE ARE GIVEN SOCIETIES LOCATED ON THESE DIMENSIONS?
A CULTURAL GEOGRAPHY OF THE WORLD

In most respects, the two dimensions in figure 3.2 show a good fit with the attributes we would expect to find if they reflected the shift from Traditional to Modern values, and from Modern to Postmodern values, respectively. But in one important way the pattern seems wrong: the growth of big government was a central aspect of Modernization. For many decades, the all-encompassing socialist state was thought to be the wave of the future: it was the logical culmination of the trend toward bureaucratization and state authority. If so, we would expect to find emphasis on "State/employee management" and "State responsibility" located near the top of the vertical dimension. Instead, we find them occupying roughly neutral positions on this dimension. Why? In order to understand the answer, let us examine the specific national cultures underlying this pattern.

Figure 3.5 shows the location of each society on the two dimensions we have been examining. To locate them in this space, dummy variables were created for each of our 43 societies; these variables were mapped onto the two dimensions shaped by the worldviews of the respective publics. Because these dummy variables are extremely skewed (each having one country coded "1" and 42 countries coded "0"), the correlations with the cultural dimensions are modest; but if we combine countries into larger groups (such as the Nordic group or the Latin American group) the correlations with the ideological space become quite strong. The societies that show similar cultural orientations in our surveys (and therefore are near each other on this figure) fall into intuitively plausible clusters.

Our broadest generalization is that the value systems of richer countries differ systematically from those of poorer countries. The poorer countries tend to be located toward the lower left on figure 3.5, with the richer ones falling into the upper right-hand quadrant. Although there are some deviant cases (the United States having much more traditional values than its GNP per capita would predict), the overall correlation between values and economic development is very strong.

But the pattern is coherent in many additional respects. For example, all four of the Latin American societies included in the 1990 World Values Survey fall into one cluster, reflecting the fact that, in global perspective they have relatively similar value systems. The two African societies fall into another cluster; and the three Confucian-influenced societies of East Asia fall into another cluster—which partly overlaps with another cluster containing the former communist societies. The historically Catholic societies of Western Europe fall into another compact cluster. Although church attendance in Western Europe has collapsed, the historically Protestant societies of Northern Europe fall into another cluster (with Eastern Germany located at the intersection of the Northern European cluster and the ex-communist cluster, as its historical experience might suggest). The United States and Canada constitute a North American

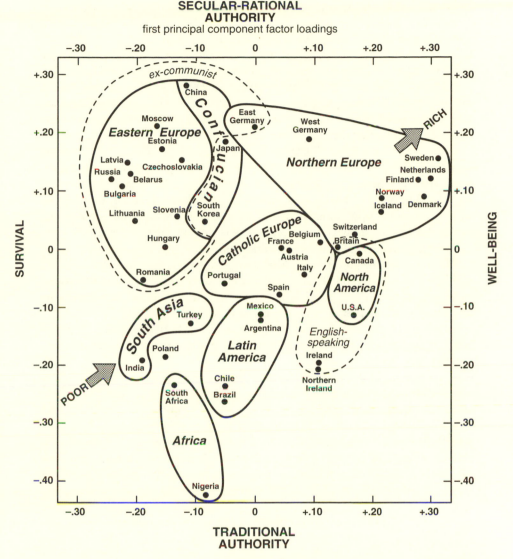

Figure 3.5. Where given societies fall on two key cultural dimensions. *Source*: 1990–93 World Values Survey. Positions are based on the mean scores of the publics of the given nation on each of the two dimensions.

cluster—that could be expanded to include the other English-speaking societies. Poland is an outlier, having more traditional values than the other ex-communist societies of Eastern Europe: it does not fit into any coherent cluster. But on the whole, the value systems of a majority of the world's people are anything but random: though shaped by a variety of factors, they manifest a remarkably coherent pattern that can be interpreted parsimoniously.

Societies that are close to each other on figure 3.5 show relatively similar responses to most of the questions that were asked in the World Values survey. For example, though the peoples of the United States and Canada differ in many ways, they have relatively similar basic values in comparison with most other societies: accordingly, they are located close to each other on figure 3.5.

Just how close are they? To answer this question, let us examine the responses to the first six questions asked in the survey. The publics of each society were asked "Please say, for each of the following, how important it is in your life." They rated the relative importance of "Work," "Family," "Friends," "Leisure," "Politics," and "Religion." This list covers a broad range of human concerns, and the various publics differed a great deal in how much importance they attached to the respective aspects of life. The cross-national rankings for nearly 350 variables are shown in Basanez, Inglehart, and Moreno (1997), and they support the claim that societies that are close to each other on figure 3.5 tend to show similar values and beliefs in many other ways; here, we will limit ourselves to these six variables.

Since 43 societies are ranked here, the greatest possible distance between any two societies would occur if one of them were ranked first and the other were ranked forty-third: all 41 of the other societies would fall between them. Conversely, the smallest possible distance would occur if the two societies had consecutive ranks, with *none* of the other societies falling between them. Finally, if the two societies were randomly distributed, about 20 societies would fall between them.

The publics of the United States and Canada give relatively similar ratings to these six aspects of life: on the average, only 3.3 other societies fall between them. The values of Canadians and Americans are much more similar to each other than they are to those of most other peoples. The British are also relatively close to the Americans, but by no means as close as the Canadians. On the other hand, the publics of the United States and China generally give these six domains quite different ratings: on the average, they are separated by nearly 24 societies, as the following ratings show:

CULTURAL DISTANCE FROM THE UNITED STATES
(mean number of societies between the
United States and given society)

United States–Canada	3.3
United States–Britain	9.0
United States–France	16.7
United States–Japan	21.8
United States–Russia	22.2
United States–China	23.8

This principle applies generally. One finds a similar pattern if one views the world from a Swedish perspective, for example. Sweden, Norway, and Denmark are located relatively near each other on figure 3.5, and they make rather similar ratings of the six aspects of life. On the average, only 3.8 societies fall between Sweden and Norway in these rankings, and only 5.8 societies fall between Sweden and Denmark. On the other hand, Sweden and France are separated by a mean of 13.6 societies, while Sweden and Russia are separated by an average of 17.8 societies, Sweden and Japan by 18.2 societies, and Sweden and China are separated by an average of more than 19 societies.

Given groups of nations take coherent positions on the two dimensions. For example, Norway, Iceland, Denmark, Finland, and Sweden—the five Nordic countries—form a compact cluster located in the upper right-hand quadrant of figure 3.5: all five have related histories and similar cultures, ranking fairly high on the cultural outlook associated with rational-legal authority, and ranking very high on Postmodern values. To some extent, these countries are geographically proximate, but the fact that they are prosperous and traditionally Protestant welfare states seems more important than their geographic proximity. Thus the Netherlands, which is not a Nordic country but was historically Protestant and is today a prosperous welfare state, falls squarely into the middle of the Nordic group. Although geographically located next door to Belgium and sharing a common language with half of Belgium, the Netherlands is culturally much closer to the Nordic countries than to Belgium. Historically, the Netherlands has been shaped by Protestantism; even the Dutch Catholics today are remarkably Calvinist. And although the churches themselves are now a fading influence in Western European society, religious traditions helped shape enduring *national* cultures that persist today. Thus, culturally, the Netherlands is located somewhere between Norway and Sweden.

Belgium, France, Italy, Spain, Portugal, and Austria constitute another cluster in the cultural space of figure 3.5. Although church attendance has declined drastically, all of these countries were historically Roman Catholic. Furthermore, this cluster is adjacent to a Latin American (and overwhelmingly Catholic) cluster containing Mexico, Argentina, Chile, and Brazil. These predominantly Catholic countries form a fairly coherent group. One could even expand it to include the four other historically Roman Catholic countries, Poland, Hungary, Slovenia, and Lithuania. The last four countries are outliers, probably because of their divergent histories since 1945: the rising prosperity experienced by Western European Catholic countries in recent decades had much less impact on them, and they are more permeated by survival values than are the rest of the Catholic group. On the Modernization dimension, however, their values are almost as traditional as those of other Catholic countries (and they have more traditional values than the other exsocialist countries). As Basanez (1993) demonstrates, the Protestant-Catholic differences do not simply reflect the fact that the historically Protestant countries tend to be richer than the Catholic ones: controlling for GDP/capita, the value differences between them remain significant at the .001 level.

Nevertheless, there is no question that traditional orientations *are* closely related to a society's level of economic development. Almost all of the economically less-developed countries fall into the lower left-hand quadrant of figure

3.5, with cultures that emphasize traditional authority and survival values. But interestingly enough, all five of the English-speaking societies (Britain, Canada, the United States, Ireland, and Northern Ireland) fall into a cluster located in the lower right-hand quadrant: these countries have relatively strong security values, but much more religious-traditional values than most other countries at their economic level. This is particularly true of Ireland and Northern Ireland, which have a traditional/religious outlook that is fully as strong as that found in India, South Africa, or Brazil—with only Nigeria being markedly more traditional.

The former West German and East German regions of Germany were still independent states when these surveys were carried out and were sampled separately. Although West Germany falls into the upper right-hand quadrant with the other Western European societies, and East Germany into the upper left-hand quadrant containing most of the historically communist societies, the two societies are relatively close to each other on the two main cultural dimensions. This is significant. From 1945 to 1990, the communist regime made a massive effort to reshape East German culture to support a Marxist and atheistic authoritarian regime. Simultaneously, the Western powers launched massive efforts in West Germany to remake political culture to support a market-oriented Western liberal democracy. The evidence indicates that 45 years under radically different regimes did have an impact: by 1990 the two societies were some distance apart, especially along the Postmodernization dimension. But even more impressive is the fact that, in global perspective, the basic cultural values of the two societies were still relatively similar. This natural experiment indicates that, even when it makes a conscious and concerted effort to do so, the ability of a regime to reshape its underlying culture is limited. After 45 years under diametrically opposed political and economic institutions, in their basic values East Germany and West Germany remained as similar to each other as are the United States and Canada.

Almost all of the socialist or ex-socialist societies fall into the upper left-hand quadrant: these societies are characterized by survival values and a strong emphasis on state authority, rather than traditional authority. Poland is a striking exception, distinguished from the other socialist societies by its strong traditional-religious values. China is an outlier in the opposite direction—the least religious and most state-oriented society for which we have data. These societies' positions reflect their distinctive cultural heritages. On one hand, adherence to the Catholic church has been a mainstay of the Polish struggle for independence since 1792. The church continued to play a vital role in this struggle throughout the 1980s, revitalizing the role of religion in the national culture.

China, on the other hand, has had a relatively secular cultural system for 2,000 years; and bureaucratic authority developed within the Confucian system long before it reached the West. Thus China and the other Confucian-influenced societies of East Asia have had one major component of modern culture for a very long time. Until recently, they lacked the emphasis on science and technology and the esteem for economic achievement that are its other main components; but their secular, bureaucratic heritage probably helped to facilitate their rapid economic development once these were attained. China's traditional emphasis on the state may have been reinforced by four decades of socialism. Japan, another Confucian-influenced society, and both Eastern and Western Germany are also characterized by relatively strong emphasis on rational-legal authority.

Most of the socialist and ex-socialist societies are oriented toward rational-legal, rather than traditional-religious, authority. Their people have experienced four to eight decades of socialist regimes in which religion has been systematically repressed and in which it is perfectly realistic to consider politics important because economic life, cultural life, and even one's chances of survival depend on the state. The socialist states were probably the most heavily bureaucratized, centralized, and secularized societies in history, and they held science and technology in such esteem that their elites legitimated their power by the claim that they ruled, not through the unscientific and fallible process of majority rule, but according to the principles of scientific socialism. By these standards, the socialist states represented the culmination of Modernization—and the fact that, on figure 3.5, they are located near the Modernization pole of the Traditional Authority–Rational-Legal Authority dimension seems appropriate. But figure 3.2 revealed one surprising anomaly: one would expect that such key ideological components of the socialist state as its tendency to hold the "State responsible" for providing for everyone's needs should *also* cluster near the Modernization pole and gain maximum support in the socialist societies. It does not. Why?

We suspect that if these surveys had been carried out a decade or two earlier, support for state management and state responsibility *would* have been relatively strong in the ex-socialist societies. Most of them had experienced relatively high economic growth rates from 1945 to 1975 or 1980. Up to this point, they seemed to be functioning well: they had done a good job of providing the basic necessities for nearly everyone and were able to conceal or repress criticism of their shortcomings in other aspects of life. Support for a state-run economy and society was probably a good deal higher then, in socialist countries, than it was in 1990. In this simpler, more orderly world, we would have found "State responsible" located near the Modernization pole. And the empirical picture may now again be closer to this model than it was in 1990: as the transition to market economies proved unexpectedly traumatic, reform communist elites returned to power in a number of ex-communist societies during the early 1990s.

But reality is complex. In 1990–91, when these surveys were carried out, the socialist economic and political systems were collapsing; and mass support for state-run economies had withered away in these societies. The classic model of state socialism was surviving only in North Korea and Cuba, and paradoxically mass support for socialism was no longer the wave of the future for industrial society, but had become a Third World phenomenon.

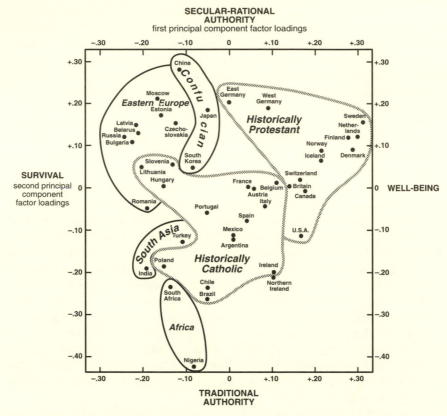

Figure 3.6. Where given societies fall on two key cultural dimensions: religious influences. *Source*: 1990–93 World Values Survey. Positions are based on the mean scores of the publics of the given nation on each of the two dimensions.

INSTITUTIONAL DETERMINISM OF CULTURE?

As we have seen, the historically Protestant countries of both Northern Europe and North America tend to cluster together to form one large group; similarly, the historically Roman Catholic countries of Western Europe, Latin America, and Eastern Europe tend to cluster together, forming another broad but reasonably cohesive cluster. Despite the enormous recent changes linked with economic and social Modernization, and despite the tremendous sociopolitical changes linked with communist domination of four traditionally Catholic societies throughout the Cold War, in global perspective the historically Catholic societies still have relatively similar cultural values—as do the historically Protestant societies. As figure 3.6 illustrates, the Catholic societies form a group characterized by more traditional values, and by greater emphasis on survival values, than holds true of most Protestant societies. At first glance, this might seem to constitute strong evidence for an institutional determinist interpretation: the religious institutions of these societies led them to develop different cultures.

If institutional determinism is simply taken to mean that a society's institutions are among the factors that help shape its culture, it is undoubtedly correct. But institutional determinism is often pushed to a much more extreme claim than this. It is taken to mean that institutions alone determine a society's cultural values, so one need not really take cultural factors into account: if one changes the institutions, the culture automatically changes to fit it. If one examines the evidence more closely, it is clear that this position is untenable.

There are tremendous cultural differences between Protestant and Catholic societies, but for the most part they do not reflect the direct influence of the Catholic and Protestant churches today. For the direct influence of the church today is very slight in many of these countries. Although church attendance remains relatively high in Poland and Ireland (and the United States), it has fallen drastically in most of the historically Catholic countries of both Western and Eastern Europe; and it has fallen even more drastically in most historically Protestant European societies, to the point where some observers now speak of the Nordic countries as post-Christian societies: church attendance has plummeted toward zero. The societies that were traditionally Catholic still show very distinct values from those that were traditionally Protestant—even among segments of the population who have no contact with the church. But these values persist as part of the cultural heritage of given nations, and not through the direct influence of the religious institutions. This cultural heritage has been shaped by the economic, political, and social experience of the people, including the fact that the Protestant societies industrialized earlier than most of the Catholic societies—which at an even earlier stage of history may, in turn, have been linked with religious differences (as Weber suggests), but is certainly not a case of mere institutional determinism.

There is a remarkable degree of coherence to this pattern. Forty of the 43 societies fall into compact and historically meaningful clusters, such as Latin America or Eastern Europe or East Asia. There are only three outliers from this perspective: Poland plus Ireland and Northern Ireland (with the two parts of Ireland being closely linked). Both Poland and Ireland might be described as hyper-Catholic societies: they are Roman Catholic societies that for centuries were occupied and dominated by more powerful non-Catholic neighbors and that responded to pressures toward cultural assimilation by an intense reemphasis on their Roman Catholic heritage as a means of preserving their national identity. Ironically, this may have led to a similar reaction on the part of the Irish Protestants, who constitute a small minority within Ireland as a whole and might be described as hyper-Protestants. Poland and both parts of Ireland strongly emphasize traditional cultural values concerning not only religion, but also politics, gender roles, sexual norms, and family values. They illustrate the fundamentalist reaction to threat.

In most countries, these cultural differences reflect the entire historical experience of given societies, and *not* the influence of the respective churches today. This point becomes vividly evident when we examine the value systems of such societies as the Netherlands and Germany—both of which were historically predominantly Protestant societies, but (as a consequence of different birth rates and different rates of religious attrition) have about as many practicing Catholics as Protestants today. Despite these changes in their religious makeup today, both the Netherlands and Germany manifest typically Protestant values. Moreover, the Catholics and Protestants *within* these societies do not show markedly different value systems: the Dutch Catholics today are as Calvinist as the members of the Dutch Reformed Church.

The historically Protestant and Catholic societies are not randomly distributed on our cultural map—far from it, they constitute coherent clusters. The communist ideology has been described as a secular religion, and the historically communist societies also make up a coherent cluster, which partly overlaps with the Catholic cluster: 13 of the 14 formerly communist societies fall into a compact cluster in the upper left-hand quadrant, and this Eastern European cluster could easily be expanded to include China and Eastern Germany. And as we have noted, though they are located on two different continents and span the Catholic-Protestant divide, the five English-speaking societies are also relatively near to each other on this cultural map: a common language is the unifying factor in this case. But the most pervasive influence of all seems to be economic development. If one draws a diagonal from the lower-left corner to the upper-right corner of figures 3.5 or 3.6, it traces the transition from poorer to richer societies. Both the Modernization dimension and the Postmodernization dimension are strongly correlated with a society's level of economic development: the values of richer societies differ systematically from those of poorer societies on both dimensions. Clearly, institutional determinism would be a far too simple interpretation of the evidence. Although the impact of religious institutions is evident, economic, political, geographic, linguistic, and other factors also play important roles. The worldview of a given people reflects its entire historical heritage.

To What Extent Was Modernization Theory Correct?

Coherent Cultural Patterns Exist

We have found that constraint *does* exist among cultural patterns. To get a sense of just how true this is, let us imagine two extreme models, ranging from a world wholly without cultural constraint, to one with total constraint. In the former model, each society goes its own way: the fact that it possesses one specific cultural attribute has no influence on whether other attributes are present. Cultural components are randomly related. The other extreme model is one of total determinism: only a few cultural patterns are possible, and if one major component of a pattern is present, all the other elements are also present in every case.

As one would expect, the empirical findings do not fit either extreme model, but they come much closer to the constrained model than to the random one. Fully half of the cross-cultural variation among this broad array of variables can be captured in just two dimensions. This picture is certainly not one of complete determinism: these two dimensions do not explain *all* of the variation among these 43 cultural indicators. But they do account for 51 percent of the variance—vastly more than the less than 5 percent that they would explain in a random model.

These Coherent Cultural Patterns Are Linked with a Society's Level of Economic Development

The fact that constrained cultural patterns exist does not, by itself, demonstrate that Modernization theory is correct: coherent cultural patterns might be found exclusively in given regions (such as Western Europe) as a result of given historical or religious traditions (such as Protestantism or Buddhism) without having any relationship to economic and technological change. Modernization theory, by contrast, implies that economic development *is* strongly linked with given cultural patterns—either because economic development produces specific types of culture, or because certain cultural patterns produce economic development. In short, Modernization theory implies that coherent cultural patterns exist, *and* that these patterns are linked with a given society's level of economic development. As figure 3.7 demonstrates, this clearly *is* the case.

We argued that the vertical dimension on figures 3.2 and 3.3 reflects the Modernization process, while the horizontal dimension reflects Postmodernization. The evidence presented in figure 3.7 indicates that economic development is conducive to *both* Modernization and Postmodernization, which are two successive stages of development: a society's per capita GNP is correlated with Modernization values at the .60 level, and at the .78 level with Postmodernization values. But other economic indicators show quite different relationships to these two respective dimensions. For example, the percentage of the labor force in the manufacturing sector is strongly correlated with the vertical (Modernization) dimension ($r = .63$) but much less strongly linked with the horizontal (Postmodernization) dimension ($r = .22$); but Postmodern values are strongly linked with the percentage of the labor force in the *service* sector ($r = .79$).

Bell argues that Postindustrial society has arrived when a majority of a society's workforce is employed in the service sector. There is a good deal of overlap between Postmodern society and Postindustrial society. But Bell's concept of Postindustrial society emphasizes changes in the structure of the workforce, while the term "Postmodern society" emphasizes cultural changes linked with economic security; we have argued that existential security is a key factor underlying Postmodernization. In keeping with this contention, we find that prosperity has as strong a relationship with Postmodern culture as does the composition of the workforce.

Similarly, the percentage of a given society's population having a secondary

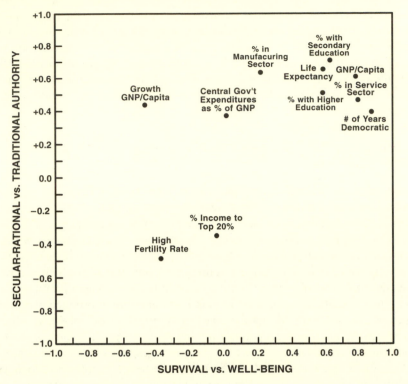

Figure 3.7. Economic and social correlates of two key dimensions of cross-cultural variation. *Source*: 1990–93 World Values Survey.

or higher education shows a .71 correlation with the Rational-Legal pole of the Modernization dimension—and a .63 correlation with the Well-being pole of the Postmodernization dimension. These findings support the claim by Lerner (1958), Inkeles and Smith (1974), and others that rising educational levels have contributed to major cultural changes.

The consequences of growing up in a setting in which one can take satisfaction of one's survival needs for granted, rather than in a society of scarcity, seems to have been underestimated by Bell, Inkeles and Smith, and others. The strong linkage between Postmodern values and a society's GDP/capita supports the interpretation that these are, indeed, *security* values: they have an extremely strong tendency to be found in relatively prosperous societies.

An even more striking contrast between the economic correlates of Modernization and Postmodernization is the fact that Modernization values have a substantial positive linkage with economic growth rates, while Postmodern values have a *negative* linkage with economic growth: Postmodern societies are even richer than modernizing societies, but they show lower economic growth rates.

Overall, the evidence in figure 3.7 suggests that if educational levels con-

tinue to rise and the workforce continues to move out of farming and manufacturing into the service and knowledge sectors, and if per capita income continues to rise, then we can expect to see a gradual modernization of preindustrial societies and a shift toward Postmodern values, in advanced industrial
societies.

Is Cultural Change Taking Place?

The fact that Postmodern values are strongly linked with economic development does not necessarily prove that as economic development takes place,
these values will become more widespread. The linkage might be spurious.
Long-term time series data are needed to demonstrate whether or not the predicted changes are taking place and help sort out the causal relationships. We
don't have extensive time series data for most of the variables examined here,
but we do have some—and virtually all of the available evidence points to the
conclusion that a shift toward Postmodern culture *is* taking place in advanced
industrial societies.

The most abundant time series data (by far) relate to Materialist/Postmate-
rialist values. Though this is only one component of the much larger syndrome
of Postmodern values, it is a key indicator of this broader syndrome. Evidence
of a shift from Materialist to Postmaterialist values will be presented in chapter 4; it shows that Postmaterialist values have increased in the past quarter
century, and that they have increased at almost exactly the rate predicted by
the intergenerational population replacement model (about one point on the
values percentage difference index per year).

If Postmaterialist values are moving in the predicted direction, this suggests
that the entire set of closely correlated Postmodern values may be moving in
the same direction, since theoretically they share a common set of causes: the
transition from conditions of scarcity to the relative security of Postmodern
society.

This broader shift toward Postmodern values in general *does* seem to be taking place. In chapters 7 and 8 we test the hypothesis that all values having reasonably strong correlations with Postmaterialism are part of an intergenerational shift linked with population replacement. To do so, we first identified 40
variables that were strongly correlated with Postmaterialist values and were
included in both the 1981 and 1990 World Values surveys. Our expectation was
that whatever values were positively correlated with Postmaterialism would
become more widespread over time, other things being equal. When we compare the 1981 responses, with responses to the same questions in the same
countries in 1990, we find that in the great majority of cases these values
shifted in the predicted direction. The available evidence suggests that cultural
change is taking place in the predicted direction.

As hypothesized, the apparent decline of traditional values is strongly linked
with economic growth: as figure 3.7 indicates, a country's growth rate from

1965 to 1990 shows a .44 correlation with emphasis on Rational-Legal Authority (and a corresponding negative correlation with Traditional Authority). In chapter 6 we probe into the relevant causal linkages: the findings suggest that culture shapes economic life, as well as being shaped by it. In the early stages of industrialization, achievement motivation seems to contribute to economic growth. But insofar as this growth produces prosperity, in the long run it leads to cultural changes that tend to de-emphasize achievement motivation, leading to *lower* rates of economic growth. This points to still another contrast between Modernization and Postmodernization: while the Modernization process is linked with high *rates* of economic growth, Postmodernization is not. Quite the contrary, relatively high growth rates show a *negative* linkage ($r = -.47$) with well-being values. In part, this reflects the fact that Postmaterialists do not emphasize economic growth, and they tend to give priority to protecting the environment, if forced to choose.

Traditional values are negatively linked with economic growth, but positively linked with high fertility rates, as figure 3.7 demonstrates ($r = .48$). As we saw earlier, societies with Traditional values tend to emphasize the family and have relatively large numbers of children. It seems that this is not just a matter of lip service. A society's values and its actual fertility rate are closely linked, probably in a causal relationship. This tends to set up a self-reinforcing process: traditional values not only seem to inhibit a set of norms that are conducive to economic growth, they also encourage population growth rates that tend to offset the effects of whatever economic growth *does* occur, making it still more difficult to raise per capita income. Conversely, both Modernization and Postmodernization are linked with declining birth rates, so the pie gets divided up among fewer people—another example of how cultural and economic factors constitute mutually reinforcing syndromes.

MODERNIZATION, POSTMODERNIZATION, AND DEMOCRATIZATION

Finally, the Postmodernization process has important political implications. Inkeles and Diamond (1980), Inglehart (1990), and others have argued that economic development is linked with cultural changes that are conducive to democracy, an argument that has been disputed by dependency theorists, neo-Marxists, and some rational choice theorists. As figure 3.7 indicates, there is no correlation whatever between the Modernization axis and the number of years for which a given society has been democratic. As Moore (1966) pointed out, modernization can give rise to either democratic or authoritarian regimes.

But there is an amazingly strong correlation between the Postmodernization dimension and democracy: $r = .88$. We suggested earlier that high levels of subjective well-being, coupled with Postmodern values, including interpersonal trust, tolerance, and Postmaterialist values, should be conducive to democracy. The empirical evidence is remarkably strong: this cluster of cultural traits clearly *is* linked with stable democracy. One could argue that this cultural syndrome is conducive to democracy, or that democracy somehow gives rise to a culture of trust, tolerance, subjective well-being, and Postmaterialist values, or that the cultural syndrome and the political institutions are mutually supportive. We will analyze the causal linkages more closely in chapter 5; for the moment, we will simply observe that Postmodern values and stable democracy go together very closely.

It has been known for some time that democracy is more likely to be found among relatively prosperous countries than among poorer ones (Lipset, 1960). The present body of evidence supports that conclusion. But the linkage between culture and democracy found here is even stronger than the linkage between economic development and democracy. This finding suggests that economic development by itself does not automatically produce democracy; it does so only insofar as it gives rise to a specific syndrome of cultural changes.

Putnam (1993) supports this interpretation, using aggregate time series data from 20 regions of Italy, extending from 1860 to the mid-1980s. He finds that given regions have varying degrees of a cultural syndrome termed "Civic Community" (characterized by trust, tolerance, solidarity, civic engagement, political equality, and civic associations), which is strongly correlated with the effectiveness of democratic institutions in the given regions. Economic development is also related to democratic effectiveness; but controlling for civic traditions, economic development has no impact whatever. On the other hand, a region's level of civic involvement in 1900 not only predicts subsequent civic involvement and institutional performance, but also helps explain subsequent economic development.

WHY DOES CHANGE FOLLOW PREDICTABLE PATTERNS?

Coherent trajectories of cultural change exist, with some cultural patterns being far more probable than others. Why?

The evidence suggests that in the long run, cultural change behaves as if it were a process of rational choice—subject to substantial cultural lags, and subject to the fact that the goals being maximized vary from one culture to another and can only be understood through empirical knowledge of the specific culture. In this loosely rational process, peoples are maximizing a variety of goods, the most basic of which is survival—and their cultures are survival strategies for a given people. Cultural variation tends to follow predictable patterns because some ways of running a society work better than others. If one is willing to concede that most people prefer survival to nonsurvival, then both Modernization and Postmodernization are linked with outcomes that almost anyone would consider "better." As figure 3.7 indicates, there is a .59 correlation between a society's female life expectancy and its level of Modernization, and a .65 correlation between life expectancy and Postmodernization. Neither process bestows moral superiority, but both Modernization and Postmodernization are linked with a markedly lower likelihood of dying prematurely from disease or malnutrition. Life expectancy today ranges from as low as 39 years in the poorest countries to almost 80 years in developed ones. This is a difference that few people would fail to appreciate, regardless of cultural orientation. It is one reason why the modernization syndrome had such pervasive appeal. Successful industrialization requires a relatively competitive, impersonal, bureaucratic, achievement-oriented form of social relations that tends to be dehumanizing and stressful; but in societies of scarcity around the globe, it came to be viewed as a worthwhile trade-off. Islamic fundamentalism remains an alternative model insofar as oil revenues make it possible to obtain many of the advantages of modernization *without* industrializing; but we would not expect this model's credibility and mass appeal to outlast the oil reserves.

The Modernization process brought substantial gains in life expectancy by maximizing economic growth, making it possible to sharply reduce the two leading causes of death in preindustrial societies—malnutrition and disease. But the linkage between economic development and rising life expectancy eventually reached a point of diminishing returns.

Postmodernization represents a shift in survival strategies, from maximizing economic growth to maximizing survival and well-being. Modernization focused on rapid economic growth, which provided a means to maximize survival and well-being under the conditions that emerged when rationalization and industrialization first became possible. But no strategy is optimal for all time. Modernization was dramatically successful in raising life expectancies, but it has begun to produce diminishing returns in advanced industrial societies. By emphasizing competition it reduced the risk of starvation—but it probably also increased psychological stress. As we have seen, subjective well-being levels are lower in the communist and ex-communist societies—which are, by some criteria, the most "modern" of all societies—than in the most traditional societies. These low levels of subjective well-being in the ex-socialist world are almost certainly linked with the current crisis in the former communist societies, but the 1981 World Values Survey found low levels there even before the collapse of communism. During the decade before 1990, symptoms of severe demoralization and psychological stress were evident in the former Soviet Union and were manifest in high rates of alcoholism and declining life expectancies.

Postmodernization, on the other hand, has a mildly negative linkage with economic growth, but a strong positive linkage with subjective well-being. With the transition from Modernization to Postmodernization, the trajectory of change seems to have shifted from maximizing economic growth to maximizing the quality of life.

CROSS-SECTIONAL EVIDENCE OF SOCIAL CHANGE

Cross-sectional data can be a useful supplement to time series data in understanding processes of socioeconomic change. Although time series data provide the only reliable measurements of changes over time, appropriate cross-sectional data can extend the scope of one's perspective in time and space: its configuration may reflect processes that occurred over many decades or even centuries.

Interpreted in connection with the available time series data, the cultural configurations found in the 43-nation World Values survey suggest that coherent, and even to some extent predictable, trajectories of political and cultural change are linked with given socioeconomic developments. These trajectories are not deterministic: the leaders and institutions, and the cultural and geographic heritage, of a given society also help shape its course. And development does not move in a simple, linear fashion: all trends eventually change direction.

But neither is socioeconomic change random and unpredictable, with each society following its own idiosyncratic course. On the contrary, change tends to follow clear configurations, in which specific clusters of cultural characteristics go together with specific types of political and economic change. The familiar Modernization syndrome of urbanization, industrialization, and mass literacy tends to have foreseeable consequences such as increasing mass mobilization. Modernization is linked with given cultural changes, such as a growing emphasis on Achievement Motivation, and a shift from Traditional to Rational-Legal Authority, which encompasses dozens of more specific changes.

Similarly, the emergence of advanced industrial society, with an increasing share of the public having higher education, being employed in the service sector, and feeling assured that their survival needs will be met, gives rise to a process in which high levels of subjective well-being and Postmodern values emerge—and in which a variety of attributes, from equal rights for women to democratic political institutions, become increasingly likely.

Measuring Materialist and Postmaterialist Values

MATERIALIST/POSTMATERIALIST VALUE PRIORITIES are only one component of the much broader configuration that constitutes the Postmodernization dimension. But Materialist/Postmaterialist values are by far the best documented aspect of this broader configuration, having been measured in cross-national surveys carried out regularly since 1970. The initial research on intergenerational value change was based on this dimension, and it continues to play an important role in research on cultural change. This chapter examines the nature of Postmaterialist values and the controversy over how these values can be measured most effectively; the next chapter analyzes the intergenerational shift from Materialist to Postmaterialist priorities during the past quarter century.

Over the years since these values were first investigated, there has been considerable controversy about what they were tapping, how values should be measured, and how many dimensions one should use to analyze Materialist/Postmaterialist value priorities. This controversy continues; several important critiques of measurement techniques have appeared recently. The 1990 World Values Survey measured Materialist/Postmaterialist value priorities by asking the respondents in more than 40 societies a series of questions that began as follows: "There is a lot of talk these days about what the aims of this country should be for the next ten years. On this card are listed some of the goals which different people would give top priority. Would you please say which one of these you, yourself, consider the most important? And which one would be the next most important?"

Twelve goals were rated, but in order to reduce the task to manageable proportions, they were presented in three groups of four items; each set of four goals contained two items designed to tap Materialist priorities, and two designed to tap Postmaterialist priorities. These 12 goals are shown in abbreviated form in figure 4.1; the full text of this battery appears in Appendix 2.

The choices deal with broad societal goals rather than the immediate needs of the respondent: we wanted to tap long-term concerns, not one's response to the immediate situation. Among these 12 goals, six items were intended to emphasize survival needs: "Rising prices," "Economic growth," and "Stable economy" designed to tap emphasis on economic security, and "Maintain order," "Fight crime," and "Strong defense forces" designed to tap emphasis on physical security. These items tap two distinct types of needs, but both are "Materialist," in that they are directly related to physiological survival. We hypothesized that they would tend to go together, with only those who feel secure about the satisfaction of both needs being likely to give top priority to belonging, self-expression, and intellectual and aesthetic satisfaction—Post-

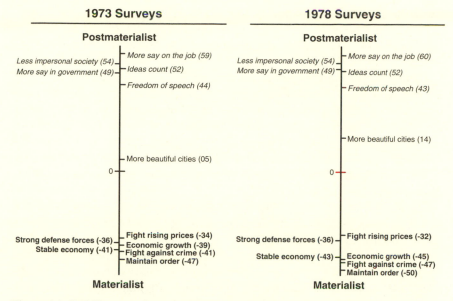

Figure 4.1. Stability over time: the Materialist/Postmaterialist dimension in nine Western nations in 1973 and 1978.

Mean factor loadings from each of the nine European Union countries surveyed in September 1973 and October–November 1978. Items with Materialist polarity are in boldface type; items with Postmaterialist polarity are in italics. Based on principal components analyses of ranking of the 12 goals. *Source*: Inglehart, 1990: 140.

materialist needs that the remaining six items are designed to tap. We view all of these needs as universal: every human being needs sustenance and safety—but also desires self-expression, esteem, and aesthetic satisfaction and has a sense of intellectual curiosity. Thus one finds art and music and other products of the search for beauty in all societies, and one finds magic, religion, myths, or philosophy, reflecting the desire to understand and interpret the meaning of life in even the poorest societies. Hungry people may not give top priority to self-expression and intellectual concerns, but given some respite from the struggle for survival, people will act on these needs unless circumstances stifle them. Our expectation, therefore, is that emphasis on the six Materialist items will tend to form one cluster, with the Postmaterialist items in another distinct cluster.

All cultures are multidimensional. Change can occur in sexual norms, tastes in food or music, political party preferences, trust in government, religious outlook, and numerous other aspects of life. The question is not whether the Materialist/Postmaterialist dimension is the only dimension along which change can occur, but whether such a dimension exists—and if so, whether significant change has been taking place in the predicted direction.

Our theoretical framework implies that emphasis on economic security and on physical security will tend to go together—and that those who feel insecure about these survival needs have a fundamentally different outlook and political behavior from those who feel secure about them. The latter are likely to give top priority to nonmaterial goals such as self-expression, belonging, and intellectual or aesthetic satisfaction.

Emphasis on economic and physical security were expected to go together for two reasons: (1) From a macrosocietal perspective, war tends to produce both economic and physical insecurity—both hunger and loss of life. Consequently, those generations that have experienced war are likely to feel less secure about both. (2) From a microsocietal perspective, poor individuals tend to be exposed to both economic and physical insecurity—both poverty and relatively high crime rates. The more affluent strata have resources that shield them, to some extent, from *both*.

Satisfaction of the survival needs, we hypothesized, leads to growing emphasis on nonphysiological or "Postmaterialist" goals. A large share of the public in Western societies have been socialized in an environment that provides an unprecedentedly secure prospect that one's physiological needs will be met. Consequently, Western publics' responses should tend to polarize along a Materialist/Postmaterialist dimension, with some individuals consistently emphasizing Materialist goals, while others tend to give priority to Postmaterialist goals.

To test this hypothesis, we performed principal components analyses of the rankings of these goals in each of the countries surveyed in 1990–93. For this analysis, each item was recoded as a separate variable with codes ranging from "1" to "3," indicating whether the given item was ranked as most important in its group of four items, as second most important, or as one of the two least important items.

Our variables are based on relative rankings, not absolute scores. This is crucial to operationalizing our hypothesis, but it means that the items are not independent, which raises problems for factor analysis. If one were rating only two items, for example, the rank of the first item would determine the rank of the second, automatically generating a -1.0 correlation between them. With three items, one would expect negative correlations of about .5. With a pool of four items, random answering would generate negative correlations of about .3 between all four items. Thus, there is a tendency for the ratings of all these items to be negatively correlated, which tends to spread any four items over more than one dimension. Nevertheless, as our empirical results show, this effect is dominated by an even stronger tendency for Materialist items to be chosen together, on one hand, and for Postmaterialist items to be chosen together, on the other.

The Materialist/Postmaterialist dimension has proven to be remarkably robust over time. As figure 4.1 demonstrates, factor analyses of survey data from the nine countries that were members of the European Community in 1973 reveal two clear clusters: at the top of the continuum, five Postmaterialist items cluster together, showing positive polarity; and at the opposite pole, all six Materialist items cluster together, showing negative polarity. This pattern is remarkably uniform across all nine nations (detailed country-by-country results appear in Inglehart, 1977: 44–47). Moreover, this battery was used again in a subsequent survey in these same countries in 1978, and as figure 4.1 shows, the results were very similar to those from 1973. The results show a cross-national consistency that is truly remarkable. In survey after survey, five items—the same five items in every country—cluster near the positive end of the continuum. Six items—again, the same six in every country—are grouped near the negative pole. The remaining item falls near the midpoint.

The items that cluster toward the negative pole are the six Materialist items, and five of the six Postmaterialist items fall into the opposite group. A single item—the one concerning "More beautiful cities"—does not fall into either cluster. This item does not behave according to our expectations, a fact that we must explore in more detail. But the other 11 items live up to expectations to an almost uncanny degree. The consistency of responses to these items cannot be attributed to such common sources of spurious correlation as response set, which often occurs when respondents simply rate a series of items as either "good" or "bad" (or "very important" or "less important"): some respondents give similar ratings to a whole series of items. In the present case, this is impossible: one must rank each goal as being *more* important or *less* important than the others, in a format that gives no cues to the "right" answer.

Given respondents tend to be preoccupied with a consistent set of needs located toward either the Materialist or Postmaterialist side of the continuum. Eleven of the 12 items fall into two separate clusters, reflecting Materialist and Postmaterialist priorities, respectively. The item designed to tap aesthetic needs ("more beautiful cities") fits into neither cluster; with the same consistency by which the eleven other items did fit into their expected places, this one fails to show a strong positive loading in any of these countries. Why?

The answer is that this item does not simply evoke aesthetic needs, as it was intended to do. Instead, it also taps an Urban/anti-Urban dimension on which collective economic development is seen as conflicting with one's personal security. Here, this item shows a surprisingly strong relationship with the safety needs (see Inglehart, 1977:45–50). For many people, the term "cities" evokes fears of crime.

The relationship between aesthetic concerns and Postmaterialist values is clarified by another analysis utilizing the Rokeach Terminal Values Survey (see Rokeach, 1973) together with the Materialist/Postmaterialist battery, both of which were included in the American component of the Political Action study (Barnes et al., 1979). Factor analysis of the 12-item Materialist/Postmaterialist battery plus the 18-item Rokeach battery reveals an interesting structure. As we would expect, a number of dimensions are needed to capture the configuration of responses. But the Materialist/Postmaterialist dimension remains clearly recognizable, and several of Rokeach's items show substantial loadings on it. In the Postmaterialist cluster of this dimension, we find "Equality" and "Inner Harmony," plus a pair of items relating to the intellectual and aesthetic needs—"Wisdom" and "A World of Beauty." Ironically, the item we

TABLE 4.1
The Materialist/Postmaterialist Dimension in 15
Western Nations, 1990 (Loadings on First Principal
Component in Factor Analysis)

Less Impersonal Society	.60
More Say on Job	.62
More Say in Government	.50
Ideas Count More than Money	.51
Freedom of Speech	.34
More Beautiful Cities	.18
Strong Defense Forces	−.26
Fight Rising Prices	−.28
Fight against Crime	−.39
Maintain Order	−.55
Economic Growth	−.59
Maintain Stable Economy	−.63

Note: Items with Materialist polarity are in boldface type; items with Postmaterialist polarity are in italics.

Source: 1990–91 World Values Survey data from France, Britain, West Germany, Italy, the Netherlands, Denmark, Belgium, Ireland, Norway, Sweden, Denmark, Finland, Iceland, Canada, and the United States.

designed to tap the aesthetic needs fails to show the expected empirical relationships—but the item developed by Rokeach *does*. Analysis of the responses to our own item concerning "more beautiful cities" revealed an unexpected tendency for this item to be linked with emphasis on "the fight against crime." Including the word "cities" in this context seems to evoke a concern with safety among some respondents; for them, the cities are unbeautiful not only because they are dirty but because they are dangerous. Rokeach's item makes no reference to cities and evokes aesthetic concerns in unmixed form—and consequently falls into the Postmaterialist cluster as the need hierarchy hypothesis would suggest. In short, the anomalous results obtained with this item seem to reflect imperfect formulation of our "aesthetic" alternative, rather than an indication that aesthetic concerns are not part of the Postmaterialist syndrome. When unambiguously formulated, they *are*.

The pattern found in 1973 and 1978 continues to manifest itself in the 1990s. The loadings on the first factor in 15 Western countries are shown in table 4.1 (the detailed results for each country are shown in Abramson and Inglehart, 1995). In this table, the goals designed to tap Materialist priorities appear in boldface; the goals intended to tap Postmaterialist priorities appear in italics. With almost incredible consistency, in nation after nation, emphasis on the six items designed to tap economic and physical security goes together, forming a coherent Materialist cluster; in every case, emphasis on the five items designed to tap belonging, self-expression, and intellectual satisfaction also goes together, forming a clearly defined Postmaterialist cluster.

A "UNIDIMENSIONAL" THEORY OF VALUE CHANGE?

The Materialist/Postmaterialist thesis postulates that an intergenerational value shift is taking place along a dimension defined by two poles, termed "Materialist" and "Postmaterialist" values, respectively. This space is, by definition, one-dimensional and, though human values are almost infinitely multidimensional, the theory focuses on this one dimension. In this sense only, the theory might be called "unidimensional," though this is a potentially misleading label.

Just how misleading this label can be becomes evident in a recent analysis by Buerklin, Klein, and Russ (1994). Claiming that the Materialist/Postmaterialist value change theory is "unidimensional," they interpret this term to mean that we believe *all* human values constitute one dimension. If this claim were true, then the analysis carried out by Buerklin et al. would be a valid test of the theory: if the Materialist/Postmaterialist value change thesis actually *did* hold that all human values constitute a single dimension and that everything on it is undergoing intergenerational change, then if one can find any value that *is not* undergoing an intergenerational shift, the thesis would be disproven. Buerklin et al. analyze a battery of questions that measures a number of different things and have no difficulty in finding various values that are *not* undergoing intergenerational change, so, they conclude, they have refuted the thesis.

But do we really believe that human values are unidimensional, in the sense that Buerklin et al. claim? Demonstrably, no: though our analyses focus mainly on the Materialist/Postmaterialist dimension, we have, from the start, also analyzed various other value dimensions.

Our analysis of the Materialist/Postmaterialist shift focuses on one dimension. It does so because the theory generates clear predictions about the type and direction of change one should find along this specific dimension: unprecedentedly high levels of security are producing an intergenerational shift from giving top priority to security, to giving top priority to self-expression. The investigation focuses on this one dimension because the theory does not predict what might be happening in other value domains. The Materialist/Postmaterialist dimension is a central and important part of mass value systems, but (obviously) it does not cover everything. There are almost limitless numbers of other values, and changes might conceivably be occurring in almost any of them, ranging from communism versus capitalism, to whether people prefer Madonna to Mozart, or chocolate to vanilla, but the theory does not deal with them. Nevertheless, it is clear that we recognized from the start that other value dimensions also exist and discussed them at some length (Inglehart,

1977: 45–51). In subsequent publications, (Inglehart, 1978, 1979) we analyzed the relationships between Materialist/Postmaterialist values and the 18 Rokeach Terminal Values which are designed to tap the full range of human concerns. And in Inglehart (1990) we explored the relationships between Materialist/Postmaterialist values and a wide variety of other values, extending from religion to politics to sexual norms. Clearly, the claim that the theory is "unidimensional" in the sense of considering the Materialist/Postmaterialist dimension to be the only value dimension that exists, or the only dimension worth analyzing, is groundless.

THE STUDY OF VALUE PRIORITIES: RANKINGS VERSUS RATINGS

The Materialist/Postmaterialist thesis deals with priorities, not levels: this a crucial distinction. We did not think that people had never before valued freedom of expression: history makes it clear that it has been valued for centuries. Nor did we think that the new generation no longer valued economic security and order, but now preferred crime and deprivation: it is pretty obvious that most Postmaterialists want peace and prosperity, like everyone else. In other words, we did not think it likely that there had been a reversal of polarity in core societal goals. But it did seem possible that a more subtle change had occurred: though both old and young still valued both prosperity *and* freedom, there had been a change in the relative priority attached to such goals. While the older generation were likely to give top priority to economic and physical security over self-expression if they had to choose, we hypothesized that a growing segment of the postwar generation would give self-expression priority over economic and physical security, if it came to a crunch.

In short, the shift is *not* a reversal of polarities, in which most people formerly were opposed to freedom of speech or having more say on the job, but now favor them; nor is it one in which the Postmaterialists no longer like the items with Materialist priority, but have come to prefer crime and high inflation. It is, instead, a shift in priorities—something that would not necessarily be revealed in favorable/unfavorable ratings of given goals but would, nevertheless, have a crucial impact on the choices they made.

The intergenerational change is based on a shift in *priorities*. Consequently, we set out to determine which, among a set of almost universally desired goods, have top priority among different generations. Priorities reflect the way in which one *ranks* various goals (all of which may be considered desirable and important). Consequently, they are best measured by a ranking method. One can, under some circumstances, infer priorities from ratings, but ratings are generally not well suited to that task.

Building on criticisms made earlier by Herz (1979), Flanagan (1982, 1987), and Klages (1988, 1992), Buerklin et al. imply that the ranking technique is a means of forcing respondents to say things they do not really mean: "We wish to make it clear that the so-called 'Ranking' procedure violates the principle of Independence of Measurement. One obtains from this 'extreme forced-choice situation' (Klages, 1992: 26) only a distorted and imperfect picture of the value space. . . . The ranking procedure forces the respondent to differentiate value items along a single dimension" (Buerklin et al., 1994: 585; my translation).

Contrary to this claim, the use of ranking techniques is a commonly used and widely accepted method in survey research. It is virtually unavoidable in any well-designed study of basic values. Thus, it was used by Milton Rokeach in his classic studies of human values. Rokeach is quite explicit about why he used ranking instead of ratings. Even though rankings are a far more time-consuming method than simple ratings, he required his respondents to rank each of his 18 terminal values and 18 instrumental values because he realized that practically everyone attached positive polarity to all 36 items and would score almost all of them as "important" or "very important" if they were simply asked to rate them. He did so because he understood that one's value *priorities* are a genuine and crucial aspect of one's motivation—and something quite distinct from what is measured by ratings.

As we have noted, the ranking method tends to cause each item in a given pool to be negatively correlated with all of the other items in that pool. With random answering, each item in a pool of four items would have a negative correlation of about $-.33$ with each of the other items. This means that the first two items will tend to fall at the opposite poles of the first dimension; but the third item will be negatively correlated with *both* of them, which tends to force it off the first factor and onto another. The same is true of all additional items: ipsivity tends to force them *off* the first factor. We get a Materialist/Postmaterialist dimension not because of, but *in spite of*, the ranking format. The fact that we nevertheless obtain a clear Materialist-Postmaterialist dimension as the first principal component in survey after survey reflects the fact that people are not answering these items randomly: certain people tend to choose Materialist goals consistently, while others tend to emphasize Postmaterialist goals consistently. The format gives no cue concerning which are which: they cluster together because of their content, not their format.

By contrast, the rating method tends to produce a one-dimensional solution: insofar as it encourages response set, it produces a first principal component on which everything is positively correlated with everything else, regardless of content, so that all items have high positive loadings on the first principal component. As we will see below, this is exactly the pattern that appears in the data collected by both Buerklin et al. and Bean and Papadakis (1994) when they employ the rating technique (see table 4.4, first unrotated factor). These authors interpret this as simply meaning that people want all of these goals, overlooking the fact that this tendency is inflated by response set.

It is perfectly true that most people would like to eat their cake and have it too—and this poses no problem when no choice is necessary. But the crucial situations in politics (and life in general) arise when choices are necessary—when one must choose between civil liberties and maintaining order, or between building highways and protecting the environment, or choosing which of two attractive people one will marry. In such situations, ratings may provide little or no guidance: one may like both alternatives. The choice is determined by one's priorities.

We certainly do not claim that the rating method is never useful; we often use it. But any battery designed to measure changes in *basic value priorities* will, almost inevitably, be extremely vulnerable to response set. This is true because any such battery will (and should) consist of items that have the following characteristics: (1) almost everyone considers them desirable, and (2) almost everyone considers them important. They would not *be* basic human values unless they had these characteristics.

It is conceivable that one might, for some reason, want to measure people's priorities among superficial and unimportant values, but it would make no sense to do so in connection with the study of intergenerational change. Such values would not be central and deep-rooted enough to show enduring intergenerational differences: they would change readily, in response to the immediate environment.

Ratings are a perfectly valid means of collecting some types of information, but they are not well suited to measuring priorities: people can and do give equally high ratings to many goals, without revealing their underlying priorities. This does not mean that one does not *have* any underlying priorities—they can be readily and reliably measured with properly framed questions. The question is not whether one should always use ratings or always use rankings: both techniques are useful, but it is important to be aware that they measure two different aspects of reality.

THE PROBLEM OF RESPONSE SET

One of the classic methodological problems associated with having respondents rate a long series of items in identical format is the danger that the ratings will be shaped, not by the items' content (as the investigator assumes), but by the fact that they are asked in an identical format: the similarity of format cues the respondent into giving similar responses to a whole series of items, especially if they appear near each other in the questionnaire. Respondents with relatively little education are especially prone to do this, since this way of responding requires no cognitive effort or information—but, of course, it yields misleading data. This problem has been well known for decades, having been revealed as a major problem in the research underlying the classic *Authoritarian Personality* study; partly because the problem was already recognized so long ago, it is sometimes lost sight of in contemporary research. It remains as real as ever.

The ratings obtained from the battery used by Buerklin et al. seem to reflect the questionnaire format as much as the content of the items used. The ranking method is much less vulnerable to response set: by its very nature, one cannot simply run down the list, giving similar scores to a series of consecutive items: one is forced to select one item for top priority, another for second priority, and so on. This method has the disadvantages of ipsivity, but it is capable of measuring values or attitudes with much less noise than tends to be present in responses to rating scales.

It also is more useful for testing a specific theory. It targets the inquiry much more sharply than do ratings. It enables one to focus on measuring the respondents' priorities along a specific dimension. This, of course, implies that one has a specific theory in mind that one wishes to test: it is too tightly focused to be useful at the exploratory stage, or if one is not guided by some clear theory.

Rankings versus Ratings: An Empirical Comparison

As we have pointed out, this theory is about priorities, not levels of support. Consequently, the items in the Materialist/Postmaterialist battery need to be ranked, not simply rated. The ranking method has two real disadvantages: (1) it is much more time consuming than ratings, and (2) it produces ipsitive data, which violate one of the assumptions of some statistical models; this is a difficulty, though not an insuperable one (Jackson and Alwin, 1980). Ranking, however, has two major advantages that, for present purposes, far outweigh the disadvantages: first, rankings are not determined by response set: when the respondent ranks the items, it is impossible to simply race down the list, giving relatively high (or relatively low) ratings to all of them. One is forced to consider each item separately, in relation to the others. Response set seems to be such a serious problem in the ratings obtained by Buerklin et al. that it is unclear if any but the first item in their battery is rated primarily in terms of its content: after the first item in the series, all of the succeeding items get uniformly high ratings (Inglehart and Klingemann, 1996). Second—and even more important—rankings are a fundamentally different approach, which is more suitable for the measurement of priorities than are ratings: rankings enable one to measure an aspect of reality that ratings may completely fail to uncover.

Buerklin et al. (1994) have raised an important and basic methodological question, but their database does not enable them to answer it since they employed neither the format nor the items used to measure Materialist/Postmatearialist values. What would they have found if they had used items that actually *did* tap the Materialist/Postmaterialist dimension—and then had also taken the precaution to ask them as both ratings and rankings, to test the effects of response set? Fortunately, this question is not merely hypothetical: exactly this was done in an article published almost simultaneously with the one by Buerklin et al. The results are extremely interesting.

Bean and Papadakis (1994) also argue that the Materialist/Postmaterialist dimension can better be measured by ratings than by rankings, and they pro-

TABLE 4.2
Factor Analysis of Materialism-Postmaterialism
Items Based on Rankings: First Principal Component

Less Impersonal Society	.61
Ideas Count More than Money	.58
More Say in Government	.48
Freedom of Speech	.45
More Say on Job	.44
More Beautiful Cities	.21
Maintain Stable Economy	−.19
Fight Rising Prices	−.22
Strong Defense Forces	−.29
Fight against Crime	−.35
Economic Growth	−.48
Maintain Order	−.55

Note: Items with Materialist polarity are in boldface type; items with Postmaterialist polarity are in italics.

Source: National survey of Australians' Attitudes toward Welfare, 1988 (N = 1,814), in Bean and Papadakis, 1994: 275.

ceed to carry out an appropriate and well-designed test of this claim. To do so, they first administered a national survey in Australia that measured Materialist/Postmaterialist values both by rankings (as advocated by Inglehart) and by ratings. They find that when the respondent uses the ranking method, one obtains a first principal component on which all six of the items designed to tap Materialist priorities form a cluster having negative polarity, and all six items designed to tap Postmaterialist priorities show positive polarity. In short, the authors find a clear Materialist-Postmaterialist dimension, with the Materialist items near one pole and the Postmaterialist items near the other pole. Table 4.2 shows their results. As this table indicates, the fit with theoretical expectations is virtually perfect. Although two of the items have relatively weak loadings on their respective factors, all 12 items show the polarity predicted by the theory. And although these results come from Australia, they show a pattern that is almost identical to results obtained by other investigators using the same methodology, in dozens of other countries.

Using a rating format, however, the authors get a completely different set of results: the first principal component is one on which all 12 items are given relatively high (or relatively low) ratings. When subjected to varimax rotation, this factor breaks down into a Materialist factor and a Postmaterialist factor (which are uncorrelated since varimax rotation was used). Using this approach, there seems to be no such thing as a Materialist/Postmaterialist dimension. Table 4.3 shows the results obtained from ratings.

The results seem contradictory. The authors argue that the rating approach reflects reality better than the ranking approach because most respondents are really in favor of all 12 goals: they want freedom of speech *and* law and

TABLE 4.3
Factor Analysis of Materialism-Postmaterialism Items Based on Ratings:
First Principal Component Analysis with Varimax Rotation

	First Unrotated Factor	Rotated Factors	
		Postmaterialism	Materialism
Materialist Items			
Maintain Order	.47	.06	.67
Fight Rising Prices	.56	.39	.41
Economic Growth	.46	.04	.69
Strong Defense	.42	.04	.63
Stable Economy	.56	.24	.59
Fight Crime	.51	.09	.70
Postmaterialist Items			
More Say in Government	.53	.52	.19
Protect Free Speech	.49	.51	.14
More Say in Jobs	.61	.70	.11
Beautify Cities and Countryside	.54	.65	.05
More Humane Society	.64	.75	.08
Society Where Ideas Count	.56	.74	−.04

Source: National survey of Australians' Attitudes toward Welfare, 1988 (N = 1,814), in Bean and Papadakis, 1994: 278.

order—*and* economic growth *and* environmental protection *and* low inflation *and* more say in government *and* strong defense forces. The rating approach is more "flexible" than the ranking approach because it enables respondents to give high ratings to all 12 goals. Most respondents give priority to the Materialist goals over the Postmaterialist goals (or vice versa) only when they are constrained to do so by a ranking format.

Which approach captures reality? It depends on which aspect of reality you want to capture. Ultimately, it comes down to the question, Do you want to measure priorities or response levels?

It is perfectly true, as Bean and Papadakis point out (together with Klages and Buerklin et al.), that nearly everyone would like to attain all of these goals. All 12 goals were designed to tap things that nearly everyone considers desirable: this is inherent in any battery designed to measure changing priorities among basic values. Thus, in an unconstrained format, people can give positive ratings to virtually everything. This tendency is strengthened by the fact that a rating approach puts a dozen positive goals in an identical format, creating a series where the easiest thing to do is run down the list, giving similar ratings to item after item. This is a perfect setting for response set to occur. The rating list is a convenient way to quickly elicit a long stream of responses. It seems extremely quick and efficient. The problem is that it can yield virtually meaningless responses. This format systematically tends to create or inflate positive correlations between the items in a series. Furthermore, it provides a systematic bias: less-educated people are particularly likely to be influenced by response set. It is cognitively undemanding: one need not differentiate between the items—one can simply give a series of high (or low) ratings.

The less educated are particularly prone to response set, and in keeping with this fact it is very significant that Bean and Papadakis find (when, and *only* when they use ratings) that the less educated constitute the high scorers on both their Materialist dimension and their Postmaterialist dimension (Bean and Papadakis, 1994: 280). In striking contrast to this finding, in virtually every survey ever carried out, the Postmaterialists identified by the *ranking* method consist of those with relatively high educational levels—to such an extent that some analysts have even suggested that Postmaterialist values simply reflect high educational levels (Duch and Taylor, 1993). This is a remarkably clear illustration of the fact that the rating method fails to identify those with Postmaterialist priorities: the "Postmaterialists" identified by ratings have a mean educational level *below* that of the sample as a whole. Needless to say, the "Postmaterialists" identified in this manner do not show the other demographic characteristics of true Postmaterialists: most strikingly, they are not concentrated among the young.

Ratings elicit information quickly—but they are not well suited to measuring priorities. Rankings, on the other hand, are much more time-consuming and difficult than ratings. With this format, the respondent cannot simply race down the list giving similar (usually high) ratings to every item. He or she must painstakingly decide which, among a series of desirable goals, is most important, which ranks second, and which are least important. This is a more demanding method. But for analyzing politics, this provides much more useful information than simply knowing that given individuals rate almost everything as "extremely important."

This is true because politics is, above all, a question of choices. True, environmental protection does *not* always conflict with economic growth; nor does maximizing individual freedom necessarily conflict with maintaining order. But these are the easy situations, when the solution is obvious and everyone can be satisfied. The crunch comes when two or more highly important and desirable goals *do* conflict with each other: it is precisely then that important political issues arise. Sometimes you cannot eat your cake and have it too. Under these circumstances, one is forced to make choices. And it is then that priorities become crucial.

The ratings approach is quite appropriate for many purposes. But it is not an appropriate way to measure value priorities—which is the topic on which the Materialist/Postmaterialist value change thesis focuses. The theory does not hypothesize that some people are opposed to economic and physical security, while others like it. It assumes that these are goals sought by almost everyone. The shift from Materialist to Postmaterialists priorities occurs when a given segment of the population has been raised with a sufficiently high level of economic and physical security that further emphasis on them has diminishing marginal utility. It is precisely because Postmaterialists have security (and *not* because they reject it) that they give top priority to other goals.

Thus, Bean and Papadakis (1994) and Buerklin et al. (1994) are perfectly correct in saying that most people (Materialists and Postmaterialists alike) would like to have all of these goals—and that, if they were unconstrained, they would give positive ratings to nearly all of them. The ratings results that they obtain from Australia and Germany, respectively, demonstrate this point. This is, indeed, one aspect of reality. Hence, the ratings approach produces a first principal component on which all 12 goals have positive polarity.

But this does not mean that there is no such thing as Materialist-Postmaterialist priorities. Quite the contrary, the data collected by Bean and Papadakis (1994) demonstrate clearly that these very same respondents are perfectly capable of differentiating between Materialist and Postmaterialist priorities, and they do so when the question is posed in a way that measures priorities. Priorities tap a different aspect of reality from that measured by ratings; and priorities are important because reality often constrains individuals to make choices.

Priorities are not an artifact of survey research. They exist inside people's minds and can be measured reliably—and they emerge even when (as with Bean and Papadakis) the investigators have a skeptical attitude toward them. Indeed, their data replicate the pattern that was predicted by the theory of Materialist/Postmaterialist value change with a remarkable fidelity. This theory was developed 25 years ago, by an American working in Western Europe. Over the past two decades, literally scores of surveys in dozens of countries have discovered an almost identical configuration, in which one segment of the population (which tends to be the older and the economically less secure strata) gives top priority to the items that were designed to tap Materialist priorities; while another segment (the younger, more prosperous and better educated) give priority to a set of items that were designed to tap Postmaterialist priorities. These findings, from 43 societies not including Australia, are presented below. This latest set of findings, from a survey in Australia, indicates that a virtually identical configuration of societal priorities emerges in yet another country on another continent.

The study by Bean and Papadakis (1994) adds a well-executed methodological study to the picture, and it provides convincing evidence that the format in which the questions are posed is crucial. The authors conclude that the rating method is a more appropriate way to measure Materialist/Postmaterialist values than the ranking method, since it "allows for a more flexible and realistic account of the choices made by most social actors." The authors have demonstrated that, free from any constraint, people will give high ratings to both Materialist and Postmaterialist goals. They interpret this to mean that the rating format taps reality more faithfully than the ranking format.

But it depends on which aspect of reality one wishes to understand. If one is asking the question, Do people want to attain all of these goals, or only some of them? then the rating format is appropriate, and the answer is clear: most people want all of them. But if one is interested in the question, What priorities do people act on, when forced to choose between two desirable goals? then the ranking method is appropriate.

Comments on Bean and Papadakis's study by both Inglehart (1994) and Hellevik (1994) appeared with the original article. Both comments noted, independently, that the results from the ratings approach gave strong indications of response set. Hellevik commented,

> Bean and Papadakis see the correlated indexes of Materialism and Postmaterialism as a substantively interesting result of allowing a choice of "both-and" instead of forcing the respondent to make priorities. In my view they overlook methodological problems of the rating method, problems which actually may explain their results. Through my work with national and comparative analyses of cultural indicators, using mainly scales, we have reached exactly the opposite conclusion: ranking is preferable to rating. The reasons for this are both substantive and methodological. The two measurement methods give information on separate aspects of value preferences which are both of interest. Rating indicates absolute levels of support, while ranking indicates the *priorities* among values—even if they have similar levels of support. (Hellevik, 1994: 293)

In their reply to these critiques, Bean and Papadakis (1994) reported that they had tried to correct for response set by using a standard method—anchoring the responses around each respondent's mean score across the set of items and analyzing the extent to which a given response was higher or lower than this mean. When they did so, they found, to their surprise, that their result mirrors the result based on rankings, with the Materialist items at one pole, and the Postmaterialist items at the opposite pole (Bean and Papadakis, 1994: 297). They took this to mean that their correction for response set had failed. There is no reason to believe that it had: a more straightforward interpretation is that response set is, indeed, responsible for the pattern they get using ratings—and that when it is corrected, one obtains the Materialist/Postmaterialist dimension that these items were designed to tap.

WHAT IS THE RIGHT LEVEL OF ANALYSIS: ONE DIMENSION?
OR TWO, FOUR, OR N DIMENSIONS?

The Materialist/Postmaterialist concept is unidimensional by definition and operates at a relatively high level of generality. This level of analysis has proven productive. It is perfectly possible, however, either to ascend to higher levels of generality—examining the degree to which Materialist/Postmaterialist values are themselves part of a still broader configuration of values (as we did in chapter 3)—or to descend to lower levels of generality, examining its component subclusters, as Herz (1979), Flanagan (1982, 1987), and Van Deth (1984) have done.

Herz (1979) used multidimensional scaling to obtain a two-dimensional structure from the Materialist-Postmaterialist rankings. But this two-dimensional array revealed a clear watershed, with all of the Materialist items on one side and all of the Postmaterialist items on the other side (see Inglehart, 1990:143).

Van Deth (1986) went even farther: he used factor analysis, smallest space analysis, multidimensional scaling, and unfolding techniques to explore the structure of the standard 12-item battery Materialist/Postmaterialist values battery based on rankings. He found that, although the detailed placement of individual items varied, these methods all produced basically the same result: here, too, the most prominent feature was a clear watershed, with all of the Materialist items at one side of the graph and all of the Postmaterialist items at the other side. The results indicated that the use of an additive index, based on the distinction between Materialist and Postmaterialist items, was justified.

As all of these analyses demonstrate, the Postmaterialist dimension can, indeed, be broken down into its constituent subclusters. But, at the same time, they confirm the robustness of the broader Materialist-Postmaterialist dimension: if one measures people's priorities, then no matter how you slice the data, one comes up with an overall pattern on which the Materialist items are at one side, and the Postmaterialist items are on the opposite side.

Klages (1988, 1992) prefers to deal with two dimensions that he describes as "Duty/Acceptance" and "Self Realization." His analysis does not deal with a change in priorities, but with high or low levels of support for two more or less unrelated dimensions. He is free to do so, and he may well come up with interesting findings concerning changes in levels of support for these goals: it is not an either/or choice.

Varimax rotation will usually do what it was designed to do—break a dimension down into its components; but it is absurd to interpret this fact as meaning that the dimension in question "really" has two or more subcomponents, and that, consequently, one is obliged to operate at the lower level of generality. The reality is not only that the battery used to measure Materialist/Postmaterialist values has subclusters that were designed to tap economic and physical security, respectively, but that each of these subclusters can also be broken down further, until one reaches the individual items that make them up. It is perfectly legitimate to operate at the lowest possible level of generality, examining attitudes toward "The fight against crime," for example, or any other individual item that interests one. Similarly, it is perfectly possible to operate at Flanagan's slightly higher level of generalization, or at the level of the Materialist/Postmaterialist dimension, or (since Materialist/Postmaterialist priorities prove to be correlated with a broad range of other values) to examine whether these values themselves fit into a still broader configuration such as "Survival Values" versus "Well-being Values." It depends on the theoretical purpose one has in mind.

To date, dimensional analysis of data from more than 40 countries around the world has demonstrated that, underlying the value systems of many different peoples, a Materialist/Postmaterialist dimension *does* exist. Furthermore, as the Materialist/Postmaterialist value change theory implies, and as we will see in the next chapter, the values measured by this dimension are linked with economic security, both at the microlevel—with individuals from relatively prosperous families being more likely to be Postmaterialists—and at the macrolevel—with Postmaterialist values being far more widespread in rich countries than in poor ones. In addition, as the theory implies, these values show evidence of intergenerational change, with Postmaterialist values being far more widespread among the young than among the old.

A number of critics implicitly assume that one must *either* focus on levels of support for given values, as measured by ratings; *or* value priorities, which are best measured by rankings. They overlook the fact that value priorities and levels of support reflect two distinct aspects of reality. One is free to measure either. A good deal of empirical evidence indicates that the most important intergenerational value change now taking place involves a change in priorities: this does not rule out the possibility that important changes may *also* be occurring in levels of support for given goals. For value *priorities* and relative levels of support for given goals are two distinct aspects of reality. Both are worth studying. It is not an either/or choice.

THE POSTMATERIALIST DIMENSION IN GLOBAL PERSPECTIVE

The 1990 World Values Survey measured Materialist/Postmaterialist priorities in 43 societies, using the ranking method. As we saw above in figure 4.1, the results from 16 Western democracies show remarkable cross-national similarity. In every case, the same five items clustered near one pole of the first principal component. These items deal with such goals as freedom of expression and having more say on the job or in political life. All five of these items had been designed to tap Postmaterialist priorities. Six items—again the same six in every country—clustered near the opposite pole. These items emphasize economic and physical security. All six were designed to tap Materialist priorities. The remaining item fell near the midpoint.

Exactly the same pattern holds true in 16 Western European and North American societies—including several that had not previously been surveyed. People respond to the five Postmaterialist items (shown in italics) as if they tapped a similar underlying value, placing them in one cluster. People also respond to the six Materialist items (shown in boldface type) as if they tapped something very different. The one remaining item is ambivalent. The detailed results for each of the 43 societies included in the 1990 World Values Survey are reported in Abramson and Inglehart (1995).

There is strong evidence that the Materialist/Postmaterialist battery taps a cross-nationally comparable phenomenon throughout the Western world. Is it *merely* a Western phenomenon, however, or does it, as the theory implies, emerge in any society that is undergoing an intergenerational shift toward higher levels of prosperity and security?

TABLE 4.4

The Materialist/Postmaterialist Dimension in Four
Latin American Countries (Loadings on First
Principal Component in Factor Analysis)

More Say in Government	.67
More Say on Job	.60
Less Impersonal Society	.52
Freedom of Speech	.36
Ideas Count More than Money	.34
Economic Growth	−.15
More Beautiful Cities	−.27
Strong Defense Forces	−.27
Maintain Stable Economy	−.31
Fight Rising Prices	−.37
Fight against Crime	−.49
Maintain Order	−.56

Note: Items with Materialist polarity are in boldface type;
items with Postmaterialist polarity are in italics.
Source: 1990–91 World Values Survey data from Mexico,
Argentina, Brazil, and Chile.

Do non-Western publics see things from a completely different perspective? Apparently not. Four Latin American societies were included in the 1990–91 World Values Survey, and the same basic structure applies (see table 4.4). There are some variations from the pattern found in advanced industrial societies: already known to be a deviant item, "More beautiful cities" shows negative polarity here, and "Economic growth" is only very weakly linked with the Materialist cluster. But all five of the Postmaterialist items show positive polarity and fall into the predicted cluster.

More strikingly still, the pattern that emerges in Japan and South Korea is practically identical to the pattern we find in Western Europe and Latin America. Although these two East Asian societies started with profoundly different cultural traditions from those of the West, they have both become advanced industrial societies—and their publics respond in a fashion that is almost indistinguishable from that of Western respondents. As table 4.5 demonstrates, the five Postmaterialist items cluster at one pole, and the six Materialist items cluster at the opposite pole. Moreover, the item concerning "More beautiful cities and countryside," which gave ambiguous results in the West, shows a clear Postmaterialist polarity in both Japan and South Korea. The two East Asian countries not only conform to theoretical expectations, they actually show a slightly better fit than do most Western countries. This is a very interesting finding. It indicates that the emergence of a polarization between Materialist goals and Postmaterialist goals is *not* a uniquely Western phenomenon. It is a phenomenon of advanced industrial society that emerges with high levels of

TABLE 4.5
The Materialist/Postmaterialist Dimension in East
Asia (Loadings on First Principal Component in
Factor Analysis)

Less Impersonal Society	.70
More Say on Job	.60
More Say in Government	.50
More Beautiful Cities	.38
Freedom of Speech	.45
Ideas Count More than Money	.24
Fight against Crime	−.30
Fight Rising Prices	−.31
Strong Defense Forces	−.45
Maintain Order	−.50
Maintain Stable Economy	−.61
Economic Growth	−.62

Note: Items with Materialist polarity are in boldface type;
items with Postmaterialist polarity are in italics.
Source: Pooled 1990–91 World Values Survey data from
Japan and South Korea.

economic development—even among societies that started with very different
cultural heritages.

There are societies in which the polarization between Materialist and Postmaterialist values is less distinct, but the division is *not* between Western and
non-Western cultures. The countries that deviate most from the Materialist/
Postmaterialist configuration are the ex-socialist countries, even those that
have historically had close ties with the West.

The 1990–91 World Values Survey includes samples from 11 societies of
the former Soviet bloc, as well as China (see table 4.6). In 11 of these 12
countries the five Postmaterialist items cluster together in one group. Poland
is the sole exception, and even there, four of the five Postmaterialist items
cluster together. Thus, even in the communist and ex-communist societies,
we find a clear and consistent Postmaterialist cluster. But there is a tendency
for emphasis on "economic growth" to fall into the Postmaterialist cluster.
This is a striking deviation from what we find everywhere else, and it would
be surprising if we found it in societies with market economies. But within
the societies that have had state-run economies, it is understandable. "Economic growth" (like everything connected with the economy) has quite different connotations in a state-socialist society from what it has in a market
economy.

In 1990 the socialist societies had authoritarian political systems and state-
run economies that had become stagnant to the point of paralysis. The existing system of state controls had widely come to be seen as incompatible with
economic growth. Even in China, which continued to experience rapid growth,

TABLE 4.6
The Materialist/Postmaterialist Dimension in 11
Ex-socialist or Socialist Countries (Loadings on
First Principal Component in Factor Analysis)

More Say in Government	.73
Less Impersonal Society	.46
More Say on Job	.44
Freedom of Speech	.27
Economic Growth	.18
Ideas Count More than Money	.17
Maintain Stable Economy	−.02
Strong Defense Forces	−.37
More Beautiful Cities	−.38
Fight Rising Prices	−.43
Maintain Order	−.50
Fight against Crime	−.57

Note: Items with Materialist polarity in Western countries
and East Asia are in boldface type; items with Postmaterialist
polarity in Western countries and East Asia are in italics.

Source: Pooled 1990–91 World Values Survey data from
Belarus, Bulgaria, China, Czechoslovakia, East Germany, Es-
tonia, Hungary, Latvia, Lithuania, Poland, Russia, and greater
Moscow.

this growth was taking place entirely in the private sector. State-run industries
were stagnant. In this context, as of 1990, economic growth had come to be
seen as something that could only be attained by breaking free from a massive
and sclerotic state bureaucracy and turning the economy over to individual initiative. In contrast with the West, where an emphasis on economic growth was
linked with loyalty to the established order, in the state-socialist world many
viewed economic growth as a goal that could only come through radical socioeconomic change. Moreover, these changes were closely linked with the
Postmaterialist emphasis on individual autonomy: they required the liberation
of the individual from state authority. Hence we find the apparent paradox that,
in many of the former state-socialist societies and in China, respondents who
gave high priority to economic growth were the same people who emphasized
"giving the people more say in government," "more say on the job," "freedom
of speech," and "a less impersonal, more humane society."

Further analyses support the conclusion that in these societies Postmaterialist values are linked with support for reduced government involvement in the
economy. In the 1990–91 World Values Survey, respondents were asked to
place themselves on a 10-point scale measuring their attitudes toward governmental versus private ownership of business and industry. In the non-socialist
countries, people with Postmaterialist values tend to be slightly more favorable to the idea of a state-run economy than are those with Materialist values.

This is not a strong relationship, but it reflects the traditional ideological heritage of the Left.

The situation is dramatically different in Eastern Europe, the societies of the former Soviet Union, and the People's Republic of China. In all 12 of these societies, people with Postmaterialist values are *less* favorable to a state-run economy than are the Materialists. The polarity of "progressive" values has reversed. Throughout the ex-socialist societies, people who place themselves on the Left *and* those with Postmaterialist values reject the idea of a state-run economy.

There are also cross-national differences in the polarity of the goal of "trying to make our cities and countryside more beautiful." This item was designed to tap aesthetic values. But analyses of Western societies showed that it had a surprisingly strong linkage with safety needs.

The "beautiful cities" goal has differing associations in different societies in the World Values survey. The variations follow a consistent pattern. When the 12-item measure was first developed in 1973, the "beautiful cities" item was more or less neutral, with a slight Postmaterialist polarity (Inglehart, 1977). In the 1990 surveys, this item has a slightly stronger Postmaterialist polarity than it had previously, in most Western societies. And, as we noted, the goal has an even clearer Postmaterialist polarity in Japan and South Korea. In the four Latin American countries, on the other hand, the goal of "more beautiful cities" clearly emerges as a Materialist value; and it is even more clearly a Materialist goal in the societies of the former Soviet bloc.

In the West this goal, originally designed to tap aesthetic values, now appears to be performing its original mission, though still only weakly. The fact that this item falls into the Materialist cluster in Eastern Europe seems to reflect severe environmental deterioration in these societies (see Inglehart and Abramson, 1992b). In these societies, environmental pollution has become a massive and life-threatening problem, one that is far more severe than in the West. In the former state socialist countries, pollution is not perceived primarily as an aesthetic problem, but as one that is directly life-threatening. This perception is far from groundless. The death rates in some regions of Russia, the former East Germany, Poland, and the former Czechoslovakia are shockingly high, for reasons attributable to massive industrial pollution. In the West the goal of "more beautiful cities" has an ambivalent meaning, tapping aesthetic needs to some extent, but also having secondary connotations of urban disorder and crime. In Japan and Korea, where urban crime rates are much lower than in most Western countries, this item unequivocally taps Postmaterialist concerns. In the former Soviet bloc countries, with life-threatening levels of pollution, it tends to tap basic Materialist concerns for the effects of industrial pollution on human survival.

In the former communist world, economic and physical security cannot be taken for granted nearly as much as in the rich industrial societies of the West and East Asia. Hence, as one might expect, the Materialist-Postmaterialist dimension is less consistent, and less clearly crystallized in the ex-socialist so-

TABLE 4.7

The Materialist/Postmaterialist Dimension in India
(Loadings on Second* Principal Component in
Factor Analysis)

More Say in Government	.61
Less Impersonal Society	.58
More Say on Job	.43
Ideas Count More than Money	.38
Freedom of Speech	.06
Strong Defense Forces	−.01
Economic Growth	−.08
Maintain Order	−.19
Maintain Stable Economy	−.34
More Beautiful Cities	−.35
Fight Rising Prices	−.46
Fight against Crime	−.49

Note: Items with Materialist polarity are in boldface type; items with Postmaterialist polarity are in italics.

Source: Pooled 1990–91 World Values Survey data from India.

*In India, the first principal component reflects a polarization between emphasis on economic priorities and emphasis on maintaining military and domestic order; all of the Postmaterialist items are neutral on this dimension.

cieties than it is in the West and East Asia. Although a recognizable Materialist/Postmaterialist dimension does emerge in the former Soviet bloc, it accounts for less variance than it does in richer advanced industrial societies. In three of these societies (Lithuania, Czechoslovakia, and Hungary) this dimension emerges only as the second principal component in the factor analysis.

The Postmaterialist phenomenon is only marginally present in such low-income societies as India and Nigeria, both of which had per capita incomes of approximately $300 in 1990. As the theory implies, there are very few Postmaterialists in these countries, and mass values do not crystallize along this dimension as strongly as they do in richer societies (see Abramson and Inglehart, 1995, for country-by-country results). A recognizable Materialist/Postmaterialist dimension emerges in India, but it accounts for less variance than in almost any other country and is the second principal component instead of the first (see table 4.7).

Although interesting cross-national differences in the structure of these values exist, the evidence suggests that the core meaning of Materialism/Postmaterialism is similar across this wide range of societies. The quest for economic security is much more politicized in societies with state-run economies than in societies with market economies, which gives a distinctive meaning to items that refer to the economy. Apart from this, however, the Materialist goals show consistent results, and the five Postmaterialist items behave in a similar way in all types of societies, East and West, as well as North and South. The results indicate that an additive index, based on summing up the five Postmaterialist items (producing an index having scores ranging from 0 to 5) can be used in virtually any of the 43 societies included in the World Values survey. Consequently, we can construct a cross-nationally comparable index of Materialist/Postmaterialist values, based on the nine items that do have globally consistent polarity (assigning neutral polarity to the two items referring to the economy, and the item referring to "more beautiful cities"). This index is used throughout this book, except when only the original four-item index is available.

On the whole, the cross-national similarities underlying mass responses to the Materialist/Postmaterialist values items are far more striking than the cross-national differences.

CHAPTER 5

The Shift toward Postmaterialist Values, 1970–1994

INTRODUCTION

The basic values of publics throughout advanced industrial society have been undergoing a gradual intergenerational shift during the past several decades. Although different countries have shifted at different rates, economic and technological changes have had a broadly similar impact across these societies. As Postmodernization theory implies, the process applies to advanced industrial society in general.

In 1970 we hypothesized that the value priorities of Western publics were shifting from Materialist values toward Postmaterialist values—from giving top priority to physical sustenance and safety, toward heavier emphasis on belonging, self-expression, and the quality of life (Inglehart, 1971). The predicted intergenerational value shift could not be demonstrated until many years had passed; and whether or not it was occurring has been hotly disputed (Böltken and Jagodzinski, 1985; Thomassen and Van Deth, 1989; Trump, 1991; Clarke and Dutt, 1991). Only in recent years has a sufficiently long time series become available to test the prediction reliably. This chapter examines cross-national survey data over a 24-year period. The results show a clear and statistically significant trend toward Postmaterialist values in almost all of the societies for which we now have detailed time series measurements over this period. These values also show short-term fluctuations linked with changing rates of inflation and unemployment, as the value change thesis implies; but the long-term trend seems to result mainly from intergenerational replacement.

Evidence from the 43 societies surveyed in the World Values surveys enables us to test the value change hypothesis on a broader basis than has ever before been possible. The thesis implies that we should observe two quite different findings, both of which are important: societies with high *levels* of economic development should have relatively high *levels* of Postmaterialist values, and societies that have experienced relatively high rates of economic *growth* should show relatively large *differences* between the values of younger and older generations. As we will see, the evidence supports both hypotheses. It appears that this value shift occurs in any society that has experienced sufficient economic development in recent decades so that the preadult experiences of younger birth cohorts have been significantly more secure than those of older cohorts. Large intergenerational differences are found in societies that have experienced rapid growth in GNP per capita and are negligible in societies that have had little or no growth. And these value differences are enduring characteristics of given birth cohorts. Accordingly, as intergenerational population replacement has occurred, Materialist priorities have become less prevalent and Postmaterialism has increased in 18 of the 20 societies for which we have comparable data over the past decade.

The shift toward Postmaterialist values has far-reaching implications. It is only one part of a broader shift toward Postmodern values, involving changing orientations toward politics, work, family life, religion, and sexual behavior. Far more data are available on the evolution of Postmaterialist values than on any other component of this cultural shift, but a broad range of orientations are linked with Materialist/Postmaterialist values, and most of them seem to be moving on the same trajectory. Thus, charting the transition to Postmaterialist values can help us understand the entire Postmodern shift.

The Rise of Postmaterialist Values

As noted earlier, research on the Materialist/Postmaterialist value change has been guided by two key hypotheses (Inglehart, 1977):

1. *A Scarcity Hypothesis.* An individual's priorities reflect the socioeconomic environment: one places the greatest subjective value on those things that are in relatively short supply.

2. *A Socialization Hypothesis.* The relationship between socioeconomic environment and value priorities is not one of immediate adjustment: a substantial time lag is involved, because, to a large extent, one's basic values reflect the conditions that prevailed during one's preadult years.

The scarcity hypothesis is similar to the principle of diminishing marginal utility. And it implies that recent economic developments have significant consequences. During the period since World War II, advanced industrial societies have attained much higher real income levels than ever before in history. Coupled with the emergence of the welfare state, this has brought about a historically unprecedented situation: most of their population does *not* live under conditions of hunger and economic insecurity. This has led to a gradual shift in which needs for belonging, self-expression, and a participant role in society became more prominent. Prolonged periods of prosperity tend to encourage the spread of Postmaterialist values; economic decline tends to have the opposite effect.

But there is no simple one-to-one relationship between economic level and the prevalence of Postmaterialist values. These values reflect one's *subjective* sense of security, not one's economic level per se. While rich people tend to feel more secure than poor people, one's sense of security is also influenced by the cultural setting and social welfare institutions in which one is raised. Thus, the scarcity hypothesis must be supplemented with the socialization hypothesis: a basic personality structure tends to take shape by the time an individual reaches adulthood, and changes relatively little thereafter.

Taken together, these two hypotheses generate a set of predictions concerning value change. First, while the scarcity hypothesis implies that prosperity is conducive to the spread of Postmaterialist values, the socialization hypothesis implies that neither an individual's values nor those of a society as a whole will change overnight. For the most part, fundamental value change takes place as younger birth cohorts replace older ones in the adult population of a society. Consequently, after a long period of rising economic and physical security, one should find substantial differences between the value priorities of older and younger groups: they have been shaped by different experiences in their formative years.

This thesis was first tested in surveys carried out in 1970 with representative national cross sections of the publics of Great Britain, France, West Germany, Italy, the Netherlands, and Belgium. The people interviewed chose the goals they considered most important among a set of items designed to tap economic and physical security, on the one hand, or self-expression and the nonmaterial quality of life, on the other hand.

In the original four-item Materialist/Postmaterialist values battery, each respondent was asked to select what their country's two top goals should be among the following choices: (1) maintaining order in the nation, (2) giving the people more say in important government decisions, (3) fighting rising prices, (4) protecting freedom of speech. Respondents who select "maintaining order" and "fighting inflation" are classified as Materialists; those who choose "giving the people more say" and "freedom of speech" are classified as Postmaterialists. The four remaining combinations are classified as "Mixed."

As the preceding chapter indicates, the Materialist/Postmaterialist dimension travels well cross-culturally. It taps an almost universal concern: feeling secure or insecure about survival is meaningful in virtually any culture. Consequently, the Materialist/Postmaterialist dimension emerges in such societies as South Korea or Turkey with a basic structure roughly similar to that found in Western industrial societies. There are very few Postmaterialists in low-income societies, so the dimension is less important and less strongly structured there, accounting for a smaller percentage of the variance than it does in advanced industrial societies. But these items seem to tap comparable concerns in poor countries and in rich countries.

Not only do the Postmaterialist items have similar connotations within this 12-item battery, but they also have similar demographic correlates: in all societies that have experienced substantial increases in economic security during the past several decades, these values tend to be emphasized more heavily by the younger birth cohorts.

Our theory of value change generates a number of predictions. The most basic prediction specifies what kind of cultural change should take place under given conditions: existential security leads to the rise of Postmodern values. This chapter focuses on the shift from Materialist to Postmaterialist values, while chapters 9 and 10 test this prediction concerning various other aspects of the Postmodern shift. In addition to predicting what kinds of values should become more widespread, chapter 1 spelled out a series of detailed predictions concerning when, where, and how fast value change should occur. This chapter tests the following predictions, connected with the shift from Materialist to Postmaterialist values:

1. Postmaterialist and other Postmodern values will be most widespread in the richest and otherwise most secure societies. The publics of impoverished and insecure societies will emphasize survival values to a much greater extent.

2. Within any given society, Postmodern values will be most widespread among the more secure strata: the wealthier and better educated will be most likely to hold a whole range of security values, including Postmaterialism; the less secure strata will emphasize survival priorities.

3. Short-term fluctuations will follow the scarcity hypothesis: prosperity will enhance the tendency to emphasize well-being values; economic downturn, civil disorder, or war will lead people to emphasize survival values.

4. Long-term changes will also reflect the scarcity hypothesis: in societies that have experienced high levels of security for several decades, we should find a long-term shift from survival values toward well-being values. This shift is not universal: it should occur only in those societies that have attained sufficient existential security so that a substantial share of the population takes survival for granted; but it is not uniquely Western: it appears in any society that *has* experienced the transition to high mass security.

5. In those societies that have experienced a long period of rising economic and physical security, we will find substantial differences between the value priorities of older and younger groups, with the young being much likelier to emphasize well-being values than the old.

6. These intergenerational value differences should be reasonably stable over time: though immediate conditions of security or insecurity will produce short-term fluctuations, the underlying differences between younger and older birth cohorts should persist over long periods of time.

7. In cross-national perspective, large amounts of intergenerational *change* will be found in countries that have experienced relatively high rates of economic *growth*; conversely, the difference between the values of young and old will be small or nonexistent in countries that experienced relatively little increase in per capita income. Thus, high *levels* of prosperity should be conducive to high *levels* of Postmaterialism and other Postmodern values; high rates of economic *growth* should produce relatively rapid rates of value *change*, and relatively large intergenerational *differences*.

8. If one knows the distribution of values across birth cohorts in a given nation at a given time, one can estimate how much change will be produced in a given time span as a result of intergenerational population replacement. Thus for Western Europe, using the four-item Materialist/Postmaterialist values battery, population replacement should produce a shift toward Postmaterialism of approximately one point per year on the Materialist-Postmaterialist percentage difference index.

The 1970 European Community surveys were the first to test the value change thesis. The results showed the age group differences that the social-

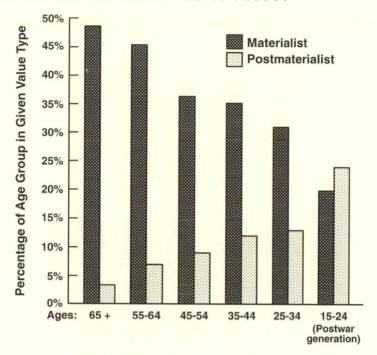

Figure 5.1. Value type by age group, among the publics of Britain, France, West Germany, Italy, Belgium, and the Netherlands in 1970. *Source*: European Community survey of February 1970; based on original four-item Materialist/Postmaterialist values battery. Reprinted from Inglehart, 1990: 76.

ization hypothesis predicts. Figure 5.1 depicts this pattern in a pooled sample of six Western European publics. The basic pattern is similar in all six countries: among the older groups, Materialists outnumber Postmaterialists enormously; as we move to younger groups, the proportion of Materialists declines and that of Postmaterialists increases. Thus, among the oldest cohort, Materialists outnumber Postmaterialists by more than 12 to 1; but among the youngest cohort, Postmaterialists are more numerous than Materialists.

The age differences shown here are striking. But does this pattern reflect life-cycle effects, birth cohort effects, or some combination of the two? Our theory predicts that we will find birth cohort differences; but these differences between the priorities of young and old *could* reflect some inherent tendency for people to become more materialistic as they age. If so, then as time goes by, the values of the younger groups will eventually become just like those of the older groups, producing no change in the society as a whole. Does aging make one place ever-increasing emphasis on economic and physical security? The only way to answer this question is by following given birth cohorts over time, to see if they become more Materialist as they age. We can do so: the four-item Materialist/Postmaterialist values battery has been asked in cross-national sur-

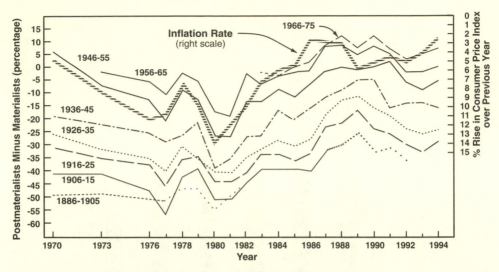

Figure 5.2. Cohort analysis with inflation rate superimposed (using inverted scale on right): percent Postmaterialists minus percent Materialists in eight birth cohorts in six Western European societies, 1970–94. *Source*: Based on combined weighted sample of European Community surveys carried out in West Germany, France, Britain, Italy, the Netherlands, and Belgium, in given years (N = 243,356), and based on the four-item values index, which was included in each of these surveys. Inflation data from statistical office of the European Communities.

veys carried out by the European Community at least once a year in almost every year from 1970 to the present.

Figure 5.2 traces the balance between Materialists and Postmaterialists within given birth cohorts from February 1970 to fall 1994, using the pooled data from the surveys carried out in Britain, France, West Germany, Italy, Belgium, and the Netherlands (an analysis based on more than 240,000 interviews). Each cohort's position at a given time is calculated by subtracting the percentage of Materialists in that cohort from the percentage of Postmaterialists. Thus, at the zero point on the vertical axis, the two groups are equally numerous (the cohort born in 1946–55 was located near this point in 1970). On this graph, the proportion of Postmaterialists increases as we move up the vertical axis; the proportion of Materialists increases as we move down. If the age differences reflected a life-cycle effect, then each of the cohort lines should move downward, toward the Materialist pole, as we move from left to right across this 24-year period.

We find no such downward movement. Instead, the younger birth cohorts remain relatively Postmaterialist throughout the period from 1970 to 1994: given cohorts did not become more Materialist as they aged by almost a quarter of a century—instead, many of these cohorts were slightly *less* Materialist at the end of this period than they were at the start.

WHAT CAUSES THE PERIOD EFFECTS?

In addition to presenting the results of a cohort analysis from 1970 to 1994, figure 5.2 shows the current rate of inflation, superimposed as a heavy shaded line. Since the theory predicts that Postmaterialist values will rise when inflation falls, the inflation index runs from low rates at the top of the graph to high rates toward the bottom. This makes it easy to see that (as predicted) inflation and Postmaterialist values move up and down together, bearing in mind that a *downward* movement of the inflation line indicates *rising* rates of inflation on this graph.

Striking period effects are evident: there was a clear tendency for each cohort to dip toward the Materialist pole during the recession of the mid-1970s and again during the recessions of the early 1980s and the early 1990s. These effects are implicit in the theory, which links Postmaterialist values with economic security. High inflation rates tend to make people feel economically insecure, and as the graph demonstrates, there is a remarkably close fit between current economic conditions and the short-term fluctuations in Materialist/Postmaterialist values. High levels of inflation depress the proportion of Postmaterialists. But these period effects are transient; they disappear when economic conditions return to normal. In the long run, the values of a given birth cohort are remarkably stable. Despite the fluctuations linked with current economic conditions, the intergenerational differences persist: at virtually every point in time, each younger cohort is significantly less Materialist than all of the older ones. These enduring generational differences reflect differences in the formative conditions that shaped the respective birth cohorts: the older ones were influenced by the hunger and insecurity that prevailed during World War I, the Great Depression, and World War II; the younger ones have grown up in an era of historically unprecedented prosperity.

Strictly speaking, these data do not prove that generational change is taking place: one can never distinguish between cohort effects, period effects, and aging effects on statistical grounds alone, since any one of them is a perfect linear function of the other two. Theoretically, the pattern in figure 5.2 might reflect a combination of life-cycle (or aging) effects plus some mysterious period effect that somehow prevented each cohort from becoming more Materialist as it aged from 1970 to 1994. So far, no one has identified a period effect that might have done this (for a debate on this point, see Clarke and Dutt, 1991; and Inglehart and Abramson, 1994); and if someone did, it would be an ad hoc explanation, designed to fit an existing set of observations.

The generational change hypothesis, on the other hand, was published long before these data were collected—and it predicted both the robust cohort differences subsequently observed, and the period effects. If one agrees that the downward swings toward Materialist values found in the mid-1970s, the early 1980s, and the early 1990s were probably due to the economic fluctuations that occurred in those years (and the empirical fit is very good), then the pattern looks like a clear case of intergenerational value change. If this is true, it has

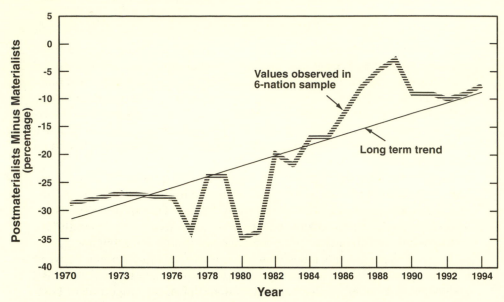

Figure 5.3. The trend toward Postmaterialist values in six Western European societies, 1970–94. The trend toward Postmaterialism is significant at the .001 level. Beta = .61, p < .001. *Source*: Based on combined weighted sample of European Community surveys carried out in West Germany, France, Britain, Italy, the Netherlands, and Belgium, in given years (N = 243,356).

far-reaching implications: in the long run the values of these societies should shift in the predicted direction.

VALUE CHANGES OBSERVED IN WESTERN COUNTRIES, 1970–1994

A good deal of intergenerational population replacement has taken place since 1970. The intergenerational value change thesis predicts that in the long run this should produce a shift from Materialist toward Postmaterialist values among the populations of these societies. More than a quarter century has passed since these values were first measured in 1970. Do we find the predicted value shift? As the following evidence demonstrates, we do indeed. In a companion volume to this book, Abramson and Inglehart (1995) present a far more detailed analysis of the shift from Materialist to Postmaterialist values than is given here. This chapter summarizes and updates the key findings.

Figure 5.3 shows the overall trend among the populations of the six nations first surveyed in 1970. Like the cohort trajectories in the preceding figure, the trend line shown here dips steeply downward in each of the three recent recessions; but the long-term trajectory shows a clear upward trend, and regression analysis reveals that this trend is statistically significant at the .001 level (see Abramson and Inglehart, 1995: ch. 4). Although each given birth cohort in the preceding figure shows relatively little net movement upward or downward from 1970 to 1994, the line for the *total* sample shows a strong upward movement, reflecting intergenerational population replacement: by 1994, the two oldest cohorts had almost completely disappeared from the sample and had been replaced by two younger (and much more Postmaterialist) cohorts. In 1970, the mean position for the sample as a whole was located about halfway between the cohort born in 1916–25 and the cohort born in 1926–35; by 1994 this point had moved up more than two cohorts and was located slightly below the position of the 1946–55 birth cohort. A substantial value shift had occurred in the population as a whole.

In 1970, Materialists outnumbered Postmaterialists overwhelmingly in all of these countries, but by 1994, the balance had shifted markedly toward Postmaterialist values. In 1970, within these six Western European nations as a whole, Materialists outnumbered Postmaterialists by a ratio of about 4 to 1. By 1994, this ratio had fallen to less than 1.5 to 1: Postmaterialists had become almost as numerous as Materialists.

Figure 5.3 shows the trend in six European countries for which detailed time series data are available from more than 40 European Community surveys that were carried out in *each* of these countries from 1970 to 1994. An almost equally detailed time series is available for Denmark and Ireland, from the surveys that were carried out in each country from 1973 to 1994. Figure 5.4 shows the net shift in these eight countries, plus the United States. Eight of the nine countries show a shift from Materialist toward Postmaterialist values, with only Belgium remaining unchanged. In the early 1970s, Materialists heavily outnumbered Postmaterialists in all nine of these countries. By the early 1990s, Postmaterialists had increased almost everywhere and had become more numerous than Materialists in the United States, Denmark, and the Netherlands.

If one knows the relative proportions of Materialists and Postmaterialists in each birth cohort of a given nation, plus the size of each cohort (obtainable from census figures), one can calculate the amount of value shift that would take place each year as a result of intergenerational population replacement. Abramson and Inglehart (1987) have done so, finding that in Western Europe, the population replacement process would bring a shift toward Postmaterialism of slightly more than one point per year in the percentage difference index or PDI (this constitutes the vertical axis in figures 5.2, 5.3, and 5.4). This is a relatively modest gain; in any given year, it could easily be swamped by fluctuations in current conditions linked with security or insecurity. But these short-term fluctuations move in both directions: in the long run, they tend to cancel each other out. The impact of intergenerational population replacement, on the other hand, moves in one continuous direction for decades. In the long run, its cumulative effects can be substantial. This seems to be the case with the data at hand. For these nine countries as a whole, over the 24-year period from 1970 to 1994 the PDI shows a mean shift toward the Postmaterialist pole

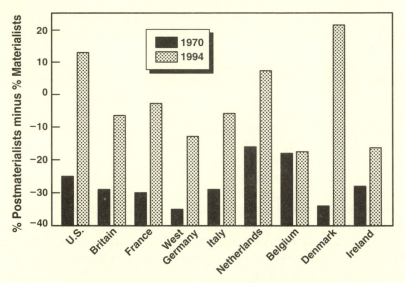

Figure 5.4. The shift toward Postmaterialist values among the publics of nine Western Societies, 1970–94. *Source*: European Community surveys, February 1970 and fall 1994; and U.S. national election surveys from 1972 and 1992.

of 23 points: this is almost exactly the amount of change that would be expected to occur solely as a result of intergenerational population replacement.

Economic conditions were *not* more favorable in 1994 than they were at the start of the series, in 1970; they were worse. The early 1990s were a period of recession, and as figure 5.2 indicates, the levels of Postmaterialism in most cohorts reached a peak about 1989 and declined during the next few years. Nevertheless, as younger, more Postmaterialist cohorts replaced older ones, the population as a whole showed a long-term shift toward Postmaterialist values in almost every country. Despite substantial short-term fluctuations, and despite the fact that the surveys in our most recent year, 1994, occurred when Western Europe was still recovering from a major recession, the predicted shift toward Postmaterialist values took place—and its magnitude was just about the size that would be predicted by an intergenerational population replacement model.

Figure 5.4 shows only the starting point and the end point of each country's time series from 1970 to 1994. In a more detailed analysis of this time series, consisting of at least 33 surveys for each nation, Inglehart and Abramson (1994) examine the trends in each of the eight countries; then, using regression analysis, they demonstrate that Britain, France, West Germany, Italy, the Netherlands, Ireland, and Denmark all show large and statistically significant long-term trends from Materialist to Postmaterialist values over this period. In the eighth case (Belgium), they find no trend. But a time series analysis controlling for the joint effects of inflation and unemployment demonstrates that there is a statistically significant trend toward Postmaterialism in *all eight* of the Western European countries for which a detailed time series is available over the past two decades: Belgium showed no shift toward Postmaterialism because it has suffered much higher levels of unemployment in recent years than in the 1970s, which has largely offset the effects of intergenerational population replacement. When they control for inflation and unemployment, Belgium is no longer a deviant case: it too shows a significant shift toward Postmaterialism. Controlling for inflation and unemployment largely explains the period effects: as the theory implies, high levels of inflation and unemployment encourage an emphasis on economic security, rather than on Postmaterialist values (Inglehart and Abramson, 1994). As we have seen, a substantial shift toward Postmaterialist values also took place in the United States. These data come from the six NES presidential election surveys carried out from 1972 to 1992. Six surveys do not provide a sufficient number of time points to test the trend's statistical significance, but the net effect in the United States seems to be about as large as in most Western European countries.

THE POSTMATERIALIST PHENOMENON: EVOLVING OVER TIME

Much of the literature on Postmaterialism deals with whether it is a deep-rooted phenomenon having a long-term impact on political behavior or simply a transient epiphenomenon. We will reexamine this issue in the light of recent evidence. If a society's basic values change mainly through intergenerational population replacement, we would expect them to change at a gradual pace. But though short-term changes may be small, close examination of their societal location can provide valuable insight into their long-term implications. Contrary to what some observers assumed (Kesselman, 1979), Postmaterialism did not dwindle away in the face of diminished economic and physical security. In most countries its numbers grew, and in many ways its political influence is greater now than it was a decade or two ago; but its character and tactics have changed significantly.

By 1970, Postmaterialists had attained numerical parity with Materialists only among the postwar generation. Furthermore, they were concentrated among the more affluent strata of this age group: among university students, they heavily outnumbered the Materialists. This helps explain the widespread popular perceptions of a generation gap that emerged in the late 1960s and early 1970s. Even among the postwar generation, Materialists were about as numerous as Postmaterialists. But in this age group's most articulate and most visible segment—the university students—there was an overwhelming preponderance of Postmaterialists. The students lived in a distinct milieu: they had highly developed communications networks with other students but were largely isolated from their nonstudent peers. The priorities prevailing in this milieu were fundamentally different from those shaping the society as a whole.

The existence of such a milieu can play an important part in the evolution and propagation of a given set of values. Indeed, Habermas (1979) argues that the rise of Postmaterialism is not due to the different formative experiences of different generation units, but to exposure to the specific worldviews inculcated by distinct communications networks (see also Jaeggi, 1979). But this explanation seems to complement, not substitute for, the one proposed here. It helps account for the spread of values in a given milieu, but provides no explanation of *why* given generation units were disposed to accept given values in the first place, while others rejected them. It seems clear that in virtually all Western nations, the student milieu of the late 1960s *did* constitute a distinct communications network, propagating a distinctive viewpoint. Given these circumstances, it is not surprising that the student elite saw themselves as part of a counterculture that was engaged in an irreconcilable clash with the culture of an older generation: From their viewpoint, the dictum "Don't trust anyone over 30" seemed plausible. Our hypotheses imply that as time went by, the Postmaterialists would become older and more evenly distributed across the population. Hence, the plausibility of a monolithic generation gap would fade away. But in 1970, conditions were optimal to sustain belief in a generation gap, with all youth on one side and all older people on the other.

One of the most important changes derives from the simple fact that, today, Postmaterialists are older than they were when they first emerged as a major political factor in the 1960s. Initially manifested mainly through student protest movements, their most important impact now comes through the activities of elites. For the students have grown older, and Postmaterialism has penetrated deeply into the ranks of professionals, civil servants, managers, and politicians (Inglehart, 1990: ch. 9). It seems to be a major factor in the rise of a "new class" in Western society—a stratum of highly educated and well-paid young technocrats who take an adversarial stance toward their society (Ladd, 1978; Gouldner, 1979; Lipset, 1979). The debate between those giving top priority to economic growth, versus those who emphasize environmentalism and the quality of life, reflects persisting value cleavages.

The Postmaterialists among the protest generation of the 1960s were much more likely to enter academic life, the mass media, and nonprofit foundations than were Materialists: these occupations provided relatively great opportunities for self-expression. By contrast, the Materialists were more likely to go into career paths that maximized one's earning power and financial security, such as business, engineering, and technical fields.

One consequence has been that, as they aged and moved into adult careers, Postmaterialists have become the dominant force in most universities. In the 1960s, they were student protesters; by the 1990s, they were the department chairs and deans. The emergence of the phenomenon of Political Correctness reflects this transition in the dominant culture within universities: values that were controversial in the 1960s had became the values of the establishment in the 1990s. Although some of these values were still controversial in the society as a whole, there was pressure to conform to them within the universities.

VALUE CHANGE BEYOND WESTERN DEMOCRACIES

Although the highly industrialized democracies of Western Europe and North America historically led the shift toward Postmaterialist values, our theory implies that this process should also occur in other nations that develop high levels of prosperity and advanced social welfare networks. Consequently, it should be at work in East Asia (parts of which have now attained Western levels of prosperity) and even in Eastern Europe. The value change theory implies that we should find a higher proportion of Postmaterialists among the younger cohorts than among the old, in *any* society that has had sufficient economic growth during the past four or five decades so that the younger cohorts experienced substantially greater economic security during their preadult years than did those who are now in their fifties, sixties, or seventies.

At first glance, it might seem unlikely that intergenerational value change would be at work in Eastern European countries, since they are far less prosperous than Western Europe and the United States, and their economies are currently in decline. But a country's absolute level of wealth is not the crucial variable: the value change thesis implies (1) that countries with high *levels* of prosperity should have relatively high *levels* of Postmaterialist values, and (2) that countries that have experienced relatively high rates of economic *growth* should show relatively large *differences* between the values of young and old, reflecting the fact that the formative conditions of the respective generations have undergone relatively large amounts of *change*.

Thus, we would indeed expect Russia and other Eastern European countries to show relatively low absolute *levels* of Postmaterialism. But they should also show substantial intergenerational *change* in these values, reflecting the massive differences between the conditions that shaped the formative years of those who grew up during World War I, the Great Depression, and World War II and those who grew up subsequently. The crucial factor governing the emergence of Postmaterialist values is whether one experienced a sense of economic and physical security during one's formative years. Accordingly, we would expect Postmaterialist values to have developed during the past 50 years in Eastern Europe and the former Soviet Union. Though their GNP per capita lags behind that of Western countries, it is far above the subsistence level (and several times as high as that of such countries as China, Nigeria, or India). Throughout the ex-socialist world, the younger birth cohorts have generally experienced greater security during their formative years than did older ones.

In the Russian case, for example, those born in 1920 experienced the civil war and the mass starvation linked with forced collectivization during the 1920s, followed by the terror and Stalinist purges of the 1930s, and mass starvation and the loss of 27 million lives in the Soviet Union during World War II. The 1950s and 1960s, by contrast, were an era of recovery and rapid economic growth at rates that exceeded those of most Western countries. This was the era that led Khrushchev to boast "We will bury you" economically—and at the time, many Western observers thought it a plausible claim. Recent years have been calamitous, creating a period effect that tends to drive all of the Russian cohorts downward toward the Materialist pole. But the formative years of the younger cohorts were far more secure than those of the older cohorts, and if the intergenerational *differences* reflect differences in preadult experience rather than current conditions, we would indeed expect to find evidence of intergenerational change in Eastern Europe.

From 1945 to about 1980, most Eastern European countries had impressive rates of economic growth; in the early decades, it seemed likely that they would catch up with and surpass the West. Since 1980, their economies have decayed, but there is no question that the average Pole or Russian experienced far greater economic and physical *security* during the era from 1950 to 1980 than during the period from 1915 to 1945.

The emergence of Postmaterialist values in Eastern Europe might be reinforced by the fact that the welfare systems of socialist states partially compensated for their relatively low levels of prosperity. The key factor in value change is not one's absolute income, but the degree of *security* experienced during one's formative years. The communist regimes of Eastern Europe provided a relatively secure existence during most of the postwar era: job security was very high, rents were low, basic foods were provided at subsidized prices, and medical care and education were free. The quality of what one got was poor, but one was sure of getting it.

East Asia contrasts with Eastern Europe. Fifty years ago, it was far less developed than Eastern Europe; as recently as 1950, Japan's annual per capita income was only a fraction of that in such Eastern European countries as Czechoslovakia, Poland, or Hungary—and the Chinese and South Korean per capita incomes were a fraction of Japan's. But in recent decades, East Asia (including China, since the pragmatists took power in 1976) has shown the most rapid economic growth rates in the world. By 1990, per capita income in South Korea and Taiwan had reached Eastern European levels and Japan was one of the richest countries in the world. Even China was experiencing annual growth rates of around 10 percent, enough to double GNP every seven years.

Thus, the older East Asian birth cohorts grew up under conditions of extreme scarcity, while the youngest ones have experienced relatively secure circumstances throughout their formative years. Consequently, we would expect these countries to show low proportions of Postmaterialists overall, but relatively steep rates of intergenerational change. The Eastern European countries, by comparison, started out at much higher levels but have grown less rapidly: we would expect to find higher proportions of Postmaterialists than in East Asia, but less intergenerational change. Figure 5.5 shows the value differences across the respective birth cohorts, using 1990 World Values Survey data from countries in Eastern Europe and East Asia, together with the European Union and the United States, using the 12-item values indicator.

As figure 5.5 illustrates, the younger birth cohorts do, indeed, show considerably higher proportions of Postmaterialists than the older cohorts in most of these societies. The intergenerational shift from Materialist to Postmaterialist

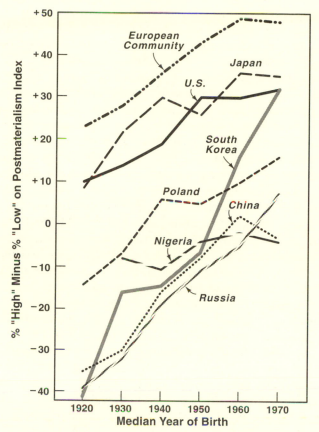

Figure 5.5. Values by birth cohort in Western democracies, Eastern Europe, East Asia, and Africa. *Source*: 1990–93 World Values Survey. *Note*: Respondents are classified as "high" on the 12-item Materialist/Postmaterialist values index used here if they gave high priority to at least three of the five Postmaterialist goals (ranking them among the two most important in each group of four goals). They are classified as "low" if they gave high priority to none of the five Postmaterialist goals.

values is not limited to Western democracies: it is found across advanced industrial societies with a wide variety of political and economic institutions, and a wide variety of cultural traditions. Although the richer countries have much higher absolute proportions of Postmaterialists than the poorer ones, we also find a steep slope reflecting intergenerational value differences in poor countries that have experienced a rapid increase in prevailing standards of living during the past several decades.

Results from several European Union countries have already been examined in detail and are combined into a single line on figure 5.5 to simplify the picture. Overall, the European Union shows the highest proportion of Postmaterialists on this graph, with the United States and Japan also ranking high. Even the oldest birth cohorts in these advanced industrial societies rank higher than even the youngest cohorts in most other countries. But an upward slope, reflecting a rising proportion of Postmaterialists to Materialists as we move from old to young, is also found in Eastern Europe and East Asia.

In virtually every case, from North America to Western Europe to Eastern Europe to East Asia, as we move from the oldest cohorts at the left of the graph to the youngest cohorts at the right, the ratio of Postmaterialists to Materialists rises. This is exactly what we would expect to find if intergenerational value change were occurring. To prove that it is, we would need data from a long time series, and thus far such data are available only for Western Europe and, to a lesser extent, the United States and Japan. But in every country for which substantial time series data *are* available, the evidence indicates that these age differences reflect intergenerational change, rather than life-cycle effects: there is no tendency for given birth cohorts to become more Materialist as they age. Furthermore, as this finding implies, the ratio of Postmaterialists to Materialists has gradually risen over time. We believe that the other countries shown in figure 5.5 are on a trajectory similar to that on which Western nations and Japan have been moving in recent decades.

Figure 5.5 presents a great deal of information, reflecting the twentieth-century history of each nation; it could be discussed at considerable length. The data reveal huge cross-national differences. Thus, there are far more Postmaterialists in the United States and the European Union than in South Korea, but the slope rises steeply in South Korea, suggesting that a very rapid process of intergenerational change is taking place there. During the past quarter century, only one country in the world (Singapore) has had a higher rate of economic growth than South Korea, which shows the steepest slope in the graph. Among its oldest birth cohort there are literally *no* Postmaterialists; 70 percent fall into the pure Materialist category and 30 percent are mixed types (producing an index of −40 on the vertical axis). Among its youngest cohort, Materialists outnumber Postmaterialists by only 10 points.

If Postmaterialist values simply reflected current conditions, one would not expect to find a shift from Materialist to Postmaterialist values in such countries as Russia and Poland, which experienced economic stagnation during the decade preceding these surveys and by 1990 were in a state of economic collapse. But the theory postulates a long-term process of intergenerational change based on the differences experienced during a given cohort's preadult years. From this perspective, we *would* expect to find intergenerational value differences in Eastern Europe, for it is clear that the formative experiences of the cohorts born in the 1950s, the 1960s, and the 1970s were characterized by far more secure circumstances than is true of those who experienced the traumatic upheavals of the 1920s, 1930s, or 1940s. And we do find evidence of intergenerational change. As figure 5.5 demonstrates, the Russian results show an upward slope. Although the Russian cohort line starts and ends at a level far below that of the richer countries, intergenerational differences in Russia are even steeper than those found in Western Europe, the United States, or Japan.

China shows an equally steep slope, reflecting sharp intergenerational differences that may have contributed to the spring 1989 clash between young intellectuals and the aging leadership still in control of the army. These intergenerational differences reflect the massive differences between the formative experiences of the older generation in China, who lived through an era of mass starvation and civil war that went on almost continuously from the 1920s to 1949, and those of the younger cohorts, brought up in conditions of relative stability and prosperity—broken by the severe but relatively brief upheavals of the Great Leap Forward and the Cultural Revolution in the late 1960s. China has had a series of wild swings since 1949, including periods of extremely rapid economic growth and periods of severe economic decline. As recently as 1959–60, millions of people starved to death; but this was a relatively brief period, compared with the decades of slaughter and starvation that dominated the warlord period, the civil war, and World War II. By these standards, the communist victory in 1949 brought a distinct improvement. And for the past two decades, China has experienced exceptional economic growth, with an average rate higher than Japan's. Our data reflect these facts: China starts out with an extremely low proportion of Postmaterialists among its oldest cohorts, but then shows a steep upward slope (though not as steep as that found in South Korea) as we move to its younger cohorts. Although its absolute level of Postmaterialism remains far below that of most Western countries, China seems to be on a similar trajectory, and (as we will argue in the following chapter) further economic development should bring expanding mass support for democratization.

The European Union countries show a steeper rate of change than does the United States, reflecting their higher growth rates since World War II. While among the older Western European cohorts, Materialists substantially outnumber Postmaterialists (and thus fall well below the zero level on this graph), all three of the cohorts born after 1945 rise above this threshold—indeed, the two youngest European Union cohorts rank well above their American counterparts.

The value differences across age groups are greater in Western Europe than in the United States—which implies that Western Europe is manifesting a more rapid rate of value change over time. This has indeed been the case. In 1972, when the American public was first surveyed, it showed a considerably higher proportion of Postmaterialists than did the combined six European Union countries for which data were then available; but subsequently, Western Europe has caught up. Nevertheless, the United States has shown a significant movement in the predicted direction.

For the most part, the findings from Japan fit theoretical expectations. Its overall proportion of Postmaterialists ranks just after the United States and Western Europe and well above most of the other countries in figure 5.5, as one would expect of a country that has now attained a high per capita income. Moreover, in Japan as in virtually all advanced industrial societies, Postmaterialist values are more widespread among the younger cohorts than among the

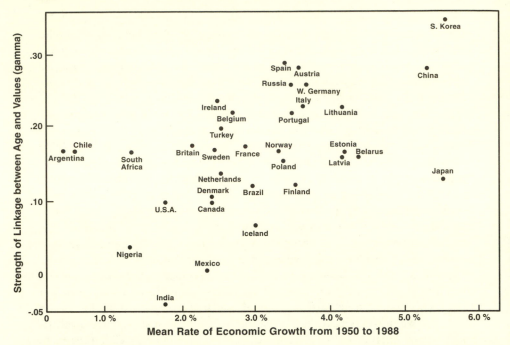

Figure 5.6. Societies with fast-growing economies have relatively large differences between the values of young and old.
r = .52, p < .001. *Source*: 1990–93 World Values Survey. Based on 12-item Materialist/Postmaterialist values index. *Note*: Data on economic growth were not available for several Eastern European countries.

older ones. Furthermore, the ratio of Postmaterialists to Materialists has gradually risen over time, in Japan as in the United States and Western Europe. In 1972, the first Japanese survey to measure these values found 43 percent Materialists and only 5 percent Postmaterialists—a preponderance of more than 8 to 1 (Watanuki, 1977). In the 1981 World Values Survey, the figures had shifted to 37 and 6 percent, respectively, a ratio of 6 to 1. And the 1990 World Values Survey found 29 percent Materialists and 10 percent Postmaterialists: the ratio had fallen to less than 3 to 1. In these respects, the Japanese findings confirm the theory's predictions. One finding is surprising, however: as one of the world's most rapidly growing economies, we would expect to find a steeper slope for Japan than for most other countries, but we do not.

Figure 5.5 would be unreadable if it included the results from all 43 societies for which data are available, but we should note that two important countries do *not* show any indication of intergenerational change: India and Nigeria. The data for Nigeria are plotted on figure 5.5. The line is almost horizontal, reflecting virtually no intergenerational change. The Indian data are not shown here, but as figure 5.6 demonstrates, the relationship between values and age is even weaker there, with younger groups being slightly *less* Postmaterialist than the old. A combination of relatively slow industrialization and rapid population growth during most of the period from 1945 to 1990 kept India from developing at anything approaching the East Asian rate. Nigeria has had virtually no increase in GNP per capita since 1965, and its public also shows a flat relationship between age and values. These findings indicate that intergenerational value change is not inherent in the human condition: as our theory implies, we find it in those countries where the formative years of the younger cohorts were shaped by significantly higher levels of economic security than those of the older cohorts. In countries that have *not* experienced economic development, intergenerational value differences are absent.

Economic Growth and Value Change

The value change thesis implies that large amounts of intergenerational *change* will be found in countries that have experienced relatively high rates of economic *growth*. Figure 5.6 tests this hypothesis against the data from all of the societies for which we have data, and not just the selected examples just discussed. To present the findings from more than 40 societies on one graph, figure 5.6 condenses the relationship between age and values for each country into a single coefficient. As this figure demonstrates, the selected examples shown in figure 5.5 reflect the overall pattern: intergenerational value differences tend to be largest in countries that have experienced the greatest amounts of economic growth during the past 40 years. Accordingly, the correlation between age and values is strongest in such countries as South Korea and China, and weak or even negative in such countries as Nigeria and India—which have not only experienced much lower rates of economic growth than China or South Korea, but which also have much more unequal income distributions, so that substantial proportions of the population live at the edge of starvation.

Note that the intergenerational value differences are also relatively weak in the United States: though it has a relatively high absolute *level* of Postmaterialism, its rate of intergenerational *change* is relatively small. Although the United States has been one of the world's richest countries since the nineteenth century, it has not experienced dramatic changes between the formative experiences of younger and older cohorts like those found in Europe and East Asia. The United States has been a relatively rich country throughout the lifetime of everyone in the sample and was not devastated by World War II—but the United States has had relatively slow growth in recent decades.

As usual, we find deviant cases. Argentina and Chile are "overachievers," showing larger intergenerational differences than their economic growth rates would predict; and, as we have seen, Japan is an "underachiever," showing smaller intergenerational value differences than its historic economic growth rate would predict. But overall, the pattern fits our theoretical expectations. High rates of economic growth tend to go with large intergenerational value differences (r = .41, statistically significant at the .01 level).

Economic Security and Value Change:
New Evidence from 40 Societies

The value change thesis also implies that high *levels* of prosperity should be conducive to high *levels* of Postmaterialism, so rich countries should tend to have more Postmaterialists than poor ones.

Disputing this thesis, Trump (1991) and Duch and Taylor (1993), drawing on data from only three societies, have claimed that Postmaterialist values are *not* more likely to be found in prosperous countries or regions than in poor ones. The World Values surveys provide strong evidence that they *are*. These surveys cover an unprecedentedly broad range of the economic spectrum, with data from low-income nations, middle-income countries, and advanced industrial democracies having per capita incomes 60 or 70 times as high as those of the poorest countries.

Our theory implies that the shift from Materialist to Postmaterialist priorities is potentially universal: it should occur in any country that moves from conditions of economic insecurity to relative security (though during a transitional period, older generations will continue to reflect the conditions that characterized their preadult experiences). This has clear implications: people living in rich countries generally experience more economic security than those in poor nations, where the pie is not only smaller but also tends to be less evenly distributed, and many people live on the edge of starvation. Accordingly, we would expect high levels of GNP/capita to be linked with relatively high levels of Postmaterialist values.

Although this implication is straightforward, until recently it was not possible to test it adequately because most of the surveys exploring values (like most surveys in general) have been carried out in relatively developed societies. Using the 1990–91 World Values Surveys we can now test this hypothesis across the full range of economic development. The results confirm that hypothesis, as figure 5.7 demonstrates (using the 12-item values index). Rich countries tend to have much higher proportions of Postmaterialists than poorer countries. Although some rich countries such as Norway and the United States are "underachievers" and some poorer countries such as Mexico and Turkey are "overachievers," the overall correlation is remarkably strong: r = .68, significant at the .0001 level.

Diez Nicolas (1994) demonstrates that this relationship also holds true at the regional level, within a given nation. He has included the Materialist/Postmaterialist values battery in *monthly* national surveys of the Spanish public since 1988, obtaining nearly 55,000 interviews in the period 1989–92. Cumulating large numbers of interviews from each region enables him to perform statistically reliable analyses of the relationship between values and economic security at the regional level, in a country that has large amounts of regional variation. This provides a much more reliable base on which to test this hypothesis than the 741 secondary school students on which Trump (1991) relied for ev-

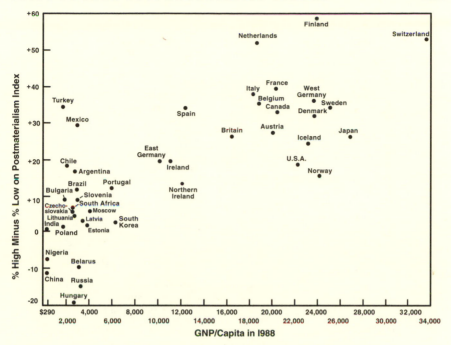

Figure 5.7. Economic development and Materialist/Postmaterialist values.
r = .68, p < .0001. *Source*: 1990–93 World Values Survey. GNP/capita from World Bank, *World Development Report, 1993. Note*: Respondents are classified as "high" on the 12-item Materialist/Postmaterialist values index used here if they gave high priority to at least three of the five Postmaterialist goals (ranking them among the two most important in each group of four goals). They are classified as "low" if they gave high priority to none of the five Postmaterialist goals.

idence that regional economic variations in the United States are unrelated to Postmaterialist values.

Diez Nicolas finds that the relative level of Postmaterialism varies a good deal from region to region and is quite stable from one year to the next. The wealthiest regions (the Basque country and greater Madrid) consistently have the highest proportions of Postmaterialists; and the poorest regions (Andalusia, Extremadura, and Castille-La Mancha) show the lowest proportions of Postmaterialists in virtually every year. As figure 5.8 shows, this relationship is very strong, and it shows a particularly good fit with a given region's level of economic development 25 years prior to the survey, during the median respondent's preadult years (r = .83). Here again, the evidence indicates that economic security has a powerful linkage with the emergence of Postmaterialist values.

Duch and Taylor (1993) and Davis (1996) suggest that the value shift we observe is due simply to rising levels of education. Do richer countries and richer

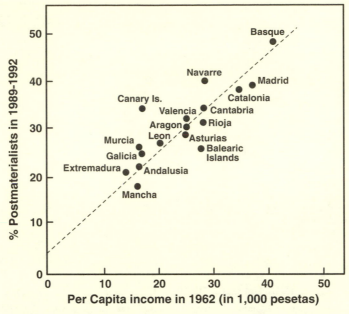

Figure 5.8. Postmaterialist values by economic level of Spanish regions one generation before surveys.
N = 54,557, r = .83. *Source*: Juan Diez Nicolas, "Postmaterialismo y Desarrollo Economico en Espana," paper presented at World Conference on Social Values, Madrid, September 27–October 1, 1993.

regions have larger numbers of Postmaterialists simply because their publics are better educated?

As our theory implies, we do indeed find that the better educated in every country are likelier to have Postmaterialist values than the less educated. In large part, this reflects the fact that one's educational level is an excellent indicator of how economically secure one was during one's *formative* years. For the great majority of people, one's education is completed in their preadult years; and how much education they get is closely related to how well-off their parents were during that period: economically secure families give their children more years of education than economically insecure ones. We would also expect the upper-income and occupational groups to be more Postmaterialist than the lower ones, but one's educational level is a considerably better indicator of security during one's formative years than is one's *current* income or occupation. Education gets closer to the key causal factor, which is *formative* security. One's income or occupation reflects one's *current* economic level. But one's education not only taps current prosperity but is also an excellent indicator of how prosperous one's *parents* were.

An alternative explanation would focus on some form of indoctrination: the better educated are more likely to have Postmaterialist values because their teachers teach them these values. Some version of this seems to be what Duch and Taylor, and Davis have in mind—though this interpretation fails to explain why (as our data demonstrate) those who received a higher education in the era before World War II are *not* predominantly Postmaterialists.

Still another possible explanation for why we would expect the better educated to be more Postmaterialistic lies in the fact that the better educated generally have better jobs and higher incomes than the less educated: they have relatively high levels of *current* economic security, which, the theory implies, should also be conducive to Postmaterialist values. We don't rule out either indoctrination or current prosperity as possible contributing factors: our theory holds that security during one's formative years is conducive to the emergence of Postmaterialist values, and not that it is the *only* influence on these values. The question is "What is the relative importance of these factors?"

Our theory emphasizes the role of formative security. But one's educational level is linked with current prosperity, exposure to indoctrination, and how well-off one's family was during a person's formative years. In order to separate these mingled influences, we will perform a multiple regression analysis. But we have a problem in doing so: this approach will almost inevitably underestimate the impact of formative experiences. The reason why it will do so is simple: recall data virtually always contain a good deal more measurement error than do reports of one's own current characteristics. Most respondents can give pretty accurate information concerning their own income, occupation, or educational level at the time of the survey. But their report of their parents' characteristics when they were growing up almost inevitably is contaminated with a good deal of measurement error. First, there is the simple fact that they are not reporting their own characteristics now—they are reporting someone else's characteristics when they were growing up—which may have been 30 or 40 years ago. These problems are especially acute with recall data concerning one's parents' *income*: this is something that may have varied a good deal from one year to the next and, quite often, was something that the parents did not discuss with their children. We ask the reader, "What was your parents' income level when you were growing up?" Hardly anyone can give a precise figure—but most people can provide a pretty accurate account of their *own* income at the time of the survey. Consequently, recall data on parental income will almost certainly explain less of the variance in one's attitudes than data on one's own current income: its explanatory power is weakened by a great deal of measurement error. Recall data on one's parents' occupation has some of these same problems—it deals with something that may be quite distant in time, may have varied, and may not have been clearly conveyed to the child; but most people can give at least a fairly accurate idea of what their parents' occupation was when they were growing up. The same is true of one's parents' educational level: it suffers from the measurement problems inherent in recall data about someone else's characteristics, possibly a long time ago; but one's parents' educational level was a fixed characteristic in most cases, and one can get a more accurate measurement of it than of parental income during one's formative years.

In short, it is considerably more difficult to get an accurate measure of "formative security" than it is to get one of one's current economic characteristics—which tends to weaken the relative explanatory power of formative security in any regression analysis that runs one against the other. Nevertheless, let us carry out the test, using the best measure of formative security that we can get. For this purpose, the best data we know of are those from the *Political Action* surveys (Barnes et al., 1979) carried out in the 1970s. In order to obtain a relatively good indicator of formative security, we construct a multi-item index based on the reported educational level of the respondent's mother and father, plus the reported occupation of the respondent's father (most respondents' mothers didn't have one, when they were growing up). Table 5.1 shows the results of multiple regression through the origin, in each of the six countries for which these data are available.

As table 5.1 demonstrates, our theory is clearly upheld in every one of the six societies. For our indicator of formative security not only reduces the correlation between the respondent's educational level and his or her values: in all six societies, our indicator of formative security, based on recall data concerning the respondent's parents' educational and occupational level when the respondent was growing up, actually explains *more* of the variance in his or her values than does the respondent's own educational level.

This is a truly remarkable set of findings. Normally, one would expect an individual's own current characteristics to provide a far stronger explanation of his or her own values or attitudes than the status of some other person—particularly since our measure of parental SES is based on recall data reporting the status of another person at a time that may be several decades in the past. But despite all the problems inherent in recall data, we find that the respondent's *parents'* SES consistently provides an even stronger explanation of the respondent's values, than does his or her *own* educational level.

These two variables, by themselves, explain most of the variance in Materialist/Postmaterialist values in every country; across the six societies, they account for 79 percent of the variance. And the most important factor is Formative Security, not the respondent's education. This holds true only rather narrowly in Italy, where (as the respective beta coefficients demonstrate) Formative Security accounts for slightly more of the variance in values than does the respondent's educational level. In Germany, the Netherlands, Austria, the United States, and Finland, the predominance of Formative Security is one-sided; and for the six nations as a whole, the beta coefficient for Formative Security is .635—more than twice the size of the coefficient for respondent's educational level, which is .266.

One could scarcely hope for a clearer demonstration of the fact that these values are *not* simply the result of indoctrination in the schools, or a reflection of the fact that the better educated tend to have higher incomes. The impact of one's *formative* experiences seems to have a considerably greater impact on Materialist/Postmaterialist values than the individual's educational level. For-

TABLE 5.1
Dependent Variable   VAR0340
Independent Variables   INDEX1

Materialist/Postmaterialist Values: 4 pt
Formative Security, Computed According to the Following Formula:
INDEX1 = [2 × (VAR0162/25) + VAR0168 + VAR0172]/4,
where   VAR0162—Father's Occupation: Standard Prestige Scores
        VAR0168—Father's Education Type
        VAR0172—Mother's Education Type
VAR0214   Respondent's Educational Level

| | | | | Simple Regression Beta Coefficients (for Respondent's Educational Level) | Multivariate Analysis | | | | |
| | | | | | Regression Coefficients | | Beta Coefficients | | |
Number	Country	Number of Cases	Number of Valid Cases		Formative Security	Educational Level	Formative Security	Educational Level	R Square
1	Germany	2,307	1,841	.868	.724 (.040)	.427 (.040)	.566	.338	.794
2	Netherlands	1,201	993	.871	1.171 (.059)	.485 (.062)	.665	.260	.828
3	Austria	1,585	1,205	.872	.956 (.054)	.411 (.051)	.628	.286	.812
4	United States	1,719	1,246	.857	.788 (.056)	.328 (.045)	.590	.305	.783
5	Italy	1,779	1,385	.876	.742 (.046)	.601 (.040)	.475	.442	.808
6	Finland	1,224	1,005	.870	1.113 (.065)	.443 (.062)	.649	.268	.816
	All Countries	12,558	7,675	.858	.952 (.021)	.365 (.020)	.635	.266	.789

Notes: Standard errors in parentheses. All regressions are significant at 1% level (based upon regression through the origin). No data available for VAR0172 (Mother's Education Type)
in the British and Swiss surveys.
Source: "Political Action—An Eight Nation Study," 1979.

mative Security seems to play a key role in the emergence of Postmaterialist values.

Changes in the World Values Survey, 1981–1990

Data from a long time series would be needed to demonstrate directly that economic development tends to produce an intergenerational shift toward Postmaterialist values globally, and such data are not available for most of these countries. Although the time series evidence that *is* available has a remarkably good fit with the predictions of the Postmaterialist value shift thesis, most of it comes from nine Western nations. We can supplement it with a modest amount of additional time series data from the World Values surveys: for 21 of these countries, data from the four-item values battery is available from both the 1981 and the 1990–91 surveys.

Table 5.2 shows the distribution of Materialist and Postmaterialist values in 1981 and 1990 for 21 countries. We also have World Values survey data from these time points for one additional country, Denmark, but we do not present them here. The 1981 Danish sample seems to have been unrepresentative: its results are far out of line with the results from other countries, and also with the results from other Danish surveys carried out at the same time. Consequently we do not use this survey as a basis of cross-time comparisons in this book (details concerning the 1981 Danish sample are presented in Appendix 2).

As table 5.2 shows, 18 out of these 21 countries show a shift in the predicted direction, from 1981 to 1990–91. South Korea shows no net shift, which is surprising. Only two countries (Iceland and South Africa) show shifts in the opposite direction from the one predicted. We have no explanation for why Iceland is a deviant case, but it is not surprising that South Africa shows a shift toward Materialist goals. A society's values at any given time point reflect a combination of long-term trends and current period effects—and South Africa experienced a period of severe insecurity during the 1980s. Its economy, suffering from international boycott and low commodity prices, experienced economic stagnation throughout the 1980s. Moreover, widespread violence and political instability gave rise to growing concern for physical security among both blacks and whites. Powerful period effects were working to produce a sense of insecurity, rather than the security that contributes to Postmaterialist values.

A generalized shift toward Postmodern values seems to be taking place. With only two time points available, the World Values surveys database does not enable one to distinguish period effects from long-term trends, but it does provide data from a wide range of nations. Here again, the findings show a shift from Materialist to Postmaterialist values, complementing the findings from the much more detailed time series available from eight Western European countries.

TABLE 5.2

The Shift Toward Postmaterialist Values: Results from the 1981 vs. 1990 World
Values Surveys (Percentage Postmaterialist Minus Percentage Materialist)

	1981	*1990*	*Net Shift*
Finland	21	23	+2
Netherlands	−2	26	+28
Canada	−6	14	+20
Iceland	−10	−14	−4
Sweden	−10	9	+19
W. Germany	−11	14	+25
Britain	−13	0	+13
France	−14	4	+18
Belgium	−16	2	+18
S. Africa	−16	−33	−17
Mexico	−19	−14	+5
Ireland	−20	−4	+16
Argentina	−20	−6	+14
Norway	−21	−19	+2
U.S.*	−24	6	+30
Japan	−32	−19	+13
S. Korea	−34	−34	0
Italy	−39	7	+46
Spain	−41	−6	+35
N. Ireland	−45	−7	+38
Hungary	−50	−41	+9

*The values question was not asked in the U.S. in the 1981 survey; results are from the 1980
NES survey.

Source: 1981 and 1990 World Values surveys.

CONCLUSIONS

The value change thesis predicts a gradual intergenerational shift from Materialist values toward Postmaterialist values. During the years from 1970 to
1994, a statistically significant shift toward Postmaterialist values took place
in all eight Western European countries for which a detailed time series is
available; similar shifts seem to have occurred in the United States, Japan, and
many other countries around the world.

The trend toward Postmaterialism is not automatic. It does not seem to be
taking place in Nigeria or India. Although generational replacement tends to
push Postmaterialism upward throughout advanced industrial society, such
economic factors as inflation and unemployment also affect value change. The
consequences of the breakup of the Soviet Union have been massive, and current conditions there are harrowing. In settings of extreme uncertainty such as
the former Soviet Union, with falling living standards and declining life ex-

pectancy, we would *not* expect to find a movement toward Postmaterialism. On the contrary, our theory implies that current conditions in Russia or Belarus would bring increasing emphasis on Materialist values.

The data we have examined make two points clear: first, the shift from Materialist to Postmaterialist values is not a uniquely Western phenomenon. It is found in societies with widely different institutions and cultural traditions. The rise of Postmaterialist values is closely linked with prosperity and seems to occur wherever a society has experienced enough economic growth in recent decades so that the younger birth cohorts have experienced significantly greater economic security during their formative years than did the older cohorts. In societies that are not yet well launched on industrialization, on the other hand, there are few Postmaterialists and little difference between the values of young and old: intergenerational value differences reflect a society's rate of economic growth. Economic growth, of course, is only one factor that contributes to security or insecurity. Other events such as war, domestic upheaval, and ethnic conflict can also have a major impact, but they tend to be situation-specific (and are less readily quantified), making them more difficult to analyze empirically.

Second, where value change has occurred, intergenerational differences are remarkably robust. In Western Europe, clear and sizable differences between the values of younger and older birth cohorts persisted through the recessions of the mid-1970s and the early 1980s. More remarkably still, in Russia and Eastern Europe sizable intergenerational value differences have persisted through the collapse of the economic and political systems in recent years. These values show predictable period effects in response to current economic conditions. But the Postmaterialist value shift does not simply reflect current conditions. It also has a long-term component that seems to reflect the distinctive formative circumstances that given birth cohorts experienced as much as 40 or 50 years ago.

As we have seen, cultural change has a rational component: it tends to follow the principle of diminishing marginal utility. But the enduring intergenerational differences found here undermine any simplistic version of rational choice theory that would seek to explain behavior as a response to one's immediate situation, unshaped by internal cultural differences. For we find persisting generational differences that seem to reflect the enduring legacy of the distinctive formative experiences of given generations. At any point in time, the respective birth cohorts in a given society are in the same situation as their elders but respond to it in fundamentally different ways because they evaluate it by different values. These different responses to the same situation do not simply reflect that fact that the respective cohorts are of different ages, for their distinctive values continue to characterize given cohorts even after they have aged over many years.

Inglehart (1990) found that orientations concerning a wide variety of domains, from politics to religion, to sexual norms to childrearing values, were correlated with Materialist/Postmaterialist values. Evidence presented in chapters 9 and 10 indicates that this broader cluster of Postmodern values is undergoing an intergenerational value shift, similar to the shift from Materialist toward Postmaterialist values. Thus, the detailed evidence now available about the Postmaterialist shift may help us understand the far broader cultural shift from survival values to Postmodern values.

Economic Development, Political Culture, and Democracy: Bringing the People Back In

A GENERATION AGO, Lipset (1959), Rostow (1961), Dahl (1971), and others argued that economic development leads to democracy. This claim was disputed by dependency school writers, who argued that development was more likely to lead to bureaucratic authoritarianism than to democracy; and more recently, Arat (1988) and Gonick and Rosh (1988) claimed to have disproven Lipset's thesis on the basis of empirical analyses. Nevertheless, the evidence indicates that development is indeed conducive to democracy (Bollen, 1979, 1980, 1993; Bollen and Jackman, 1985; Brunk, Caldeira, and Lewis-Beck, 1987).

Figure 6.1 shows one piece of the evidence. It reveals that as of 1987, out of the 42 countries with per capita incomes under $500 only one (India) was democratic. Among countries with incomes from $500 to $1,000, only four out of 15 were democracies. But among countries with incomes over $6,000, 20 of the 26 were democratic (the exceptions being then East Germany, Czechoslovakia, Kuwait, Saudi Arabia, United Arab Emirates, and Singapore). Although there is no one-to-one relationship between economic development and democratization, rich countries are much likelier to have democratic institutions than are poor countries.

This relationship between democracy and economic development is not merely cross-sectional—it helps predict which countries are most likely to *become* democratic. Thus, during the avalanche of democratization that took place during the four years after 1987, most of the countries that began the transition to democracy were drawn from the upper middle income group, with per capita incomes from $1,000 to $6,000. This includes such countries as Chile, Nicaragua, Turkey, South Korea, and most of Eastern Europe (including both Czechoslovakia and East Germany). By 1992, democracy remained very rare in low-income countries, but a majority of the countries in the upper middle income group had governments that came to power through free elections.

Burkhart and Lewis-Beck (1994) have provided the latest and most conclusive demonstration of the fact that economic development is conducive to democracy, using more reliable time series data and more rigorous methodology than that of Arat (1988) or Gonick and Rosh (1988), and finding (1) that economic development is conducive to democracy, and (2) but democracy is *not* conducive to economic development. On the latter point they confirm Helliwell's (1994) finding that, despite the spectacular success of the authoritarian model of development in East Asia, economic development is about as likely to take place in democratic as in authoritarian regimes.

These are important findings, but they leave a major question unanswered:

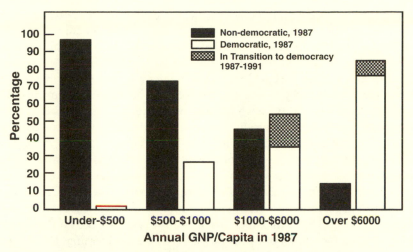

Figure 6.1. Economic development and the transition to democracy. *Source*: GNP per capita from World Bank, *World Development Report, 1989*, pp. 164–65. "Democracies" consist of countries coded as "free" in Raymond D. Gastil (ed.), *Freedom in the World*, 1986–87 (New York: Freedom House, 1987): 30–34. This figure includes only those countries for which data are available for both variables.

Why does economic development lead to democracy? Is the linkage between development and democracy due to wealth per se? Apparently not: if democracy automatically resulted from simply becoming wealthy, then Kuwait and Libya would be model democracies. It is important to bear this point in mind: wealth *alone* does not automatically produce democracy. It seems clear that additional steps are involved. This chapter argues that economic development is conducive to democracy *provided* that it brings certain changes in culture and social structure.

Lerner (1958), Deutsch (1964), and others had argued that modern economic development brings social mobilization, facilitating mass participation in politics, which helps prepare the way for democracy. We believe that they were right, but this is only part of the story. Building on the work of Almond and Verba (1963), Inglehart (1988, 1990), Diamond, Linz, and Lipset (1990), and Putnam (1993), we will demonstrate that economic development is conducive to democracy not only because it mobilizes mass publics, but also because it tends to give rise to supportive cultural orientations. Our analysis utilizes empirical measures of culture from the 1990–93 World Values surveys carried out in 41 societies around the world representing 70 percent of the world's population, to demonstrate that both social structure and political culture play important roles in the emergence and survival of democracy.

The idea that political culture was linked with democracy had great impact following the publication of *The Civic Culture* (Almond and Verba, 1963), but went out of fashion during the 1970s for a variety of reasons. The political culture approach raised an important empirical question: whether given societies had political cultures that were relatively conducive to democracy. Some critics alleged that this approach was "elitist" in finding that some cultures were more conducive to democracy than others: any right-minded theory should hold that all societies are equally likely to be democratic. The problem is that by tailoring one's theory to fit a given ideology, one may come up with a theory that does not fit reality, in which case, one's predictions will eventually go wrong, and the theory will provide misleading guidance to those who are trying to cope with democratization in the real world.

By the 1980s, though the concept of political culture was still unfashionable in American academic circles, observers in other countries, from Latin America to Eastern Europe to East Asia, were coming to the conclusion that cultural factors played an important role in the problems they were encountering with democratization. Thus Mikhail Gorbachev observed, "We are now, as it were, going through the school of democracy afresh. We are learning. Our political culture is still inadequate. Our standard of debate is inadequate; our ability to respect the point of view of even our friends and comrades—even that is inadequate" (Gorbachev, cited in Brzezinski, 1989: 44). Even in Latin America, where the dependency perspective had been extremely influential, cultural factors are now being accorded a key role in democratization. Thus in 1990, a conference of leading politicians and intellectuals from throughout Latin America concluded

> Democracy and sustainable development will depend in large measure on the ability of individual societies to modernize from within. . . . Changes in the practical exercise of power and the reorganization of systems of production give rise to changes not only in political, social and economic institutions, but also in culture and in the behavior of individuals molded by that culture. The other vital dimension of the challenge facing societies in the early stages of democratization is the forging of a democratic political culture. (Declaration of Montevideo, 1990, cited in Albala-Bertrand, 1992: 156–57)

Cultural factors have been omitted from most empirical analyses of democracy—partly because, until now, we have not had reliable measures of them from more than a handful of countries. When cultural factors *are* taken into account, as in Inglehart's (1990) and Putnam's (1993) work, they seem to play an important role.

We will briefly describe which factors are important to democracy and why, and discuss the nature of our dependent variable, democracy, in presenting the theory underlying this analysis. We claim that economic development leads to two types of changes that are conducive to democracy: it gives rise to social structural changes that *mobilize* mass participation; and cultural changes that help *stabilize* democracy.

Structural changes. Industrialization tends to transform a society's social structure, bringing urbanization, mass education, occupational specialization, growing organizational networks, greater income equality, and a variety of associated developments that mobilize mass participation in politics. Two aspects of this "Modernization" syndrome are particularly relevant to democracy:

1. Rising educational levels, which produce a more articulate public that is better equipped to organize and communicate, and

2. Rising occupational specialization, which first shifts the workforce into the secondary sector and then into the tertiary sector. These changes produce a more autonomous workforce, accustomed to thinking for themselves on the job and having specialized skills that enhance their bargaining power against elites.

Cultural changes. Economic development is also conducive to *cultural* changes that help stabilize democracy. We find two particularly central factors:

1. *A culture of trust.* In authoritarian regimes, the usual way to handle opposition is to imprison or execute its leaders. A crucial element in the rise of democracy is the emergence of the norm of the "loyal opposition": instead of being viewed as traitors who are conspiring to overthrow the government, the opposition is trusted to play by the rules of the democratic game. This means that if the opposition wins an election, the governing elite will turn power over to them, trusting that they will not be imprisoned or dispossessed, and that (after a given time) the new elite will hold elections in which they can freely compete for power.

2. *Mass legitimacy.* Legitimacy, or diffuse mass support, can help sustain democratic institutions through difficult times. It is an asset to any regime, but it is crucial to democracies. Democratic institutions can be imposed by elites or even by foreign conquest—but whether they survive depends on whether they take root among the public. With democratization, the public becomes a crucial political factor.

Positive outputs from a political system can generate mass support for the political incumbents. In the short term, this support is based on calculations concerning "What have you done for me lately?" But if a given regime's outputs are seen as positive over a long time, the regime may develop "diffuse support" (Easton, 1963)—the generalized perception that the political system is inherently good, quite apart from its current outputs. This type of support can endure even through difficult times. As we will demonstrate, a sense of subjective well-being among the public of a given society is an excellent indicator of whether or not that regime possesses legitimacy—indeed, it is a *better* indicator than responses to direct questions about how strongly one supports democratic political institutions.

THREE ASPECTS OF DEMOCRACY: STABILITY, LEVEL AT A GIVEN TIME, AND SHORT-TERM SHIFTS

Democracy is a multidimensional phenomenon. But to date, most empirical analyses have focused on a single aspect of democracy as the dependent variable. Thus, Inglehart (1990) analyzed the *stability* of democracy—operationally, the number of years that democratic institutions had functioned continuously in a given society. But this is just one aspect of democracy; many other analyses have focused on *levels* of democracy at a given time. This chapter examines the linkages between economic development, sociocultural change, and three different aspects of democracy:

1. The long-term *stability* of democracy,
2. The *level* of democracy at given points in time, and
3. Short-term *changes* in levels of democracy: for example, the causes of the sudden surge of democracy that followed the collapse of socialist regimes in Eastern Europe and the former Soviet Union in 1989–91.

Careful specification of the aspect of democracy to be examined is crucial, since different causal factors are important with each aspect of democratization. These factors may even reverse their polarity in connection with different aspects of democratization. Thus, though there is strong evidence that prosperity is conducive to democracy, the fall of authoritarian regimes may be precipitated by economic *collapse*. Political culture tends to be most important in consolidating democracy and enabling it to endure through difficult times. Situation-specific factors (such as the death of Franco) are often the immediate cause of the transition to democracy. But once democratic institutions are in place, their long-term survival depends on the presence or absence of supportive orientations among the citizens. The growing importance of mass preferences is inherent in the very nature of democracy. If democratic institutions do not attain enough deep-rooted mass support to weather difficult times, the citizens can simply vote democracy out of existence: they did so in Weimar; they would have done so in Algeria if democracy had not been suspended there; and they may do so in some of the Soviet successor states.

Long-Term Stability of Democracy

Mass political culture's most crucial role concerns the long-term *stability* of democracy: political culture stabilizes democracy by providing an enduring base of mass support.

Democratic institutions can be implanted by a handful of elites or even imposed by foreign conquest, as they were in Germany and Austria at the end of World War I, and in Germany, Japan, and elsewhere at the end of World War II. Democracy can be imposed from above or from outside, but whether or not it survives through good times and bad depends on whether its institutions have built up deep-rooted cultural attachments among the citizens. Various writers have stressed the importance of this factor. Weber emphasized the importance of legitimacy; Easton spoke of "diffuse support"; Almond and Verba discussed the "Civic Culture"; Putnam (1993) showed how "Civic Orientations" contributed to the effectiveness of democracy in Italy; and in an analysis based on data from 24 societies surveyed in the 1981 World Values Survey, Inglehart (1990) demonstrated that interpersonal trust and subjective well-being were closely linked with the long-term survival of democratic institutions.

The appropriateness of analyzing the stability of democracy has been debated. Lipset (1959), Muller (1988), and others measured democracy in ways that included stability along with measures of political rights and civil liberties. This practice was criticized by Jackman (1973), Bollen (1980), and Bollen and Jackman (1985). "The fusion of stability and democracy measures," Bollen and Jackman argue, "makes it impossible to interpret observed associations of 'democratic stability' with other variables, because it is never clear whether degree of stability or degree of democracy is the operative factor at work" (Bollen and Jackman, 1985: 612). For example, in answering the question "Does democracy lead to greater income equality?" this procedure can be confusing—possibly leading one to conclude that *democracy* leads to income equality, when it is actually due to *stability*. Bollen and Jackman's writings make a strong case for not confusing the *stability* of democracy with the *extent* of democracy—which, we emphatically agree, are two distinct things. But they do not constitute a blanket injunction against studying the stability of democratic institutions—which is an important variable in itself.

Our analysis does not confuse these two aspects of democracy: we will carry out analyses in which the dependent variable is the *extent* or level of democracy. But we will also analyze the *stability* of democracy. This analysis does not use democratic stability as a proxy for *degree* of democracy; instead, it is explicitly designed to focus on the factors that enable democratic institutions to survive over time, addressing the question "What factors enable given societies to remain above the threshold at which the top political leaders are chosen by free and competitive elections?"[1]

Levels of democracy at a given point in time and the stability of democracy in given societies are both significant. Whether or not democratic institutions survive through good times and bad depends on whether they have built up deep-rooted cultural attachments among the citizens. Weimar Germany had a constitution that was, on paper, as democratic as that of any society on earth; the *level* was high. But democratic norms did not take root, and these institutions proved unstable. In 1933 the German people turned power over to Adolf Hitler. Similarly, although Bulgaria and Slovenia today are coded by Freedom House as having virtually the same levels of democracy as Britain and Swe-

---

[1] Our measure of the stability of democratic institutions is the number of continuous years from 1920 to 1990 during which top leadership was chosen by free and competitive elections and ranges from 0 to 70. Accordingly, it reflects a wide range of degrees of *stability* (without attempting to simultaneously capture the relative *extent* of democracy across the various societies). Coding it requires that one determine whether top leadership was selected by free and competitive elections. This is a judgment call, which may be uncertain in marginal cases, but in most instances there is almost universal agreement on whether or not given elections were free and competitive. But any system for measuring either the extent *or* the stability of democracy requires human judgments about whether or not given societies fall above given thresholds. Competent coders usually *can* decide whether a given society did, or did not, hold genuinely competitive elections—and probably can do so with even greater reliability than they would attain in judging whether a given society falls at level "3" or level "4" on the Freedom House ratings of political rights or political liberties—which many analysts (ourselves included) use.

den, democratic institutions have functioned much longer in Britain and Sweden than in Bulgaria or Slovenia—a fact that no prudent analyst would ignore in assessing the prospects for survival of democratic institutions in the respective societies. Stability and levels of democracy are two different things, and both are important.

Levels of democracy have risen repeatedly during the nineteenth and twentieth centuries. When modern democracy first emerged in Great Britain and the United States, suffrage was limited to the middle class. In subsequent waves, it was extended to the lower middle class, the working class and to exslaves; in the 1920s, it was extended to women; and in the 1970s, to 18–20-year-olds. In subsequent years, mass political participation has continued to become more active and more issue-specific, as increasingly educated electorates have extended their repertory of techniques designed to influence elite decision making.

Jackman and Miller (1996) claim that this expansion of mass participation makes it impossible to measure democratic stability: one cannot start counting the number of years during which a given society has been "democratic" until it has become completely democratic by today's standards. In fact, this constitutes a problem only if one adheres to a unidimensional concept of democracy. Dahl (1971) distinguishes between two key aspects of democracy, contestation and inclusion; and he argues that democracy is more likely to survive over time if contestation *precedes* broad mass inclusion. Thus, in British history, elite contestation began with the Magna Charta, which forced the king to share power with the nobility, and which constitutional authorities accord an important role in introducing pluralist norms into the British political culture. Mass democracy began to emerge in the nineteenth century, and democratic norms had become widespread and generally accepted long before the latest major extension of the franchise, to 18-year-olds in the 1970s. It would be absurd to claim that British democracy began only in the 1970s (or even in the 1920s, when women obtained suffrage). These were indeed important stages in the extension of mass inclusion, but genuine contestation (in the form of freely contested elections) existed well before that time. To insist that democracy does not exist until the process of mass inclusion has been completed would be to define democracy as an empty cell: the process is probably not yet complete even now, because levels of democratic participation will almost certainly continue to rise.

Shifts to (and from) Democracy

In contrast with its role in sustaining democracy over the long run, political culture has a very different relationship to short-term changes to and from democracy. Indeed, the same cultural factors that stabilize and sustain democracy can also help stabilize authoritarian regimes. Thus, though high levels of legitimacy and trust are crucial to the survival of democracy, they would not explain short-term shifts toward democracy. Instead, one would expect *low* levels of legitimacy and trust to be linked with the collapse of authoritarian regimes, possibly opening the way for a transition to democracy. Thus, the short-term consequences of cultural factors are very different from their long-term functions. Gradual cultural changes can give rise to conditions that become increasingly favorable to the rise of democratic institutions, but the immediate precipitating factor is likely to be some macroevent such as defeat in war or an intergenerational transfer of power from hard-line leaders to reformist leaders. Accordingly, the literature on transitions to democracy tends to focus on elite-level events rather than on underlying changes in culture or social structure (e.g., O'Donnell, Schmitter, and Whitehead, 1986).

Levels of Democracy at a Given Time Point

Most empirical analyses of the factors conducive to democracy have used the level of democracy at a given point in time as the dependent variable. Although the most crucial function of cultural factors is their role in sustaining democratic institutions over time, they are also linked with the level of democracy found at given points in time. But clearly, the strength of this relationship will vary from one time point to another.

In 1790, there were three democracies in the world. In 1900, there were about a dozen. In 1919, there were about two dozen, and by 1991 there were more than 60. After each wave of democratization, many of the new democracies failed to survive. Thus, the number of democracies declined sharply during the period between the two World Wars, and again in the 1960s and 1970s; and some of today's new democracies will probably not survive.

Each major wave of democratization weakens the correlation between cultural factors and democracy, because a massive surge of democratization tends to bring into the "democratic" category a large new group of societies that rank lower on prodemocratic culture than the long-established democracies: the latter are societies in which democracy has survived for a long time partly *because* they have high levels of these cultural characteristics. If, by some happy stroke, every nation in the world were suddenly to adopt democratic constitutions, the correlation between culture and democracy would automatically drop to zero—but this would probably be a temporary situation. Unless the new democracies developed such cultural attributes as interpersonal trust and legitimacy, their democratic institutions would be unlikely to survive major economic or political crises; and the processes of cultural change and attrition would eventually bring back a correlation between civic culture and democracy. Thus (as we will demonstrate) the strength of the relationship between polit-ical culture and democracy differs sharply before and immediately after a major wave of democratization. This means that when one uses *levels* of democracy as a dependent variable, the time point one chooses is crucial.

The number of democracies in the world has been increasing and, in the long run, we think the trend will continue. It will do so because economic development tends to bring changes in social structure and culture that are favorable to democracy. Let us examine these processes in more detail.

CHANGES IN SOCIAL STRUCTURE: COGNITIVE MOBILIZATION
AND THE RISE OF CITIZEN INTERVENTION

The literature on social mobilization has chronicled how industrialization and urbanization led to mass literacy, the rise of organized labor, mass political parties, and the emergence of universal suffrage (Lerner, 1958; Deutsch, 1964; Inkeles and Smith, 1974). These were profoundly important developments that brought previously parochial masses into political relevance. These processes increased mass political participation, but they did not necessarily bring about democracy. Instead, depending on the social and economic context of the given society, they could either give rise to mass democracy, or to fascism or communism. All three forms of government emphasized mass participation; indeed, both fascism and communism regularly attained higher levels of mass attendance at political rallies and higher voting turnout than liberal democracies ever did. But with fascism and communism, it was almost entirely elite-led participation, designed to mobilize mass support for policies already chosen by the elites—and not participation through which the masses chose between competing elites and alternative elite policies.

Democratic theory emphasizes two central elements: elite competition and mass participation. In the first half of the twentieth century, democracy (unlike fascism and communism) was based on genuine elite competition; but mass participation was still largely orchestrated by elites even in the democracies. Democracy continues to evolve. In advanced industrial society, the process of cognitive mobilization gives rise to more active and more demanding types of mass participation. This makes it increasingly difficult for democracies to limit mass publics to an elite-directed role, and increasingly difficult for authoritarian systems to *survive*: they face rising mass pressures for liberalization.

The coming of advanced industrial society leads to a syndrome of intergenerational changes that bring significant further increases in citizen intervention in politics. A long-term rise in educational levels and in mass political skills has characterized all industrial societies. An extension of social mobilization beyond the transformations brought by urbanization and early industrialization, this process has been termed "cognitive mobilization" (Inglehart, 1977). While social mobilization manifested itself in visible changes of location and occupation, cognitive mobilization is based on invisible changes that upgrade individual skills. These changes have momentous political consequences.

Cognitive Mobilization reflects rising levels of education and changes in the nature of work, from simple routine operations to tasks requiring specialized knowledge and autonomous judgment. The publics of advanced industrial societies become accustomed to thinking for themselves in their everyday jobs; at the same time, they become more articulate and skilled at organizing people. The skills they learn through higher education and in their work life make them increasingly skillful political participants.

Democracies existed before the industrial era. But in polities that are too large for face-to-face interaction, political participation was limited to a minority of the population. Ancient Athens was a democracy by the standards of its time, but one that excluded a large slave population, a large foreign population, and all women. Even as recently as the eighteenth century, democracy in the United States was limited to a minority of the population which excluded Blacks, women, and, in some states, those who fell below certain property-ownership thresholds. By contemporary standards, neither classical Athens nor the early United States would qualify as democracies. Mass mobilization is a prerequisite for the contemporary version of democracy.

Mass political participation develops in two major stages, one based on an older mode of elite-led political participation, and the other on a newer mode linked with cognitive mobilization. The institutions that mobilized mass political participation in the late nineteenth and early twentieth century—labor union, church, and mass political party—were hierarchical organizations in which a small number of leaders or bosses led masses of disciplined troops. These institutions were effective in bringing large numbers of newly enfranchised citizens to the polls in an era when universal compulsory education had just taken root and the average citizen had a low level of political skills. But while these elite-directed organizations could mobilize large numbers, they produced only a relatively low *level* of participation, rarely going beyond mere voting.

By itself, voting is not necessarily an effective way for citizens to exert their control over national decisions. It can be, and sometimes is, manipulated by elites. The extreme example is the communist people's democracies which regularly attained far higher levels of electoral participation than any liberal democracy—but did so in an institutional framework that kept real decision making entirely in the hands of the elites. Voting can be an effective step toward empowering the citizens, but it is not a very discriminating one. In one-party states, it is nothing more than a way for the ruling elite to elicit mass endorsement. And even when competing parties are present, it may only mean that the citizens get to choose one set of elites or another, and then let them make the actual decisions for the next several years.

A newer elite-challenging mode of participation is emerging that expresses the individual's preferences with far greater precision than the old. It is issue-oriented and based on ad hoc groups rather than on established bureaucratic organizations. It seeks specific policy changes, rather than simply giving a blank check to the elites of a given party. This mode of participation requires relatively high skill levels.

The most readily available indicator of political skills is one's level of formal education. In part, participation levels reflect skill levels, and sheer literacy seems sufficient to produce voting. The citizens of most Western democracies reached this threshold generations ago. But while mere literacy may be sufficient to produce high rates of voting, taking the initiative to seek specific policy changes at the national level seems to require higher education. This is particularly true of the more elite-challenging types of political behavior: as Barnes et al. (1979) demonstrate, high educational levels are closely associated with participation in elite-challenging forms of political action. But the

Barnes et al. study goes a step farther and develops measures of political skills; they prove to be an even stronger predictor of unconventional political behavior than is education—and far stronger than social class.

Educational statistics give a good indication of the progress of cognitive mobilization over time, since governments have kept records of the numbers of students enrolled at various levels for many decades. These statistics tell a dramatic story. Early industrial society introduced universal primary education, bringing widespread literacy, and as industrial societies have developed knowledge-based economies, enrollment in higher education has increased enormously.

As a result of the explosive expansion of higher education during the past 50 years, younger cohorts have much higher educational levels than older ones, throughout advanced industrial society. In the United States, for example, only about a third of the cohort born during the decade before 1925 received any secondary or higher education. Among the cohort born from 1966 to 1972, over 90 percent have done so. In Russia, the rise is even steeper, moving from about 10 percent among the oldest cohort, to almost 90 percent among the youngest.

Because its educational attainment is a relatively stable attribute of a given birth cohort, intergenerational population replacement has foreseeable consequences. One can project the educational level of a given population 10 or 20 years into the future with considerable accuracy. And the consequences are significant.

The rise of postindustrial society or information society (Bell, 1973, 1976) leads to a growing potential for citizen participation in politics. Increasingly, not only one's formal education but also one's job experience helps develop politically relevant skills. The assembly-line worker produced material objects, working in a hierarchical system that required (and allowed) very little autonomous judgment. Workers in the service and information sectors deal with people and concepts; operating in an environment where innovation is crucial, they need autonomy for the use of individual judgment. It becomes inherently ineffective to attempt to prescribe innovation from above, in hierarchical fashion. Accustomed to working in less hierarchical decision-structures in their job life, people in the tertiary, or information and service, sectors are relatively likely to have both the skills and the inclination to take part in decision-making in the political realm as well.

Inglehart (1990) presents evidence of a long-term rise in mass skills in coping with politics that is transforming the mass basis of politics in Western industrial societies. Throughout advanced industrial society, publics are becoming more apt to *want* democratic institutions, and more adept at applying pressures to *get* them. These changes in mass skills and values are not the only factors that matter. A determined elite can repress public demands for democratization for a long time. But as an industrial society matures, the costs of repression rise: it stultifies initiative, bringing a demoralized, inefficient economy, and a technology that falls behind world standards.

The new mode of political participation is far more issue-specific than voting is, and more likely to function at the higher thresholds of participation. It is new in the sense that only recently has a large percentage of the population possessed the skills required for this form of participation. And it is new in that it makes the public less dependent on permanent, oligarchic organizations.

Thus, as cognitive mobilization proceeds, the established organizations become progressively less effective. Possessing a wide range of alternative channels of information and input, people rely less and less on permanent organizational networks such as labor unions, churches, and urban political machines. Both union membership rates and church attendance have been falling in most Western countries, and traditional political party ties have also been weakening. This tends to depress voter turnout, which is heavily dependent on elite-directed mobilization, and may require little or no cognitive response to current issues. High rates of voter turnout are a good thing, to be sure. But we should bear in mind that the one-party communist regimes regularly reported voting rates of 98 or 99 percent. Electoral turnout is desirable, but it is *not* a reliable indicator of citizen input. Although electoral turnout has stagnated, elite-directing types of participation, aimed at influencing specific policy decisions, are becoming more widespread.

The Iron Law of Oligarchy is being weakened. Advanced industrial society brings an increasingly educated and occupationally specialized public. As the workforce shifts from doing routine tasks, toward becoming specialists, doing tasks that require individual judgment and autonomy, they become less amenable to centralized hierarchical control.

CULTURAL CHANGES CONDUCIVE TO DEMOCRACY

The spread of democracy reflects not only changes in social structure, but also cultural changes. The study of political culture grew out of the tragic events that led up to World War II. In the aftermath of World War I, democratic regimes were set up in Germany, Italy, Poland, Spain, and many other formerly authoritarian societies. On paper, some of them looked like ideal democracies. But when they encountered the severe economic difficulties of the 1920s and 1930s, democracy failed to survive in many cases. Why did this happen? Great Britain, the United States, and the Nordic countries also experienced severe economic distress during the Great Depression, but democracy survived there; in contrast, democracy gave way to fascist regimes in Germany, Italy, Japan, Spain, Hungary, and elsewhere, preparing the way for the greatest bloodbath the world had ever known.

The classic Civic Culture study (Almond and Verba, 1963) addressed the question "Why did democratic institutions survive in some countries but not in others?" Manifestly, it was not just a question of constitutional engineering. The laws and constitution of the Weimar Republic were as democratic as those of any nation in the world—but they did not take root. An authoritarian outlook remained widespread throughout German society, and when distress and insecurity became severe, the Germans voted Hitler into power in free elections. Facing comparable problems, the British, Americans, and various other peoples were relatively steadfast in their support for democracy. Democracy, apparently, is not just a matter of elite-level arrangements; the basic cultural orientations of the citizens also play a crucial role in its survival. Almond and Verba set out to measure the relevant orientations empirically, to determine whether there really were underlying differences in the political cultures of stable democracies, as compared with those of unstable democracies.

Ideally, to explain the role of cultural factors in the survival of democracy, Almond and Verba would have used data on cultural conditions from the period *before* the rise of fascism: a cause must precede its effect. But survey research techniques had not yet been developed in that period, and they would have needed a time machine in order to go back and collect such data. However, culture is by definition a relatively stable aspect of a society. If so, one would expect to find significant elements of the cultural differences that contributed to the survival of democracy in Britain and the United States, and to its failure in Germany and Italy, that were still visible in the orientations of the respective mass publics in 1959, when their fieldwork was carried out. Almond and Verba set out to determine whether such differences existed.

Democratic institutions had recently been transplanted to Germany, Italy, and Japan. Would they take root this time, or would they fail again?

This basic question is of far more than academic interest again today, when democratic institutions have recently been installed in scores of formerly authoritarian societies, from Argentina to Russia—and where their fate remains uncertain. Authoritarian forces seem to be making a comeback in a number of the Soviet successor states; and a protofascist party won more votes than any other party in the 1993 Russian parliamentary elections, which gives rise to the chilling question: Will Russia's fate be like that of the Weimar Republic?

THE IMPORTANCE OF SOCIETAL TRUST

Partly, the answer depends on the development of a culture of trust. Interpersonal trust plays a crucial role in democracy. Democratic institutions depend on trust that the opposition will accept the rules of the democratic process. One must view one's political opponents as a *loyal* opposition who will not imprison or execute you if you surrender political power to them, but can be relied on to govern within the laws, and to surrender power if your side wins the next election.

Banfield (1958) found that Southern Italian society had much lower levels of trust than Northern Italy; this severely hindered the large-scale cooperation between strangers that is essential to both economic development and successful democratic institutions. Almond and Verba (1963) also argued that a sense of interpersonal trust is a prerequisite for effective democracy. They found that the publics of Italy and West Germany were characterized by lower levels of interpersonal trust, readiness to participate, and other attitudes conducive to democracy than were the British and American publics. The relative weakness of the "Civic Culture" in Germany and Italy presumably contributed to the failure of democracy in those societies in the period before World War II.

Testing these ideas in a broader cross-national context, Inglehart (1990) found that interpersonal trust and related cultural orientations were strongly linked with both economic development and with stable democracy. He emphasized, however, that culture is a variable, not a constant: though cultural characteristics tend to change slowly, they can and do change. Thus, while Southern Italians were still markedly less trusting than Northern Italians in 1990, and the Italian public still had lower levels of interpersonal trust than the British or Americans, levels of trust had gradually risen in Italy. Starting from an almost incredibly low level in the 1959 Almond and Verba survey, only 8 percent of the Italian public had agreed that "most people can be trusted"; but this figure rose to 27 percent in 1981 and to 30 percent in 1986. Even in 1990 Italy ranked lower than the United States or Britain, but it showed a gradual upward trend.

As the classic literature on political culture implied (but could not demonstrate directly), trust is linked with the survival of democratic institutions. The 1990 World Values data reveal a strong positive correlation between interpersonal trust and the functioning of democratic institutions throughout the world, as figure 6.2 demonstrates. The vertical axis reflects the number of years during which democratic institutions have functioned continuously in a given country. This measure ranges from long-established stable democracies to authoritarian states and societies in which democratic institutions have just been established—and may or may not survive.

The overall pattern in figure 6.2 confirms theoretical expectations that have never before been tested against a global database. Levels of interpersonal trust among mass publics are closely linked with the number of years for which democratic institutions have functioned continuously in those societies, showing a highly significant .72 correlation globally. In most stable democracies, at least 35 percent of the public express the opinion that "most people can be trusted"; in almost all of the nondemocratic societies, or those that have only recently started to democratize, interpersonal trust is below this level.[2]

It seems likely that democratic institutions are conducive to interpersonal

---

[2] Because the 1990 World Values Survey finds a surprisingly high level of interpersonal trust among the Chinese public (higher than in any other nondemocratic society), we checked these results against another national survey carried out in China, using the same question. An October 1993 survey of urban China carried out for Ichiro Miyake and Kazufumi Manabe by the Institute for Public Opinion Research of the People's University of China, with an N of 1,920, also shows higher levels of interpersonal trust in China than in any other nondemocratic or newly democratic society (for further details, see Manabe, 1995). The level of interpersonal trust shown for China in figure 6.2 reflects the combined results from the 1990 World Values Survey and the 1993 survey by Manabe and Miyake.

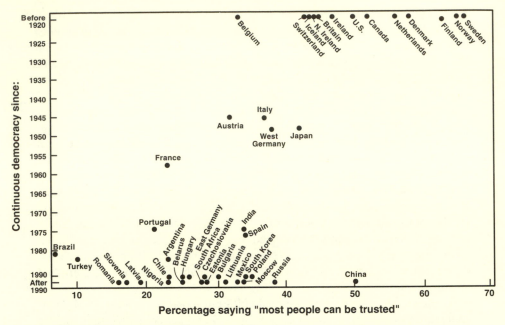

Figure 6.2. Stable democracy and interpersonal trust.
r = .72, N = 43, significant at .0000 level. Number of years for which democratic institutions have functioned continuously in given country, by percentage saying that "most people can be trusted." *Source*: 1990–93 World Values Survey.

trust, as well as trust being conducive to democracy. We do not have the long time series database that would be needed to sort out the causal linkages between culture and institutions. But there is no reason to simply assume that institutions determine culture, rather than the other way around. As Putnam (1993) has demonstrated in the Italian case, cultural patterns already present in the nineteenth century seem to have helped shape the economic and political developments of given regions in the twentieth century. We suspect that culture and social structure tend to have a mutually supportive relationship in any stable social system. The available evidence cannot determine the causal direction, but it does indicate that culture and political institutions have a strong tendency to go together—with trust and stable democracy being closely linked, as the political culture literature has long claimed.

STABLE DEMOCRACY AND LEGITIMACY

In recent years, formerly authoritarian regimes from East Asia to Central Europe and the former Soviet Union have held their first free elections. But it is one thing to adopt formal democracy and another to attain stable democracy.

Immediately after World War I, a number of new democracies were established, many of which did not survive the stresses of the interwar era. The most tragic and fateful case was that of Germany. Democratic institutions were seen by many Germans as a foreign element that had been forced on them by defeat in World War I. Authoritarian elites still held influential positions, and the underlying mass political culture was not congruent with democratic institutions (Eckstein, 1961, 1988). Democracy failed to develop the deep-rooted allegiance among the mass public that might have enabled it to weather difficult times. Formal democracy can be established by elites—but once politics is decided by free elections, the orientations of the masses become crucial. In Weimar Germany, Hitler became chancellor through free elections.

The Weimar Republic collapsed in the face of economic difficulties because it lacked legitimacy and because an authoritarian political culture persisted. But culture is a variable, not a constant. It can change gradually, as the history of Germany after World War II demonstrates. Democracy slowly established roots among the West German people after 1945 (Boynton and Lowenberg, 1973; Baker, Dalton and Hildebrandt, 1981). By the 1980s, West Germany had become a stable democracy.

Weimar Germany never had a chance to develop this kind of legitimacy. Associated with defeat from its start, it soon faced the hyperinflation of the 1920s; it was unable to maintain internal order; and it finally collapsed under the impact of the Great Depression in the 1930s. Several decades later, the Bonn regime did develop legitimacy, but it did so gradually. Throughout the first decade of its existence, a large proportion of the German public continued to agree with the statement that "the Nazi regime was a good idea, badly carried out." As recently as 1956, a plurality of the West German public still rated Hitler as one of Germany's greatest statesmen; 1967 was the first year in which an absolute majority of respondents rejected that claim (Conradt, 1993: 51–52).

Democratic institutions gradually won acceptance. At first this acceptance was based on the postwar economic miracle; by the late 1950s, the Bonn republic had achieved remarkable economic success. The 1959 *Civic Culture* survey showed that while many British and American citizens expressed pride in their political institutions, few Germans did. But the West Germans *did* take pride in their economic success (Almond and Verba, 1963). Mass support for the democratic regime in Bonn continued to grow with continued economic achievement, though economic success was not the only reason for its growing legitimacy. The institutions of the Federal Republic (unlike those of Weimar) maintained domestic order and provided for a peaceful transfer of political power from a hegemonic party to the opposition in the 1960s. By the late 1970s, the West German public was *more* apt to express satisfaction with the way their political system was functioning than were most other Western European peoples, including the British. Democracy had finally developed roots in West German society.

SUBJECTIVE WELL-BEING AND LEGITIMACY

Political economy research deals with similar processes leading to the development of mass support, but it normally has a short-term focus. If the economic cycle has been going well, support for the incumbents increases; if the economy has done poorly, support for the incumbents declines. In the short run, the response is to "throw the rascals out" (Kramer, 1971; Lewis-Beck, 1986; Markus, 1988). Support for a democratic regime has similar dynamics but is based on deeper long-term processes. Recent economic success may enhance support for the individuals in office. But if, in the long run, people feel that *life* has been good under a given regime, it enhances feelings of diffuse support for that regime. Thus, feelings of overall subjective well-being play a key role in the growth of legitimacy. Legitimacy is, of course, helpful to any regime, but authoritarian systems can survive through coercion; democratic regimes *must* be legitimate in the eyes of their citizens, or, like the Weimar Republic, they are likely to collapse.

In preindustrial society, chronic poverty was taken for granted as a normal part of life. But in industrial society, mass publics have come to expect their governments to provide for their well-being. Thus, in industrial society, reasonably high levels of subjective well-being have become a necessary though not sufficient condition for stable democracy: societies with high levels of subjective well-being *can* function as democracies, though they do not necessarily become democratic unless they also have high levels of trust and other preconditions; societies with low levels of subjective well-being are likely to have coercive governments or to collapse in the face of mass demands for radical change.

Satisfaction with one's life as a whole is one of the best available indicators of subjective well-being, and it has been surveyed regularly in the Euro-Barometer studies. A society's prevailing level of subjective well-being is a reasonably stable cultural attribute—and one that has important political consequences. If a society has a high level of subjective well-being, its citizens feel that their entire way of life is fundamentally good. Their political institutions gain legitimacy by association.

Surprising as it may seem at first glance, satisfaction with one's *life as a whole* is far more conducive to political legitimacy than is a favorable opinion of the political system itself. Mass satisfaction with the way the *political system* is currently functioning has only a modest linkage with stable democracy; but satisfaction with one's life as a *whole* is a strong predictor of stable democracy (Inglehart, 1990). On reflection, it makes sense that satisfaction with one's life as a whole is a stronger predictor of stable democracy than is satisfaction with the political system. For politics is a peripheral aspect of most people's lives; and satisfaction with this specific domain can rise or fall over night. But if one feels that one's life as a *whole* has been going well under democratic institutions, it gives rise to a relatively deep, diffuse, and enduring basis of support for those institutions. Such a regime has built up a capital of mass support that can help the regime weather bad times. Precisely because overall life satisfaction is deeply rooted and diffuse, it provides a more stable basis of sup-

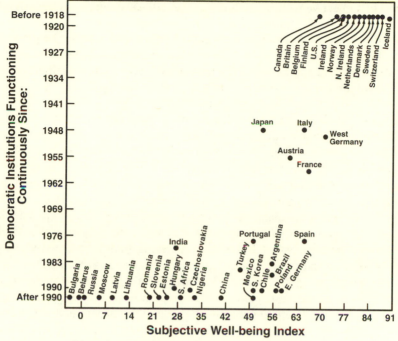

Figure 6.3. Stable democracy and subjective well-being.
r = .82, N = 42, significant at .0000 level. Number of years for which democratic institutions have functioned continuously in given country, by percentage ranking "high" on subjective well-being index. *Source*: 1990–93 World Values Survey.

port for a given regime than does political satisfaction. The latter is a narrower orientation that taps support for specific incumbents at least as much as support for the regime. Accordingly, political satisfaction may fluctuate rapidly over time, with adherents of the Left expressing higher levels when their party is in office, and supporters of the Right showing higher levels when their party is in power—but overall life satisfaction is relatively stable. Political satisfaction mainly taps support for the current incumbents; life satisfaction taps support for the type of political system, or regime.

Figure 6.3 shows levels of subjective well-being in more than 40 societies, based on combined responses to questions about life satisfaction and personal happiness. It examines a broader range of societies than ever before, including a number of authoritarian societies and new democracies. As this figure shows, societies characterized by a relatively strong sense of subjective well-being are far likelier to be stable democracies than societies characterized by a low sense of well-being, confirming earlier findings (Inglehart, 1990). The correlation (r = .82) is remarkably strong. Our interpretation is that, because a sense of subjective well-being is diffuse and deep-rooted, it provides a relatively stable basis of support for a given type of regime.

When people are dissatisfied with politics, they may change the parties in office. When the people of a given society become dissatisfied with their *lives*, they may reject the regime—or even the political community, as in the case of the Soviet Union and Yugoslavia. Only rarely does mass dissatisfaction reach this level.

Research on subjective well-being in many countries has virtually always found that far more people describe themselves as "happy" than as "unhappy" and far more people describe themselves as satisfied with their lives as a whole than as dissatisfied (see, for example, Andrews, 1986). The data from the 1990 World Values Survey reveal the lowest levels of subjective well-being ever recorded in research on this subject. In the surveys carried out in Russia, Belarus, and Bulgaria, as many people described themselves as "unhappy" as "happy"; and as many said they were "dissatisfied with their lives as a whole" as said they were "satisfied." This is an alarming finding. Normally, people tend to describe themselves as at least fairly satisfied with their lives as a whole, even in very poor societies. But in 1990, these three societies ranked far below even the poorest countries such as India, Nigeria, or China. Subjective well-being had fallen to unheard-of levels. It seems significant that in all three societies, the system of government collapsed during the year following these surveys—and in the Soviet case, the political community itself also collapsed, breaking up into successor states.

POSTMATERIALIST VALUES, PEOPLE POWER, AND DEMOCRACY:
THE INTERACTION BETWEEN MASS PUBLICS AND ELITES

Democratization is not something that automatically occurs when a society's people attain given skill levels and a given threshold of value change. The process can be blocked or triggered by societal events. For Eastern Europe, Gorbachev's accession to power was important: he made it clear that the Red Army would no longer intervene to stop liberalization in these countries. This, together with economic failure, was a triggering event that explains why liberalization suddenly took place throughout the region in 1989–91, rather than a decade earlier or later. But this catalyst would not have worked if underlying societal preconditions had not developed. These preconditions were not present earlier: with the possible exception of Czechoslovakia (the most developed society), none of the Eastern European countries were stable democracies before World War II.

Ironically, an unintended consequence of the relative security and rising educational levels provided by four decades of communist rule was to make Eastern European publics less willing to accept authoritarian rule and increasingly adept at resisting it. Such cultural changes can be repressed by domestic elites or by external military force. But by the late 1980s, such countries as Poland, Czechoslovakia, Hungary, and East Germany were ripe for democratization.

Once it became clear that the threat of Soviet military intervention was no longer present, mass pressures for democracy surfaced almost overnight.

These forces interact with the elites in control of a given society. The generational transition that brought Gorbachev to power could, conceivably, have brought some other less flexible leader to the top. This might have delayed the process of reform for some years, but it would not have held back the clock forever.

The impact of changing values on mass potential for unconventional political action is not limited to Western societies. East Asian societies show the same phenomenon; indeed, rising mass participation began to manifest itself in South Korea *before* the recent surge of democratization in Eastern Europe. In 1987 an unprecedented wave of demonstrations swept South Korea, demanding direct election of the president. The government yielded, and the ensuing elections in December 1987 were the fairest in South Korean history, with the opposition actually winning a clear majority of the vote. Only the fact that the two main opposition candidates split their vote almost evenly enabled the governing party's candidate to win. In the early 1990s, Taiwan, facing similar pressures from an increasingly educated and articulate populace, also adopted freely contested elections.

China went through a somewhat similar crisis in 1989, but it ended with bloody repression of the dissidents. This illustrates an important point: democratization is never automatic. It reflects the interaction of underlying social changes and specific historical events and leaders. A resolute authoritarian elite can respond to demands for reform by slaughtering the citizens involved. But in choosing this course, one pays a price: the loss of legitimacy and citizen cooperation. In part, the Chinese leadership's choice of this option was feasible because China was still at a considerably less advanced level of development than the other nations we have discussed. Its per capita income was only a fraction of that in South Korea, Taiwan, or most of Eastern Europe. China's prodemocracy movement, in 1989, was mainly based on the younger and better educated strata in the urban centers. Its repression brought little repercussion among China's vast rural masses, which still comprise the great majority of the population.

Subjective well-being levels seem to have been falling throughout the socialist world during the 1980s. The most reliable evidence comes from Hungary, the only ex-socialist nation in which the World Values survey was carried out in 1981 as well as 1990. Both happiness and life satisfaction fell by about 20 points from 1981 to 1990: in the former year, Hungary ranked at about where Turkey and Mexico are on figure 6.3; but by 1990, it had fallen to the level of India. A local survey was also carried out in one region (Tambov oblast) of the Russian republic in 1981, using the World Values survey questionnaire. Comparing these results with those from the 1990 survey of Russia indicates that subjective well-being fell even more markedly in Russia than in Hungary.

A large decline in the subjective well-being of a given public is unusual and may portend major changes in the society. The decline in subjective well-being in Hungary and Russia probably was linked with the deepening economic and political crises of the socialist world in the 1980s. In the Soviet case, it is clear that the decline of subjective well-being was not simply a mass reaction to elite-level events, for our findings of unprecedentedly low subjective well-being among the Russian people were registered *before* the economic and political system broke down in August 1991. The decline of subjective well-being among mass publics *preceded* the collapse of communism and the breakup of the Soviet Union.

We suspect that under the Weimar Republic, the German public also manifested low levels of subjective well-being. It is too soon to say whether the former Soviet Union will follow the path of Weimar or that of Bonn. The Russian economy is beginning to recover. But it is clear that in 1990–91 diffuse support was at alarmingly low levels; it would be rash to assume that democracy is safely installed in the former Soviet Union.

Although dependency theory itself has largely been abandoned, the heritage of its efforts to discredit political culture still lingers. Recent interpretations of democratization tend to focus on elite bargaining or on economic factors outside the individual, de-emphasizing the role of mass publics. This is one-sided. It is also ironic, because democracy is, by definition, a system in which mass preferences determine what happens. Mass political culture is certainly not the only factor; but, we argue, it plays a crucial role—particularly in consolidating democracy and enabling it to survive over the long term. It is time to reevaluate the role of political culture. We are in a better position to do so than ever before, because we now have a database that makes it possible to examine the linkages between mass belief systems and political institutions in global perspective.

EMPIRICAL ANALYSES: THREE ASPECTS OF DEMOCRACY

Let us summarize our key theoretical points. Our central claim is that economic development is linked with democracy because it tends to bring social and cultural changes that help democracy emerge and flourish. The assertion that *cultural* factors play an important role in sustaining democracy is the most controversial part of this claim, but we believe that social change is also important. These two types of change play quite different roles in relation to different aspects of democracy. Economic development may encourage democracy, but democracy does not emerge automatically. It emerges and flourishes insofar as economic growth produces the social and cultural changes we have just discussed. These factors impact differently on three different aspects of democracy: (1) the amount of *change* toward democracy in a given period, (2) the *level* (or extent) of democracy, and (3) the *persistence* of democracy over time.

Table 6.1 examines the impact of cultural factors on each of these three aspects of democracy, using multiple regression analysis. We have already seen (in figures 6.1 and 6.2) that well-being and trust are closely linked with the stability of democratic institutions. Table 6.1 demonstrates that (controlling for each other's effects) they both have powerful linkages with stable democracy,

TABLE 6.1
Cultural Values and Democracy: Multiple Regression Model

Independent Variable	Stability of Democracy 1920–95	Level of Democracy 1990	Level of Democracy 1995	Change in Level 1990–95
Culture				
Well-being	0.74**	0.14**	0.05**	−0.09**
	(6.34)	(7.77)	(2.95)	(−4.08)
Trust	82.91**	−1.17	−0.07	1.10
	(4.00)	(−0.35)	(−0.02)	(0.28)
Intercept	−37.13	3.09	8.82	5.73
Adjusted R²	.76	.66	.20	.33
Number of Cases	41	43	43	43

Notes: Entry is unstandardized OLS coefficient. Coefficient divided by standard error is in parentheses.
  *Variables significant at .05 level
  **Variables significant at .01 level

giving preliminary support to Inglehart's (1990) findings from the narrower range of countries in the 1981 World Values Survey, that trust and well-being are conducive to stable democracy. But well-being and trust have quite different relationships with each of our three dependent variables. They explain a very large proportion (76 percent) of the variance in stability of democracy, and a large proportion (66 percent) of the variance in levels of democracy in 1990; but their linkage with levels of democracy in 1995 is much weaker (explaining only 20 percent of the variance). The relatively weak linkage between culture and levels of democracy in 1995 reflects the fact that a major historical change took place from 1989 to 1995: an avalanche of new democracies emerged, partly through the collapse of communism in the former Soviet Union and Eastern Europe, but also through a major wave of democratization in other societies from South Korea to South Africa. Among the 41 independent polities in the 1990–93 World Values Survey, more than *one-third* began a transition to democracy during this period.

Virtually all of these new democracies had much lower levels of well-being and trust than the already established democracies, which greatly weakened the relationship between political culture and democratic institutions in 1995. But whether or not democratic institutions survive in these new democracies will depend, in large part, on the extent to which their publics develop a sense of well-being and interpersonal trust.

The change in the relationship between these cultural variables and *changes* in level of democracy from 1990 to 1995 is even more dramatic. Subjective well-being shows a strong *negative* linkage with this variable: the societies that were most likely to shift toward democracy were those in which the public

TABLE 6.2
Social Structure and Democracy: Multiple Regression Model

Independent Variable	Stability of Democracy 1920–95	Level of Democracy 1990	Level of Democracy 1995	Change in Level 1990–95
Social Structure				
Percent Service Sector	1.50** (3.54)	0.33** (6.51)	0.12** (2.96)	−0.21** (−3.24)
Percent Higher Education	0.82** (2.95)	0.03 (1.02)	0.08** (2.85)	0.04 (0.97)
Intercept	−62.50	−6.84	3.86	10.70
Adjusted R^2	.55	.65	.48	.19
Number of Cases	41	42	42	42

Notes: Entry is unstandardized OLS coefficient. Coefficient divided by standard error is in parentheses.
  *Variables significant at .05 level
  **Variables significant at .01 level

showed the *lowest* levels of subjective well-being. Thus subjective well-being shows strong relationships with all four dependent variables, but reverses its role in connection with short-term changes. While *high* levels of well-being are linked with stable democracy and high levels of democracy, *low* levels of well-being are linked with short-term shifts away from authoritarian institutions. This finding supports our interpretation that subjective well-being is crucial to the legitimacy of political institutions: when it is absent, neither democratic nor authoritarian institutions are likely to endure.

Table 6.2 shows the linkages between democracy and our two indicators of cognitive mobilization, occupational structure, and educational level. As hypothesized, both variables have strong positive linkages with the stability of democratic institutions: societies with a large service sector and societies in which a relatively large proportion of the given age cohort receives "tertiary" education (as defined by the World Bank) are much likelier to be stable democracies than are other societies. Both variables are also linked with levels of democracy in both 1990 and 1995 (though the linkage with education falls below significance in the former year). But these two variables explain relatively little of the variance in the *changes* that took place from 1990 to 1995—and here again, we find a reversal of polarity: the proportion of the economy in the service sector shows a rather strong but negative relationship with change.

Let us now undertake a more comprehensive analysis of how culture and social structure relate to economic development, and to each of the three aspects of democracy. Table 6.3 shows the results of OLS regression analyses measuring the impact of culture, social structure, and economic development on democratic stability. Model 3.1 includes all three types of independent variables,

TABLE 6.3
Stability of Democracy: Multiple Regression Model

Independent Variable	Model 3.1	Model 3.2	Model 3.3	Model 3.4
Culture				
Well-being	0.25	—	0.36**	0.44**
	(1.90)		(3.09)	(3.03)
Trust	57.07**	—	47.51**	82.43**
	(3.08)		(2.74)	(4.02)
Social Structure				
Percent Service Sector	0.51	0.53	—	0.78*
	(1.59)	(1.67)		(2.00)
Percent Higher Education	0.05	0.12	—	0.30
	(0.30)	(0.56)		(1.47)
Economic				
GNP/capita, 1990 ($100s)	0.15**	0.25**	0.18**	—
	(3.91)	(6.87)	(5.23)	
Intercept	−44.40	−24.96	−24.02	−66.19
Adjusted R²	.86	.80	.86	.81
Number of Cases	41	41	41	41

Notes: Dependent variable is the number of years for which democratic institutions functioned continuously in the given society from 1920 to 1995. Entry is unstandardized OLS coefficient. Coefficient divided by standard error is in parentheses.
*Variables significant at .05 level
**Variables significant at .01 level

and it explains fully 86 percent of the variance in the number of years for which democratic institutions have functioned consecutively in these 41 societies. Taking the other variables into account, interpersonal trust and GDP/capita emerge as the key factors, both being significant at well above the .01 level. Subjective well-being also seems important, being significant at very near the .05 level. Neither occupational structure nor educational level shows significant effects.

When we drop the two cultural variables (in model 3.2), the proportion of explained variance drops to .80 and the impact of economic development rises markedly, taking up most of the slack. But when we drop the two social structural variables (in model 3.3), the proportion of explained variance remains unchanged, at .86; the cultural and economic variables take up all of the slack, with subjective well-being and interpersonal trust both being significant at above the .01 level. Finally, when we drop GNP/capita from the regression, the proportion of explained variance falls to .81; the two cultural variables take up most of the slack, though the percentage in the service sector also rises to the .05 level of significance.

Our model is robust and indicates that the impact of economic development on stable democracy seems to work mainly through its tendency to bring cultural and (to a lesser degree) social changes. Dropping GNP/capita from the model reduces the explained variance by only five percentage points; though the linkage between development and democratic stability is very strong, most of its impact seems to pass through the cultural variables (and excluding them reduces the explained variance even more than does excluding GNP/capita).

Burkhart and Lewis-Beck (1994) have argued convincingly that economic development leads to democracy, and not the other way around. Building on their analysis, we would conclude that the most plausible interpretation of these results is that economic development leads to stable democracy mainly (though not entirely) insofar as it brings changes in political culture and social structure. This model could be depicted as follows:

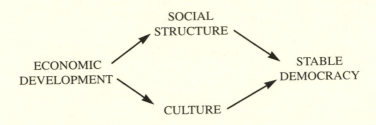

Can We Use 1990 Measures of Trust and Well-being as Indicators of Their Levels at an Earlier Time? The Stability of Cultural Variables

Before we go any farther, let us take up a basic problem involved in any endeavor to measure the impact of political culture on long-term democratic stability. Empirical measures of political culture from most of the world's societies have not been available until quite recently; consequently, any analysis of culture's impact on long-term stability must necessarily use recent measures to help explain events that took place in earlier years. Thus, the analysis in table 6.3 uses cultural measures carried out in 1990 to explain democratic stability from 1920 to 1995: obviously, we would prefer to have cultural measures from 1920 or earlier for this analysis, but such data are not available.

Using a 1990 measure of culture to explain the stability of democracy from 1920 to 1995 depends on the assumption that the cultural variables are relatively stable. But this assumption (though fortified by countless anecdotes about the stability of the cultural characteristics of given nationalities through the ages) has never been proven empirically. As we will show, there is strong empirical evidence that the cultural characteristics dealt with here actually *are* relatively stable. We have already seen one piece of this evidence: the fact that, from the Almond and Verba study in 1959 to the present survey in 1990, South-

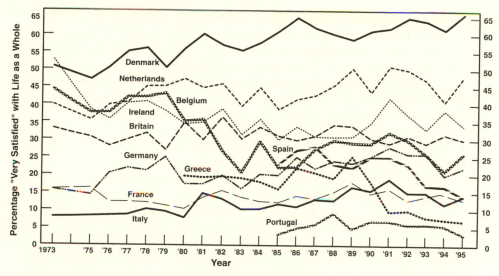

Figure 6.4. Cultural differences are relatively enduring but not immutable: cross-national differences in satisfaction with one's life as a whole, 1973–95. *Source*: Euro-Barometer surveys carried out in each respective year.

ern Italy has been characterized by much lower levels of interpersonal trust than Northern Italy—a finding that is entirely consistent with Putnam's (1993) evidence that the contemporary differences in political performance that he found between Northern and Southern Italy can be traced back to cultural differences that already existed more than a century earlier.

Although we have only fragmentary evidence concerning the long-term persistence of interpersonal trust, we have much more detailed evidence concerning another of our key variables. Overall life satisfaction has been measured in the Euro-Barometer surveys carried out in the member countries of the European Union every spring and fall from 1973 to the present. As figure 6.4 demonstrates, overall life satisfaction shows an impressive degree of cross-national stability in the European Union countries, from 1973 to 1995. Although a society's level of subjective well-being can and does change gradually over time, high or low levels are a relatively stable attribute of given societies. The correlation between a given country's level of life satisfaction at the first time point for which data are available, and its level in 1995 (the latest time point for which we have data), is .81: for most societies, this covers a 22-year time span, and it represents a truly impressive level of stability. Furthermore, as inspection of figure 6.4 demonstrates, this stability maintains itself throughout the period from 1973 to 1995, and not just at the two endpoints: in every year for which we have data, the Dutch and the Danes always rank near the top, while the Italians, French, and Portuguese always rank near the bottom.

To provide a yardstick by which to evaluate the stability of this basic cultural orientation, let us ask: How does it compare with the stability of the most frequently used of all economic indicators, per capita GNP? Relative levels of wealth are generally considered to be very stable. This assumption is well founded: with few exceptions, the relatively rich nations of 1900 were also the relatively rich nations of 1995; and most of the societies that were relatively poor in 1900 were still relatively poor in 1995. Accordingly, during the 20-year period from 1970 to 1990, GNP/capita was relatively stable, showing a correlation of .73 among the societies in the 1990 World Values Survey. But—surprising as it may seem to those who view economic data as "hard" and cultural data as "soft"—our cultural indicator shows even *greater* stability over time than does the economic indicator!

The data from the 1981 and 1990 World Values surveys enable us to test the stability of key cultural characteristics on a broader scale, using the data from the 24 societies on five continents included in both of these surveys. The results are impressive. Our index of subjective well-being (based on overall life satisfaction and reported happiness) shows a correlation of .86 between the levels measured in 1981 and the levels measured in 1990: this is even higher than the .81 correlation shown in figure 6.4. Moreover, interpersonal trust (as measured in the 1981 surveys) shows an amazingly high correlation of .91 with interpersonal trust in 1990. By comparison, the per capita GNP of these same countries in 1980 shows a correlation of .88 with their per capita GNP in 1990: a stability level about as high as that of our two cultural indicators. All of these figures are high. When one speaks of "rich countries" versus "poor countries," one is indeed dealing with a relatively stable attribute of most societies. But this is equally true of our two political culture variables. Relative levels of interpersonal trust and subjective well-being seem to be as stable attributes of given societies as are their economic levels.

Cultural variables are often thought of as vague and ethereal simply because we usually have only vague, impressionistic *measures* of them. When measured quantitatively, basic orientations such as these display impressive stability. This is an important finding, which supports the claim that cultural variables have an autonomy and momentum of their own.[3] Moreover, it suggests that our measures of political culture carried out in the 1980s and 1990s may be reasonably good indicators of how these societies ranked in earlier decades: though we cannot go back in time and measure the orientations of these publics in the 1920s, we need not abandon the effort to understand how political culture contributes to the long-term survival of democratic institutions.

Let us examine this problem from another perspective. The question is "How well can data from 1990 be used in multivariate analysis, to stand in for data measuring the same variable at an earlier point in time?" In table 6.3 we

---

[3] Culture has a significant degree of autonomy from economic factors. Though affected by economic events, culture is not simply a consequence of economic change: (1) it is shaped by many other factors besides economic ones, including wars, great leaders, major diseases, and other historical events; and (2) even insofar as they *are* shaped by economic factors, cultural changes have significant time lags. Thus culture has a momentum of its own and can influence economic factors as well as being influenced by them.

TABLE 6.4

Stability of Democracy, Using GNP/Capita in 1990, 1980, 1970, and 1957 as Independent Variables: Multiple Regression Model

Independent Variable	Model 4.1	Model 4.2	Model 4.3	Model 4.4
Culture				
Well-being	0.25	0.34**	0.45**	0.46**
	(1.90)	(2.59)	(3.42)	(3.35)
Trust	57.07**	63.75**	66.86**	73.33**
	(3.08)	(3.43)	(3.51)	(3.77)
Social Structure				
Service Sector	0.51	0.57	0.68*	0.67
	(1.59)	(1.79)	(2.06)	(1.95)
Higher Education	0.05	0.07	−0.06	−0.09
	(0.30)	(0.35)	(−0.26)	(−0.37)
Economic				
GNP/capita, 1990 ($100s)	0.15**	—	—	—
	(3.91)			
GNP/capita, 1980 ($100s)	—	0.25**	—	—
		(3.56)		
GNP/capita, 1970 ($100s)	—	—	1.20**	—
			(3.11)	
GNP/capita, 1957 ($100s)	—	—	—	0.02*
				(2.53)
Intercept	−44.40	−54.96	−62.05	−60.31
Adjusted R^2	.86	.85	.84	.83
Number of Cases	41	41	41	41

Notes: Dependent variable is the number of years for which democratic institutions functioned continuously in the given society from 1920 to 1995. Entry is unstandardized OLS coefficient. Coefficient divided by standard error is in parentheses.

*Variables significant at .05 level

**Variables significant at .01 level

used 1990 GNP/capita to measure the impact of economic development on cultural and social change, and on democracy. We used the 1990 data to be on the same footing with the cultural variables, which were also measured in 1990. But this means that the economic data have the same problem of chronology as the cultural data: causes precede effects, and we are using economic data from 1990 to explain democratic stability from 1920 to 1995.

In fact, we get essentially the same results when we employ economic indicators from much earlier time points: GNP/capita is a relatively stable attribute of given societies and, although absolute levels of income vary from one year to the next, the relative positions of given societies are reasonably stable. Thus, our regression model yields virtually identical results when we use GNP/capita in 1990, as when we use GNP/capita from earlier times.

Table 6.4 shows the results of multiple regression analyses of democratic stability, using GNP/capita in 1990, 1980, 1970, and 1957, respectively, as our indicators of economic development levels. Although the coefficients vary slightly, the same basic model emerges: GNP/capita, subjective well-being, and interpersonal trust are the key variables in every case. Moreover, our various models all explain approximately the same amounts of variance, ranging from a low of 83 percent (using GNP/capita in 1957) to a high of 86 percent (using GNP/capita in 1990).

As we have seen, our two cultural variables are fully as stable over time as is GNP/capita. Although we do not have measures of well-being and trust from earlier decades, we suspect that if we could obtain them our analysis would produce similar results, with the same basic model emerging. This, at any rate, is what happens when we use economic indicators from earlier points in time. Our model proves to be robust, suggesting that relatively stable cultural indicators from 1990 can serve as surrogates for cultural indicators from earlier points in time.

TESTING ADDITIONAL VARIABLES

Let us now examine the impact of a variety of additional variables that the literature suggests may play important roles in democracy. After preliminary discussion, each of these variables will be tested in multivariate analyses.

The Importance of Organizational Networks

Alexis de Tocqueville stressed the importance of networks of voluntary associations, arguing that democracy had emerged and flourished in America because its people participated in numerous and extensive networks of voluntary associations. This fostered cooperation and trust, which were essential to the successful functioning of democratic institutions. Putnam (1993) also emphasized this factor, arguing that Social Capital plays a crucial role in both political and economic cooperation. Social Capital consists of a culture of trust and tolerance, in which extensive networks of voluntary associations emerge. These networks provide contacts and information flows that are, in turn, supportive of a culture of trust and cooperation: economics does not unilaterally determine culture *nor* does culture determine economics. The two are intimately intertwined and mutually supportive in any society that flourishes for any length of time.

Putnam's work makes an important contribution to sorting out the causal linkages between economic and cultural factors, facilitated by his development of an exceptionally long time series of economic and cultural indicators. Analyzing Italian regional-level data from the nineteenth century to the 1980s, Putnam found that certain regions had relatively high levels of social capital, while others had much lower levels. These levels were fairly stable attributes of given regions; and they were strongly linked with the economic development level of those regions. But Putnam's analysis dispels any assumption that these regional cultural differences are simply a consequence of their respective levels of economic development. Putnam found that levels of civic involvement around 1900 predicted civic involvement levels 60 or 70 years later far better than did economic factors. More strikingly still, he also found that levels of civic involvement around 1900 predicted subsequent levels of *economic* development even better than did economic variables. Putnam's analysis indicates that cultural factors help shape economic life, as well as being shaped by it.

The World Values surveys provide information about organizational memberships. The respective publics were shown or read a list of 16 types of voluntary associations and asked, "To which, if any, of these organizations do you belong?" The surveys cover the following types of organizations: labor unions, religious organizations, sports/recreation organizations, educational/cultural organizations, political parties, professional associations, social welfare organizations, youth groups, environmental organizations, health volunteer groups, community action groups, women's organizations, Third World development groups, animal rights groups, and peace movements.

Rates of organizational memberships vary greatly across societies. The lowest level of membership was recorded in Argentina, where only a cumulative 23 percent belonged to *any* of the 16 types of organizations: the average rate of membership was slightly over 2 percent. The society with the highest rate of organizational membership was the Netherlands, where membership in these organizations averages 16 percent.

These data underrepresent the low-income societies. This battery was not asked in India or Turkey because many of these organizations scarcely existed there; it was asked in Nigeria, but was framed to imply "Do you *sympathize* with these organizations?" Consequently, we do not have comparable data from these cases. These questions *were* asked in a number of relatively low-income countries, however, with particularly interesting results from China. Although China shows a lower rate of organizational memberships than most advanced industrial societies, it has a high rate for a largely rural society.

These data enable us to examine the relationship between organizational membership and stable democracy in an unprecedentedly broad perspective. Figure 6.5 shows the overall relationship between rates of membership in these 16 types of organizations and the number of years for which democratic institutions have functioned in the given society.

Our findings support the Tocqueville-Putnam hypothesis: membership in voluntary associations is strongly linked with stable democracy. The overall regression coefficient is .65, significant at the .0001 level. Societies with high

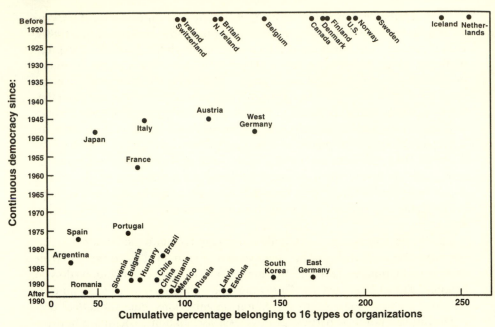

Figure 6.5. Democracy and voluntary associations.
r = .65, N = 35, significant at .0001 level. Number of years for which democratic institutions have functioned continuously in given nation since 1920, by cumulative percentage belonging to 16 types of voluntary associations (e.g., the Dutch public report a cumulative 259 percent belonging to the 16 types of organizations, for a mean 16 percent belonging to each type). *Source*: 1990–93 World Values Survey.

rates of membership are far more likely to be stable democracies than those with low rates of membership. Subsequent analyses will examine whether this holds up in multivariate analysis.

Support for Revolutionary Change and Support for Gradual Reform

Inglehart (1990) used a political culture index composed of interpersonal trust, subjective well-being, and the percentage supporting revolutionary change to explain democratic stability, finding that societies characterized by relatively high levels of support for revolutionary change are less likely to be stable democracies than other societies. Muller and Seligson (1994), in a reanalysis of Inglehart's data (plus six Central American countries), used support for gradual reform in their analysis instead of support for revolutionary change, arguing that the former provides a stronger explanation of shifts toward democracy than does the latter. Both of these variables show reasonably high levels of stability over time—though not as high as that found with subjective well-being and interpersonal trust. Among the 24 societies included in both the

1981 and 1990 World Values surveys, the correlations between levels in 1981 and levels in 1990 for each of these four variables were:

Interpersonal trust	.91
Subjective well-being	.86
Support for gradual reform	.80
Support for revolutionary change	.74

Thus, although there is an enduring tendency for certain societies to be characterized by relatively high levels of support for revolutionary change, this is a less stable variable than interpersonal trust or subjective well-being. These variables will also be examined in multivariate analyses.

Income Inequality

Much of the literature on democracy has emphasized income equality as an important factor in connection with stable democracy. This literature points out that very high levels of income inequality lead to extremist politics in which the dispossessed have nothing to lose and a great deal to gain by radical change—and the privileged elite has an enormous stake in maintaining the status quo at almost any cost. This is a recipe for extremist politics. Conversely, a reasonable degree of income equality is conducive to the spirit of compromise and moderation that is crucial to democratic politics. Furthermore, a diverse economy with many attractive jobs in the tertiary sector makes the elite more willing to accept rotation out of office: in such a setting, government is not the only route to prosperity and power; one may even have greater opportunities to earn a high income out of office than in office. Cross-sectional evidence suggests that economic development tends to produce greater income equality—which could be one reason why economic development is linked with democracy. We would expect income equality to be positively correlated with democracy.

Ethnolinguistic Fractionalization

Muller and Seligson (1994) used an Index of Ethnolinguistic Fractionalization from Taylor and Jodice (1983) in their analysis, finding that ethnic diversity makes democratization less likely. We will examine whether this finding holds up when tested in the context of the much broader database provided by the 1990 World Values Survey.

EMPIRICAL RESULTS

As table 6.5 demonstrates, none of these additional factors has a significant impact on stable democracy; and in no case does adding them to the regression analysis increase the percentage of variance explained. The basic model shown in table 6.3 explains 86 percent of the variance in democratic stability; none

TABLE 6.5

Stability of Democracy: Multiple Regression Models Testing Impact of Support for Revolutionary Change, Support for Gradual Reform, Income Equality, and Organizational Memberships

Independent Variable	Model 5.1 (Revolution)	Model 5.2 (Reform)	Model 5.3 (Income Equality)	Model 5.4 (Organizational Membership)
Culture				
Well-being	0.27	0.32	0.32*	0.25
	(1.90)	(2.05)	(1.96)	(1.46)
Trust	59.90**	56.49**	54.79*	49.44*
	(3.01)	(2.88)	(2.27)	(2.24)
For Revolutionary Change	0.16 (0.51)	—	—	—
For Gradual Reform	—	−0.22 (−0.90)	—	—
Social Structure				
Percent Service Sector	0.59 (1.71)	0.56 (1.71)	0.51 (1.25)	0.62 (1.62)
Percent Higher Education	0.02 (0.09)	0.04 (0.21)	0.05 (0.23)	0.02 (0.01)
Percent Income to Top 20%	—	—	−0.36 (−0.95)	—
Membership, 16 Types of Organizations	—	—	—	0.05 (1.05)
Economic				
GNP/capita, 1990 ($100s)	0.16** (3.47)	0.16** (3.42)	0.14** (3.18)	0.14** (3.31)
Intercept	−52.44	−35.01	−30.87	−51.21
Adjusted R²	.85	.85	.86	.85
Number of Cases	39	39	32	34

Notes: Dependent variable is the number of years for which democratic institutions functioned continuously in the given society from 1920 to 1995. Entry is unstandardized OLS coefficient. Coefficient divided by standard error is in parentheses.

*Variables significant at .05 level

**Variables significant at .01 level

of the models shown in table 6.5 explain more than this proportion of the variance. Thus, neither support for revolutionary change nor support for gradual reform has a significant independent impact on stable democracy.

It seems likely that income equality is conducive to democracy. To test this hypothesis, the percentage of a country's income going to the top 20 percent of the population was included as an explanatory factor in this analysis.[4] The findings were interesting. There is a clear tendency for advanced industrial democracies to have higher levels of income equality than preindustrial or newly industrializing societies, most of which are not stable democracies. But the *highest* levels of income equality were found among the ex-socialist countries—and when they are included in the analysis, the zero-order correlation between income inequality and stable democracy dwindles almost to zero ($r = -.06$). Democracies tend to have reasonably high levels of income equality, and we believe that this is conducive to democracy (though it may also be a consequence of democracy to some extent, since democracy shifts political power to the public, enabling them to press for more egalitarian social policies). But income equality does not seem to be the main cause of democracy.

Moreover, the relationship between income equality and democracy is not linear. Very low levels of income inequality lead to economic inefficiency and political instability. But, apparently, extremely high levels of income equality can only be attained by coercive governments.

We also tested the impact of membership in voluntary associations, our indicator of Putnam's concept of Social Capital. Although it is strongly correlated with stable democracy, this variable did not show a statistically significant impact when we control for the effects of other variables. This does not prove that it plays no role; it simply indicates that it is not among the two or three variables most strongly linked with stable democracy. Putnam (1993) views organizational membership as contributing to democracy largely because it is conducive to interpersonal trust and cooperation: consequently, we would expect organizational membership to be highly correlated with interpersonal trust, and it is. With only 41 observations and a good deal of overlapping variance (as is the case here), only a few variables are likely to have a statistically significant impact, and in this analysis organizational membership shows a positive but not statistically significant linkage with stable democracy. It also shows positive but not statistically significant linkages with levels of democracy in 1990 and 1995; but, as we will see below, organizational membership *does* show a statistically significant linkage with changes in levels of democracy from 1990 to 1995.

Although the results are not shown in table 6.5, we also examined the impact of ethnolinguistic fractionalization, finding that it does not show a signif-

---

[4] Data on income equality are from World Bank (1993). These data were not available for the Soviet successor states, which were assigned the mean score observed across the Eastern European ex-communist societies. This is only roughly accurate but should be in the right ballpark: income equality was certainly higher in these societies than in non-communist societies.

icant effect on stable democracy, and that adding it to the model does not increase the percentage of variance explained. Although one can point to horror stories about the difficulties that ethnic diversity may pose for democratic governance, from Nigeria in the 1960s to Bosnia in the 1990s, diversity does not seem to rank among the most crucial factors. In global perspective, multiethnic societies are only slightly less likely to be stable democracies than are more homogeneous societies.

Interpersonal trust, subjective well-being, reasonable levels of income equality, low levels of extremism, relatively high levels of political participation and organizational membership, and Postmaterialist values are all part of a highly intercorrelated syndrome that might be called a "prodemocratic culture." And all of these variables are closely correlated with stable democracy. But interpersonal trust and subjective well-being have the highest correlations with stable democracy. In this regression analysis, with a huge amount of shared variance and only 40 cases, only these two variables show statistically significant relationships with stable democracy. We think it highly unlikely that trust and well-being are the only relevant parts of this syndrome. Social reality is usually more complex than that. Quite possibly, all or many of the other elements of this closely related cluster of variables help sustain democratic institutions. The present analysis indicates that cultural variables play an important role in the survival of democracy over time, with trust and well-being constituting the two most prominent cultural variables. It seems unlikely that these two variables alone shape the outcome: more probably, they serve as indicators of a broader cultural configuration that is conducive to democracy.

LEVELS OF DEMOCRACY: 1990 AND 1995

Table 6.6 analyzes the factors linked with level of democracy in 1990, using the five variables in our basic model. There are some interesting changes from the results in table 6.3. Subjective well-being has a highly significant linkage with levels of democracy in 1990, as it does with democratic stability. But social structure plays a more important role, and economic development a less important one, than it did with stable democracy. The percentage of the economy in the service sector is the most important single factor shaping levels of democracy in 1990.

Interpersonal trust does not have a significant impact on levels in 1990—indeed, it shows a weakly negative linkage with it. The same occurs with the percentage receiving higher education: though it has a strong positive zero-order relationship with democracy in 1990, it shows a weakly negative relationship in this regression analysis. The education finding seems to reflect a familiar phenomenon: education and the size of the service sector are highly correlated, and under certain conditions, including both of them in the regression causes a reversal of the sign on the variable with the larger measurement error—in this case, education (Achen, 1985).

TABLE 6.6
Level of Democracy in 1990: Multiple Regression Model

Independent Variable	Model 6.1	Model 6.2	Model 6.3	Model 6.4
Culture				
Well-being	0.07**	—	0.11**	0.08**
	(2.93)		(3.98)	(3.49)
Trust	−1.30	—	−4.75	0.29
	(−0.39)		(−1.40)	(0.09)
Social Structure				
Percent Service	0.18**	0.27**	—	0.20**
Sector	(3.18)	(5.31)		(3.44)
Percent Higher	−0.01	−0.02	—	0.01
Education	(−0.18)	(−0.51)		(0.42)
Economic				
GNP/capita, 1990	0.01	0.02**	0.02**	—
($100s)	(1.60)	(3.08)	(2.64)	
Intercept	−2.79	−4.40	4.10	−4.12
Adjusted R^2	.76	.71	.70	.75
Number of Cases	42	42	42	42

Notes: Dependent variable is the level of democracy in 1990 as measured by the Freedom House ratings for Political Rights and Civil Liberties, combined into an additive index. Entry is unstandardized OLS coefficient. Coefficient divided by standard error is in parentheses.
*Variables significant at .05 level
**Variables significant at .01 level

The importance of economic level diminishes markedly here, by comparison with its linkage to democratic stability. When both culture and social structure are included in the model, GNP per capita does not show a significant impact on the 1990 level of democracy (though it does show a powerful linkage when either of these factors is dropped). Moreover, eliminating GNP/capita from the model reduces the percentage of explained variance by only one percentage point, from 76 to 75: here again, we find indications that, although economic development is strongly linked with democracy, its effects work mainly through the changes it brings in culture and social structure.

We also examined the impact of several additional variables, including support for revolutionary change, support for gradual reform, levels of income inequality, organizational memberships, and ethnolinguistic fractionalization. None of these variables shows a statistically significant linkage with level of democracy in 1990, and none of them greatly increases the proportion of variance explained.

TABLE 6.7
Level of Democracy in 1995: Multiple Regression Model

Independent Variable	Model 7.1	Model 7.2	Model 7.3	Model 7.4
Culture				
Well-being	−0.01	—	0.01	−0.01
	(−0.64)		(0.55)	(−0.02)
Trust	−3.20	—	−4.34	−1.23
	(−1.03)		(−1.36)	(−0.40)
Social Structure				
Percent Service	0.10	0.10*	—	0.12*
Sector	(1.90)	(2.16)		(2.20)
Percent Higher	0.06	0.05	—	0.08**
Education	(1.89)	(1.79)		(2.72)
Economic				
GNP/capita, 1990	0.01*	0.08	0.02**	—
($100s)	(2.11)	(1.52)	(3.74)	
Intercept	5.76	4.90	10.94	4.11
Adjusted R^2	.50	.50	.39	.46
Number of Cases	42	42	42	42

Notes: Dependent variable is the level of democracy in 1995 as measured by the Freedom House ratings for Political Rights and Civil Liberties, combined into an additive index. Entry is unstandardized OLS coefficient. Coefficient divided by standard error is in parentheses.

*Variables significant at .05 level

**Variables significant at .01 level

Table 6.7 analyzes the factors linked with level of democracy in 1995. When we compare the percentage of variance explained by these variables with the percentage explained by the democracy level in 1990, the proportion drops from .76 to .50. Although this analysis is based on levels of democracy only five years later than the previous analysis, it reflects the state of the world after an avalanche of changes that brought democratization to fully one-third of the nations in our sample. Consequently, structural factors explain much less than they did in the analysis of levels of democracy in 1990: in the new democracies that had emerged by 1995, democratic institutions were less firmly anchored in social structure and culture, and much more contingent on situation-specific factors (such as historical events, elite maneuvering, and the role of specific leaders) than they were in the longer-established democracies. The only statistically significant influence on levels of democracy in 1995 is level of economic development: richer societies were likelier to be democracies than were poorer ones. But when GNP per capita is dropped from the regression, social structural variables take up most of the slack: societies with a relatively large service sector and (even more important) societies with a relatively well-educated population were likelier to show high levels of democracy than were those with lower levels of these variables.

Our indicators of political culture are virtually unrelated to levels of democracy in 1995. The massive number of new democracies washes out the linkage between culture and democracy: as we have argued, democratic institutions can be *adopted* in virtually any setting. But our interpretation implies that democracy is most likely to survive and flourish in societies that rank high on subjective well-being and interpersonal trust. A culture of trust and well-being will probably develop in some of the new democracies; and democracy may fail to survive in others that rank low on trust and well-being. In the long run, both processes tend to reinstate the linkage between political culture and democracy.

As additional analyses indicate, none of the additional variables examined in table 6.5 (support for revolution, support for gradual reform, income inequality, organizational membership, and ethnolinguistic fractionalization) has a statistically significant impact on levels of democracy in 1995, although income inequality comes close to the .05 level of significance: societies with relatively low levels of income inequality were likelier to have higher levels of democracy in 1995 than those with greater inequality.

ANALYZING RECENT CHANGES IN LEVELS OF DEMOCRACY

Inglehart (1988, 1990) argued that political culture plays a crucial role in sustaining democratic political institutions: economic development is linked with democracy, in large part, because it leads to changes in social structure and political culture that are conducive to democracy.

Muller and Seligson (1994) argue that Inglehart's political culture data were collected in 1981 and therefore cannot be used to explain the persistence of stable democracy before that time (unless, of course, they tap stable cultural differences that were present even earlier). Consequently, they drop Inglehart's dependent variable and analyze changes in levels of democracy that occurred after 1981. They claim to be testing Inglehart's thesis, but their analysis is based on a model in which the dependent variable is democracy at time 2 (the 1980s), controlling for democracy at time 1 (the 1970s). This means that they are not analyzing either the *extent* of democracy or the *stability* of democracy among the societies in their sample: they are analyzing recent *changes* (from the 1970s to the 1980s). The authors do not attempt to conceal this fact: they refer to their dependent variable as "change in level of democracy." But their choice of recent *change* as a test of whether political culture is conducive to democracy has important implications that they seem to have overlooked. They use this dependent variable to address the question "Is political culture conducive to democracy?" But their analysis actually addresses the question "Is political culture conducive to the *shifts* in levels of democracy observed

TABLE 6.8

Shifts in Levels of Democracy, Muller-Seligson Model: Impact of Income Inequality, Support for Gradual Reform, and Ethnolinguistic Fractionalization

Independent Variable	Model 8.1 (1970s–1980s shifts) (Muller-Seligson, 1994: 642)	Model 8.2 (1990–95 shifts)
Culture		
For Gradual	.62**	−.05
Reform	(2.82)	(−.75)
Social Structure		
Ethnolinguistic	−.17*	−.01
Fractionalization	(2.13)	(−.59)
Income to Top 20%	−1.60**	−.09
	(4.10)	(−1.23)
Level of Democracy,	.32*	.61**
1980s (1990)	(2.46)	(3.11)
Intercept	93.1	13.1
Adjusted R²	.87	.37

Notes: Dependent variable is the level of democracy in 1980s (1995), controlling for level in 1970s (1990). Entry is unstandardized OLS coefficient. Coefficient divided by standard error is in parentheses.

*Variables significant at .05 level

**Variables significant at .01 level

from one decade to another?" It does not and cannot determine whether a given political culture is conducive to stable democracy or to high levels of democracy during a given period.

Table 6.7 replicates the Muller-Seligson analysis, using their model to analyze shifts in levels of democracy from 1990 to 1995. Model 8.1 in table 6.8 shows the results they obtained, using the data from the 1981 World Values Survey (plus six Central American societies) to analyze shifts from the 1970s to the 1980s. In their analysis, they found that income inequality was the most important influence on democratization from the 1970s to the 1980s. Support for gradual reform, ethnolinguistic fractionalization, and level of democracy at the earlier time point also had statistically significant effects. Their model explained fully 87 percent of the variance in democratization during this time period.

But their model is completely time bound. The factors governing *shifts* in levels of democracy from one decade to the next are largely situation-specific (in the period they analyzed, such events as the death of Franco and Argentina's defeat in the Falklands War triggered democratization). Accordingly, their model does not hold up when used to analyze the shifts toward democracy in other time periods. As model 8.2 demonstrates, using the same variables with the 1990 World Values Survey data, we get completely different results when we apply their model to analyze shifts toward democracy during the period from 1990 to 1995. Neither income inequality nor support for gradual reform nor ethnolinguistic fractionalization has a statistically significant impact on the shifts that took place in this broader sample of countries from 1990 to 1995. Not surprisingly, level of democracy at time 1 *does* have a significant linkage with level of democracy at time 2, but this is the only element of their model that survives. And the proportion of variance explained by their model drops precipitously—falling from 87 to 37 percent. A completely different group of countries shifted toward democracy in the 1980s, from those that shifted toward democracy during the 1990s—and the two groups of countries were very different in social structure and culture.

Is the breakdown of the Muller-Seligson model due to the fact that we use a broader set of nations in the analysis in model 8.2? No, it is not. Table 6.9 replicates their analysis, using the *same* set of nations that they examined. The results demonstrate that their findings are indeed time bound. When we focus on the same time span that they examined, we get similar results (see model 9.1). But when we analyze shifts toward democracy among these same societies during other time periods, we get quite different results. Income equality, support for gradual reform, and level of democracy at time 1 were the main influences on the shifts toward democracy that took place from the 1970s to the 1980s, in Muller and Seligson's analysis (with ethnolinguistic fractionalization approaching the 0.05 level of significance). None of these variables consistently shows a significant impact on democratization during the other time periods. Level of democracy at time 1 has a significant effect in two of the four other time periods; income equality has a significant effect in one of the four other time periods; and neither support for gradual reform nor ethnolinguistic fractionalization has a significant effect in any of the four other time periods. The factors that explain shifts toward democracy from the 1970s to the 1980s are *not* the same as those that explain shifts toward democracy in those same countries from the 1980s to the 1990s, or from the 1970s to the 1980s, or from the 1970s to 1995, or from 1990 to 1995. Situation-specific factors dominate structural factors, in explaining short-term change.

To understand why we get such volatile results, let us look more closely at the changes on which the Muller and Seligson analysis focuses. Figure 6.6 shows which societies changed the most during the period Muller and Seligson analyzed, based on their own data. As figure 6.6 makes clear, their approach does not analyze which nations are most democratic, or which nations have the most stable democratic institutions. Instead, their analysis focuses on the difference between two distinct sets of countries: one group consisting of Spain, Argentina, Honduras, Portugal, Greece, and Panama, which had experienced large recent changes; and another group of 21 societies that showed little or no change in level of democracy from the 1970s to the 1980s—and which lumps together the stable democracies *and* the stable authoritarian states and any marginally democratic societies that did not undergo major changes

TABLE 6.9
Effects of Civic Culture Attitudes and Macrosocietal Variables

Independent Variable	Equations Explaining Level of Democracy		
	Model 9.1 1970s–1980s (Muller-Seligson Analysis)		Model 9.2 1980s to 1990
Level, 1970s	0.32	(2.23)*	—
Level, 1980s	—		0.96 (6.36)**
Level, 1990	—		—
Gradual Reform	0.62	(2.49)*	0.16 (0.78)
Interpersonal Trust	0.04	(0.20)	−0.19 (−1.44)
GDP/capita	−0.01	(−0.05)	−0.07 (−0.72)
Income Inequality	−1.61	(−3.21)**	−0.20 (−0.44)
Ethnolinguistic Fractionalization	−1.62	(−1.78)	0.65 (0.91)
Intercept	93.13		14.10
Adjusted R^2	.85		.92
Number of Cases	25		25

Independent Variable	Equations Explaining Level of Democracy		
	Model 9.3 1970–95	Model 9.4 1980s–95	Model 9.5 1990–95
Level, 1970s	0.01 (0.07)	—	—
Level, 1980s	—	0.53 (2.83)**	—
Level, 1990	—	—	0.15 (0.76)
Gradual Reform	−0.13 (−0.47)	0.50 (−1.93)	−0.25 (−0.80)
Interpersonal Trust	0.12 (0.57)	0.06 (0.35)	0.13 (+0.66)
GDP/capita	0.07 (0.46)	0.03 (0.23)	0.07 (+0.50)
Income Inequality	−1.20 (−2.20)*	−0.08 (−0.14)	−0.89 (−1.38)
Ethnolinguistic Fractionalization	−0.39 (−0.39)	0.08 (0.88)	−0.19 (−0.19)
Intercept	144.47	76.57	125.45
Adjusted R^2	.61	.73	.62
Number of Cases	25	25	25

Notes: Entry is unstandardized OLS coefficient. Coefficient divided by standard error is in parentheses. Estimates are based on 25 cases. Greece and Luxembourg are excluded because data on income inequality is unavailable.
*Significant at .05 level
**Significant at .01 level

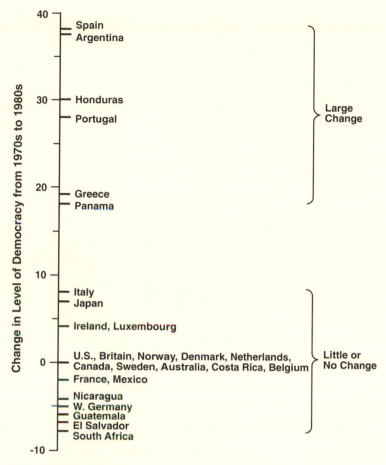

Figure 6.6. Changes in level of democracy from 1970s to 1980s in 27 nations. *Source*: calculated from Muller and Seligson, 1994: 648 (appendix A).

in this period. Most of the variance on which Muller and Seligson's analysis is based reflects the contrast between six societies that, for various reasons, showed major changes in the 1980s—and a heterogeneous group of societies that did not. Their analysis ranks Spain and Argentina at the top of the scale, far above the Nordic countries or the English-speaking democracies, even though the latter countries rank much higher on both *level* of democracy and *stability* of democracy: for Spain and Argentina happen to be the societies that showed the most dramatic *changes* during this period. Their analysis focuses on recent fluctuations that cultural differences would be unlikely to explain since culture is, by definition, relatively stable.

Muller and Seligson's dependent variable is so volatile that any cultural variables that *did* explain the pattern they find in the 1980s could not very well explain the pattern found in the 1970s or 1990s: the societies that make a breakthrough to democracy in one decade are not likely to be the same ones that make it a decade earlier or a decade later. For example, Spain falls at the high end of the scale in Muller and Seligson's analysis, since it adopted democratic institutions during this period. South Africa falls at the *opposite* end of the scale. Nevertheless, shortly after 1990 South Africa began a transition to democracy: today it would rank near the high end of their scale, having shown large recent changes. Conversely, Spain and Argentina would now drop toward the low end of the scale, since they did not show large *shifts* toward democracy in the last few years but declined slightly in the Freedom House ratings. When applied to a different time period, their dependent variable becomes radically different from the one they examined in the 1980s.

Muller and Seligson present a thoughtful analysis that addresses a very real problem: causes precede effects, which means that any attempt to analyze the contributions of political culture to democratic stability before 1960 (when political culture began to be measured empirically) faces difficult measurement problems. But their analysis has two flaws, either of which would be fatal to a test of political culture theory.

First, it is based on a dependent variable that does not address the question of whether cultural factors are responsible for the long-term survival or failure of democracy—instead, it focuses on the fluctuations from the 1970s to the 1980s. By their very nature, cultural differences are relatively stable aspects of given societies and hence unlikely to explain fluctuations in a given society's level of democracy from one decade to the next. Muller and Seligson's analysis controls for the long-term component of democracy and analyzes *only* the recent fluctuations. This gives them a dependent variable that was measured after the 1981 surveys were carried out, but it is clearly the wrong dependent variable to test the role of culture.

Their analysis is further distorted by an artifact of the data they use. The Freedom House codings of levels of democracy use the stable democracies to define the top level of their scales: from the start, they have been assigned the maximum possible score. This means that they literally *cannot* rise any farther—and since Muller and Seligson's analysis is based on change, this means that they cannot attain high scores on their dependent variable. This explains the bizarre pattern that is visible in figure 6.5: in virtually every case, the stable democracies get scores near (or exactly at) zero, reflecting no change. Muller and Seligson nevertheless argue that the cultural characteristics associated with stable democracy should be linked with large amounts of *change* on this measure. Their model specification virtually guarantees that they will not find it, and they don't.

It is perfectly legitimate and useful to analyze short-term changes in levels of democracy, as Muller and Seligson have done; but when one does so, it is important to be aware that this is a very different dependent variable from either *levels* of democracy or *stability* of democracy—and one that is mainly shaped by situation-specific factors.

With this in mind, let us examine the shifts in levels of democracy that took

TABLE 6.10

Shifts in Levels of Democracy from 1990 to 1995: Multiple Regression Model

Independent Variable	Model 10.1	Model 10.2	Model 10.3	Model 10.4
Culture				
Well-being	−0.09*	—	−0.10**	−0.08*
	(−2.49)		(−3.68)	(−2.56)
Trust	−1.90	—	0.41	−1.53
	(−0.41)		(0.09)	(−0.35)
Social Structure				
Service Sector	−0.08	−0.18*	—	−0.08
	(−0.99)	(−2.50)		(−0.97)
Higher Education	0.06	0.07	—	0.07
	(1.38)	(1.46)		(1.60)
Economic				
GNP/capita, 1990	0.01	−0.01	0.01	—
($100s)	(0.26)	(−1.26)	(0.67)	
Intercept	8.55	9.30	6.19	8.23
Adjusted R^2	.32	.20	.32	.34
Number of Cases	42	42	42	42

Notes: Dependent variable is the shift from 1990 to 1995 on the Freedom House combined index of Political Rights and Civil Liberties. Entry is unstandardized OLS coefficient. Coefficient divided by standard error is in parentheses.

*Variables significant at .05 level

**Variables significant at .01 level

place from 1990 to 1995, using change scores instead of level at time 2, controlling for level at time 1, as Muller and Seligson do: change scores provide a more straightforward measure of change, and one that is comparable to the other dependent variables used in this analysis.

Table 6.10 shows the results of a regression analysis of changes in level of democracy from 1990 to 1995, using the same cultural and social structural explanatory variables as in our previous analyses. One striking contrast with these previous analyses is the relatively small proportion of variance that these variables explain: while our analyses of levels of democracy and stability of democracy explained from 50 to 85 percent of the variance, the same variables explain only 32 percent of the variance in the shifts from 1990 to 1995. This reflects the fact that these recent shifts are not firmly rooted in the social or economic structure of the societies. Controlling for other factors, rich societies were as likely to shift as were poor ones, and highly educated publics were as likely to shift as were poorly educated ones. The most important influence on change is subjective well-being, but it has a reversed polarity in comparison with the previous analyses: the societies that underwent regime changes were

TABLE 6.11

Shifts from 1990 to 1995 (Change Scores): Multiple Regression Models Testing Impact of Support for Revolutionary Change, Support for Gradual Reform, Income Inequality, and Organizational Memberships

Independent Variable	Model 11.1 (Revolution)	Model 11.2 (Reform)	Model 11.3 (Income Inequality)	Model 11.4 (Organizational Membership)
Culture				
Well-being	−.07	−.08*	−.09*	−.08*
	(−1.91)	(−1.99)	(−2.33)	(−2.60)
Trust	−.69	−1.48	.54	−11.6*
	(−.01)	(−.29)	(.10)	(−2.68)
For Revolutionary Change	.13	—	—	—
	(−1.75)			
For Gradual Reform	—	−.02	—	—
		(−.29)		
Social Structure				
Service Sector	−.03	−.07	.04	−.11
	(−.35)	(−.83)	(.45)	(−1.60)
Higher Education	.06	.08	.02	.02
	(1.23)	(1.44)	(.41)	(.46)
Income to Top 20%	—	—	−.13	—
			(−1.45)	
Membership, 16 Types of Organizations	—	—	—	.03*
				(2.74)
Economic				
GNP/capita, 1990 ($100s)	.004	.001	.001	.005
	(.32)	(.09)	(−.09)	(.65)
Intercept	3.02	8.99	8.32	11.93
Adjusted R^2	.34	.28	.36	.62

Notes: Dependent variable is the shift in level of democracy from 1990 to 1995. Entry is unstandardized OLS coefficient. Coefficient divided by standard error is in parentheses.

*Significant at .05 level

**Significant at .01 level

societies in which the mass publics had *low* levels of subjective well-being. When well-being and trust are dropped from the analysis, the percentage of variance drops to only 20 percent (see model 10.2). When this is done, the role of the occupational structure becomes significant: societies with a relatively *low* proportion of the economy in the tertiary sector are most likely to have shifted. But when the social structure variables are dropped and well-being and trust are restored, the percentage of variance explained recovers fully, returning to 32 percent. Dropping GNP/capita from the analysis does not reduce the explanatory power of the model (it actually rises slightly). Far from confirming Muller and Seligson's finding that subjective well-being is irrelevant to democracy, this analysis suggests that the authoritarian regimes fell, in part, because they had lost mass legitimacy.

We also tested the impact of a number of other variables, with the results shown in table 6.11. When we add "support for revolutionary change" to the regression (in model 11.1), this new variable almost reaches the .05 level of significance, while subjective well-being drops just below that threshold: both of these variables tap regime legitimacy and they share a good deal of variance, reducing each others' explanatory power.

When we drop "support for revolutionary change" and add "support for gradual reform," however, the latter variable has very little explanatory power (and subjective well-being rises above the .05 significance level). Contrary to the findings of Muller and Seligson (1994), support for revolutionary change seems to have a stronger impact on short-term changes than does support for gradual reform, though neither of them increases the proportion of explained variance significantly.

Model 11.3 shows what happens when we add income inequality to the regression model. Countries with less inequality are somewhat more likely to change than those with greater inequality, but the effect is not significant and this variable does not add much to the percentage of variance explained.

Model 11.4 adds our indicator of Social Capital, organizational memberships, to the regression. Doing so increases the percentage of variance explained markedly, almost doubling the adjusted R^2. In this model, interpersonal trust, subjective well-being, and organizational memberships all have significant effects: societies that are low on trust and well-being, but high on social capital, are the ones that are most likely to have shifted toward democracy from 1990 to 1995. Social Capital had shown the predicted polarity but had not attained a significant level in our previous analyses. Its inclusion here brings a dramatic change, producing what seems to be a model that is much stronger than those that lack it. This analysis is based on a significantly smaller number of cases than the other models, because we have data on organizational memberships for eight fewer societies than those included in the other analyses in table 6.11. Nevertheless, these findings tend to support the hypothesis that social capital plays a significant role in democratization.

WHICH COMES FIRST: DEMOCRATIC POLITICAL CULTURE OR DEMOCRACY?

We have found strong evidence that political culture and the level and stability of democracy are closely linked. But determining the causal direction of relationships in social science is always difficult. One way to explain away the linkages between culture and democracy would be to argue that they reflect a spurious effect of economic determinism, in which economic development gives rise to a specific type of culture, *and* to democratic institutions, without culture being an intervening variable. This interpretation does not hold up in the light of the analyses we have just carried out: economic development is indeed important, but its effect seems to work mainly through changes that it brings in culture and social structure.

Another interpretation that might explain away the relationships we have observed between culture and democracy could be termed Institutional Determinism. This interpretation would argue that the linkages between culture and democracy exist because democratic institutions determine the underlying culture.

This model contains a grain of truth: institutions *do* help shape their society's culture—along with many other factors. But the plausibility of the interpretation that institutional determinism is the major explanation is severely undermined by the findings of Burkhart and Lewis-Beck (1994) that economic development leads to democracy, but democracy does not bring economic development. The causal process seems to run from economic factors to institutions, rather than the other way around—and, as we have seen, the economic factors work mainly through changes in culture and social structure.

Institutions do influence politics and economics. But they do not explain them by themselves, and the importance of their role varies greatly according to the kind of behavior in question. For example, institutions have a major impact on relatively narrow and highly formalized behavior such as voting turnout. Voting is an activity that engages the average citizen briefly once every four or five years and is highly amenable to institutional control. By simply changing the laws, for example, one can expand the electorate overnight to include women or 18–20-year-olds. Or by applying severe sanctions against nonvoting, one can produce extremely high rates of turnout. Thus, the ex-communist societies regularly reported voter turnout rates of 98 or 99 percent, and Albania may hold the world's record for electoral participation, with a reported turnout of 99.99 percent in one of Enver Hoxha's last elections. Although they were voting for a one-party slate, the regime got almost every living citizen to the polls. The point is that voting turnout is relatively easily manipulated by elites: it does not necessarily reflect any real choice or deep-rooted preferences on the part of the masses.

Stable democracy, by contrast, depends on a deeply rooted sense of legitimacy among the public. Simply making it illegal not to trust people or legally requiring everyone to be satisfied with their lives would not produce governmental legitimacy or a society of trust.

Trust and legitimacy are much more diffuse characteristics than voter turnout, and much less amenable to institutional manipulation. They reflect the entire historical heritage of the given society, with the political institutions being only one of many relevant factors. Similarly, economic growth does not seem to result from simply getting the right institutions: societies with a wide variety of institutions have failed to attain it. And conversely, high rates of economic growth have been achieved by societies with institutions ranging from democratic to authoritarian ones, with market economies or state-run economies, and with small-scale enterprises or huge industrial conglomerates.

The same is true of stable democracy: if it were simply a question of getting the right institutions, the world would be much nicer. One could simply xerox the U.S. Constitution and mail it out to all the governments of the world. Unfortunately, reality is not that simple: the fact that each society has a distinctive economic and social structure and cultural heritage can have a decisive impact on whether or not democracy survives in that society.

Thus, the former Soviet Union had one of the most democratic constitutions in the world (on paper), guaranteeing high levels of civil rights and political freedom, together with referenda, recall of judges, and other enlightened features. Great Britain, on the other hand, has no written constitution: the basic rules of democracy exist only as unwritten norms. But in the Soviet Union, the constitutional guarantees had no real effect, while in Britain, they were generally observed—with results that were as different as day and night. The current debate between advocates of an institutional approach and the advocates of a behavioral approach wrongly assumes that the two are separable. They are not. Formal institutions and political culture have a symbiotic relationship, with institutions becoming a behavioral reality only insofar as they become a part of the political culture.

An Institutional Determinist interpretation of these findings would argue that a society's level of interpersonal trust is determined by how long it has lived under democratic institutions. Our position, by contrast, is that interpersonal trust reflects a society's entire historical heritage, with its political institutions being merely one contributing factor. Although we lack sufficient time series data for a conclusive test, the institutional determinist model fails to hold up in those cases where we do have a substantial time series. For example, the peoples of Northern and Southern Italy have lived together under the same political institutions since unification 125 years ago. Nevertheless (as we have seen), Northern Italian society continues to show much higher levels of interpersonal trust than Southern Italy: clearly, these differences in trust levels reflect something other than the presence or absence of democratic institutions. The United States furnishes an even stronger refutation of the institutional determinist thesis. It is one of the oldest democracies in the world and shows relatively high levels of interpersonal trust (though by no means the highest in the world). But are these high levels of trust due to its democratic institutions? Apparently not—for trust in government has shown a sharp decline among the American public during the past few decades: in 1958, only 24 percent of the American public expressed distrust in the national government; in 1992, fully 80 percent expressed distrust. But this collapse of trust in government was *not* mirrored in a similar collapse of interpersonal trust which was relatively stable, declining only slightly. Interpersonal trust apparently moved on a different trajectory, which suggests that interpersonal trust was *not* determined by the American people's experience in the political sphere. Moreover, it is perfectly clear that stable democracy does not necessarily produce high levels of trust. In the United States, it has actually been declining.

In addition to these empirical findings, there are theoretical grounds to doubt the institutional determinism model. To illustrate this point, let us turn to our other main variable, subjective well-being. There are clear reasons why democratic regimes cannot survive unless they are supported by the masses: if they are not, the public can simply vote them out of existence. The classic example was that of Weimar Germany, when Hitler came to power in 1933; this happened again most recently in Algeria, where the military took over to prevent a democratically elected Islamic Fundamentalist party from taking power; and it came close to happening in Russia in 1996 and could still conceivably happen there. But when we try to reverse the causal arrow, there is no obvious reason why democratic regimes would necessarily be more successful than authoritarian regimes in *producing* high levels of subjective well-being for their citizens. History indicates that they sometimes do and sometimes do not. In Germany, the Weimar regime apparently did not produce high levels of subjective well-being, but the Bonn regime did. Subjective well-being was higher under the authoritarian Soviet regime than it is under the current, more democratic, Russian regime. The World Values survey data show that in 1990 (the year before the collapse of the Soviet dictatorship), 33 percent of the Russian public were dissatisfied with their lives as a whole (scores of 1–4 on a 10-point scale). A 1995 survey of the Russian public replicated this question; it found that 51 percent of the Russian public—an absolute majority—were dissatisfied with their lives as a whole.[5] Far from automatically producing subjective well-being, the experience of the Russian people with democracy so far has been linked with a *decline* in overall life satisfaction.

The Euro-Barometer surveys provide a less dramatic but more broadly based demonstration of the fact that living under democratic institutions does not automatically produce rising life satisfaction. As we saw in figure 6.4, subjective well-being levels were remarkably stable among established Western European democracies throughout the period from 1973 to 1995. More than 20 years of being democracies *did not* significantly raise their levels of subjective well-being. The evidence suggests that high levels of subjective well-being are a prerequisite for stable democratic institutions, rather than an automatic consequence of them.

Even apart from this strong empirical evidence, it seems highly unlikely that the extremely strong correlation ($r = .82$) that we find between subjective well-being and democracy is *simply* a consequence of having democratic institutions: to accept this interpretation, one would need to believe (1) that whether the masses are experiencing desperate misery or high levels of well-being has no impact on the survival of democratic institutions, but (2) that democratic institutions have almost magical powers to make people happy.

[5] Results from a representative national survey of the adult population of the Russian Republic (N = 2,040), carried out by the Russian Institute of Public Opinion (ROMIR) in November 1995.

The latter proposition simply is not plausible. To assume that a society's subjective well-being is determined by its political institutions is to assume that the tail is wagging the dog. Andrews and Withey (1976) have demonstrated that among the American public, subjective well-being is determined mainly by one's level of satisfaction with one's family life, one's marriage, job, home, friends, and leisure time—with politics making only a relatively minor contribution to overall subjective well-being. This accords with a large body of evidence that politics plays only a peripheral role in most people's lives.

Findings from the 1990 World Values Survey demonstrate that this holds true not only in America but in the world as a whole: politics is only of relatively minor subjective importance to most people. When asked how important various things were in their lives, the following percentages of the publics of our 43 societies rated the six following domains "very important":

1. Family   83%
2. Work   59%
3. Friends   38%
4. Leisure   33%
5. Religion   28%
6. Politics   13%

Politics ranked dead last, with only one person in eight considering it very important. Six times as many people emphasized the family, as emphasized politics. This may be dismaying to political scientists, but it seems to be a global reality. Politics was rated least important in almost every country.

Unlike totalitarian systems, democracies make only modest efforts to reshape their underlying cultures: the very essence of democracies is that they *reflect* the preferences of their citizens, rather than attempting to dictate them. It seems highly unlikely that the powerful correlation that we have found between culture and democracy exists because democratic institutions somehow create a new culture. Democratic institutions probably encourage feelings of interpersonal trust to some extent and may have some tendency to enhance subjective well-being, but the process seems to work mainly in the opposite direction: mass well-being and trust are crucial to the viability of democratic institutions.

Postmaterialist Values and the Future of Advanced Industrial Society

In advanced industrial society, prolonged prosperity and the welfare state contribute to an increasingly widespread sense that survival can be taken for granted, giving rise to another cultural factor conducive to democracy: the spread of Postmaterialist values. This is a relatively recent development, and it may be a major reason why, although early industrial societies were almost equally likely to mobilize their publics into democratic, fascist, or communist forms of political participation, advanced industrial society gives rise to democracy almost exclusively, rather than to either of the two other forms of modern political regimes.

Both theory and empirical evidence indicate that Postmaterialist values did not become a significant factor in politics until about two decades after World War II; clearly, Postmaterialist values cannot explain the stability of democracy throughout the period since 1920. Moreover, even today these values are widespread only in advanced industrial societies; they could not very well be the main factor explaining the *levels* of democracy found throughout the world. Nevertheless, there is reason to believe that they are conducive to democracy in advanced industrial societies, contributing to a growing demand for higher levels of mass participation in politics.

Our theory implies that a shift toward Postmaterialist values should occur in any nation that develops high levels of economic security. As we have seen, this process seems to be at work not only in the West but also in East Asia (parts of which have now attained Western levels of prosperity) and even to some extent in Eastern Europe.

Postmaterialist values are conducive to democracy for three reasons: (1) They entail an emphasis on self-expression and participation that is inherently conducive to political participation, and, as we will see, Postmaterialists are relatively likely to act to attain democracy. (2) Postmaterialists view democracy as something that is intrinsically desirable—and not just as a possible means to become wealthy and successful. Thus, their support for democracy is more secure than that of Materialists, many of whom were initially attracted to democracy simply because it was associated with being rich. (3) In addition to their emphasis on participation and free speech, Postmaterialists tend to hold a wide range of basic democratic norms, as recent research demonstrates. Thus, Rohrschneider (1993) finds that Postmaterialist values are an important factor accounting for the presence or absence of democratic attitudes among the elites of both the former German Democratic Republic and the Federal Republic of Germany.

Research by Gibson and Duch in the former Soviet Union also demonstrates this point. Gibson and Duch (1994) developed a broad based scale of support for democratic values. This scale integrates seven subscales measuring (1) valuation of liberty, (2) support for democratic norms, (3) rights consciousness, (4) support for dissent and opposition, (5) support for independent mass media, (6) support for competitive elections, and (7) political tolerance. In their 1990 survey of the European Soviet Union, Gibson and Duch find that

> Those who hold Postmaterialist values are markedly more likely to support these democratic values. In the European USSR data the percentage high in support for democratic values ranges from 14 percent for the Materialists to 80 percent for the Postmaterialists, a truly remarkable difference. This is quite strong support for Inglehart's theory: Postmaterialists are much more likely to support core democratic values such as tolerance, competitive elections, etc. To what degree, though, are these findings

spurious—that is, are they a function of other factors that contribute to the development of *both* democratic and Postmaterialist values? We can consider the effect of Postmaterialism on democratic values controlling for a number of attributes of the respondents that might well account for both sets of values. . . . We find that Postmaterialism has a substantial impact on democratic values beyond the effect of these demographic attributes. Those who are more highly educated, and who are younger are more likely to support democratic processes and institutions, and these variables alone can account for a respectable amount of variance in the dependent variable. Yet when the Postmaterialism indicator is added to the equation, *an additional 10 percent of the variance can be explained.* Even while controlling for age, education, social class, etc., Postmaterialists are considerably more supportive of democratic values than are Materialists. (Gibson and Duch, 1994: 20–21)

Since Postmaterialists emphasize individual freedom and self-expression, it is not surprising that Postmaterialist values correlate with democratic values, but Gibson and Duch's finding is far from tautologous. By demonstrating the linkages between democratic values and Postmaterialist values, Gibson and Duch help integrate democratic theory and the theory of value change. Their findings imply that we should find an intergenerational trend toward increasing support for basic democratic values in societies that experience economic growth and attain higher levels of mass security.

The Growing Role of Mass Political Action

Value change has important behavioral implications. In any setting, Postmaterialists are relatively ready to act to attain their political goals—but in authoritarian systems, they are the ones most likely to act in order to attain democracy.

Representative samples of the publics interviewed in the World Values survey were asked about their readiness to take part in four forms of political action: (1) joining in boycotts, (2) attending lawful demonstrations, (3) joining unofficial strikes, (4) occupying buildings or factories. Using similar questions in eight Western democracies, Barnes et al. (1979) demonstrated that Materialist/Postmaterialist values are strongly related to one's willingness to participate in unconventional political activities such as these, in order to press for some political goal.

The spread of citizen activism is not merely a Western phenomenon. Postmaterialist values show the same linkages with unconventional political protest potential in Eastern Europe and East Asia as they do in Western countries. The data from the World Values surveys reveal that in country after country, Postmaterialists are two to four times as likely to engage in unconventional political action, as are Materialists. Figure 6.7 shows the percentage of the Russian public who said (in 1990–91) that they "have done" or "might do" all four of these activities.

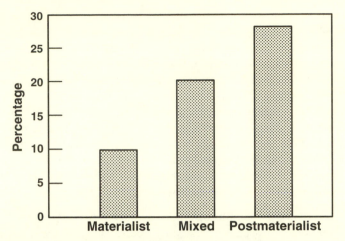

Figure 6.7. Readiness to undertake unconventional political action, by value type: Russia, 1990–91.
Percentage saying they "have done" or "might do" all four of the following: (1) join in boycotts, (2) attend lawful demonstrations, (3) join unofficial strikes, and (4) occupy buildings or factories.
Source: World Values Survey carried out in Russia, December 1990–January 1991.

The spread of Postmaterialist values seems to be increasing the degree to which mass publics engage in elite-challenging political action. From 1981 to 1990, public readiness to engage in these activities became more widespread in the great majority of societies for which we have data, as we will see in chapter 10. In nondemocratic regimes, unconventional political action may play an even *more* important role than it does in the West: it may serve as the proximate cause by which the public obtains democratization. From Seoul to Warsaw to Budapest to East Berlin, mass participation in strikes, demonstrations, and boycotts—precisely the activities examined here—played a crucial part in the transitions to democracy launched throughout Eastern Europe in 1989, and in recent moves toward democratization in East Asia and Latin America.

People power has become an unprecedentedly important factor in politics. It proved its effectiveness again six months after these surveys, in August 1991, when hard-liners in the Soviet Union attempted to seize power, arresting Gorbachev and rolling tanks into Moscow. But to widespread surprise, this time the Russian people did not resign themselves to authoritarian rule. Instead, citizens poured into the streets, defying the reactionary coup's leaders and building barricades around the Russian Parliament building where Yeltsin had organized resistance. Crowds of citizens brought armored columns to a halt. Miners went on strike. And entire units of tanks and paratroops went over to the resistance.

Both economic and noneconomic motives played a part in motivating mass resistance to communism. Its economic failures contributed to its downfall.

But it is equally important that the desire for freedom of speech and self-determination have become high-priority goals, for more people, than ever before in history. Postmaterialists are far likelier than Materialists to have taken part in the strikes, demonstrations, and other unconventional protest actions which brought down the communist regimes (or helped maintain the reform regime, in the Soviet case).

As the younger, better-educated, and more Postmaterialistic birth cohorts replace the older, less-educated ones in the adult population, we would expect elite-challenging political action to increase. Does it? In virtually all societies for which we have time series data, the answer is yes. In almost every country included in both waves of the World Values surveys, we find the predicted shift. The proportion of people who have actually done elite-challenging political actions during the past five years rose substantially from 1981 to 1990, as we will see below. One frequently reads journalistic accounts that mass publics have become politically apathetic, citing evidence that voter turnout has stagnated or declined. These accounts are accurate about voting, but miss the point that people display a rising potential for elite-challenging action. Voting turnout statistics convey a misleading impression of political apathy. Mass publics *are* becoming less likely to vote, which is a relatively elite-controlled form of participation; but throughout industrial society they are becoming *more* likely to engage in elite-challenging behavior.

THE IMPACT OF MASS VALUES ON DEMOCRATIZATION, POLITICAL CULTURE, AND STABLE DEMOCRACY

Do individual-level values have an impact on the societies in which people live? The evidence we have just examined suggests that democracy should be more likely to emerge (and survive) in societies with relatively large numbers of Postmaterialists than elsewhere. Is this the case?

The horizontal axis on figure 6.8 reflects the balance between Materialists and Postmaterialists in each country. The pattern is clear. Nations with relatively high proportions of Postmaterialists are much more likely to have had continuously functioning democratic institutions than other societies. Those with heavily Materialist publics tend to be not democratic, or to be recent (and possibly unstable) democracies. All but one of the countries that were not yet democratic in 1990 show scores *below* +10 on the Materialist/Postmaterialist values index on figure 6.8 (the sole exception being Mexico). All but one of the democracies had scores *above* that level (the sole exception being India).

One consequence of this cultural transformation is rising mass pressure for more democratic and participatory institutions. Although mass preferences *alone* do not determine when democratization takes place, there is a remarkably strong correlation between the ratio of Postmaterialists to Materialists and the existence of stable democracy ($r = .71$). Correlation is not causation. But the evidence of a causal link between Postmaterialist values and stable democ-

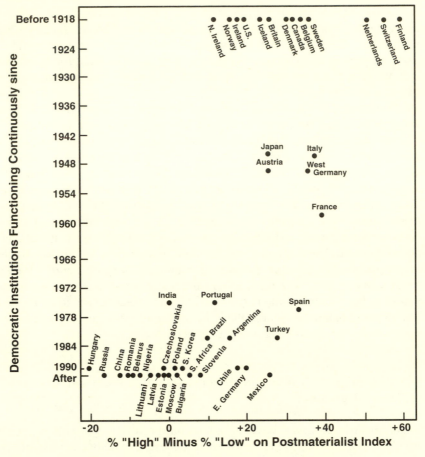

Figure 6.8. Stable democracy and Materialist/Postmaterialist values.
N = 43, r = .71, significant at .0000 level. *Source*: 1990–91 World Values Survey. *Note*:
Respondents are classified as "high" on the 12-item Materialist/Postmaterialist values
index used here if they gave high priority to at least three of the five Postmaterialist
goals (ranking them among the two most important in each group of four goals). They
are classified as "low" if they gave high priority to none of the five Postmaterialist goals.

racy goes well beyond cross-sectional evidence. It is reinforced by individual-
level findings that suggest *why* countries with relatively Postmaterialist publics
should be likelier to become stable democracies: (1) their publics give relatively high priority to individual freedom and to democratic values, and (2)
their publics are relatively likely to engage in direct political action that can
help bring a shift from authoritarian to democratic regimes.

    When we entered Postmaterialist values into the regression analyses above,
they showed positive but not significant linkages with stable democracy and
high levels of democracy. These values are part of a highly intercorrelated syn-

drome consisting of interpersonal trust, subjective well-being, a large tertiary sector, a highly educated population, and well-developed organizational networks. This syndrome is strongly linked with democracy; but Postmaterialism is not among the two or three independent variables that show significant effects. Thus far, it seems to have played only a secondary role in the emergence and spread of democracy. But if advanced industrial societies continue to produce an increasingly widespread feeling that survival can be taken for granted among a growing proportion of their populations, the political implications of Postmaterialist values may be far-reaching.

CONCLUSION

The evolution of industrial society makes democracy more likely. It brings gradual cultural changes that make mass publics increasingly likely to want democratic institutions and more supportive of them once they are in place. This transformation does not come easily or automatically. Determined elites, in control of the army and police, can resist pressures for democratization. But the emergence of prosperous welfare states leads to gradual long-term changes in which mass publics give an increasingly high priority to autonomy and self-expression in all spheres of life including politics. And as they mature, industrial societies develop increasingly specialized and educated labor forces, which become increasingly adept at exerting political pressure. It becomes more difficult and costly to repress demands for political liberalization. Moreover, economic development is also linked with relatively high levels of subjective well-being and interpersonal trust, which also seem to play a crucial role in democracy. With rising levels of economic development, cultural patterns emerge that are increasingly supportive of democracy, making mass publics more likely to *want* democracy, and more skillful at *getting* it.

Although rich societies are much likelier to be democratic than poor ones, wealth alone does not automatically bring democracy. But the process of industrialization does have an inherent tendency to produce changes that are conducive to democracy. In the long run, the only way to avoid the growth of increasingly articulate and effective mass demands for democratization would be to reject industrialization. Very few ruling elites in the contemporary world are willing to do so. Those societies that do move onto the trajectory of industrial society will eventually face increasingly powerful pressures for democratization.

Our findings suggest that political culture plays a much more crucial role in democracy than the literature of the past two decades would indicate. Although it does not seem to be the immediate cause of the *transition* to democracy, political culture does seem to be a central factor in the survival of democracy. In the long run, democracy is not attained simply by making institutional changes or through clever elite-level maneuvering. Its survival also depends on what ordinary people think and feel.

CHAPTER 7

The Impact of Culture on Economic Growth[1]

INTRODUCTION

Do cultural factors influence economic development? If so, can they be measured and their effect compared with that of standard economic factors such as savings and investment? This chapter examines the explanatory power of the standard growth model based on economic variables and compares it with that of cultural variables such as achievement motivation, Postmaterialist values, and social capital factors such as membership in associations. We argue that it is not an either/or proposition: cultural and economic variables play complementary roles and both are needed to produce growth. This hypothesis is tested empirically, using recently developed econometric techniques to assess alternative interpretations of economic growth.

In chapter 2 we found that a major dimension of cross-cultural variation—the Modernization dimension—was closely linked with the long-term economic growth rates of the 43 societies examined there. Although this suggests that basic values may be an important factor in economic development, we did not analyze causal relationships in that chapter, which simply presented a broad overview of the cross-national patterns. We return to that finding here, probing more deeply into the linkages between values and economic growth.

It is clear that cultural factors alone do not explain all of the cross-national variation in economic growth rates. Every economy experiences yearly fluctuations in growth rates as a result of short-term factors; these are not attributable to cultural factors, which fluctuate relatively little. It is evident that a given society's economic and political institutions are also important: for example, North Korea and South Korea had a common culture until 1945, but South Korea's economic performance has been vastly superior since then. Similarly, though China experienced some periods of high growth rates during the Maoist era, its economic performance has been much stronger since the pragmatists took control after the death of Mao. And Chile experienced low growth rates throughout the period from World War II to the 1970s, but has shown high growth rates since adopting structural reforms. Obviously, cultural factors *alone* do not explain why economic growth rates vary.

But there is equally strong evidence that cultural differences are an important part of the story. For example, during the 45 years of the Cold War, West Germany had the strongest economy in Western Europe, while East Germany had the most advanced economy in the Soviet bloc. Even more strikingly, over

---

[1] Ronald Inglehart, James Granato, and David Leblang are coauthors of this chapter.

the past five decades the Confucian-influenced societies of East Asia have out-performed the rest of the world by a wide margin. This holds true despite the fact that they have had an enormous variety of economic and political institutions—ranging from the extreme laissez-faire capitalism of Hong Kong to the state-run economy of Maoist China, and from the highly concentrated capitalist conglomerates of South Korea to the fragmented small enterprises of Taiwan, and under political institutions that ranged from liberal democracy to some of the world's most authoritarian regimes. The linkage between Confucian culture and economic achievement also manifests itself at the individual level, under a variety of institutional settings. East Asian minorities throughout the world—operating under a wide range of political and economic institutions—have achieved remarkable rates of social mobility and economic achievement. The performance of East Asian minorities has been a striking success story from Southeast Asia to Western Europe, North America, and Latin America. Institutions alone do not determine economic growth, any more than do cultural factors alone. Both societal-level and individual-level evidence suggests that a society's economic and political institutions are shaped by cultural factors as well as by economics.

We hypothesize that cultural and economic factors play complementary roles in economic growth. Surprisingly enough, this position has rarely been taken previously: the literature has tended to present culture and economic determinants of growth as mutually exclusive. One reason for this is because until now we have had inadequate measures of the cultural factors. Most previous attempts to establish the role of culture have either inferred culture from economic performance, which is circular and proves nothing, or have attempted to estimate cultural factors from impressionistic historical evidence. Since this evidence was not quantitative, it was usually used to support sweeping all-or-nothing claims: its relative impact could not be measured against that of economic factors, so its advocates felt obliged to assert that it was decisive all by itself. Debate centered on the question whether cultural factors determined economic growth, or whether economic factors were decisive. It is perfectly conceivable that *both* types of factors are important, but until cultural factors could be used in quantitative analysis, this possibility could not be tested.

By culture, we refer to a system of common basic values that help shape the behavior of the people in a given society. In most preindustrial societies, this value system takes the form of a religion and changes very slowly; but with industrialization and accompanying processes of Modernization, these worldviews tend to become more secular, rational, and open to change.

For reasons discussed earlier, the cultures of virtually all preindustrial societies are hostile to social mobility and individual economic accumulation. Thus, both medieval Christianity and traditional Confucian culture stigmatized profit-making and entrepreneurship. But (as Weber argued) a revised Protestant version of Christianity played a key role in the rise of capitalism; and at a later stage of history, a modernized version of Confucian society encouraged economic growth through its support of education and achievement.

We will first discuss theories that deal with the impact of culture on economic growth; next we will present some data demonstrating the surprisingly strong empirical linkages between cultural variables measured in the World Values survey and economic growth rates. We will then discuss the baseline endogenous growth model, which attempts to explain economic growth on the basis of economic factors alone. This approach has demonstrated that a given country's investment rate plays a key role in economic growth rates. But it has been unable to explain why some countries have high investment rates while others have low ones: standard economic variables, such as GNP per capita, are only weakly related to growth rates and explain very little. Why do some societies save and invest to a much greater extent than others? And why have the investment rates of some societies (such as the United States) gradually declined over time? We suggest that cultural factors help provide answers to both questions. Finally, we will integrate cultural and economic variables into a multivariate analysis that analyzes the contributions of both sets of factors.

Theories dealing with the impact of culture on economic development go back to Max Weber and Alexis de Tocqueville, respectively. The first set of ideas stresses the importance of motivational factors while the second emphasizes the importance of networks of voluntary associations. We will refer to these two bodies of theory as dealing with motivation and social capital, respectively.

MOTIVATIONAL FACTORS AND ECONOMIC GROWTH

The motivational literature stresses the degree to which given cultures emphasize or stigmatize economic accumulation and achievement. It grows out of Weber's (1904–5) Protestant Ethic thesis, which has been controversial for 90 years and continues to be influential. This school of thought gave rise to historical research from Tawney (1922) to Harrison (1992), and to empirical work by McClelland (1953, 1961) on Achievement Motivation, and continued with Inglehart's (1971, 1977, 1990) work on the shift from Materialist to Postmaterialist value priorities—a process that could be viewed as the erosion of the Protestant Ethic among populations that have experienced high levels of economic security.

Chapter 1 proposed a modified interpretation of Weber's thesis concerning the role of the Protestant Ethic in economic development. Briefly, we argued that Weber was correct in viewing the rise of Protestantism as a crucial event in modernizing Europe. He emphasized the fact that the Calvinist version of Protestantism encouraged norms favorable to economic achievement. But the rise of Protestantism was only one case of a more general phenomenon. It was important not simply because of the specific content of early Protestant beliefs, but because it undermined a set of religious norms that inhibit economic achievement and that are common to most preindustrial societies. Let us consider how this works.

Preindustrial economies are zero-sum systems: because they experience little or no economic growth, upward social mobility can only come at someone else's expense. Traditional cultural norms generally reflect this fact: social status is hereditary rather than achieved, and social norms encourage one to accept one's social position in this life, emphasizing that the denial of one's worldly aspirations will be rewarded in the next life. Aspirations toward social mobility are sternly repressed. Such value systems help to maintain social solidarity and discourage economic accumulation in a variety of ways, ranging from norms of sharing and charity, to the norms of noblesse oblige, to the potlatch and similar institutions found from pre-Columbian North America to Africa, in which one attains prestige by recklessly giving away one's worldly goods.

The traditional value systems of agrarian societies are adapted to maintaining a stable balance in an unchanging technological environment. They discourage social change in general and accumulative entrepreneurial behavior in particular, which tends to be relegated to pariah groups if tolerated at all. Economic accumulation is viewed as greed. To facilitate the economic accumulation needed to launch industrialization, these cultural inhibitions must be relaxed.

In Western society, the Protestant Reformation helped break the grip of the medieval Christian worldview on a significant part of Europe. Throughout the first 150 years of the Industrial Revolution, industrial development took place almost entirely within the Protestant regions of Europe and the Protestant portions of the New World. This began to change only during the second half of the twentieth century, when precisely those regions that had been most strongly influenced by the Protestant Ethic—and had become economically secure— began to de-emphasize economic growth, gradually turning toward Postmaterialist values. Meanwhile, an entrepreneurial outlook had emerged in Catholic Europe and (even more strikingly) in the Far East, both of which now show higher rates of economic growth than Protestant Europe. Today, the concept of the Protestant Ethic would be outdated if we took it to mean something that can only exist in historically Protestant countries. But Weber's more general insight that cultural factors can influence economic growth is valid.

McClelland's (1953, 1961) work on Achievement Motivation built on the Weberian thesis but focused on the values that were encouraged in children by their parents, schools, and other agencies of socialization. He hypothesized that some societies (whether Protestant, Catholic, Islamic, or other) tend to emphasize economic achievement as a positive goal, while others give it little emphasis. Since he could not directly measure the values emphasized in given societies through representative national surveys, McClelland attempted to measure them indirectly, through content analysis of the stories and school books used to educate children in various societies. He found that some cultures *did* emphasize achievement in their school books more heavily than others— and that the former showed considerably higher rates of economic growth (as measured by rates of electric power consumption) than did the latter.

McClelland's work has been criticized on various grounds. It was questioned whether his approach really measured the values actually taught to children, or simply those of textbook writers. And subsequently, writers of the dependency school argued that any attempt to trace differences in economic growth rates to factors within a given culture, rather than to global capitalist exploitation, was simply a means of justifying capitalist exploitation of the peripheral economies. Such criticism served to denigrate this type of research but was hardly an empirical refutation.

Survey research by Lenski (1963) and by Alwin (1986) found that Catholics and Protestants in the United States showed significant differences in the values they emphasized as the most important things to teach children, and that these differences followed the lines of the Protestant Ethic thesis, with Protestants being more likely to emphasize determination and individual autonomy, while Catholics tended to emphasize obedience. But Alwin also demonstrated that these differences have been eroding over time, with Protestants and Catholics in the United States gradually converging toward a common belief system (somewhat as Catholic Europe and Protestant Europe gradually became less dissimilar).

Building on this line of research, the World Values survey asked representative national samples of the publics in 43 societies, "Here is a list of qualities that children can be encouraged to learn at home. Which, if any, do you consider to be especially important?" This list included qualities that reflected emphasis on autonomy and economic achievement, such as "thrift, saving money and things" and "determination," and others that reflected emphasis on conformity to traditional social norms, such as "obedience" and "religious faith."

We constructed an index of Achievement Motivation that sums up the percentage in each country emphasizing the first two goals, minus the percentage emphasizing the latter two goals. This method of index construction offsets the tendency of respondents in some societies to place relatively heavy emphasis on *all* of these goals, while respondents in other countries mention relatively few of them. We thus obtain an index that ranges from -200 (which would result if 100 percent of the people in a given society emphasized "obedience," and 100 percent emphasized "religious faith," while no one emphasized either "thrift" or "determination") to $+200$ (which would result if everyone emphasized "thrift" and "determination" while no one emphasized "obedience" or "religious faith"). A score of zero results if there is exactly as much emphasis on the two traditional goals, as on the two achievement motivation goals.

Do different societies emphasize different qualities in raising their children? And are these values related to their economic growth rates? The answer to both questions is Yes. The societies examined here show tremendous variation, ranging from scores of -100 on the achievement motivation scale, to scores of $+100$. And the relationship that we find between childrearing values and economic growth is surprisingly strong. Our four-item Achievement Motivation index shows a .66 correlation (significant at the .001 level) with the economic growth rates observed from 1960 to 1990 in these societies.

Our dependent variable in this analysis is the given society's mean annual rate of real growth in GDP per capita, using data from Levine and Renelt (1992) covering the period from 1960 to 1990. Using a long time period such as this is appropriate when testing the linkages between economic growth and long-term attributes such as culture and social structure: this minimizes the impact of short-term fluctuations. We end the series in 1990, the year in which the World Values surveys were carried out.

The ex-socialist societies other than China are excluded from the analysis shown here because data on their economic growth rates are of uncertain reliability; including them, using the best available data, produces similar results (which are reported in Appendix 3).[2]

Although frequently stereotyped as having authoritarian cultures, China, Japan, and South Korea all emerge near the pole that emphasizes thrift rather than obedience. The three East Asian societies in this survey rank highest on Achievement Motivation, while the two African societies included in this survey rank near the opposite end of the continuum, emphasizing obedience and religious faith. The publics of India and the United States also fall toward the low end of the achievement motivation scale. This scale reflects the balance between two types of values: one type of values—emphasizing thrift and determination—supports economic achievement, while the other—emphasizing

---

[2] In Appendix 3, we include 11 ex-socialist societies in a similar analysis, using growth rates from the *World Handbook of Political and Social Indicators* (1st, 2d, and 3d editions). Figure A.3 shows the overall relationship between values and economic growth rates in this larger pool of societies. For the period 1965–88, our data for most countries come from the *World Development Report, 1990* (World Bank, 1990), but the data for all ex-communist societies (not including China) come from the *World Bank Atlas, 1992* and cover only 1980–91. The data for China in the earlier period cover only the period from 1952 through 1961. Our analysis is based on a weighted average of the growth rates for the earlier and later time periods.

The data from the ex-communist countries are less reliable than those from market economies. They are based on different accounting systems and tend to exaggerate growth rates. Furthermore, since separate growth figures are not available for the Soviet (or Yugoslav) successor states prior to 1980, we use the Soviet (or Yugoslav) growth rates for these societies in the earlier period. Clearly, these data are imperfect. But they reflect the best available estimates, from widely recognized sources; and we believe that they are in the right ballpark for purposes of global comparisons. Soviet sources claimed a 13 percent annual growth rate for the Soviet Union during the 1950s. The *World Handbook* credits the USSR with a much more plausible 4.9 percent growth rate in 1950–65; this is a higher rate than that of most Western democracies, but considerably lower than the 7.8 percent rate which the World Handbook estimates for Japan, or the 5.5 percent rate given for West Germany. In recent years, the Soviet economy slowed down, stagnated, and then, during the transition from a command economy to a market economy, collapsed: the World Bank estimates that Russia had a growth rate of only 1.3 percent during 1981–90 and negative growth more recently (China continued to grow at an estimated 7.8 percent). The recent collapse of most communist economies has been dramatic, but it should not obscure the fact that these societies once had some of the world's highest growth rates. Though the growth rates for the ex-socialist societies and China from 1950 through 1988 have relatively high error margins, few informed observers doubt that these countries experienced much higher growth during most of this period than did such countries as Argentina, Chile, Nigeria, and India; or the United States, Canada, and Great Britain.

obedience and religious faith—tends to discourage it, stressing conformity to traditional authority and norms. These two types of values are not necessarily incompatible: some societies rank high on both, while others rank relatively low on both. But the relatively *priority* accorded to these two types of values is strongly related to a society's growth rate.

Correlation is not causation, of course. In the remainder of this chapter, we will examine other possible causal factors that might account for the striking linkage we have found between Achievement Motivation and economic growth. Unless we can prove these linkages to be spurious, the no-relationship thesis seems untenable. But what third factor could be causing a spurious relationship here?

One possible candidate is suggested by the dependency school, which holds that the dominant factor is international economic exchanges: foreign investment and trade undermine economic growth in peripheral countries. This is the opposite of what economic theory would predict. Economists, citing the benefits of comparative advantage, argue that foreign investment and trade work to *enhance* the wealth of any country. While certain jobs and occupations will lose out, they tend to be replaced by new jobs and occupations that have even higher productivity levels than their predecessors. This increase in productivity leads to greater prosperity. This theoretical expectation is borne out empirically: Hein (1992) and Dollar (1992) analyze economic data from 150 countries and demonstrate that foreign trade and investment variables actually have a rather modest relationship to growth—but that their polarity is the opposite of that proposed by dependency theory: those nations that traded more and had more investment from capitalist countries showed higher, not lower, subsequent rates of economic growth.

Another possible way to explain away the strong linkage between culture and economic growth shown in figure 7.1 would be by arguing that economic growth determines values, rather than the other way around. Do cultural factors lead to economic growth, or does economic growth lead to cultural change? We believe that the causal flow can work in both directions, with the predominant influence varying from case to case. For example, there is strong evidence that Postmaterialist values emerge when a society has attained relatively high levels of economic security: in this case, economic change reshapes culture. On the other hand, once these values become widespread, they are linked with relatively low subsequent rates of economic growth. Here, culture seems to be shaping economics.

In the present case, the most plausible interpretation is that determination and thrift are conducive to economic growth. For some time, economists have been aware that a nation's rate of gross domestic investment is a major influence—generally, the *most* important influence—on its long-term growth rate. Investment, in turn, depends on savings. Thus, a perfectly straightforward reading of the evidence would be that a society that encourages thrift, produces savings; this leads to investment, which brings economic growth.

Emphasis on obedience is negatively linked with economic growth for the

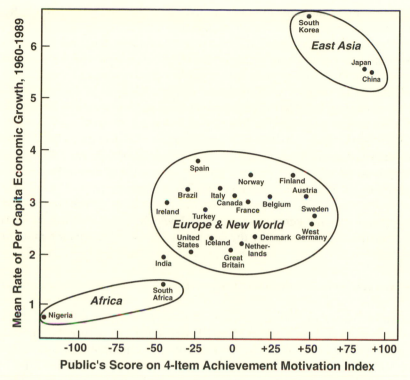

Figure 7.1. Economic growth rate by achievement motivation scores of publics.
Note: Achievement Motivation index is based on percentage in each society who emphasized "Thrift" and "Determination" as important things for a child to learn, *minus* the percentage emphasizing "Obedience" and "Religious faith."

converse reason. In preindustrial societies, obedience means conformity to traditional norms that stigmatize economic accumulation and instead emphasize obligations to share with one's relatives, friends, and neighbors. Such communal obligations are strongly felt in preindustrial societies; within the given culture, they are important virtues. But from the perspective of a bureaucratized rational-legal society, these norms are antithetical to capital accumulation and conducive to nepotism. Furthermore, this conformity to authority inhibits innovation and entrepreneurship.

The motivational component is also tapped by Materialist/Postmaterialist values, with Postmaterialism having a negative linkage with growth. Achievement motivation has a moderate negative linkage with the Materialist/Postmaterialist dimension (r = −.39). Although both Achievement Motivation and Postmaterialist values have significant linkages with economic growth, they affect it in different ways: Achievement Motivation seems to reflect the transition from preindustrial to industrial value systems, linked with the Modernization process. Materialist/Postmaterialist values, on the other hand, reflect the transition from industrial to postindustrial society, bringing a shift *away* from emphasis on economic growth, toward increasing emphasis on protection of the environment and on the quality of life in general. Previous research demonstrates that (1) a gradual shift from Materialist toward Postmaterialist goals has been taking place throughout advanced industrial society, (2) this shift is strongly related to the emergence of democracy, but (3) Postmaterialist values tend to be *negatively* linked with economic growth.

Do these cultural variables add anything to an explanation of economic growth, beyond what is explained by the standard economic variables? To answer this question, we will perform multivariate analyses below. But, first, let us examine the impact of "social capital," that is, propensities toward membership in voluntary associations—something distinct from the "human capital" factor in the endogenous growth model, which refers to skills and is usually operationally measured by the educational level of the given population.

SOCIAL CAPITAL AND ECONOMIC GROWTH

The importance of social capital was first stressed by Tocqueville, who argued that democracy had emerged and flourished in America because the American people participated in numerous and extensive voluntary associations. This fostered cooperation and trust, which were essential to the successful functioning of democratic institutions. Almond and Verba (1963) made similar findings.

In contemporary social science, this idea was reprised by Banfield (1958), who found that Italian society was characterized by low levels of interpersonal trust, especially in Southern Italy, where the prevailing outlook was "amoral familism": the absence of feelings of trust or moral obligation toward anyone outside the nuclear family. The Southern Italian subculture seemed to lack such norms, which severely hindered the large-scale cooperation among strangers that is essential to both economic development and successful democratic institutions.

Testing these ideas in a broader cross-national context, Inglehart (1990) found that interpersonal trust and related cultural orientations were strongly linked with both economic development and stable democracy. He emphasized, however, that culture is a variable, not a constant: though cultural characteristics tend to change slowly, they can and do change. Thus, while the Italian public in the 1980s continued to be characterized by relatively low levels of interpersonal trust (and Southern Italians remained much less trusting than Northern Italians), overall levels of trust had gradually risen.

Putnam (1993) argued that Social Capital plays a crucial role in both political and economic cooperation. Social Capital consists of a culture of trust and tolerance, in which extensive networks of voluntary associations emerge. These networks, in turn, provide contacts and information flows that are supportive of a culture of trust and cooperation: it would be mistaken to assume that economics unilaterally determines culture *or* that culture determines economics. The two are intimately intertwined, and mutually supportive in any society that flourishes for any length of time.

Putnam's work helped clarify the causal linkages between economic and cultural factors, utilizing his exceptionally long time series of both economic and cultural indicators. Analyzing Italian regional-level data from the nineteenth century to the 1980s, Putnam found that certain regions had relatively high levels of social capital, while others had much lower levels. These levels were fairly stable attributes of given regions; and they were strongly linked with the economic development level of those regions. Moreover Putnam's analysis dispels any assumption that these regional cultural differences are simply a consequence of their respective levels of economic development. He found that levels of civic involvement around 1900 predicted civic involvement levels 60 or 70 years later far better than did economic factors. More strikingly still, he also found that levels of civic involvement around 1900 predicted subsequent levels of *economic* development even better than did economic variables. While Putnam rejects cultural determinism as an interpretation of Italian development, his analysis provides strong evidence that cultural factors help shape economic life, as well as being shaped by it.

Another analysis of longitudinal data indicates that individuals' attitudes and expectancies influence their economic outcomes. Szekelyi and Tardos (1993) analyzed the 25-year database of the Panel Study of Income Dynamics carried out by the Institute for Social Research at the University of Michigan. They first identified a syndrome consisting of a long-term time perspective, confidence that one's long-term plans will work out, an emphasis on saving rather than spending now, and interpersonal trust. Analyzing the panel data, they found that those individuals who scored high on this syndrome subsequently earned significantly higher incomes than those who scored low, after controlling for initial levels of income, education, age, sex, race, residence, and region.

Tocqueville had argued that membership in voluntary associations was conducive to democracy. Putnam extends this to argue that a culture characterized by trust, cooperativeness, and extensive networks of secondary associations was conducive to *both* democracy and economic development.

Mancur Olson (1982), by contrast, argues that as a society's networks of secondary association become highly developed, they strangle economic growth. The behavior of individuals and firms in stable societies leads to the formation of dense networks of collusive, cartelistic and lobbying organizations that make economies less efficient and dynamic and polities less governable. The longer a society goes without an upheaval, the more powerful such organizations become—and the more they slow down economic expansion. Societies in which these narrow interest groups have been destroyed by war or revolution enjoy the highest rates of growth. The implications of Putnam's and Olson's theories seem diametrically opposed: does the growth of voluntary associations favor or strangle economic growth?

In fact, the two sets of ideas may not be as incompatible as they at first seem. For Olson emphasizes the negative consequences of organizational networks among *highly developed* societies; at earlier stages of development, they may play an innocuous or even useful role. Putnam, on the other hand, examines the roots of economic development in nineteenth-century Italy and even much earlier. Although he does not discuss the effects of associational networks at various stages of development, his analysis focuses on consequences that result from the presence or absence of these networks in the *early* stages. This, of course, is the phase which seems most relevant to development in contemporary developing nations.

Voluntary Associations and Economic Growth in 43 Societies

Although Tocqueville developed his thesis in the context of the nineteenth-century United States, and Putnam in the context of nineteenth- and twentieth-century Italy, their implications extend far beyond those settings. Thus, Esman and Uphoff (1984), Cernea (1993), and Landell-Mills (1992) have argued that local associations play a crucial role in the development of agrarian societies throughout the world.

Data from the 1990–91 World Values Survey enable us to examine the impact of membership in voluntary associations in a global perspective. Although this database does not have the long time series that makes Putnam's analysis so powerful, it enables us to test his hypotheses across a much broader spectrum of societies than was available to him or any previous analyst. The World Values survey provides cultural measures from societies throughout the world, covering the full range of economic and political variation.

These surveys provide information about organizational memberships: the respective publics were read a list of 16 types of voluntary associations and asked, "To which, if any, of these organizations do you belong?" They were also asked if they did voluntary work for any of these organizations. The types of organizations that were covered (listed from those with the most members to those with the fewest) are labor unions, religious organizations, sports and recreational organizations, educational/cultural organizations, political parties, professional associations, social welfare organizations, youth work (Scouts, etc.), environmental/conservation organizations, health volunteer work, community action groups, women's organizations, Third World development organizations, animal rights organizations, and peace organizations.

These data were not designed to test the Tocqueville-Putnam hypothesis. Also, they underrepresent the less developed societies, a problem that is exacerbated by the fact that comparable data are not available for three of the four lowest-income countries in our sample. This battery was not asked in India or Turkey because many of these organizations scarcely existed there. It was asked in Nigeria, but was framed to imply "Do you *sympathize* with these organizations?" Consequently, we do not have comparable data from some key cases.

These questions *were* asked in some low-income countries, however, and the results from China are particularly interesting. Although China shows a lower rate of organizational memberships than most advanced industrial societies, it has a high rate for a predominantly rural society. This may reflect the heavy emphasis that the Chinese government has placed on organizing rural populations since the start of the Maoist era.

Does associational membership have the same linkage with economic growth as it does with democracy? The answer is no. The correlates of high economic growth rates prove to be quite different from the syndrome of high levels of associational membership, plus high levels of trust, prosperity, and stable democracy.

High rates of membership in the 16 types of organizations for which we have data are *not* linked with high rates of economic growth during the period from 1950 to 1988; indeed, we find a modest *negative* correlation between associational membership and economic growth (r = −.22). What is good for democracy is not necessarily good for economic growth. As Przeworski and Limongi (1993) and Helliwell (1994) have demonstrated, there is no clear relationship between the two: democracies are no likelier (and no less likely) to have high rates of growth than are authoritarian regimes.

Thus far, the evidence seems to support Olson rather than Putnam et al.: membership in organizations is *negatively* related to economic growth (though only weakly so).

But the Olson thesis does not imply that voluntary associations are inherently detrimental to economic growth—only that they are detrimental when they become hypertrophied. Olson is mainly interested in the impact of organized interest groups in advanced industrial societies, where they tend to have stultifying effects. In the early stages of economic development, however, organizations may have a positive impact on growth, as Putnam argues.

We suspect that an interaction effect is involved in the impact of voluntary associations on economic growth. When we test this hypothesis, we find that it is confirmed. Let us compare the relationship between membership rates and economic growth, in relatively rich and relatively poor countries, respectively, dichotomizing our sample between those with a GNP/capita above $8,300 (the median income level for the 43 societies in our sample) and those with a lower GNP/capita. When we do so, we find that the correlation between cumulative membership in the 16 types of organizations included in the survey is *negative* among the more developed societies (r = −.35) but *positive* among the less developed ones (r = .24). Although neither of these correlations is very strong, they work in opposite directions, as Olson and Putnam together could be taken to imply: their net difference amounts to a substantial .59.

Our data were not designed to test Putnam's hypothesis, and, as we have noted, data are lacking for some particularly interesting cases. Moreover, different types of associations and different intensities of participation show different linkages with economic growth. In the lower-income societies in our sample, active participation in political parties, labor unions, and professional associations shows a particularly strong relationship with economic growth (r = .69) (among richer societies, this relationship disappears). Nevertheless, our findings suggest that Olson's and Putnam's theses are not actually incompatible, provided that they are specified according to a country's level of economic development. Relatively dense networks of associational membership seem to be conducive to economic growth in the earlier stages of development, as Putnam has argued; but (as Olson has argued) these associations can become hypertrophied and excessively powerful in advanced industrial societies, distorting policy to defend well-organized interests at the expense of overall economic growth.

Future research should attempt to improve our measurement of associational membership, and to obtain these measures for a larger number of less-developed societies. For now, the available evidence supports an interpretation that integrates the hypotheses of Olson and Putnam, specifying that they operate at different levels of economic development.

Let us briefly consider another factor that may be related to economic growth. Various writers have argued that reasonably equal income distributions are more conducive to economic growth than highly unequal ones. We measured income inequality using the percentage of income going to the top 20 percent of the population and examined its linkage with economic growth rates from 1950 to 1988. This thesis is supported by the data: the two variables show a significant relationship in the predicted direction (r = −.41). As anticipated, income inequality is linked with relatively low rates of economic growth; but this relationship is not nearly as strong as the relationship between Achievement Motivation and growth. Here again, we find that cultural factors can have even stronger linkages with economic growth than do purely economic variables.

Let us now test the relative impact of economic and cultural factors on economic growth.

THE BASELINE ENDOGENOUS GROWTH MODEL

Neoclassical growth models today build on the work of Solow (1956) and Swan (1956). These models focus on savings, population growth, and shifts in technology as the key influence on growth. Accordingly, one can trace the economic growth consequences resulting from a shift in the rate of saving, the population growth rate, or the level of technology. But these models all have a logical weakness: they show a paradoxical steady-state result. In these models aggregate savings produce a level of capital formation such that gross investment exceeds depreciation, and thereby increases capital per worker. Consequently, at the limit the marginal product of capital declines to the point where the savings (revenue) generated by the capital falls to a level just large enough to replace old equipment and provide new machines for new workers. The result is an unchanging standard of living.

This result is clearly not supported by evidence from the real world. Consequently, economists began searching for ways to augment the neoclassical model that would allow sustainable growth and increases in the standard of living. These models have been termed endogenous growth models. At the heart of the endogenous growth literature is an emphasis on the productivity of the population (Barro, 1990, 1991; Lucas, 1988; Romer, 1986, 1990). Unlike earlier neoclassical models, endogenous growth models show that reproducible capital need not have decreasing returns to scale; they assume constant returns to scale to a broad range of reproducible inputs, including human capital. Consequently, growth can be sustained.

The two leading schools of thought, however, differ in their emphasis. Romer (1990) argues that increased research and development spending is the key to new technological developments, which result in increasing social returns to social knowledge. Lucas (1988) argues that expansion of human capital in terms of both education and "learning by doing" also plays a pivotal role in economic growth.

Empirical endogenous growth models virtually always include initial levels of wealth and investment in human capital (as well as investment rates and growth rates), since studies by Barro (1991), Helliwell (1994), Levine and Renelt (1992), and Mankiw, Romer, and Weil (1992) all find that they have robust and positive partial correlations with economic growth.

Including initial levels of wealth (each society's Gross Domestic Product per capita) enables us to test the proposition that a society's absolute level of wealth is a significant determinant of its growth rates. There are two contrasting hypotheses concerning why this might be true. First, dependency theory implies that it is inherently easier for already developed ("core") countries to achieve growth than it is for the poorer ("peripheral") ones: the already established core economies dominate the world economy and can prevent the newcomers from developing. The second model takes exactly the opposite view: it is inherently easier for *less* developed countries to attain high growth rates than it for developed ones. The former can import already proven technology from richer countries; whereas the more developed societies can only grow by developing new technology—which is costly and often does not pay off. The empirical findings clearly support the latter interpretation: poorer countries show higher growth rates.

Levine and Renelt (1992) find that the initial level of per capita income, the initial level of human capital investment, and the period share of investment to GDP have robust correlations with economic growth. Their investigation uses a variant of Leamer's (1983) Extreme Bounds Analysis (EBA) which emphasizes the stability of various focus parameters when variables are removed or added. They find that most other exogenous variables are fragile to alterations in the conditioning set of information. Thus, the conclusions of most empirical work rest on parameter estimates that fluctuate enough to make scholars wary. Levine and Renelt's work is also useful because they provide a straightforward way to evaluate the sensitivity of the cultural variables; we implement this procedure below.

Multivariate Analysis

Our empirical approach is straightforward: we begin by using ordinary least squares regression to estimate a baseline endogenous growth model that includes the variables identified by Levine and Renelt (1992) as having robust partial correlations with economic growth. Using data for 25 countries, we first test the endogenous growth specification (model 1 in table 7.1).[3] Each nation's rate of per capita economic growth is regressed on its initial level of per capita income and human capital investment (education spending) as well as on its rate of physical capital investment. As expected, the results fit the predictions of endogenous growth theory. The results can be summarized as follows: (1) the significant negative coefficient on the initial level of per capita income indicates that controlling for human and physical capital investment, poorer nations grow faster than richer nations; (2) investment in human capital (education spending) has a positive and statistically significant effect on subsequent economic growth; and (3) increasing the rate of physical capital investment increases a nation's rate of economic growth. Overall, this baseline model performs well: it accounts for 55 percent of the variation in cross-national growth rates and is consistent with prior cross-national tests of the conditional convergence hypothesis (e.g., Barro, 1991; Mankiw et al., 1992). Model 1 also passes all diagnostic tests, indicating that the residuals are not serially correlated (LM test), are normally distributed (Jarque-Bera test), and are not heteroskedastic (White test).

Model 2 in table 7.1 regresses the rate of per capita economic growth on a constant and the two cultural variables. As expected, both achievement motivation and Postmaterialism are significant predictors of economic growth and have the expected sign: achievement motivation has a positive linkage with growth, while Postmaterialist values have a negative linkage with growth. Thus, the evidence tends to support the arguments of both the Protestant Ethic and Postmaterialist theses. Moreover, these variables, taken by themselves, account for 59 percent of the variance in growth rates—even more than is explained by the economic variables alone. A glance at the diagnostics again indicates that the residuals are well behaved.

COMPARING COMPETING EMPIRICAL MODELS: ENCOMPASSING RESULTS

Both the economic and cultural models give similar goodness-of-fit performance; and each model's regressors are statistically significant. But which model is superior? Or does each model possess explanatory factors that are missing in the other? Mizon and Richard (1986) have devised the encompassing approach, a set of statistical procedures that can guide us in building a theoretically parsimonious and statistically efficient model of economic growth

---

[3] The data used in the regression analyses in table 7.1 are provided in Appendix 3.

TABLE 7.1

OLS Estimation of Economic Growth Models Dependent Variable: Mean Rate
of per Capita Economic Growth (1960–89)

Model Variable	Model 1	Model 2	Model 3	Model 4
Constant	−0.70	7.29*	3.16	2.4*
	(1.08)	(1.49)	(1.94)	(0.77)
Per Capita GDP in 1960	−.63*	—	−0.42*	−0.43*
	(0.14)		(0.14)	(0.10)
Primary Education in 1960	2.69*	—	2.19*	2.09*
	(1.22)		(1.06)	(0.96)
Secondary Education in 1960	3.27*	—	1.21	—
	(1.01)		(1.08)	
Investment	8.69*	—	3.09	—
	(4.90)		(4.40)	
Achievement Motivation	—	2.07*	1.44*	1.88*
		(0.37)	(0.48)	(0.35)
Postmaterialism	—	−2.24*	−1.07	—
		(0.77)	(1.03)	
R^2 Adjusted	.55	.59	.69	.70
SEE	.86	.83	.72	.71
LM [$\chi^2(1)$]	.42	.65	.68	.87
Jarque-Bera [$\chi^2(2)$]	.05	.30	.18	.57
White [$\chi^2(1)$]	.28	.24	.37	.18
SC	.119	−.117	−.095	−.352

Notes: Mean of dependent variable: 3.04. N is 25 for all models. Standard errors in parentheses.
*t test: $p < .05$

that answers these questions. The encompassing principle investigates the validity of a model relative to an alternative by determining whether a model statistically accounts for the main features of a rival, enabling analysts to choose one explanation over another and to assess the relative credibility of theoretical and empirical models. Granato, Inglehart, and Leblang (1996; see also Granato and Suzuki, 1995) use encompassing analysis to test various theories of economic growth, presenting a detailed explanation of this technique and illustrates its usefulness. We summarize their findings here. They find that neither model 1 nor model 2 is an efficient substitute for the other, and both models explain aspects of growth that the other cannot. In short, growth rates are best understood as a consequence of *both* economic and cultural factors. Accordingly, they combine the two models, with the results shown in table 7.1, model 3.

Some dramatic changes take place when we analyze the joint effects of cultural factors and economic factors. The most striking finding is the fact that the coefficient for investment decreases dramatically, falling from 8.69 in model 1 to 3.09 in model 3: while it still has the expected sign, it is now well below significance. Why is physical capital investment, which was robustly correlated with economic growth in other studies, now insignificant? We have suggested that achievement motivation is conducive to economic growth partly because it encourages relatively high rates of investment (one of its components is an emphasis on thrift—and, as this suggests, achievement motivation and investment are highly correlated). Consequently, when we take achievement motivation into account, we are controlling for investment to a considerable extent. Presumably, the direct path from culture to economic growth reflects the effect of motivational factors on entrepreneurship and effort.

Model 3 in table 7.1 indicates that achievement motivation is positively and significantly related to economic growth. But the coefficient for Postmaterialist values is now insignificant. This is probably due to the fact that Postmaterialism is most widespread in relatively rich countries, as we saw in chapter 4. The bivariate correlation between Postmaterialism and initial level of wealth is .75, which means that by controlling for wealth (and education) we have largely controlled for Postmaterialism as well. Secondary school enrollment also drops below significance in model 3: it is highly correlated with primary school enrollment, which continues to show significant effects.

Model 4 eliminates the three insignificant variables from model 3 to check the stability of the remaining parameters. Model 4 is quite clearly the most parsimonious and efficient model, explaining 70 percent of the variance in economic growth rates with only three variables (considerably more than either the economic or the cultural factors did alone) and generating a Schwartz criterion (SC) value of $-.352$, which indicates that this is the most robust of our four models. In addition, the residuals are well behaved, and the model passes tests for serial (spatial) correlation, normality, and heteroskedasticity.

Granato et al. (1996) test the robustness of this model in a number of additional ways, examining what happens when influential observations are removed (see Jackman, 1987), and when alterations are made in the set of variables included (see Levine and Renelt, 1992). The robustness of these results were further validated using a variant of Leamer's Extreme Bounds Analysis and nonparametric methods including robust regression and bootstrap resampling. By all of these tests, this model proves to be robust—and, in particular, Achievement Motivation continues to have a significant impact on economic growth.

A number of theoretically interesting variables showed significant zero-order relationships with economic growth, but were dropped from these models because they did not show statistically significant relationships in competition with other key independent variables. These variables include both income inequality and organizational memberships. And, as we have seen, though Postmaterialist values showed a significant impact on economic growth, in the predicted direction, its impact drops below statistical significance in our final model. This does not prove that these variables do not have an impact on economic growth—but simply that they are not among the two or three strongest predictors. When analyzing 2,000 cases, many independent variables can have statistically significant effects. But with an N of only 25 countries and a good deal of shared variance, as we have here, only the few variables that have the strongest relationships are likely to reach statistical significance. We think it likely that these other factors also play a role; but the encompassing analysis indicates that the most *important* influences on economic growth are (1) Achievement Motivation values, (2) human capital investment, and (3) the initial level of per capita GDP.

Structural Equation Models

We have found that both Achievement Motivation and Gross Domestic Investment are closely linked to economic growth rates—and that the two are closely related. It seems likely that Achievement Motivation is conducive to economic growth at least partly because it encourages relatively high rates of investment. In order to examine the extent to which a multistage process such as this is at work, we tested a number of structural equation models based on this principle. The best-fitting model is shown in figure 7.2.

This model shows a chi-square of 3.56 and p = .313 with 3 degrees of freedom and an RMSR of .034, indicating a good fit with the data, and it explains 57 percent of the cross-national variance in economic growth. This model not only explains a higher percentage of the variance in economic growth than does a similar model based on economic variables alone (which accounts for only 45 percent of the variance), it also helps explain why gross domestic investment occurs: cultural differences lead to different investment rates. The model containing economic variables alone does not do so: investment rates are not significantly related to GNP/capita or to other purely economic variables.

This model has a number of interesting features. The most important finding, however, is that the data are consistent with a model positing that high levels of Achievement Motivation are conducive to high levels of investment, and to high levels of economic growth. Human capital (operationally, a high percentage of the population having secondary or higher education) is also conducive to investment (both represent forms of deferred gratification, building up two different types of capital for the future). But Achievement Motivation plays an even more important role, apparently having a major impact on Gross Domestic Investment. Achievement Motivation also has an important direct effect on economic growth rates, quite apart from its tendency to increase domestic investment: the direct path from Achievement Motivation to Growth

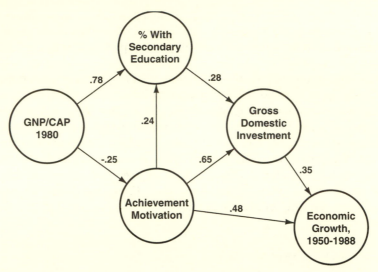

Figure 7.2. Economic and cultural influences on economic growth: structural equation model.
N = 43, Chi squared = 3.56, p = .313, df = 3, RMSR = .034. *Source*: World Bank data and 1990–91 World Values Survey data, aggregated to national level.

probably reflects the effect of motivational factors on entrepreneurship and effort.

CONCLUSIONS: CULTURAL FACTORS IN ECONOMIC GROWTH

The idea that economic growth is partly shaped by cultural factors has been highly controversial. One reason why this idea has been resisted is because culture is often thought of as a diffuse and permanent feature of given societies: if culture determines economic growth, then the outlook for economic development seems hopeless, because culture cannot be changed.

When we approach culture as something to be measured by quantitative empirical means, this illusion of diffuseness and permanence disappears. We no longer need deal with gross stereotypes, such as the idea that "Germans have always been militaristic," or "Hispanic culture is unfavorable to development." We can move, instead, to the analysis of specific components of given cultures at given times. Research carried out in this manner finds that, from 1945 to 1975, West German political culture underwent a striking transformation, from being relatively authoritarian to becoming increasingly democratic and participant (Baker et al., 1981). We find that, from 1970 to 1995, the United States and a number of Western European societies experienced a gradual intergenerational shift from having predominantly Materialist priorities toward having increasingly Postmaterialist priorities. Although these changes have been gradual, they demonstrate that central elements of culture can and do change.

Furthermore, empirical research can help identify the specific components of culture that are most relevant to economic development. One need not seek to change a society's entire way of life. The present findings suggest that one specific component—Achievement Motivation—plays a key role in economic growth. In the short run, it is not easy to change even a relatively narrow and well-defined cultural component such as this, but it seems far easier than attempting to change a society's entire culture. Simply making parents, schools, and other organizations aware of the relevant attitudes may be a step in the right direction.

As Weber suggested more than 90 years ago, cultural factors seem to play an important role in economic development: societies differ in the extent to which they emphasize thrift, savings, and individual economic achievement, as opposed to traditional communal obligations—and those that emphasize the former tend to show higher rates of growth.

Does this mean that societies that emphasize traditional values are doomed to remain permanently less developed? By no means. Only the old, carved-in-marble view of culture would point to this conclusion. As we have argued throughout this book, culture is a variable, not a constant. Although the Industrial Revolution was launched in predominantly Protestant countries, the "Protestant Ethic" spread to Catholic Europe, which today has a higher growth rate than Northern Europe. Moreover, precisely because they are less developed, low-income countries eventually develop one advantage over rich ones: they possess a pool of relatively low-cost labor, which eventually begins to attract investment from their richer neighbors. Thus, during the postwar era, the richer countries of Northern Europe began to build plants in Southern Europe, and remittances from "guest workers" in the North helped fuel the economic takeoff of the southern countries. More recently, this happened in East Asia, when the Japanese labor force became high-cost in comparison with that of its neighbors. Japanese investment (and outsourcing of components for Japanese products) flowed into the rest of East Asia—and more recently into Southeast Asia and South Asia.

This tendency for economic development to spread to countries having a cheap and efficient labor force is complemented by another process: cultural changes in the developed societies eventually bring a shift in emphasis away from economic growth at any cost, toward greater emphasis on environmental protection.

The present analysis suggests that a given society's culture plays an important role in economic growth—with a specific and clearly defined Achievement Motivation dimension being particularly significant. Although this is the only cultural variable that shows a statistically significant impact on economic growth in this analysis, much the same situation holds true here as in connection with stable democracy. Achievement Motivation is part of a cultural syndrome linked with growth. With a large amount of shared variance and only

25 cases, only this variable shows a statistically significant relationship, but it seems unlikely that it is the only relevant cultural variable. Postmaterialist values may also play an important role in shifting emphasis away from thrift and saving, though their effect tends to be confounded with the fact that they are found in relatively wealthy countries, which tend to have low growth rates for a variety of reasons. Also potentially important, though they do not show statistically significant results in this analysis, are a society's associational networks—which seem to play contrasting roles in developed and developing societies.

Since we do not yet have time series data on these values, we cannot reach definitive conclusions about the causal relations between culture and economic growth. An alternative interpretation to our own would be that high rates of economic growth somehow give rise to a culture that emphasizes thrift and determination. This is conceivable. But there is an obvious logic to the hypothesis that cultures that emphasize thrift and determination should tend to show high growth rates: thrift makes high investment rates possible. If we try to turn the causal arrow around, however, there is no obvious reason why rapid growth would bring increasing emphasis on thrift: quite the contrary, one would expect it to give rise to higher rates of *spending*. Until we have cultural time series data, we cannot regard the matter as settled, but the evidence strongly suggests that certain cultural values play an important role in economic growth.

The question "Is economic growth due to cultural factors or to economic factors?" misses the point. Cultural factors are intimately linked with economic factors; and they provide a strong explanation of why, over the long term, some societies have shown much higher rates of economic growth than others. Both the encompassing tests and the structural equation models demonstrate that a model that includes both cultural factors and economic factors has a significantly better fit and explains more of the variance than does a model that relies on economic variables alone.

Economic theory has already begun to incorporate social norms and cultural factors into its models (Cole, Malaith, and Postlewaite, 1992; Fershtman and Weiss, 1993). The logical next step is to determine how cultural and motivational factors can be used to augment existing economic models in order to gain a better understanding of economic growth.

The collapse of the Soviet economy illustrates how costly it can be in the long run to refuse to consider the importance of individual incentives and motivations. Our results indicate that both cultural and economic factors are crucial to economic growth. Neither supplants the other. Future research will be best served by treating the two types of explanation as complementary.

The Rise of New Issues and New Parties

THE GOALS OF BOTH INDIVIDUALS and of societies are changing as a result of the diminishing marginal utility of economic growth. This is changing the political agenda of advanced industrial societies, giving rise to new issues, new political movements, and new political parties. This chapter examines how this is happening at both the individual and societal levels.

CHANGING VALUES AND A CHANGING POLITICAL AGENDA

The shift toward Postmodern values has brought a shift in the political agenda throughout advanced industrial society, moving it away from an emphasis on economic growth at any price, toward increasing concern for its environmental costs. It has also brought a shift from political cleavages based on social class conflict toward cleavages based on cultural issues and quality of life concerns. Huntington (1994) has gone so far as to argue that the main basis of global political conflict from now on will no longer be economic or ideological issues, but cultural issues: world politics will revolve around a "Clash of Civilizations." While this projection may be overdrawn, there is no question that ethnic and cultural issues are becoming more prominent. Economic conflicts are likely to remain important. But, while in the past they dominated the scene to such a degree that many influential thinkers accepted the Marxist view that economics was virtually the whole story, today this seems less plausible. Economic conflicts are increasingly sharing the stage with new issues that were almost invisible a generation ago: environmental protection, abortion, ethnic conflicts, women's issues, and gay and lesbian emancipation are heated issues today—while the central element of the Marxist prescription, nationalization of industry, is almost a forgotten cause.

As a result, a new dimension of political conflict has become increasingly salient. It reflects a polarization between modern and postmodern issue preferences. This new dimension is distinct from the traditional Left-Right conflict over ownership of the means of production and distribution of income. Its growing salience is transforming the meaning of Left and Right and changing the social bases of Left and Right. Historically, the Left was based on the working class and the Right on the middle and upper classes. Today, increasingly, support for the Left comes from middle-class Postmaterialists, while a new Right draws support from less secure segments of the working class. A new Postmodern political cleavage pits culturally conservative, often xenophobic, parties, disproportionately supported by Materialists, against change-oriented parties, often emphasizing environmental protection, and disproportionately supported by Postmaterialists.

Throughout most of the twentieth century, it was generally agreed that support for more state intervention in the economy was the crucial distinction between Left and Right. From a Marxist perspective, private ownership was the root problem, and nationalization of industry and state control of the economy constituted the core solution to all social problems. Abolishing private ownership of the means of production, it was thought, would eradicate exploitation, oppression, alienation, crime, and war.

Although they called themselves "liberals," the American Left also tended to view more state regulation and control of the economy as inherently good: liberals were those who supported a growing role for the state; conservatives were those who opposed it. Well into the 1970s, Western political elites continued to define the meanings of "Left" and "Right" in terms of state intervention in the economy and society (see Aberbach et al., 1981, 115–69).

This consensus has dissolved. It no longer seems self-evident that more state authority constitutes progress, even to those on the Left. One of the key developments of recent years has been a growing skepticism about the desirability and effectiveness of state planning and control, a growing concern for individual autonomy, and a growing respect for market forces. In recent years this outlook has been endorsed not only by conservatives but also by growing segments of the Left. As early as the 1960s, New Left groups emerged in the West that were highly critical of big government, viewed bureaucracy as dehumanizing, and called for devolution of decision-making power to local communities and to those directly affected by the decisions.

In an even more dramatic change, post-socialist Eastern European governments have been drastically reducing the role of the state. And in China, the pragmatists who came to power after the death of Mao, though still nominally communists, have been allowing more and more scope for individual enterprise and an increased role for market forces, though continuing to repress political pluralism. The last attempt to apply the classic policies of the Left in a major Western nation occurred in 1981, when a socialist-communist coalition won office in France. After two years of unrewarding experience with nationalization of industry and other traditional policies of the Left, the socialists abandoned the classic Marxist approach and shifted to market-oriented policies. Similar shifts toward market economies have been occurring in Asia, Africa, and Latin America, even in states led by elites who were shaped by Marxism. Today, almost no one views nationalization of industry as a panacea. While the economic Left-Right dimension still exists, its meaning has changed radically.

The transition from a state-run economy to a market economy often entails traumatic costs. In a number of ex-communist societies, this has brought former communist elites back into power under new labels. But even in these cases, there has not been a return to a Soviet-style state-run economy; instead, the policies of former communist elites have generally been limited to slow-ing down the pace of change and attempting to soften its shock. Where change is occurring in this area today, it is predominantly a movement toward *privatization* of former state functions. The Right consists of those who are pushing for faster or more widespread privatization; the Left consists of those who resist privatization or urge that it be done more slowly.

Russia is an exception: here, in a reversal of meanings, the "Left" label now designates the reformers who are seeking a market economy with private ownership. Russia is torn between reformers on the Left, seeking a greater role for individual initiative and individual self-expression, and the still-entrenched Nomenklatura on the Right, clinging to power and privilege based on their control of the economy. Well into the 1990s, Russia was trapped between two eras, with its state-run economy collapsing but with its market economy not yet fully established. Halfway measures to move toward a more open but more competitive and less predictable society brought suffering and insecurity to a large part of the Russian people. In the 1993 elections to the Russian parliament, a majority of seats were won by a coalition of former communist hardliners and xenophobic protofascists. The future of the reform movement, and of democracy itself, is uncertain there, but the old lines of confrontation have changed irrevocably.

This change in orientations toward state authority can be analyzed on two levels. At the individual level these changes reflect the Postmodern shift in basic values; and at the societal level, they reflect the fact that the expansion of the state has reached a point of diminishing returns. The two developments are mutually supportive.

In the ex-socialist countries, overexpansion of the state eventually paralyzed innovation and economic growth, bringing their economies to the point of collapse. In the West, the problem is more limited; economic growth continues, but the welfare state is in crisis. Paradoxically, this crisis does not reflect the failure of the welfare state so much as the fact that it has succeeded in alleviating those problems it can most readily solve—and thereby helped pave the way for new types of problems to become central. The expansion of the welfare state tempered the ruthless exploitation of laissez-faire capitalism, helping it evolve into a stabler and more viable form of society. Today, in contrast with previous history, the masses do not starve even in times of severe economic decline; their standard of living has been stabilized at a modest level of economic security, reducing social class tensions. This helps explain why—in contrast to the widespread political extremism that arose during the Great Depression of the 1930s—Western nations' politics remained on a relatively even keel during the recent recessions, even though unemployment in some countries exceeded the levels experienced during the Great Depression.

But the growth of the welfare state has begun to reach its limits. When government expenditures exceed 55 percent of gross national product, as is now the case in many Western societies, there is little room for further expansion; taxation becomes massive, and the majority of the public feels the burden.

INDIVIDUAL-LEVEL CHANGES: THE POSTMODERN SHIFT AND THE RISE
OF THE POSTMODERN POLITICS CLEAVAGE

The goals of both individuals and of societies are changing as a result of the
diminishing marginal utility of economic growth. In this respect, cultural
change behaves as if it were a rational response to the changing physical and
socioeconomic environment. But culture exists in the minds and feelings of
given peoples. Accordingly, it changes only insofar as what people learn and
experience reshapes prevailing beliefs and values. It can be analyzed at both
the individual and societal levels, which are simply two sides of the same coin.

The rise of a new axis of political cleavage started with changes in the values of individuals—which then brought new issues such as abortion, environmental protection, and women's issues to a central place in the political arena.
Only gradually and a good deal later did these changes reshape political cleavages and lead to the emergence of new political parties. Long-established institutions have considerable inertia and are slow to change.

For most of the twentieth century, the dominant axis of political cleavage
was the Left-Right polarization based on economic issues, with the working
class supporting the Left and the middle class supporting the Right. In his 1960
classic *Political Man*, Lipset correctly described this polarization as the most
important single fact about political cleavages throughout the industrial world.
In a predominantly materialistic world, conflict over income and ownership of
the means of production was the central issue.

But significant numbers of Postmaterialists moved into political relevance,
as the postwar generation began to reach adulthood. Postmaterialists first became visible as student protesters, during the 1960s, bringing a variety of new
issues into the political arena. At that point in time their values differed sharply
from those of the dominant establishment; they were outsiders and invented a
whole repertory of (then) unconventional protest tactics to bring their goals to
national notice. But as they reached maturity and began to occupy positions of
power, Postmaterialists adopted new strategies. By the 1980s, they were becoming powerful within established political parties, or were founding successful political institutions of their own. As Postmaterialist elites took over
established institutions, political extremism became less and less associated
with the Left, and increasingly a tactic used by the Right.

For most of the past three decades, Postmaterialists have dominated the political agenda in most Western democracies: overwhelmingly, the new issues
that were introduced during the 1960s and 1970s reflected Postmodern priorities. It was only recently that the Right staged a counterattack, often utilizing
the same political techniques that the Postmaterialists had introduced during
the 1960s, when they were a relatively powerless minority.

The Modern/Postmodern dimension described in chapter 3 reflects the wide
array of new issues that have become prominent with the rise of Postmodern
politics: these issues range from abortion to cultural change and ethnic diversity as figure 3.2 demonstrated. Although a variety of issues became salient

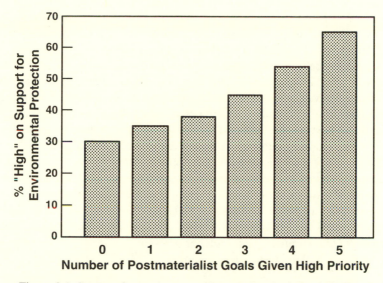

Figure 8.1. Support for environmental protection, by Materialist/Post-materialist values in five advanced industrial societies. *Source*: 1990–93 World Values Survey data from United States, Britain, France, West Germany, and Sweden (N = 7,473). *Note*: Respondents are classified as "high" on the environmental protection index if they (1) agreed with *both* of the following: (a) "I would give part of my income if I were certain that the money would be used to prevent environmental pollution," and (b) "I would agree to an increase in taxes if the extra money were used to prevent environmental pollution," *and* (2) they also disagreed with *both* of the following: (a) "The government should reduce environmental pollution but it should not cost me any money," and (b) "Protecting the environment and fighting pollution is less urgent than often suggested."

with the emergence of Postmodern culture, the central issue initially was the Peace Movement. But as the war in Vietnam receded into the past, environmental causes became the flagship issue. Throughout advanced industrial society (though not necessarily in developing societies), Postmaterialists are far more favorable to environmental protection than are Materialists, as figure 8.1 demonstrates.

Postmaterialist Values and Environmental Attitudes

The rise of Postmaterialist values helps account for the spectacular rise in the salience of environmental issues which has taken place during the past two decades. Postmaterialism became a significant political force during the past 25 years, as the postwar generation emerged into political relevance. Shortly afterward, environmental concerns took on an unprecedented salience throughout advanced industrial society.

Postmaterialist goals are not the only factor motivating concern for the quality of the environment. In advanced industrial society, environmental protection is primarily a Postmaterialist concern; but in many developing countries, from China to Mexico, air pollution and water pollution levels are far worse than in advanced industrial societies, posing immediate problems to health. In such settings, environmental protection is not a quality of life issue, but a matter of survival; it is as likely to be supported by Materialists as by Postmaterialists. The highest levels of support for environmental protection, however, are found in the Nordic countries and the Netherlands—which have the most Postmaterialist publics in the world (Inglehart, 1995).

Figure 8.1 shows the relationship between Materialist/Postmaterialist values and support for environmental protection in advanced industrial societies. This figure uses a 12-item battery in which the following five items tap Postmaterialist priorities across virtually all 43 societies included in the World Values surveys (see Abramson and Inglehart, 1995):

Protecting freedom of speech
Giving people more say in important government decisions
A less impersonal, more humane society
Giving people more say on the job and in their communities
A society in which ideas count more than money

A given individual may choose anywhere from zero to all five of these items among his or her high-priority goals.

In advanced industrial societies, these values are strongly related to support for environmental protection: as figure 8.1 demonstrates, among those who give high priority to none of the Postmaterialist goals, only 29 percent rank high on support for environmental protection; among those who give high priority to all five Postmaterialist goals, fully 68 percent rank high on support for environmental protection. This relationship has impressive strength across advanced industrial societies, especially considering the fact that none of the five Postmaterialist items makes any direct reference to environmental concerns.

It is relatively easy to give lip service to environmental protection, and many people do so. Do these attitudes have behavioral consequences? The relatively favorable attitude of Postmaterialists toward environmental causes is not just a matter of lip service: their behavior reflects their distinctive values to an even *greater* extent than do their attitudes. Although Postmaterialists are only about twice as likely as Materialists to favor environmental protection, they are four to 10 times as likely to be active members of environmental protection groups. And Postmaterialists are four to six times as likely to vote for environmentalist parties (in countries that have them) as are Materialists. Figure 8.2 shows the evidence from four Western societies.

The Materialist/Postmaterialist dimension has become the basis of a major new axis of political polarization in Western Europe, leading to the rise of the Green Party in West Germany, and to a realignment of party systems in a number of other countries (Inglehart, 1977, 1990; Dalton, Flanagan, and Beck,

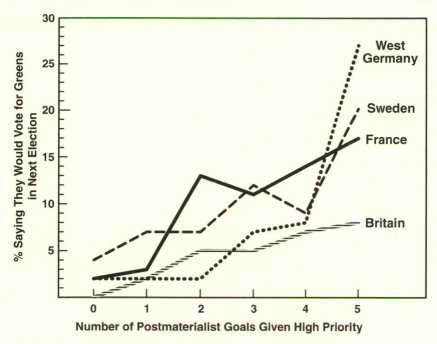

Figure 8.2. Intent to vote for environmentalist political parties, by Materialist/ Postmaterialist values in four countries having such parties. *Source*: 1990–93 World Values Survey.

1984). During the 1980s, environmentalist parties emerged in West Germany, the Netherlands, Belgium, Austria, and Switzerland. In the 1990s they made breakthroughs in Sweden and France and are beginning to show significant levels of support in Great Britain. In every case, support for these parties comes from a disproportionately Postmaterialist constituency. As figure 8.2 demonstrates, as we move from the Materialist to the Postmaterialist end of the continuum, the percentage intending to vote for the environmentalist party in their country rises steeply: from 0 to 8 percent in Britain, from 2 to 17 percent in France, from 4 to 20 percent in Sweden, and from 2 to 27 percent in Western Germany. Pure Postmaterialists are five to 12 times as likely to vote for environmentalist parties as are pure Materialists. Environmentalist parties are not yet strong enough to govern independently and may never be so; but they have successfully advocated environmental protection policies in each of these countries and have forced the established parties to adopt stronger environmental protection policies in order to compete for their voters.

A New Axis of Political Cleavage: Postmodern versus Fundamentalist Values

Although it is more difficult to change long-established institutions than individuals' attitudes, environmentalist parties have begun to emerge in many societies in which the electoral system does not tend to strangle new parties. Why? The environmentalist cause is only one of many Postmodern issues favored by Postmaterialists. This electorate is distinctive in its entire worldview: they are relatively favorable to women's rights, disabled groups, gay and lesbian emancipation, ethnic minorities, and a number of other causes. But the environmental cause has emerged as the symbolic center of this broad cultural emancipation movement: while many of the other Postmodern causes tend to be divisive, practically everyone likes clean air and green trees. Although these parties reflect an entire worldview, environmental symbols captures the issue on which they have the widest potential appeal.

Nevertheless, the rise of Postmaterialist causes has given rise to negative reactions from the very start. The French student protest movement was able to paralyze the entire country in May 1968; but it led to a massive shift of working-class voters, who rallied behind De Gaulle as the guarantor of law and order, giving the Gaullists a landslide victory in the June 1968 elections. In the same year, student protesters in the United States were able to bring down Lyndon Johnson, but they alienated much of the traditional Democratic Party electorate—many of whom threw their support to a reactionary candidate, George Wallace, enabling Richard Nixon to win the presidency. The 1972 elections were something of a replay, except that this time normally Democratic voters who were repelled by the seeming radicalism of the McGovern campaign supported Nixon: for the first time in history, white working-class voters were about as likely to vote for the Republican as for the Democratic candidate. The aftermath of these events transformed the two parties, but the United States still has a two-party system, with the same party labels as before: superficially, the system seems unchanged.

Although Postmaterialist-led parties emerged in both the Netherlands and Belgium during the 1970s, West Germany was the scene of the first breakthrough by an environmentalist party in a major industrial nation. Postmaterialist protest had manifested itself as dramatically in Germany as in the United States or France, but it was only in 1983 that the Greens were sufficiently strong and well organized to surmount West Germany's 5 percent hurdle and enter the West German parliament—bringing a significant structural change to West German politics. But more recently, the Greens have been countered by a Republikaner party characterized by cultural conservatism and xenophobia. In the 1994 national elections, the Greens won 7 percent of the vote. The Republikaner, on the other hand, were stigmatized as the heirs of the Nazis and won only 2 percent of the vote, too little to win parliamentary representation. Nevertheless, xenophobic forces have already had a substantial impact on German politics, motivating the established parties to shift their policy positions in order to co-opt the Republikaner electorate. These efforts even included an amendment to the German constitution: to cut down the influx of foreigners, the clause guaranteeing free right of political asylum was revised in 1993, in a decision supported by a two-thirds majority of the German parliament.

The rise of the Green Party in Germany has also had a major impact even

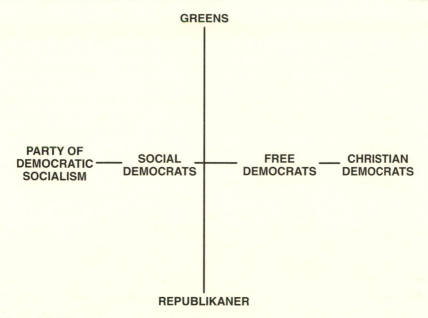

Figure 8.3. The social class-based Left-Right dimension and the Postmodern politics dimension in Germany.

though only a small portion of the electorate votes for it. For the Greens, like other New Left parties and movements, reflect an entire worldview which differs fundamentally from that of the traditional Left. Despite their name, the Greens are much more than an ecological party. They seek to build a basically different kind of society from the prevailing industrial model. During the Cold War, their most massive demonstrations were directed against nuclear weapons and NATO. They have actively supported a wide range of Postmodern causes, from unilateral disarmament to women's' emancipation, gay and lesbian rights, rights for the physically disabled, Palestinian liberation, and citizenship rights for non-German immigrants. But their greatest impact on German politics has been in forcing the established parties, from the Christian Democrats to the Social Democrats, to adopt pro-environmentalist positions in order to compete for the Greens' voters.

The Greens and the Republikaner are located at opposite poles of a new political dimension, as figure 8.3 suggests. If we simply judged by their labels, this might not seem to be the case: the Republikaner do not call themselves the Anti-Environment Party; nor do the Greens call themselves the Pro-Immigrant Party. But, in fact, their constituencies are disproportionately Materialist and Postmaterialist, respectively; and these parties adopt opposite policies on the relevant issues. The older parties are arrayed on the traditional Left-Right axis, established in an era when political cleavages were dominated by social class conflict. On this axis (the horizontal dimension of figure 8.3) both elites and mass electorates place the Party of Democratic Socialism (the Eastern German ex-communists) on the extreme Left, followed by the Social Democrats and the Free Democrats, with the Christian Democrats at the Right of the spectrum. This figure is schematic. As Kitschelt (1995) has demonstrated, the new politics dimension is not perpendicular to the long-established Left-Right dimension. Instead, the Greens are closer to the old Left on key issues, while the Republikaner are closer to the Right. But, although both elites and masses tend to think of the Greens as located on the Left, they represent a fundamentally new Left. Traditionally, the Left parties have been based on a working-class constituency and advocated a program that called for nationalization of industry and redistribution of income. In striking contrast, the Postmaterialist Left appeals primarily to a middle-class constituency and is only faintly interested in the classic program of the Left. For example, Postmaterialists are not necessarily more favorable to state ownership than are Materialists, as figure 8.12 indicates. But Postmaterialists *are* intensely favorable to the Left position on Postmodern issues—which frequently repel the traditional working-class constituency of the Left.

The vertical axis on figure 8.3 reflects the polarization between Postmodern and Fundamentalist values, reflecting differences in people's subjective sense of security. At one end, we find a Postmodern openness to ethnic diversity and changing gender roles; at the opposite pole we find an emphasis on familiar values (often rooted in traditional religion) in the face of insecurity. This cleavage tends to pit the Postmaterialists against those with traditional religious values. Although the classic interpretation of secularization attributed it to the cognitive spread of a scientific worldview, we have argued that the rise of a sense of *security* among mass publics of advanced welfare states is an equally important factor in the decline of traditional religious orientations. The cognitive interpretation implies that secularization is inevitable and more or less irreversible. By contrast, the rise of a sense of security among mass publics is far from inevitable and can be undermined by economic decline or rapid change. Fundamentalist movements continue to emerge among the less secure strata of even the most advanced industrial societies, with people reemphasizing traditional values in times of stress.

As figure 8.4 demonstrates, across five advanced industrial societies, 70 percent of the pure Materialists support a policy of reverse affirmative action— that is, the position that "When jobs are scarce, employers should give priority to [one's own nationality] over immigrants." Among the pure Postmaterialist type, only 25 percent are in favor of giving preference to native-born citizens.

Figure 8.5 presents a similar comparison, based on the proportion saying that they would not like to have immigrants or foreign workers as neighbors: 19 percent of the pure Materialists take the xenophobic position, as compared with only 3 percent of the pure Postmaterialists.

On this issue, value priorities have even more impact than they do on the environmental protection issue: Materialists are almost three times as likely as the Postmaterialists to favor employment discrimination favoring the native-

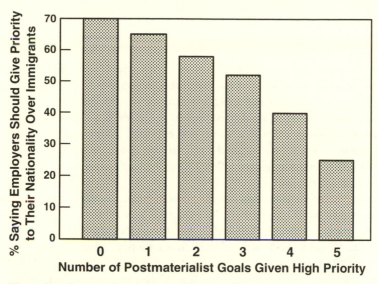

Figure 8.4. Support for giving preference to one's own nationality over immigrants when jobs are scarce, in the United States, Britain, France, West Germany, and Sweden. *Source*: 1990–93 World Values Survey. *Note*: The question was "Do you agree or disagree with the following statement: When jobs are scarce, employers should give priority to [one's nationality] over immigrants."

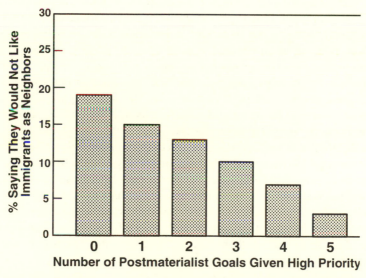

Figure 8.5. Rejection of immigrants as neighbors, in United States, Britain, France, West Germany, and Sweden. *Source*: 1990–93 World Values Survey. *Note*: The question was: "On this list are various groups of people. Could you please sort out any that you would not like to have as neighbors? Just call off the letters, please." The list included 15 groups, such as "heavy drinkers" or "homosexuals," with "immigrants/foreign workers" as one item.

born over foreigners, and six times as likely to say they would not want to have foreigners as neighbors.[1]

Like Materialist/Postmaterialist values (with which it is linked), our measure of xenophobia shows strong differences across age groups, with the younger birth cohorts being more tolerant of foreigners, homosexuals, and other outgroups. But this holds true only in societies that have experienced rising security: in societies that have not experienced economic growth, the young are *not* more tolerant than the old. In low-income societies that have not experienced economic growth, the young are actually *less* tolerant of outgroups than are the old.

A Postmodern Politics axis has also taken shape in other countries, such as France, where an Ecologist Party has recently emerged at the Postmaterialist pole, and the xenophobic National Front at the other. In contrast to Germany, where the Republikaner are unlikely to surmount the 5 percent hurdle, in France's 1993 parliamentary elections, the National Front won 12 percent of the vote. Reflecting a pervasive decline of the traditional Left in the early 1990s, the French Socialist Party won only 18 percent of the vote, and the communists won only 9 percent. Meanwhile, the Ecologists got 8 percent of the vote, the strongest performance they had ever made in elections to the National Assembly. Throughout the postwar era, the communists had been the strongest party in France. In 1993 they were outpolled by the National Front and came in only slightly ahead of the Ecologists. Figure 8.6 depicts the alignment of French parties on the two respective dimensions of political cleavage.

The once-dominant Left-Right dimension based on social class and religion is increasingly sharing the stage with a Postmodern politics dimension. Although support for environmentalist parties has grown in many Western societies, there has also been a right-authoritarian reaction at the opposite pole of the Postmodern Politics dimension. Right-wing extremist parties, such as Le Pen's National Front, have been gaining votes by appealing to antiforeign sentiments. This appeal has been particularly effective among blue-collar workers who formerly voted for parties of the Left.

The social base of such parties consists disproportionately of economically and psychologically marginal segments of society, manifesting a reaction of the insecure in the face of change. Parties of cultural autonomy, on the other hand, are not necessarily xenophobic and sometimes have a very cosmopolitan outlook: thus, though they emphasize a specific cultural identity, the Flemish and Catalan "nationalists" are actually more favorable to European integration than are most of their compatriots; and the Quebecois are more

---

[1] The "reject neighbors battery" referred to here was included in both waves of the World Values Survey, but the data are not reliable for cross-time comparisons. This battery used a scaleless format, which is very sensitive to context and interviewer effects. Moreover in 1981 it had an interviewer instruction to "code all mentions," while in 1990 each item had codes for "mentioned" or "not mentioned," with the interviewer instruction "Check a response for each item"; this attracted more choices for all items. In addition, "People with AIDS" was added to the battery in 1990.

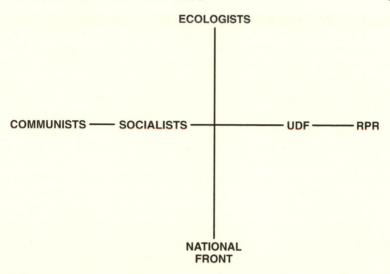

Figure 8.6. The social class-based Left-Right dimension and the Post-modern politics dimension in France.

supportive of North American free trade than are Canadians in general. These parties are motivated not by xenophobia so much as by a concern for cultural identity and for autonomy in decision making, and their social base consists disproportionately of the young, the well-educated, and Postmaterialists.

In the Netherlands—one of the most Postmaterialist societies in the world—Postmodern parties have been making growing inroads for more than two decades. In the 1994 Dutch parliamentary elections, two heavily Postmaterialist parties—Democrats '66 and the Green Left—won nearly 20 percent of the vote; while at the opposite pole of the Postmodern politics spectrum, several small fundamentalist religious parties won over 5 percent of the vote.

The ex-communist resurgence in former socialist countries reflects the fact that these parties are associated with the Good Old Days of relative stability and security in the minds of their voters. But parties tied to the classic program of the Left have been faring poorly in Western countries. This is partly due to the Postmaterialist shift, and partly due to the loss of legitimacy of the economic philosophy of socialism that accompanied the collapse of Marxism in Eastern Europe and the former Soviet Union. It also reflects the fact that the electoral appeal of the long-established Western parties was based on class-based economic issues, which have a diminishing ability to mobilize voters today.

For most of the postwar era, the Italian Communist Party won 30 to 35 percent of the vote in Italian elections, but starting in the late 1970s, it went into a steady decline. As Italy's 1994 elections approached, the situation seemed to offer a golden opportunity for the communists to stage a comeback. The Christian Democratic coalition, which had dominated Italian politics throughout the period since World War II, had finally self-destructed. Most of the top leaders of both the Christian Democrats and their socialist allies were either in jail or under indictment for flagrant corruption—a classic opportunity for the opposition to come to power. In the 1994 elections, the Christian Democratic vote plummeted to 11 percent and that of their socialist allies fell to 2 percent. But the communists were unable to capitalize on this opportunity. The Democratic Party of the Left won only 20 percent of the vote, and the hard-line communists won only 6 percent. The vacuum created by the collapse of the governing coalition was filled by new parties, some of which appeared almost overnight. The traditional Left-Right axis sunk to an unprecedented low point. The leading party was the newly established Forza Italia, with 21 percent of the vote; a regional party, the Northern League, won 8 percent; and the neo-fascist vote rose to an appalling 14 percent, while at the other pole of the Postmodern politics dimension, the Greens won 3 percent. In Italy's 1996 elections, a reform Communist Party (renamed as the Democratic Party of the Left) emerged as the largest party in parliament, but it was a profoundly transformed party, dedicated to a market economy and to Italian membership in NATO.

In Britain's 1992 general elections, the Left was in an ideal position to win. The Conservatives had been in power for three consecutive terms, and the British economy was in the throes of a deep recession; moreover, the Conservative Party had an unappealing leader who ran a dull campaign. Nevertheless, Labour lost for a fourth consecutive time. The party was widely seen as still committed to old-line policies of the Left, such as state ownership of business and industry—which it was still officially endorsing even after it had been abandoned within the ex-socialist bloc. A succession of Labour Party leaders tried to drag the party back to the mainstream, but it was only in 1995, under the leadership of Tony Blair, that the party finally officially abandoned the goal of state ownership of business and industry. With its return to the mainstream, the prospect of a Labour electoral victory was finally within reach.

The rise of Postmodern values has not led to the emergence of new parties in societies like the United States, where the absence of proportional representation makes it difficult for new parties to survive. Nevertheless, it has forced the existing parties to reposition themselves. Both major parties now claim to be pro-environmentalist, and both parties are trying to find just the right balance between cultural permissiveness and traditional family values. The success of Clinton in 1992 owed much to a skillful balancing act within the future First Family. Clinton himself, a Southern WASP male, took positions on social and economic issues that were almost indistinguishable from those of the Republicans, promising a middle-class tax cut and a balanced budget, while his wife made a subtly differentiated appeal to the Postmodern constituency. Although Postmodern political parties have not emerged in the United States, it is clear that the issues that launch such parties are as powerful here as anywhere. Concern for environmental protection has a large and active constituency; but opposition to illegal immigration also has broad and increasingly articulate support. In the United States, Postmodern politics plays itself out within the two long-established dominant parties.

In France, as we have seen, the National Front became prominent by appealing to nativist sentiment among working-class voters who formerly supported the parties of the Left. Its nearest parallels on the American scene are the Christian Coalition and the anti-immigration movements. These movements represent reactions against rapid cultural change which has been occurring throughout advanced industrial society. During the past 25 years, divorce rates rose by as much as 300 percent in Western societies, while during the same period, fertility rates fell to well below the population replacement rate. Similarly, a generation ago homosexuality was something that was only whispered about. Today, gay and lesbian groups are officially organized under government and university sponsorship and are beginning to obtain legal protection of the right to follow their own sexual orientations. This change is part of a broad intergenerational cultural shift. As we have seen, younger groups are far more permissive toward divorce, homosexuality, and abortion than older groups and place much less emphasis on having children.

In addition to these cultural changes, massive immigration flows, especially those from Third World countries, have changed the ethnic makeup of most advanced industrial societies. The newcomers speak different languages and have different religions and lifestyles from those of the native population—further compounding the impression that the culture one grew up in is being swept away. The rise of militant religious fundamentalism in the United States, and of xenophobic movements in Western Europe, represents a reaction against rapid cultural changes that seem to be eroding some of the most basic values and customs of the more traditional and less secure groups in these countries. The emergence of highly visible New Right groups has led some observers to conclude that they reflect the mainstream trend. They are important phenomena—but they do not represent the wave of the future. On the contrary, New Right groups are a reaction against broader trends that are moving faster than these societies can assimilate them. This reaction against cultural change has reinforced the Postmodern politics cleavage, pitting predominantly Materialist-oriented parties against Postmaterialist parties and giving rise to a Postmodern versus Fundamentalist cleavage dimension.

The foregoing interpretation is supported by empirical analyses by some leading scholars of comparative politics. Thus, Knutsen (1989, 1995) has demonstrated that in most Western European countries, a new dimension of political cleavage has emerged, which he describes as a Materialist/Postmaterialist values cleavage; tapping a number of issues such as environmentalism and nuclear power, the core variable in this cluster is Materialist/Postmaterialist values. This new dimension cuts across the traditional Left-Right dimension and has become an increasingly important influence on party choice in many societies—and has become the most important variable shaping political cleavages in some countries.

Similarly, in an insightful analysis of the rise of Postmodern parties in Western democracies, Kitschelt refers to parties based on Postmaterialist constituencies as "Left Libertarian parties," and those at the opposite pole, with disproportionately Materialist constituencies, as "Right Authoritarian parties" (Kitschelt, 1994, 1995). Although we use different labels, our interpretations converge with those of Knutsen and Kitschelt on the key points.

The Rise of Postmaterialist Issues and the Decline of Social Class Voting

Most of the major political parties in Western countries were established in an era dominated by social class conflict, and to a considerable extent the main established political parties are still aligned along a social class-based axis. But support for new political movements and new political parties largely reflects the tension between Materialist and Postmaterialist goals. Accordingly, social class-based voting has been declining, and there has been a growing tendency for Western electorates to polarize according to Materialist versus Postmaterialist values. This development imposes a difficult balancing act on party leaders, especially those of Left parties. If they adapt to this new polarization too slowly, they lose their young Postmaterialist activists; but if they move too fast in this direction, they risk losing their traditional working-class constituency.

The rise of a new axis of politics, based on polarization between Postmodern values and traditional cultural values and the decline of class-based polarization, has left Western political systems in a schizophrenic situation. Most of the major political parties have been aligned along the class-based axis of polarization for decades, and established party loyalties and group ties still hold much of the electorate to this alignment. But the most heated political issues today are mainly Postmodern issues, on which support for change comes mainly from a Postmaterialist, middle-class base. This creates a stress that can be resolved in two ways: by repositioning the established parties or by creating new parties. Both have been taking place.

Klingemann, Hofferbert, and Budge (1994) find that there has been a gradual repositioning of party positions along the Postmodern politics axis: in an analysis of party programs in Western democracies during the last several decades, the percentage of references to social class conflict steadily declined, and the percentage of references to Postmaterialist issues increased sharply.

In the 1940s and 1950s, socialist policies were a major theme in the political party programs of Western democracies. As figure 8.7 demonstrates, socialist economic policies were mentioned in party manifestos about 15 times as often as were environmentalist policies: during 1944–59, the average party program referred to socialist economic policy about five times (socialist parties, of course, mentioned them more often than conservative parties), while the average party platform mentioned environmental matters .3 times: two-thirds of the party platforms did not mention environmental policy at all. Since then, a radical shift in emphasis has taken place. By the 1980s, environmental policy had overtaken socialist economic policy as a campaign issue (receiving

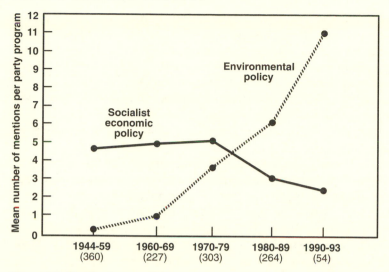

Figure 8.7. Emphasis on socialist economic policy vs. environmental policy in political party programs: 1944–93. *Source*: Comparative Manifestos Project. Based on content analysis of 1,208 party programs issued during this period by political parties in the following countries: France, Italy, (West) Germany, Austria, Switzerland, Great Britain, Ireland, the United States, Canada, Sweden, Norway, Denmark, Finland, Iceland, Belgium, the Netherlands, Luxembourg, Australia, and New Zealand. For details, see Klingemann et al., *Parties, Policies and Democracy* (Boulder: Westview Press, 1994).

almost twice as much emphasis). By the 1990s, environmental policy dominated socialist economic policy as an electoral theme: the average party program mentioned environmental policy eleven times; socialist economic policy was mentioned only 2.5 times (with much of the mention being negative).

This seems to reflect political influences moving from the microlevel to the macrolevel: though we cannot directly demonstrate that the changes at the mass level preceded the shifts at the party program level, it seems implausible that this was a case of mass values following elite cues. For, as we saw in chapter 5, the changes at the mass level reflect a deep-rooted intergenerational change that can be traced back to the postwar economic miracles and was set in motion long before the party programs began to shift. At the elite level, the changes manifest themselves only in the 1960s and 1970s, when the postwar generation became an increasingly important segment of the electorate—and of the political activists. According to Carkoglu and Blinn (1994), by 1989 the Materialist-Postmaterialist issue dimension had become the first factor in the party programs of Western democracies, explaining more of the variance in party programs than the traditional Left-Right dimension based on the classic Marxist social class polarization over ownership of the means of production and redistribution of income. Although the *parties* were still perceived as positioned along a Left-Right dimension, the dominant *issue* polarization had shifted from social class issues to Postmodern issues (Huber and Inglehart, 1995).

The rise of the Postmodern politics dimension tends to bring a reversal of social class positions: on the old Left-Right dimension, the upper income strata supported the Right or conservative position: they were the Haves and acted to preserve their economically privileged position against the Have-nots. But the Postmodern politics dimension is based not on ownership of property, but on one's subjective sense of security. It pits a Modern/Materialist worldview against a Postmodern/Postmaterialist worldview. On this dimension, those with *higher* levels of income, education, and occupational status are relatively secure, and increasingly, they tend to support the Left position.

Postmaterialists come from middle-class backgrounds, but they support change (Inglehart, 1977). This is conducive to a decline of social class voting, as middle-class Postmaterialists move left—and working-class Materialists move to the right.

For decades, one of the basic axioms of political sociology was the fact that working-class voters tend to support parties of the Left, and middle-class voters those of the Right (Alford, 1963; Lipset, 1960). This was an accurate description of reality a generation ago, but the tendency has been getting steadily weaker. As figure 8.8 illustrates, social class-based voting has declined markedly during the past 40 years. If 75 percent of the working class voted for the Left and only 25 percent of the middle-class voters did so, one would obtain an Alford class voting index of 50 (the difference between the two figures). As figure 8.8 shows, this is about where the Swedish electorate fell in 1948— but by 1990 the index had fallen to 26. The Scandinavian countries have traditionally shown the world's highest levels of social class voting, but it has declined sharply in all of them. In the United States, Britain, France, and West Germany, during the late 1940s and early 1950s, working-class voters were more apt to support the Left than were middle-class voters by margins that ranged from 30 to 45 points. By the 1990s, this spread had shrunken to the range from 1 to 25 points. In the 1992 U.S. presidential elections, social class voting had virtually disappeared. There were short-term fluctuations in given countries: the 1980s produced a partial resurgence of social class voting in Great Britain, for example. But all five of the countries for which we have data over this long time period show pronounced long-term declines in class voting. Overall, class voting indices in the 1990s were about half as large as they were in the postwar era. By the 1990s, the country with the *highest* class-voting index (Sweden) showed weaker class polarization than did the country with the *lowest* level in the 1940s (France).

The class-conflict model of politics is not just a straw man: a few decades ago it provided a fairly accurate description of reality. But that reality has changed, gradually but pervasively, and partly through intergenerational population replacement processes. Throughout Western Europe, social class vot-

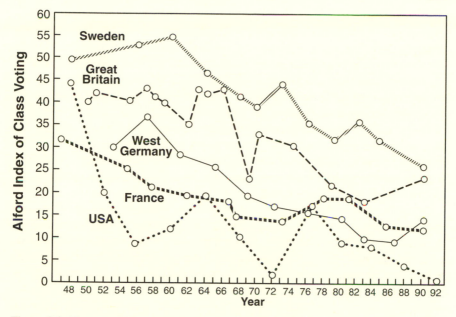

Figure 8.8. The trend in social class voting in five Western democracies, 1947–92. *Source*: Adapted from Lipset (1981): 505. Updated by author with results from France and from recent elections. American data based on whites only, for comparability over time, cited in Abramson et al., (1985, 1994). The 1990 figures for European countries are from the 1990 World Values Survey.

ing indices are about half as large among the postwar birth cohorts as they are among older groups.

There has been extensive recent debate over whether social class voting has really been declining. If one focuses on selected periods for selected countries, it is easy enough to demonstrate that there has been no decline. For example, if one focuses on Great Britain and uses the 1969 low point (shown in figure 8.8) as one's starting point, one can conclude that there has been no downward trend in that country. But if one examines the entire time series since World War II, one finds a statistically significant decline that brought class voting down to half its former size.

Another approach has been to argue that Alford's manual/nonmanual dichotomy is too simple: using various more complicated ways of measuring social class, or more complex statistical procedures than comparing the Alford index over time, various analysts have argued that they find no downward trend. The great advantage of Alford's index is precisely the fact that it *is* so simple and straightforward: the distinction between manual and nonmanual workers is theoretically clear and easy to operationalize. It indicates a clear and obvious cutting point in any industrial society. Hout, Brooks, and Manza

(1993) increase the number of measures of occupation and use logistic regression to test whether class voting has declined in the United States. Increasing the number of occupational categories does indeed increase the possibility that some combination of them may affect party choice. But their interpretation of their logistic regression results is questionable. They find, for example, that professionals voted predominantly for the Republicans in the 1950s, but for the Democrats in the 1990s. Ignoring this reversal of sign, they describe this as part of a pattern of "trendless fluctuation" because their various occupational groupings still explain about as much of the variance as ever (see Clark, 1995). Analyzing a massive database from 16 societies across four decades, and using more appropriate methodology, Nieuwbeerta and De Graaf (forthcoming) find a clear overall decline in class voting.

As social class-based voting has declined, the importance of the Postmodern political cleavage has increased. In the 1970s, Lijphart (1979) found "New Politics" parties (parties with a Postmaterialist constituency) in only three countries. In the 1989 elections to the European Parliament, New Politics parties won at least 10 percent of the vote in eight of the 12 European Community countries (Dalton, 1991b).

THE SOCIETAL LEVEL: DIMINISHING MARGINAL RETURNS
FROM ECONOMIC DEVELOPMENT

Let us turn now from analyzing cultural change at the individual level, to view it at the societal level.

Although Karl Marx died in 1883, his analysis of political conflict continued to fascinate social scientists for most of the following century. His emphasis on politics as the struggle to own the means of production captured an important part of reality in the early phases of industrial society. But with the evolution of advanced industrial society, new conflicts and new worldviews have emerged, making the economic conflicts Marx emphasized less central to political life.

This development reflects the diminishing marginal utility of economic determinism: economic factors play a decisive role under conditions of economic scarcity; but as scarcity diminishes, other factors shape society to an increasing degree. We have examined this phenomenon from an individual-level perspective; now let us examine it at the aggregate cross-national level. Forces operating at both levels converge, bringing a diminishing degree of economic determinism and class-based political conflict, as advanced industrial society emerges.

As we saw in chapter 2, human life expectancy is closely linked to a nation's level of economic development. In poor societies, life expectancies are less than 40 years, but they rise steeply with relatively modest increases in wealth, until one reaches a threshold of about $3,000 per capita income; then the life expectancy curve levels off. Economic factors become less decisive, and lifestyle factors more so. Similar patterns of diminishing returns from economic development are found with numerous other social indicators. Caloric intake, literacy rates, and other indicators rise steeply at the low end of the scale but level off among advanced industrial societies.

The pattern of diminishing marginal returns from economic development is not limited to objective aspects of life: it extends to subjective well-being as well. As we saw earlier, subjective well-being rises markedly with rising levels of economic development, and then levels off. Above a threshold of about $6,000 per capita, there is virtually no cross-national relationship between wealth and subjective well-being.

A rational strategy would dictate that at low levels of development, the individual should give top priority to maximizing one's income, and the society should give top priority to economic growth. But more of the same indefinitely is not a rational strategy. Beyond a certain threshold, there is a change in survival strategies, as Postmodern politics begins. Gradual cultural changes are feeding back into the political process of advanced industrial societies, leading to a change in their political agenda.

The Diminishing Political Base of the Traditional Left

Political life is also responding to a curve of diminishing marginal returns—in this case, the diminishing marginal utility of the classic program of the Left.

Equality of income distribution shows a curve of diminishing returns similar to those we saw for life expectancies and subjective well-being in chapter 2. Income equality increases sharply with economic development, up to a level of about $3,500 per capita in 1978 dollars (see Inglehart, 1990: 251); above that threshold, the curve levels off. In the overwhelming majority of countries with a GNP per capita below $3,500 (as of 1978), the top tenth of the population got more than one-third of the total income (in some cases as much as 57 percent). In *none* of the nations with a GNP per capita above $3,500 did the top tenth of the population get more than one-third of the total income; their share ranged from as low as 17 percent, in communist countries, to a high of 33 percent, in Finland.

Does this cross-sectional pattern reflect a longitudinal trend? The point has been debated. The most reliable longitudinal data come from economically advanced countries, most of which have shown only modest increases in income equality during the past 30 years. But if the shift is based on a curve of diminishing returns rather than a linear trend, this is exactly what we would expect. It is only in the earlier stages of economic development that we would observe large amounts of change. The United States, for example, moved toward substantially greater income equality from 1890 to 1950, but has shown some reconcentration since then. Absolute levels of income continued to rise, but relative shares changed only slightly. Most OECD countries moved toward greater income equality during the 1960s and 1970s, but the trend seems to have leveled off in the 1980s (Cusack, 1991). Conversely, Taiwan, South

Korea, Singapore, and Hong Kong all have made dramatic leaps from poverty to prosperity only recently—and all have shown substantial increases in income equality (Chen 1979).

Why do we find a curvilinear relationship between economic development and income equality? In the early phase, we believe, it reflects a process of social mobilization, engendered by economic development. Industrialization leads to urbanization and mass literacy, which facilitate the organization of labor unions and mass political parties and the enfranchisement of the working class. Economic development does not automatically bring equality, but it does tend to transform the masses from isolated and illiterate peasants into organized citizens with the power to bargain for a more equal share of the pie.

But why does the curve level off among mature industrial societies? There are two main reasons. First, as a society approaches perfect equality, it necessarily reaches a point of diminishing returns. At the point where the top tenth had only 10 percent of the income, any further transfer of income would be a move *away* from equality. None of these societies has actually reached this point, but some were getting close. In East Germany, for example, the top tenth got only 17 percent of the total income. Norway, Sweden, and Denmark have greater income equality than the United States, West Germany, or France, which suggests that the latter countries could move further toward equality without necessarily having ineffective economies or coercive societies. But the Scandinavian countries seem to be approaching the limit of what is possible in a democratic political system. By the 1980s they were already experiencing a sharp public reaction against any further expansion of the welfare state, and began to cut it back.

Why this is so reflects a second basic principle: political support for increased income equality reaches a point of diminishing returns at a level well short of perfect equality.

As a society moves closer to an equal income distribution, the political base of support for further redistribution becomes narrower. In a poor society where the top 10 percent get 80 percent of the total income, the vast majority would benefit from redistribution. In a society in which the top 50 percent get 80 percent of the total income, far fewer people will benefit from further redistribution, and they will benefit proportionately less; one eventually reaches the point at which a majority of the voters stand to lose more than they would gain by additional redistribution. This does not constitute a moral justification for not moving further toward equality, but it does constitute a major political barrier in democratic societies. Under these conditions, the political base for further development of the welfare state is simply not there—at least not insofar as the citizens are motivated solely by economic self-interest. Ironically, further progress toward equality would come *not* from an emphasis on materialistic class conflict, but through an appeal to the public's sense of justice, social solidarity, and other nonmaterial motivations. Thus in the long run, economic development makes a sense of economic deprivation both less widespread among mass publics, and a less powerful cause of political conflict.

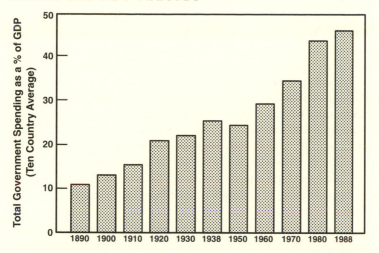

Figure 8.9. The growth of government in OECD countries, 1890–1988.

Average government spending rates over time from 10 OECD countries: Austria, Canada, Denmark, France, West Germany, Italy, Japan, Norway, United Kingdom, and the United States. *Source*: Cusack, 1991.

Stated in this way, this conclusion may seem self-evident. But it is not; it has been hotly debated and is not generally accepted even now. A quarter century ago, the "end of ideology" school concluded that growing prosperity was giving rise to the "politics of consensus in an age of affluence" (Lane 1965); the subsequent explosion of protest in the late 1960s led many to conclude that this school had been completely wrong. In fact, the "end of ideology" school's analysis of what had been happening was partly correct; like Marx, they simply failed to anticipate new developments. While economic cleavages did become less intense with rising levels of economic development, they gradually gave way to *other* types of conflict.

By 1988 government spending had risen to nearly 50 percent of GDP in OECD countries, as figure 8.9 illustrates. This is another point of diminishing returns. Obviously, this trend cannot continue much longer: it is impossible to go above 100 percent except by running large deficits, and the costs of debt service eventually eliminate even that option. But another limit begins to take effect long before a society reaches the 100 percent level: psychologically, the 50 percent level seems to be a significant threshold. As taxation moves above this level, people begin to realize that an hour spent on tax avoidance can be more remunerative than an hour spent on one's job. And the ratio shifts very rapidly as the curve rises. When government spending (and taxation) rises above 66 percent of GNP, it may become economically rational to devote two-thirds of one's time to lobbying or tax avoidance, and a third of one's time to working. One's job eventually becomes a sideline; dealing with the governmental bureaucracy becomes the major focus. For some time, people may continue to work diligently, from force of habit, but a mentality of "They pretend to pay us, and we pretend to work" increasingly permeates the society.

Consequently no economy even approaches the theoretical 100 percent limit; functional requirements call a halt well short of this point. Thus, even the USSR, though ideologically committed to the position that private enterprise was morally wrong, probably never went above the 75 percent level. The rulers were forced to tolerate a sizable private sector because private agriculture and the unofficial economy were essential in staving off economic collapse. Thus, for functional as well as political reasons, by the 1980s the growth of the state was reaching natural limits. An awareness that the Marxist model was no longer working began to permeate mass consciousness.

Diminishing Returns from the Traditional Program of the Left

We have seen indications that economic development leads to a diminishing impact of economic influences on such objective characteristics as life expectancy and economic equality. But do such changes actually reshape the subjective political preferences of mass publics? The evidence suggests that they do; at high levels of economic development, public support for the classic economic policies of the Left tends to diminish.

Everyone knows that Denmark is a leading welfare state, with advanced social legislation, progressive taxation, a high level of income equality, and well over half its GNP going to the public sector. Obviously, the Danish public must be relatively favorable to these traditional policies of the Left. Conversely, everyone knows that Ireland is a relatively rural nation, with a modest public sector and no significant communist or socialist movements. Clearly, Ireland must be a bastion of conservatism on the classic Left-Right issues.

In fact, the conventional stereotypes are wrong on both counts. These stereotypes reflect patterns that were true in the past, but precisely *because* Denmark has attained high levels of social security—and very high levels of taxation— the Danish public has little desire for further extension of these policies. Support for the classic economic policies of the Left tends to diminish as economic development rises.

As figure 8.10 demonstrates, Greece is by far the poorest country among 11 European Community societies surveyed in 1979–83, and the Greek public has by far the highest level of support for nationalization of industry, more government management of the economy, and reducing income inequality. Ireland is the second-poorest country, and overall Ireland ranks second in support for these policies. At the opposite end of the spectrum, Denmark is the richest country—and has the lowest level of support for these policies. Western Germany ranks next to Denmark in economic level—and also in support for the classic Left policies.

The principle of diminishing marginal utility applies at the societal level, as well as the individual level. Greece is an economically underdeveloped coun-

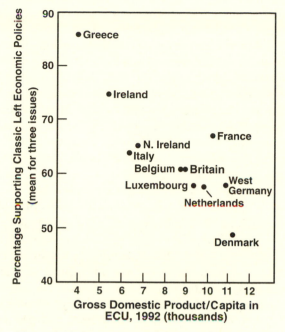

Figure 8.10. Support for the classic economic policies of the Left in 11 countries, by level of economic development.
Based on responses to three questions asked in each of three Euro-Barometer surveys in 1979, 1981, and 1983. *Source*: Inglehart, 1990: 256.

try, with many living in poverty and a small affluent elite. In such a context, the balance between rich and poor can be redressed only by strong government intervention. Denmark is a rich country that has long had some of the world's most advanced social welfare policies—and one of the world's highest rates of taxation. About 60 percent of Denmark's GNP is spent by the government; it is reaching the point at which it becomes impossible to move much further in this direction. In Denmark, further redistribution by the government seems much less urgent than in Greece—and the costs of government intervention impinge on a much larger share of the population. The incentives to press farther with the traditional economic policies of the Left become relatively weak, and public resistance becomes relatively strong.

There may be still another factor behind the decline of the traditional program of the Left. Tanzi and Schuknecht (1995) argue that the human returns on public spending are also subject to diminishing marginal returns. They analyze the increase in public spending in industrial economies over the past 125 years, assessing its social and economic benefits. They find that up to 1960, higher government spending was linked with considerable improvements in infant mortality rates, life expectancy, income equality, and educational levels. But since 1960, further increases in public spending have gone with only modest social gains—and those countries in which spending has risen most have not performed any better than those in which spending rose least. Indeed, on some indicators such as unemployment rates, the low-spending countries have done significantly better.

These findings are sure to be controversial, and they do not demonstrate a causal link: it is possible, for example, that most of the improvement in social standards up to 1960 was mainly due to rising incomes rather than public spending, and that such gains diminish once a certain income threshold is reached. But regardless of whether increased public spending brings diminishing social returns beyond a certain level, it seems clear that it does eventually bring diminishing public support.

The evidence in figure 8.10 suggests that higher levels of economic development are linked with diminishing mass support for state intervention. This figure is based on data from Western Europe. Does this pattern hold up more broadly? Data from the 1990–93 World Values Survey suggest that the phenomenon is global. As figure 8.10 indicates, throughout the industrial world public sentiment today is in favor of less, not more, government ownership. But the degree of support is closely linked to a society's level of economic development. Support for more government ownership is highest in China and Nigeria and lowest in the United States, Canada, and Western Germany. The midpoint of this scale is 5.5, about where India is located on figure 8.11. The only countries in which a majority favor more (rather than less) government ownership are China, Nigeria, Turkey, Chile, and Belarus; and the publics of Russia and India are about evenly divided. The publics of the other 35 societies favor moving away from government ownership. Marxism has become a phenomenon for which the mass appeal is found mainly in developing nations.

As figure 8.12 shows, even in Western countries, Postmaterialists are not particularly interested in government ownership of industry: though relatively enthusiastic supporters of the Left position on practically all of the Postmodern issues, the Postmaterialist constituency is not significantly more favorable to government ownership of industry than are Materialists. And in the ex-socialist societies, the situation is dramatically different: Postmaterialists are far more favorable than other groups to moving *away* from state ownership of business and industry. They see privatization as a step away from the rigid authoritarianism of the past, toward a society in which individual autonomy is enhanced.

In many ex-socialist societies such as Lithuania, Poland, and Hungary, the trauma of the transition to a market economy has brought reform communists back to power in free elections—but even the former communists are now disillusioned with government ownership. As one leader of the newly elected reform communist regime in Poland commented, "If one of our leaders proposed going back to a state-run economy, we would have to drop him from the party—not because he was a communist, but because he was an idiot."

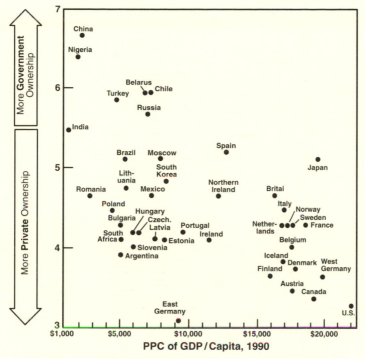

Figure 8.11. Economic development goes with diminishing support for state ownership.

Mean level of support for private vs. government ownership of business and industry, on a scale where 1 = "*Private* ownership of business and industry should be increased" and 10 = "*Government* ownership of business and industry should be increased." N = 43, r = −.54, p < .0001. *Source*: 1990–93 World Values Survey. Purchasing power estimates of GNP/capita from World Bank, *World Development Report, 1993*.

The policies that dominated the agenda of the Left throughout most of this century are running out of steam. Increased state intervention was desperately needed to alleviate starvation and social upheaval in the 1930s, was essential to the emergence of the welfare state in the postwar era, and still makes sense in some areas. But in others, it has passed a point of diminishing returns. The renewed respect for market forces that has emerged throughout most of the industrial world reflects this reality.

The neoconservative claim that the classic welfare state policies have failed is false, however. On the contrary, in such countries as Denmark these policies have largely solved the problems they are capable of solving—and have thereby reduced the demand for more of the same. Insofar as the *succeed*, they reach a point of diminishing returns, and begin to cede top priority to problems that have *not* been solved.

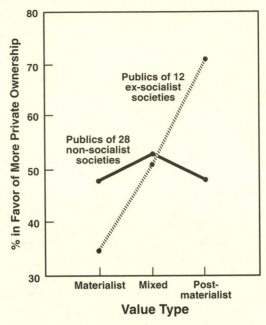

Figure 8.12. Percentage in favor of privatization of business and industry by value type, among publics of 12 ex-socialist societies vs. publics of 28 non-socialist societies.

Percentages are those placing themselves at points 1–4 on a 10-point scale on which 1 = "private ownership of business and industry should be increased" and 10 = "government ownership of business and industry should be increased."
Source: 1990–93 World Values Survey.

An attempt to turn back the clock to the savage laissez-faire policies of the early twentieth century would be self-defeating, ultimately leading to a resurgence of class conflict in all its former harshness. But the fundamentalists of the Left are equally self-defeating in their rigid adherence to a traditional program based on class conflict and state ownership and control of the means of production.

This does not mean that economic factors are no longer politically important. On the contrary, some very significant research has demonstrated strong linkages between fluctuations in the economies of Western nations and support for the incumbent political party (Kramer 1971; Tufte 1978; Hibbs, Rivers, and Vasilatos 1982). But this research has also produced a surprising finding: while support for the incumbents does reflect the performance of the national economy, it does *not* seem motivated by individual economic self-interest. The electorates of advanced industrial societies do not seem to be voting their pocketbooks, but instead seem primarily motivated by "sociotropic" concerns; rather than asking "What have you done for me lately?" they ask "What have you done for the *nation* lately?" (Kinder and Kiewiet 1979).

In short, economic factors remain an important influence on electoral behavior—but increasingly, they reflect sociotropic motivations rather than class conflict. The politics of advanced industrial societies no longer polarize primarily on the basis of working class versus middle class; and the old issues, centering on ownership of the means of production and government control of the economy, no longer lie at the heart of political polarization.

CONCLUSION

Marx set the agenda underlying modern political cleavages, which were based on ownership of the means of production and the distribution of income, and where support for the Left had a working-class base. With the emergence of advanced industrial society, the impact of economic factors reaches a point of diminishing returns. Postmodern issues take an increasingly important place on the national agenda, giving rise to a new axis based on the polarization between Postmodern and Fundamentalist worldviews; and support for sociopolitical change increasingly comes from a Postmaterialist, largely middle-class base.

The major established political parties in Western countries emerged in an era dominated by social class conflict, and to a considerable extent they are still aligned along a class-based axis. But support for new political movements and new political parties largely reflects the tension between traditional and Postmodern goals. Accordingly, social class-based voting has been declining, and there has been a growing tendency for Western electorates to polarize on a new axis, based on Postmodern issues. The established parties of the Left are trying to co-opt the Postmodern constituency, but if they move too far in this direction, they risk losing their traditional constituency, which reacts negatively to rapid change in sexual norms, gender roles, and massive immigration.

The Marxist model has lost its appeal in the industrialized world. Its emphasis on economic factors as the driving force of history provides a good first approximation of reality in the early stages of industrialization, but is of diminishing value as scarcity diminishes and new problems emerge. Similarly, the *policies* that are needed to counter the ruthless exploitation of capitalism in its laissez-faire stage reach a point of diminishing returns in advanced welfare states. Where government spending is already 40 to 60 percent of GNP, there is little potential to move further in this direction, and the massive power of big government itself becomes an increasingly serious problem. The old assumption of the Left that more government was automatically better has lost its credibility. But to elevate government nonintervention into a quasi-theological principle is equally untenable.

The meaning of "Left" and "Right" has been transformed. The key Marxist goal—nationalization of industry—has been abandoned by the publics of advanced industrial societies, though it remains attractive in less developed societies. Nationalization is not the panacea it once appeared to be. And insofar as it diverts attention from increasingly pressing problems concerning the quality of the physical and social environment, it can be downright counterproductive—for it provides no solution to these problems. Indeed, insofar as nationalization merges the political regulators with the military-industrial complex into one cozy elite, it may even make things worse. The nationalized factories of the Soviet bloc polluted even more than the private ones in the West. East Germany was the most severely polluted nation in Europe, with air and water pollutant levels two to three times as high as those in West Germany. And it is no coincidence that the only nuclear power plant accidents that have cost human lives occurred in the former Soviet Union, where environmentalist pressures for safety measures could not be freely organized. Although their environmental problems were even more severe, and their arms expenditures proportionately even higher than in Western societies, the political systems of the Eastern European countries made the emergence of independent environmentalist movements or peace movements far more difficult than in the West. It was relatively easy for the ruling elite to simply ignore such issues: officially, the problems underlying them existed only in capitalist countries.

The goals of individuals and the challenges facing society are different from those of a generation ago. For the past generation, Postmaterialists have controlled the agenda in advanced industrial societies, inserting a series of new causes into the political arena, and giving birth to new political movements and parties. After a generation of rapid social change, the opposition to Postmodern politics has become increasingly well organized and articulate, giving rise to movements and parties that systematically oppose the Postmodern agenda. The long-established political party institutions still reflect their origins in social class conflict, but the issues actually being debated today mainly concern support and opposition to Postmodernization.

The Shift toward Postmodern Values: Predicted and Observed Changes, 1981–1990

A BROADER SHIFT TOWARD POSTMODERN VALUES

Not just postmaterialist values, but a whole range of Postmodern values are shifting in a predictable direction. This chapter and the next one examine this shift. Although we do not have year-by-year evidence of these changes (as we do for the shift from Materialist to Postmaterialist values), the 1981 and 1990 World Values surveys provide at least some evidence concerning how this broader shift toward a Postmodern worldview is moving.

The 1981 World Values Surveys showed that a wide variety of values and attitudes concerning politics, work, religion, sexual norms, and childrearing values were linked with Materialist/Postmaterialist values. They also showed significant differences between the preferences of young and old, with the old having attitudes similar to those of the Materialists, and the young having attitudes similar to those of the Postmaterialists.

These findings were based on the 1981 surveys alone: time series evidence was not yet available to show whether these age differences reflected an intergenerational shift. But we argued, on theoretical grounds, that these related attitudes were influenced by the same factors as those that motivated the Postmaterialist shift and were moving on a similar trajectory:

> Far-reaching though it is, the rise of Postmaterialist values is only one aspect of a still broader process of cultural change that is reshaping the political outlook, religious orientations, gender roles, and sexual mores of advanced industrial society. These changes are related to a common concern: the need for a sense of security, which religion and absolute cultural norms have traditionally provided. In the decades since World War II, the emergence of unprecedentedly high levels of prosperity, together with the relatively high levels of social security provided by the welfare state, have contributed to a decline in the prevailing sense of vulnerability. (Inglehart, 1990: 177)

Diminishing insecurity, it was claimed, is giving rise to a broad cultural shift, embracing not only Materialist/Postmaterialist values, but an entire syndrome of related attitudes. Emphasizing this prediction, the book that presented this thesis was entitled *Culture Shift in Advanced Industrial Society*.

We now have the cross-time data needed us to test this thesis. *Is* a broad cultural shift occurring?

We would not expect to find that *all* values are changing, of course: only those that are influenced by an underlying sense of security or insecurity. This means that we are dealing with the Postmodern shift discussed in chapter 3: we would expect to find systematic change among the values linked with the Scarcity-Postmodern values dimension described there (details of question wording are provided in Appendix 2).

Furthermore, we would not expect to find this shift taking place in every country. The rate of the shift toward Postmaterialist values is influenced by two sets of factors: (1) a long-term component, based on intergenerational value change, and (2) a short-term component that reflects current conditions.

The strength of intergenerational value change varies cross-nationally. Some countries are still undergoing the process of Modernization and have scarcely begun to move onto the Postmodernization trajectory. Among the countries for which data are available for at least two time points, South Africa is least likely to be moving rapidly toward Postmodern values. There are few Postmaterialists in South Africa, and relatively little difference between the values of young and old. Consequently, intergenerational population replacement would not bring much change there. The Nordic nations and the Nether-

TABLE 9.1
Variables Correlated with Materialist/Postmaterialist Values
in 1981 World Values Surveys (Correlations above .125 Level)

I.	*Norms concerning (a) Respect for authority, (b) Sexual and marital behavior, and (c) Civil behavior*
1.	"More respect for authority would be a good thing"
2.	"Abortion is never justified"
3.	"Divorce is never justified"
4.	"Homosexuality is never justified"
5.	"Prostitution is never justified"
6.	"Sex under the legal age is never justified"
7.	"Married men/women having an affair is never justified"
8.	"Euthanasia is never justified"
9.	"Suicide is never justified"
10.	"Fighting with the police is never justified"
11.	"Using marijuana is never justified"
II.	*Religious norms*
12.	Percentage attending church at least once a month
13.	Percentage saying God is important in their lives
14.	Percentage saying they believe in God
15.	Percentage saying they believe in hell
16.	Percentage saying they believe in heaven
17.	Percentage saying they believe in sin
18.	Percentage saying they get comfort and strength from religion
19.	Percentage saying that the church in their country is giving adequate answers to moral problems

(continued)

TABLE 9.1 *Continued*

20. Percentage saying that the church in their country is giving adequate answers to problems of family life
21. Percentage saying that the church in their country is giving adequate answers to people's spiritual needs
22. Percentage saying that they "often" think about the meaning and purpose of life*

III. *Norms concerning parent-child ties*

23. Percentage saying "a child needs a home with both a father and a mother, to grow up happily"
24. Percentage saying "a woman has to have children in order to be fulfilled"
25. Percentage approving of a woman having a child as a single parent
26. Percentage believing one has a duty to love and respect one's parents, regardless of their faults

IV. *Norms concerning (a) Conventional political participation and (b) Unconventional political participation*

27. Percentage saying that they "often" or "sometimes" discuss politics with friends
28. Percentage saying that they are interested in politics
29. Percentage saying that they have signed a petition
30. Percentage saying that they have taken part in a boycott or might do so
31. Percentage saying that they have taken part in a demonstration or might do so
32. Percentage saying that they have taken part in an unofficial strike or might do so
33. Percentage saying that they have occupied a building or might do so

V. *Norms concerning (a) Control of business and industry, (b) Left-Right self-placement, and (c) Confidence in authoritarian institutions*

34a. Percentage favoring joint employee-owner participation in choosing managers in business and industry
34b. Percentage favoring state ownership of business and industry
34c. Percentage favoring owner's right to chose managers in business and industry
35. Percentage placing themselves on the Left half of a 10-point Left-Right ideological scale
36. Percentage expressing "a great deal" of confidence in the church in their country
37. Percentage expressing "a great deal" of confidence in their country's armed forces
38. Percentage expressing "a great deal" of confidence in their country's police forces
39. Percentage saying they are "very proud" of their nationality
40. Percentage saying "generally speaking, most people can be trusted"

Source: 1981 World Values survey, pooled data from 21 nations included in both 1981 and 1990 surveys.

*This item has a zero-order correlation with Materialist/Postmaterialist values of only .092 because of a tendency for older respondents to take the Postmaterialist position; controlling for age, the relationship rises above the .125 threshold.

lands are at the other extreme: Postmaterialists are numerous there, and values are strongly correlated with age, reflecting the presence of a steep gradient of intergenerational change. Most of the other nations of Western Europe and North America are well launched on the process of Postmodernization and seem likely to show relatively large amounts of change. East Asia might also show significant change on this dimension: though there are not yet many Postmaterialists there, intergenerational differences are relatively large.

Do we actually observe systematic shifts among these values? Let us begin by testing a greatly oversimplified hypothesis: that all of the values that are linked with Postmaterialism will become more widespread over time. Reality is not this simple, of course. Current conditions will cause fluctuations, both in Materialist/Postmaterialist values and in other Postmodern orientations as well: secure and prosperous conditions should be conducive to Postmodern values, and economic decline, war, or domestic strife should be conducive to survival values. Nevertheless, to begin, let us ignore the impact of short-term factors and start with the deliberately oversimplified hypothesis that "Everything that goes with Postmaterialist values will increase."

We are testing the proposition that all values having reasonably strong correlations with Postmaterialism are part of an intergenerational shift linked with population replacement. To do so, we identified 40 variables that (1) had mean correlations of at least .125 with Postmaterialism in the 1981 World Values Survey and (2) were included in both the 1981 and 1990 World Values surveys (enabling us to see whether they had changed in the predicted direction). Table 9.1 lists these 40 items. They cover a wide range of topics, but all of them are correlated with Materialist/Postmaterialist values. Figure 9.1 gives some examples, showing the relationships between four of these items and the Postmaterialism dimension. Materialists are almost twice as likely to be intolerant of both homosexuality and abortion as are Postmaterialists and much likelier to believe that a woman needs children in order to be fulfilled; but they are only half as likely as Postmaterialists to say that God is not important in their lives.

The 40 norms and values in this diverse array of items go together because they are all influenced by one's sense of security. Chapter 3 gave an overview of the values involved in this cultural shift: we would expect most of the high-loading items on the Scarcity-Postmodern values dimension depicted in figure 3.2 to be moving in the Postmodern direction, in any society that has experienced a substantial intergenerational rise in its living standard during the past few decades.

To test our prediction, we will simply compare the responses to these 40 variables in 21 countries in 1981 with the responses to the same questions in the same 21 countries in 1990 to see if the predicted shift occurred.[1] Examining the results from 40 variables in 21 different countries would produce a total

---

[1] Both World Values Surveys were also carried out in Denmark, which would provide a total of 22 countries except for the fact that the 1981 Danish survey does not seem to provide a reliable baseline for comparisons across time. See Appendix 1 for a discussion of this point.

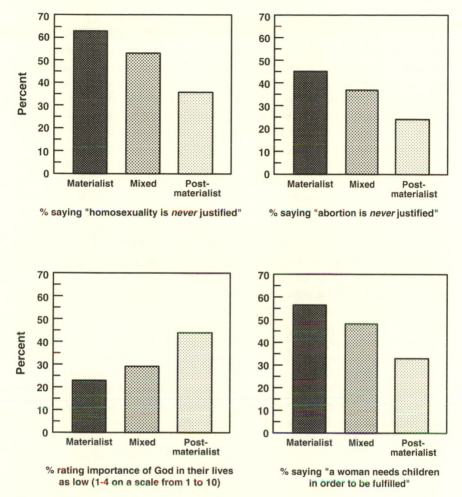

Figure 9.1. Some attitudes correlated with Materialist/Postmaterialist values. *Source*: Pooled cross-national data from 1990–93 World Values surveys.

of 40 × 21 = 840 separate tests. But since not all 40 items were asked in both years in every country, and one variable is broken down in two ways, we actually have 802 separate tests of the predicted change. This is a massive basis on which to test the hypothesized culture shift. As we are about to see, in most cases the publics did shift in the predicted direction.

CULTURAL CHANGE HAS A COMPONENT OF PREDICTABILITY

Successful prediction in the social sciences is rare, but our theory of intergenerational value change generates a set of systematic predictions that now can be tested. These predictions apply only when certain conditions are present; but (as we will see) these conditions apply widely. Our prediction is that any attitude having a reasonably strong correlation with Materialist/Postmaterialist values will move in a specified direction. And since our theory attributes these trends to intergenerational changes in perceived security, we would expect to find them in any society that has experienced rising prosperity in recent decades. When these conditions are met, our theory implies that we should observe a shift, from 1981 to 1990, toward the values espoused by the younger and more Postmaterialist respondents.

This prediction is based on population replacement effects. The fact that a given attitude (such as sexual permissiveness or interpersonal trust) is correlated with Materialist/Postmaterialist values is taken as an indication that this attitude is influenced by the degree of security that given birth cohorts experienced during their formative years. We do not assume that people are becoming more permissive or more trusting because they are Postmaterialists, but because the two orientations share common *causes*: they are shaped by one's level of security or insecurity.

The fact that a given attitude is correlated with Postmaterialist values implies that we will usually find age-related differences as well, with the younger cohorts more likely to have the Postmaterialists' attitudes. In most cases, we *do* observe such age-group differences, though a few attitudes are shaped by life-cycle effects that offset the age-linkage normally found with Postmaterialist values. For example, older people tend to spend more time thinking about the meaning and purpose of life as they approach its end; but Postmaterialists are *also* relatively likely to spend time thinking about the meaning and purpose of life, in keeping with their greater emphasis on intellectual concerns. Here we have a case in which the usual tendency of younger groups to take the Postmaterialist position is reversed by a strong life-cycle effect.

Conversely, some attitudes show age differences that reflect the human life cycle and are not correlated with Materialist/Postmaterialist values. In these cases, we would *not* expect to find any predictable trend over time. Consequently (paradoxical as it may seem), Materialist/Postmaterialist values are a better predictor of change than is age itself, even though these changes are based on population replacement effects. If a given attitude varies across age groups but is unrelated to Materialist/Postmaterialist values, we would *not* predict that it will change over time, since the age differences may simply reflect life-cycle effects. But if a given attitude is correlated with Materialist/Postmaterialist values, we *do* predict an intergenerational shift, even if we do not find age-group differences.

Short-term economic or political or social events can also have an impact on these attitudes, but they provide no basis for predicting long-term shifts. As we saw in chapter 5, short-term fluctuations influence the values of mass publics even when a long-term intergenerational shift *is* occurring: the impact of current events is superimposed on the long-term trend. This means that our predictions will not always be confirmed, especially over short time periods:

if period effects are sufficiently strong, they can neutralize the effects of inter-generational change. In the long run, however, our predictions should usually be valid. Negative period effects tend to conceal underlying intergenerational shifts, and positive period effects tend to exaggerate them. But in the long run, negative and positive period effects are likely to cancel each other out, leaving the underlying trend manifest.

The period from 1981 to 1990 is not very long from the perspective of intergenerational population replacement, but it is long enough so that at least moderate amounts of systematic change should become visible.

Predicted and Observed Changes

Norms concerning Authority

Let us examine some actual changes that were predicted and observed in the two waves of the World Values surveys. In the 1981 surveys, we found a substantial correlation between attitudes toward authority and Materialist/Post-materialist values across nearly all of the 21 countries for which we have data. Materialists tend to support the proposition that "more respect for authority would be a good thing," while Postmaterialists tend to reject it. Consequently, we predicted a gradual shift toward the values of the Postmaterialists—that is, toward less emphasis on respect for authority.

Figure 9.2 presents the evidence that tests this prediction. It shows that from 1981 to 1990, emphasis on more respect for authority became less widespread in 17 of the 21 countries for which we have data. The absolute levels of support for authority, and the size of the changes from 1981 to 1990, vary a good deal from country to country.

The prediction that this shift would occur is based on a simple population replacement model: as the younger, more Postmaterialist birth cohorts replace the older, more Materialist cohorts in the adult population, we should see a shift toward the Postmodern orientation. Moreover, since the size of the respective cohorts is known from census data, and since we have survey data on the attitudes of the various birth cohorts, we can also estimate the *size* of the attitudinal shift that population replacement should produce over a 10-year period. We do this by simply removing the oldest 10-year cohort from our sample and replacing it with a new 10-year cohort at the youngest end. In creating this new cohort, we assume that it will have values similar to those of the youngest cohort in the sample—a conservative assumption, since younger cohorts usually show *more* Postmodern values than do older ones (for a more detailed discussion of how to estimate the effects of population replacement on mass attitudes, see Abramson and Inglehart, 1995).

When we perform this calculation it indicates that, for most of these countries, we would expect to find a decline of only four or five points in the percentage favoring more respect for authority. This is a small shift. If we found it in only one case, it would be an unimpressive finding: a difference between

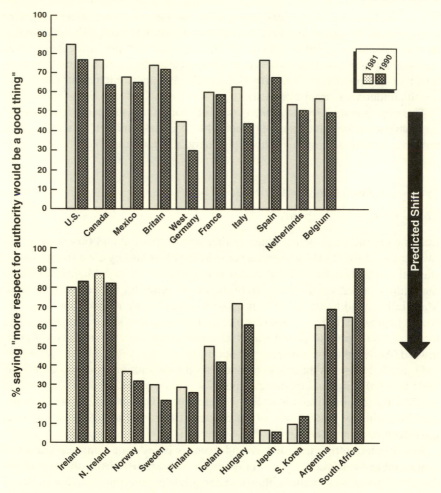

Figure 9.2. Predicted and observed shifts: percentages saying that "more respect for authority would be a good thing" in 1981 vs. 1990, in 21 countries. *Source*: 1981 and 1990 World Values surveys.

samples of this size is statistically significant at only about the .05 level. But if we observed several such consecutive shifts over 30 or 40 years, the finding would be highly significant, both statistically and substantively: over that time it could convert a 60:40 division of attitudes into a 40:60 split.

The same principle applies to a pattern of cross-cultural findings. Such a finding from only one country would hardly be worth mentioning. But if we had data from three or four countries and they all showed shifts of this size in the predicted direction, it would be highly significant. And if we found that the predicted shifts in values or attitudes generally held true across a score of societies, the probability of its being a random event would dwindle to the vanishing point. This chapter examines the shifts found with 40 variables, across

21 societies. Although the amount of change observed is usually small in any one case, the overall pattern is compelling and statistically significant at an enormously high level.

With attitudes toward authority, our theory predicts a shift of only four or five percentage points per country during this nine-year period. This is modest. In the short run, the impact of current economic or political events (or even sampling error) could easily swamp it in a given society. Thus, it would be astonishing if our predictions *did* hold up in every case. They do not: instead we find that in some countries, attitudes concerning authority moved in the predicted direction, while in others they did not. Moreover, some countries show shifts in the predicted direction that are too *large* to be due to population replacement alone: in these cases, situation-specific factors are probably adding to the results of population replacement, exaggerating the shift.

We can predict only one component of what is shaping mass attitudes, but we know that a number of factors are relevant. Consequently, we cannot predict precisely what will happen in every country. Nevertheless, because we *do* have information about one component of the process, our predictive power across many societies should be considerably better than random. And since there is a good chance that, in the long run, situation-specific factors or period effects will cancel each other out, in the long run, over many countries, our predictions should point in the right direction.

In the present case, the predicted shift toward less emphasis on respect for authority is actually observed in 17 out of 21 countries. With 81 percent success, this is far better than random prediction. We will not attempt to identify the nation-specific effects that were also at work here. Our point is that the values of most publics *did* move in the predicted direction.

Longitudinal research carried out in the United States over a much longer time confirms this finding, demonstrating that from the 1950s to the 1980s, there was a gradual decline in the American public's emphasis on conformity to authority as important things to teach a child; and there was a corresponding rise in emphasis on autonomy during this period (Alwin, 1986).[2]

Norms concerning respect for authority may be moving in the direction predicted by our theory, but does the prediction hold up in other realms as well?

The answer is yes—again and again. A wide variety of basic social norms are at least fairly strongly linked with Materialist/Postmaterialist values. And with impressive regularity, we observe shifts in prevailing values from 1981 to 1990 in which the outlook of the younger, more Postmaterialistic cohorts becomes increasingly widespread over time.

---

[2] The data from the World Values surveys show a similar shift in the relative balance between emphasis on obedience and autonomy as important values to teach a child (see figure A.3 in Appendix 3). However, these data are based on a set of unscaled questions, in which the interviewer is asked to "code all mentions." Such questions are very sensitive to interviewer effects and context. Moreover, there were changes in the other items on the list. Consequently, they cannot be considered reliable for comparisons across time and are not included in calculating the success rates of our predictions.

We find one major exception to this rule. In one domain (attitudes toward the importance of the traditional two-parent family), the values espoused by the more Postmaterialistic types did *not* become more widespread from 1981 to 1990. This is a significant phenomenon and is examined in more detail below. It reflects the fact that intergenerational population replacement is not the *only* factor that influences change. But this is a striking exception to the overall pattern. On the whole, the differences between the values of Postmaterialists and Materialists that we find in 1981 *do* generate accurate predictions of the direction in which values actually changed from 1981 to 1990.

Norms concerning Abortion, Divorce, Homosexuality, and Extramarital Sex

In face content, none of the items used to measure Materialist/Postmaterialist values makes any reference whatever to sexual or marital behavior; nevertheless, Postmaterialist values show strong correlations with a whole range of norms concerning sex and marriage. The underlying reason for this surprisingly strong linkage is the fact that both sets of values are heavily influenced by whether or not the individual feels secure concerning survival. Insecurity enhances the need for predictability and absolute norms; a sense of security, conversely, is conducive to relatively permissive and flexible norms.

Figure 9.3 shows the changes observed from 1981 to 1990 with one of these norms: attitudes toward abortion. This question (like the next several items) uses a 10-point scale, on which "1" indicates that the respondent feels that this behavior is "never justified" and "10" indicates that this behavior is "always justified." In most countries, a large share of the public felt that abortion was "never" justified and chose point "1" on this scale; figure 9.3 shows the percentages making that choice. Comparable data are not available from South Korea for this series of questions, because the 1990 survey in that country used four-point scales for these items. But across the societies for which we do have data, public attitudes moved mainly in the predicted direction, becoming more permissive toward abortion in 19 out of the 20 societies.

The South African public was the sole exception, moving against the prevailing trend both here and in the preceding case. This is part of a frequently recurring pattern that applies to both South Africa and Argentina: even when most countries were shifting in the direction predicted by the linkage with Postmaterialist values, the publics of these two societies shifted in the opposite direction. It is not surprising that South Africa and Argentina are exceptional. Theoretically, the Postmodern shift is driven by feelings of security, and during the 1980s these two societies were experiencing economic decline and a collapsing political order. They were moving from authoritarian regimes toward democracy, and the transition was filled with uncertainty.

Figure 9.4 shows the changes observed from 1981 to 1990 with attitudes toward divorce. The proportion saying that divorce is never justified was much smaller than the proportion saying that abortion is never justified, but the trend was similar: in 18 out of the 20 societies for which data are available, mass at-

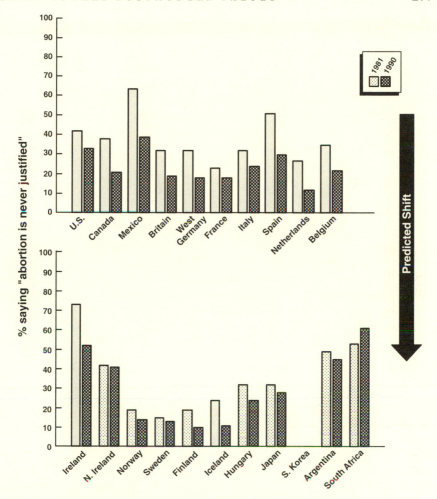

Figure 9.3. Predicted shifts and observed shifts: percentages holding that "abortion is *never* justified" in 1981 vs. 1990, in 20 countries. *Source*: 1981 and 1990 World Values surveys. Comparable data not available for South Korea (the 1990 South Korean survey used a four-point scale rather than a 10-point scale with this question).

titudes shifted in the predicted direction, becoming more permissive toward divorce (South Africa was again one of the exceptions).

Figure 9.5 shows a basically similar pattern of changes from 1981 to 1990, this time in attitudes concerning homosexuality. This attitude also is strongly correlated with Materialist/Postmaterialist values, with Postmaterialists being much less likely than Materialists to say that it is never justified. Here again, the publics of most societies shifted in the predicted direction, with 17 publics becoming more tolerant of homosexuality from 1981 to 1990: South Africa and Ireland were exceptions, moving in the opposite direction, and Northern Ireland showed no change.

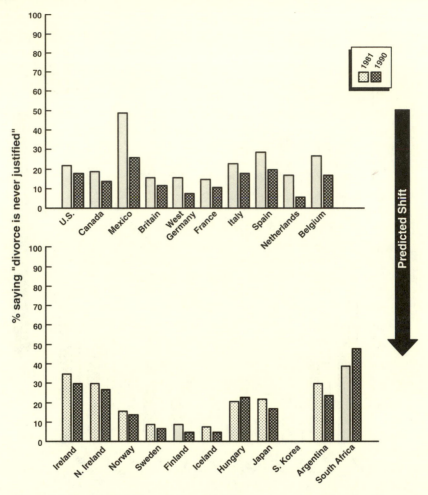

Figure 9.4. Predicted shifts and observed shifts: percentages saying that "divorce is *never* justified" in 1981 vs. 1990, in 20 countries. *Source*: 1981 and 1990 World Values surveys. Comparable data not available for South Korea.

Three more survey items in this category were strongly correlated with Post-materialist values: attitudes toward prostitution, sex under legal age, and extramarital affairs. To avoid burying the reader in an avalanche of data, and because these variables show patterns similar to those we have just seen, the relevant evidence is placed in Appendix 3, where the interested reader can examine the details (see figures A.4 through A.6). With all three attitudes, most publics shifted in the predicted direction: among those publics that showed any change, about two-thirds moved in the predicted direction. But with all three attitudes, the publics of Argentina and South Africa shifted in the opposite direction, becoming *less* permissive.

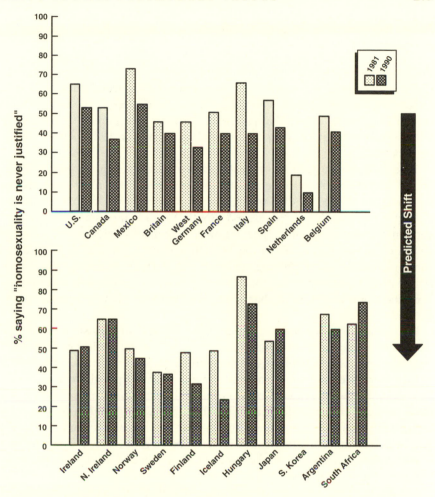

Figure 9.5. Percentages saying that "homosexuality is *never* justified" in 1981 vs. 1990, in 20 countries. *Source*: 1981 and 1990 World Values surveys. Comparable data not available for South Korea.

The publics of Norway and Sweden, who are generally rather permissive, overwhelmingly rejected "sex under the legal age." This probably reflects the fact that the translation used in these countries refers to "having sex with minors" (which could suggest child abuse), instead of the more neutral "sex under legal age." Attitudes toward sex under legal age had the lowest percentage of changes in the predicted direction among these norms, but even here 61 percent of the changes moved in the Postmodern direction. Argentina and South Africa, clearly, were *not* moving toward Postmodern values during the 1980s; nevertheless, with the seven attitudes that we have examined so far, 79 percent of the observed shifts were in the predicted direction.

Norms concerning Euthanasia, Suicide, Violence against Police, and Use of Marijuana

Four more variables that were strongly correlated with Materialist/Postmaterialist values could be described as civil norms: they concern attitudes toward euthanasia, suicide, fighting with police, and using marijuana. These questions used a 10-point scale like that just described; to avoid burdening the reader with excessive detail, the data on observed changes from 1981 to 1990 appear in Appendix 3.

Three of these four attitudes reveal a pattern of changes similar to that found above, with the overwhelming majority of publics shifting in the predicted direction from 1981 to 1990. Thus, 18 out of 20 publics became more tolerant toward euthanasia during this period (South Africa being one of the two exceptions); 16 out of 20 publics became more tolerant of suicide (with Argentina and South Africa being among the exceptions); and 17 out of 19 publics became more tolerant of fighting with the police (with Argentina and South Africa again being exceptions, and Hungary not asking this question in 1981). With these norms, observed changes are overwhelmingly in the predicted direction.

But attitudes concerning use of marijuana showed no consistent trend. The publics of nine countries became more tolerant, but the publics of nine other countries became less tolerant, and two publics showed no change. The World Values surveys do not show an undifferentiated shift toward greater permissiveness; orientations toward most norms did become more permissive, but these publics gave quite distinctive responses concerning some topics, and the use of marijuana was one of them. This finding runs counter to our predictions. Any explanation we might give for it would be ex post facto. We suspect that it may reflect a growing public awareness of the disastrous social consequences of drug abuse, but we did not predict this shift.

Despite the absence of the predicted trend with attitudes concerning use of marijuana, public responses to the four variables in this category overwhelmingly moved in the predicted direction: 78 percent of the observed shifts moved toward the position favored by those with Postmaterialist values. And more broadly, though we have encountered anomalies with some of the variables examined in this section, the responses to most items, in most countries, shifted in the predicted direction; across the norms concerning authority, sexual norms, and civil norms, fully 79 percent of the observed changes were toward the Postmodern pole.

RELIGIOUS NORMS

Most of the religious questions asked in 1981 showed strong correlations with Materialist/Postmaterialist values. Well before the 1990–91 data became available, we interpreted this as evidence that an intergenerational shift was taking place, making traditional religious values progressively less widely accepted in advanced industrial societies:

> Across the various societies included in this survey, Postmaterialists are about twice as likely as Materialists to indicate that God has little importance in their lives. From evidence presented in earlier chapters, it seems clear that an intergenerational shift is taking place from Materialist toward Postmaterialist values. Is a similar shift occurring, away from traditional Judeo-Christian religious and social values? This question cannot be answered conclusively because we do not yet have time series on these religious and cultural values that are comparable to those available on Materialist/Postmaterialist values. But the data that are available suggest that a major intergenerational shift in religious orientations is occurring. (Inglehart, 1990: 186–87)

The existence of such a trend is far from self-evident. In fact, the mass media tend to convey exactly the opposite impression—that we are witnessing a global trend toward fundamentalist religious values. Islamic fundamentalism and religious conflicts in India are cited as evidence of this trend, together with the revival of religion in Eastern Europe, and the Religious Right in the United States. Pulling together anecdotal evidence from a variety of sources, some observers have concluded that it all adds up to a worldwide fundamentalist trend. Which is taking place: a global trend toward fundamentalism—or a global trend toward secularization?

What is happening is more differentiated than either model. Our theory attributes the decline of religious values to a rising sense of security, which makes the need for the reassurance provided by traditional absolute belief systems less pressing. Thus, we *would* expect to find a trend toward secularization in advanced industrial societies. Indeed, we believe that it is precisely *because* traditional social and religious norms have been eroding rapidly in these societies during recent decades that people with traditional values (who are still numerous) have been galvanized into unusually active and disruptive forms of behavior, in order to defend their threatened values. But in advanced industrial societies, the numbers of those with traditional religious beliefs are diminishing, not growing. In these societies, fundamentalism does not represent the predominant trend, but a rearguard action by an aroused but slowly dwindling minority.

In much of the developing world, on the other hand, insecurity is pervasive. In much of Africa and some parts of Latin America, regimes are unstable and real per capita income has been declining in recent decades. The same has been true of the former Soviet states, though only recently. In such settings we *would* expect to see a heightened need for religious certainty.

So which do we find? A global trend toward traditional religious beliefs? Or two contrasting trends, with affluent and secure societies moving away from religion, but societies characterized by mass insecurity turning back to fundamentalist values?

The data from the 1990 World Values Survey helps us determine what has been happening in the realm of religion. Figure 9.6 shows one relevant indicator: reported attendance rates at religious services in 19 countries. The re-

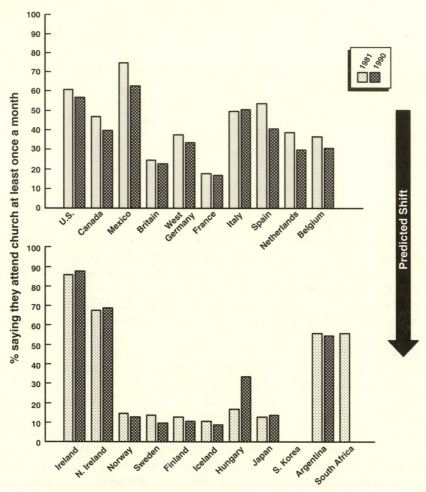

Figure 9.6. Percentages who attended church at least once a month, in 1981 vs. 1990, in 20 countries. *Source*: 1981 and 1990 World Values surveys. This question not included in 1990 South Korean survey.

sults show that from 1981 to 1990, church attendance rates *fell* in 14 of the 19 countries for which we have data. The South Korean surveys omitted most of the questions concerning religion; and data are not available for South Africa in 1981. Church attendance rose considerably in Hungary, and rose by a point or two in Ireland, Northern Ireland, Italy, and Japan. In 1981 participation in religious services already was extremely low in the Nordic countries, which are affluent welfare states—precisely the type of setting in which we would expect emphasis on religion to be minimal. In 1990 church attendance fell to even lower levels in all four countries.

Church attendance is one indicator of the priority which people accord to religion, but it measures external behavior that might be motivated by sociabil-

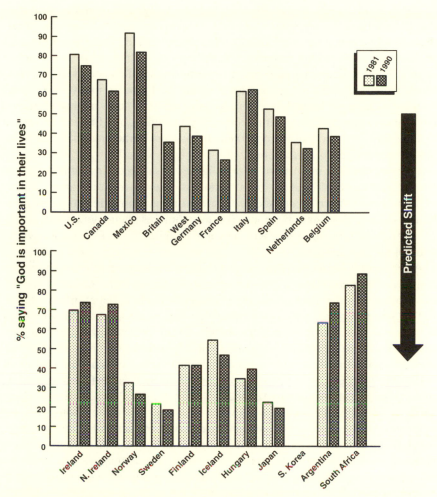

Figure 9.7. Percentages saying "God is important in their lives" in 1981 vs. 1990, in 20 countries. Based on percentage choosing cells 7–10 on a 10-point scale in which "1" means that God is not at all important in one's life and "10" means that God is very important in that person's life. *Source*: 1981 and 1990 World Values surveys. This question not included in 1990 South Korean survey.

ity, habit, or conformism, rather than genuine religious feeling. But we also have a number of indicators of how people feel about religion *internally*. Among them, the most sensitive indicator is a question that asks people to indicate how important God is in their lives, using a 10-point scale on which "1" means that God is not at all important, and "10" indicates that he is very important. Figure 9.7 shows the percentage in each country who give high ratings (scores of 7–10) to the importance of God in their lives.

This indicator of the subjective importance of religion tells the same story as the data on church attendance: emphasis on religion declined in 14 out of the 20 countries for which we have data. In keeping with the thesis that conditions of insecurity are conducive to a heightened need for the psychological reassurance that religion provides, the publics of both Argentina and South Africa showed significant *increases* in the importance attached to God in their lives. We suspect that similar changes would be found in many developing countries. Hungary, Ireland, Northern Ireland, and Italy show modest increases in the percentage placing great importance on religion, and Finland shows no change. But 70 percent of the observed changes are in the predicted direction, toward *less* emphasis on religion.

Thus we do find indications of a religious resurgence in Latin America, Africa, and Eastern Europe—but a marked *decline* in most advanced industrial societies. Within secure societies, some dramatic manifestations of militant fundamentalism have been seen recently; but this phenomenon reflects action by diminishing minorities who perceive that their way of life is threatened, and not the prevailing trend.

A substantial number of additional questions concerning religion show reasonably strong correlations with Materialist/Postmaterialist values. They include questions that measure belief in God, belief in hell, belief in heaven, belief in sin, the percentage saying that they get comfort and strength from religion, the percentage saying that the church in their country is giving adequate answers to moral problems and to problems of family life, and the percentage saying that the church is giving adequate answers to people's spiritual needs. The graphs showing the changes connected with each of these variables, in each country, are shown in Appendix 3. All but one of these variables show shifts in the predicted direction—toward less emphasis on religion—in most countries. One variable shows a countertrend: in a majority of countries, there was a rising perception that the church is giving adequate answers to people's spiritual needs. Nevertheless, the overall results are in keeping with theoretical expectations: 72 percent of the observed changes went in the predicted direction, toward *less* emphasis on religion.

Most of the countries that were surveyed in both 1981 and 1990 are relatively prosperous industrial societies that experienced modestly rising prosperity during the 1980s. This helps explain why the great majority of observed changes were in the direction of *diminishing* faith in the established religious institutions and traditional religious beliefs. Three societies were undergoing economic decay and political upheaval during this period—South Africa, Argentina, and Hungary; and in most instances, the publics of these countries shifted toward *greater* emphasis on religion.

The alleged global trend toward fundamentalist religion is based on a misconception. Fundamentalism is found mainly in less developed societies and in societies that are experiencing upheaval. In advanced industrial societies, fundamentalism has high visibility, but it seems to be a reaction by a declining minority that feels threatened by the pervasive and rapid cultural changes that are occurring in these societies.

Nevertheless, it would be inaccurate to speak of an undifferentiated trend away from religion, even in advanced industrial societies. As we commented in our analysis of the 1981 data,

> There is genuine irony in the fact that Postmaterialists seem relatively unattracted to organized religion in Western societies. Since they are less likely than Materialists to be preoccupied by the struggle for survival, theoretically they should have more intellectual and emotional energy to devote to the fulfillment of higher-order needs. And we find evidence that this is the case. Our respondents were asked, "How often, if at all, do you think about the meaning and purpose of life?" . . . Despite their relative alienation from traditional religion, in each of these societies Postmaterialists are *more* apt than the Materialists to spend time thinking about the meaning and purpose of life. This holds true despite the fact that older people are more likely to say they do so than younger ones. In this respect, Postmaterialists have more potential interest in religion than Materialists. (Inglehart, 1990: 192–93)

This implies that we should find an increase, not a decrease, in the percentage of the population who often think about the meaning and purpose of life. For religion serves a variety of functions. One of them is to provide a sense of orientation and certainty in an insecure world: no matter how threatening the situation may seem, one can have faith that things will ultimately turn out well if one adheres to a set of absolute traditional rules. For many people, that is the main function of religion. But religion has also traditionally helped satisfy intellectual and aesthetic needs, telling people where they come from and where they are going, and what is the meaning of life. Since the rise of modern science, traditional religious accounts of the origin and meaning of life have lost much of their credibility. But spiritual needs have not disappeared—indeed, interest in the meaning of life is more salient to Postmaterialists than to Materialists, and accordingly we would expect it to become *more* widespread even in advanced industrial societies. Our prediction is that interest in the meaning and purpose of life will be a rising concern, despite the general decline of traditional religious beliefs and behavior.

Figure 9.8 shows the changes observed from 1981 to 1990 in the percentage saying that they "often" think about the meaning and purpose of life. In 18 of the 21 societies, we find that a growing proportion of the population often thinks about the meaning of life; two societies show small decreases and one shows no change. Traditional beliefs and the established religious organizations may be losing their adherents, but spiritual concerns are becoming more widespread.

PARENT-CHILD TIES: A REVERSAL OF TRENDS

Now let us turn to an area in which our predictions do not hold up. This is not just a marginal failure. It is a striking reversal of the shift toward Postmodern values, not in just a few deviant cases, but across the great majority of soci-

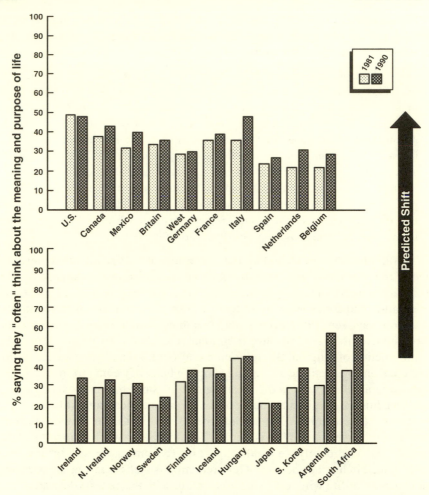

Figure 9.8. Percentages saying that they "often" think about the meaning and purpose of life, in 1981 vs. 1990, in 21 countries. *Source*: 1981 and 1990 World Values surveys.

eties for which we have data. It flatly contradicts our theoretical expectations, but the finding is clear. And sometimes, one can learn just as much from the failure of one's predictions as from their fulfillment.

The finding occurs with a set of four items concerning parent-child ties. The first of these questions asks "If someone says a child needs a two-parent home with both a father and a mother to grow up happily, would you tend to agree or disagree?" Materialists are about twice as likely to agree with this proposition as are Postmaterialists, so our prediction is clear: we would expect to find a shift in which the proportion agreeing that a child needs a two-parent family diminishes over time. Figure 9.9 shows the actual findings.

In 16 of the 19 countries for which we have data, agreement with this propo-

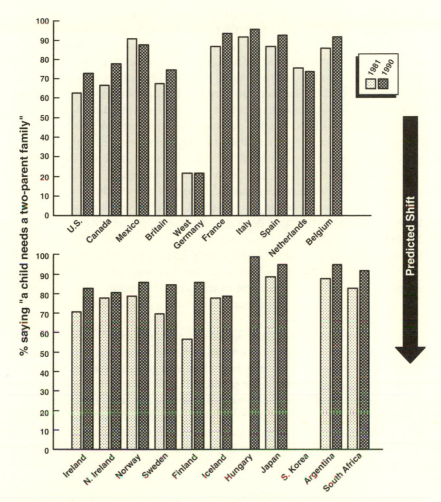

Figure 9.9. Percentages saying "a child needs a home with both a father and a mother, to grow up happily" in 1981 vs. 1990, in 19 countries. *Source*: 1981 and 1990 World Values surveys. Question not asked in South Korea, and 1981 data not available for Hungary.

sition rose, instead of falling, from 1981 to 1990. Two countries showed a slight decline and one showed no change. Overwhelmingly, the publics of these societies became more likely to believe that a child needs a home with both a father and a mother.

This is not an isolated fluke. The World Values surveys included three other questions about the importance of parent-child ties, and all three of them show roughly similar results. Figure A.19 (in Appendix 3) shows the changes over time in response to the question "Do you think that a woman needs to have children in order to be fulfilled, or is this not necessary?" Postmaterialists are much less likely than Materialists to think that a woman needs children in order to be fulfilled, so we would predict that this response would lose support; but in 14 of the 21 countries, agreement went up (with declines in six countries and no change in one). Figure A.20 (in Appendix 3) shows the changes registered in response to the question "If a woman wants to have a child as a single parent but doesn't want to have a stable relationship with a man, do you approve or disapprove?" Postmaterialists are much more likely to approve of single parenthood, so we would expect approval to rise—but it rose in 10 countries, and fell in 10 others. Finally, our respondents were asked whether they agreed that "Regardless of what qualities and faults one's parents have, one must always love and respect them" or "One does not have the duty to love and respect parents who have not earned it by their behavior and attitudes." Postmaterialists are substantially less likely to feel that one has a duty to love and respect one's parents, so we would expect this orientation to become more widespread. But, as figure A.21 demonstrates, this happened in only seven out of 21 countries.

Across the four items in this category, only 33 percent of the observed shifts were in the predicted direction. This is in startling contrast to the findings on other topics, where 75 to 80 percent of the shifts moved in the predicted direction. What accounts for the exceptional pattern of responses to questions concerning parent-child ties?

We must acknowledge that our response is ex post facto. We expected attitudes to shift toward less emphasis on family ties, but the bulk of the evidence contradicts our expectations. It may be that an intergenerational population replacement process is at work in the predicted direction, for not only is it true that Postmaterialists place less emphasis on parent-child ties, but both in 1981 and in 1990 we find clear and consistent age-group differences, with the younger cohorts placing relatively little emphasis on parent-child ties. Intergenerational differences may be present, but if so, something in the current socioeconomic environment is overwhelming their effects. What could this factor be?

Throughout advanced industrial societies, the traditional two-parent family has been breaking down. Only three decades ago, the vast majority of children were born into two-parent households. That is no longer true today, and in some countries, single-parent families have become extremely widespread. Figure 9.10 shows the rise in the percentage of children living with a never-married parent in the United States from 1960 to 1990. Figure 9.11 shows the percentage of children born to unmarried mothers in four Western European countries. The changes are dramatic. In many countries (including the United States), the proportion of children being raised by never-married parents is eight times as high as it was only 30 years ago.

A growing body of evidence from both sides of the Atlantic indicates that this phenomenon is linked with a wide range of social pathology. Recent studies show that virtually any kind of deviant behavior one can think of—from poor performance in school and early dropout rates, to drug use and criminal behavior, to obesity and psychological problems—are disproportionately high

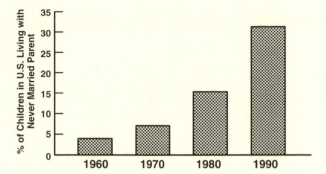

Figure 9.10. Decline of the family in the United States, 1960–90.
Percentage of children living with never-married parent.
Source: U.S. Bureau of the Census.

among the children of never-married mothers. These linkages persist when one controls for such factors as race, income, and educational differences. Thus one recent study finds that "Children who grow up in a household with only one biological parent are worse off, on average, than children who grow up in a household with both of their biological parents, regardless of the parents' race or educational background. . . . Compared with teen-agers of similar background who grow up with both parents at home, adolescents who have lived apart from one of their parents during some period of childhood are more than twice as likely to drop out of high school, twice as likely to have a child before age twenty, and one and a half times as likely to be 'idle'—out of school and out of work—in their late teens and early twenties"(McLanahan and Sandefur, 1994: 1–2).

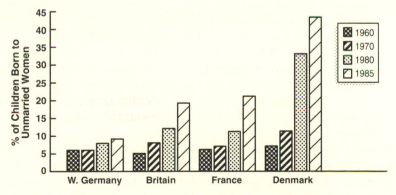

Figure 9.11. Decline of the family in Western Europe, 1960–85.
Percentage of children born to unmarried mothers. *Source*: European Community Statistical Office.

Another writer sums up recent findings as follows:

> Children in single-parent families are six times as likely to be poor. They are also likely to stay poor longer. Twenty-two percent of children in one-parent families will experience poverty during childhood for seven years or more, as compared with only 2 percent of children in two-parent families. A 1988 survey by the National Center for Health Statistics found that children in single-parent families are two to three times as likely as children in two-parent families to have emotional and behavioral problems. They are also more likely to drop out of high school, to get pregnant as teenagers, to abuse drugs and to be in trouble with the law. . . . Research shows that many children from disrupted families have a harder time achieving intimacy in a relationship, forming a stable marriage, or even holding a steady job. (Whitehead, 1993: 47)

Other recent studies present converging findings (Barton, 1992; McLanahan and Garfinkel, 1986; Wallerstein and Blakeslee, 1989): by almost any standard one might apply, children raised in single-parent families do not do as well as children raised in families where both parents are present.

It seems that social scientists are not the only people who have noticed these problems. One of the most interesting things about the resurgence of emphasis on family values is the fact that it started at the mass level and was picked up by political elites *later*. During the 1980s, mass publics throughout industrial society, reversing a long-established trend, were becoming less permissive toward parenthood outside of marriage and placing more emphasis on the importance of raising children in a setting where both a father and a mother were present.

In the late 1980s and early 1990s, growing numbers of social scientists were also coming to the conclusion that the breakdown of the traditional two-parent family was not progressive, after all, but was associated with a massive array of social pathologies.

In 1992, when Vice President Quayle criticized the mass media for irresponsibly glamorizing single parenthood, the immediate response was overwhelming ridicule. But within two years, cover stories were appearing in national magazines suggesting that the breakdown of the family really was a serious problem. And by 1994, President Clinton expressed great concern that "we are raising a whole generation of kids who aren't sure they're the most important person in the world to anybody"; while his Health and Human Services Secretary, Donna Shalala, stated in public that Dan Quayle was right when he condemned TV heroine Murphy Brown's attitude toward out-of-wedlock childbearing.

People learn from firsthand experience. Although few of them undoubtedly had read the scientific studies, it seems that on the basis of their own observations, the general publics in many countries were coming to the same conclusion as a growing number of social scientists: the traditional two-parent family was a relatively good way to raise children.

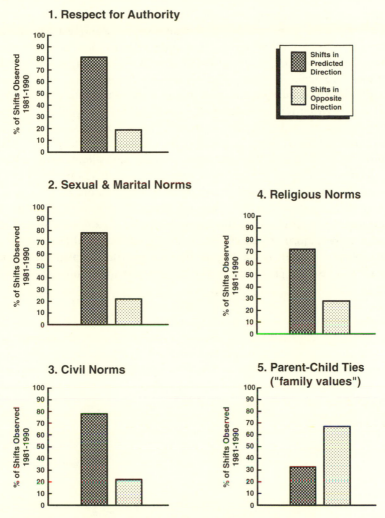

Figure 9.12. Predicted shifts and observed shifts: Overall results in five domains. *Source*: 1981 and 1990 World Values surveys.

PREDICTIONS AND OBSERVATIONS: OVERALL SUCCESS RATES

Figure 9.12 sums up the success rate of our predictions with five types of variables examined in this chapter. Across the first four categories, the great majority of the observed shifts moved in the predicted direction. This holds true for 81 percent of the shifts in respect for authority; of 79 percent of the shifts in sexual and marital norms, and also of 79 percent of the shifts in civil norms; and of 72 percent of the shifts in religious norms.

But, as we have just seen, our predictions did not hold up for the four questions dealing with parent-child ties. In response to these questions, the overwhelming majority of the publics shifted in the opposite direction from the one predicted, with only 33 percent of the observed shifts going in the predicted direction. Here again, it is clear that we are not dealing with an undifferentiated shift toward permissiveness in all things. Publics respond to what they experience in their current environment, as well as being shaped by a sense of security or insecurity during their formative years. Formative experiences remain important: the younger birth cohorts remained markedly more tolerant of single parenthood than the older ones, even though all age groups became less tolerant of it. But the influences of *both* early socialization effects and peoples' response to the contemporary environment are manifest.

To put this in perspective, however, we should bear in mind that this countershift applies to only four of the 26 items we have examined so far. In the overwhelming majority of cases, the predicted shift toward Postmodern values was observed. And, as we will see in the following chapter, the Postmodern shift was also the prevailing trend in connection with most other values.

The Erosion of Institutional Authority and the Rise of Citizen Intervention in Politics

INTRODUCTION

During the past four decades, the American public has become increasingly convinced that their government is not to be trusted. In 1958 the vast majority of Americans felt that their national government was basically honest. When asked, "Do you think that quite a few of the people running the government are crooked, not very many are, or do you think that hardly any of them are crooked?" only 24 percent of the American public said that "quite a few" of the people running the government were crooked. As figure 10.1 illustrates, this figure rose steeply during the 1960s and 1970s, leveled off during the 1980s, and reached an all time high in 1994, at which point an absolute majority—51 percent—of the American public said that quite a few of the people running the government were crooked.

A similar trend appears in response to the question "Would you say that the government is pretty much run by a few big interests looking out for themselves, or that it is run for the benefit of all the people?" In 1964 only 29 percent said that the government was run by a few big interests. This figure rose sharply until 1980, declined during the 1980s, and then reached an all-time high of 76 percent in 1994.

Figure 10.2 shows a similar pattern in response to a question concerning to what extent one can trust the government in Washington to do what is right. From 1958 to 1964, about 75 percent said that you can trust the government to do what is right "just about always" or "most of the time." A steep decline began in 1964 and continued throughout the 1970s, with a partial recovery in 1984–88, followed by further decline. By 1994 trust in the national government had fallen to an all-time low of 21 percent. In one generation, the prevailing outlook had changed from overwhelming trust to overwhelming cynicism.

This massive erosion of trust in government has given rise to a good deal of scholarly discussion since it was first noted by Miller (1974). But there is sharp disagreement about *why* it has occurred. Conservatives tend to attribute it to poor performance: the public has become fed up with the waste, corruption, and ineffectiveness of Big Government. Liberals tend to stress psychological or sociological explanations. Samuelson (1995), for example, argues that the postwar boom gave rise to expectations of economic progress that could not possibly be sustained. Both perspectives contain some truth. There is no question that good or bad performance is part of the story. For example, confidence

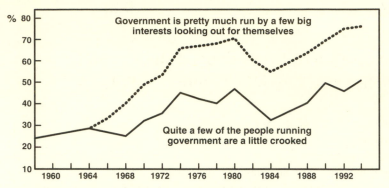

Figure 10.1. Rising distrust of government among the U.S. public, 1958–94. *Source*: University of Michigan National Election Studies, 1958–94.

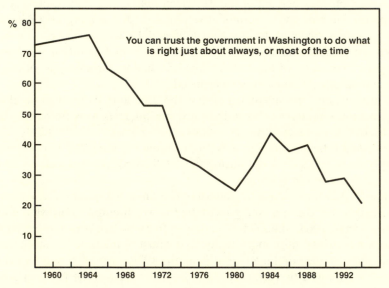

Figure 10.2. Declining trust in the federal government, 1958–94. *Source*: University of Michigan National Election Studies, 1958–94.

in the U.S. military dropped to extremely low levels during the disastrous intervention in Viet Nam—but subsequently recovered and rose to fairly high levels after the relatively quick and effective operations in Grenada and the Gulf War. But it is clearly not just a matter of government performance, for the United States was experiencing peace, steady economic growth, rising real income, low inflation, and relatively low unemployment in 1994—at which time confidence in the national government had fallen to an all-time low. It seems inconceivable that governmental performance would *not* influence public evaluations, but objective performance is always evaluated according to internalized standards—which have changed in recent decades.

If one believed in a simple one-to-one relationship between objective performance and mass evaluations, one would conclude that President Clinton must be the most inept and dishonest leader to have held office since these measurements were first taken. That interpretation doesn't hold water. The historical record suggests that governmental corruption hasn't increased over the past generation—it has probably diminished. But regardless of whether that is true, evidence presented in this chapter indicates that the phenomenon goes beyond the United States: we are witnessing a downward trend in trust in government and confidence in leaders across most industrialized societies. To explain these findings, one would need to assume that practically all of the leaders in power in the early 1990s—from Clinton to Major and Mitterrand and Gonzales and Mulroney and Andreotti and Hosokawa—all happened to be among the most incompetent and dishonest leaders their countries had ever seen. This is implausible. Instead, it seems that the rules have changed, and that the publics of these countries are now evaluating their leaders and institutions by more demanding standards than were applied in the past.

Nevertheless, there is reason to believe that governmental performance is also part of the story. Most Western governments are doing the old familiar tasks about as well as they ever did—but they are doing them in a profoundly changed setting. In the early twentieth century, industrial societies suffered from insufficient government regulation. As we argued in chapter 8, when government spending was rising from 10 percent to 20 or 30 percent of the economy, additional government regulation and redistribution had a relatively high payoff and benefited a large share of the population. But as government spending grew from 30 to 40 or 50 percent of the economy, it began to bring diminishing returns, and its costs became increasingly heavy for a growing share of the population. Entitlements tend to expand indefinitely; in the long run, the growth of government was on an unsustainable trajectory. More of the same did not have the same impact on public evaluations.

This trend has interacted with another factor: the rise of Postmodern political issues. In the 1950s, government policy was mainly aimed at securing economic growth and national security—public goods that practically everyone desired. Since the 1960s, politics has increasingly involved Postmodern issues, giving rise to a phenomenon that is sometimes described as the Culture Wars. Affirmative action, the right to abortion, and guaranteeing the rights of gays and lesbians are not viewed as public goods but involve goals that a substantial part of the public does not want to attain at all. Economic redistribution was also divisive, but was relatively amenable to compromise; issues like abortion tend to be seen as questions of good versus evil on which one cannot compromise.

Some observers have interpreted the decline of trust in government as a sign of general alienation. Pointing to declining rates of voter turnout, they argue that the American public has become disenchanted with the entire system and withdrawn from politics completely. The empirical evidence contradicts this interpretation. As we will see, though voter turnout has stagnated (largely because of weakening political party loyalties), Western publics have *not* become apathetic: quite the contrary, in the last two decades, they have become markedly more likely to engage in elite-challenging forms of political participation. Furthermore, the erosion of trust does not apply to all institutions: it is specifically a withdrawal of confidence from authoritarian institutions. During the same period that trust in political authority was fading, environmental protection movements rose from obscurity to attain remarkably high levels of public confidence: in the 1990–91 World Values survey, fully 93 percent of these publics approved of the environmentalist movement—with 59 percent approving "strongly." But support for certain types of institutions is sharply differentiated according to whether one has Materialist or Postmaterialist values, with Materialist being much more likely to support authoritarian institutions, and these institutions suffered from declining mass confidence throughout advanced industrial society.

THE AUTHORITARIAN REFLEX AND THE POSTMODERN SHIFT

Declining trust in government seems to be part of a broader erosion of respect for authority that is linked with the processes of Modernization and Postmodernization. Rapid change leads to severe insecurity, giving rise to an Authoritarian Reflex that may bring Fundamentalist or xenophobic reactions or adulation of strong leaders. As we have argued, insecurity leads to a need for strong authority figures to protect one from threatening forces and breeds an intolerance of cultural change and different ethnic groups.

Conversely, conditions of prosperity and security are conducive to greater emphasis on individual autonomy and diminishing deference to authority. Until recently, existential insecurity was a usual part of the human condition. Only recently have societies emerged in which most of the population does *not* have any fear of starvation (which is still a very real concern for much of humanity). Both premodern agrarian society and modern industrial society were shaped by survival values. The Postmodern shift has brought a broad de-emphasis on all forms of authority.

A major aspect of the Postmodern shift is a shift away from *both* religious and bureaucratic authority, bringing declining emphasis on all kinds of authority. Deference to authority has high costs: the individual's personal goals must be subordinated to those of a broader entity. Under conditions of insecurity, people are more than willing to do so. Under threat of invasion, internal disorder, or existential insecurity, people eagerly seek strong authority figures who can protect them. Conversely, the shift toward well-being values is linked with declining emphasis on political, religious and economic authority.

As we saw in figure 3.2, the idea that "more respect for authority would be a good thing" is closely linked with the Traditional pole of the Traditional-Secular-Rational values dimension. The peoples of low-income societies place much more emphasis on authority than do the peoples of advanced industrial societies: the correlation between the percentage who feel that "more respect for authority would be a good thing" and the society's per capita GNP is $-.66$. This suggests that as modernization and economic development take place, we will find declining respect for authority.

Similarly, as we saw in the preceding chapter, Materialists tend to support the proposition that "more respect for authority would be a good thing," while Postmaterialists tend to reject it. Consequently, we predicted a gradual shift toward the values linked with Postmaterialism—that is, toward less emphasis on respect for authority. And the data confirm this prediction: as figure 9.2 demonstrated, from 1981 to 1990, emphasis on more respect for authority became less widespread in 17 of the 21 countries for which we have data. Argentina, South Africa, Ireland, and South Korea were the only exceptions to this trend. The evidence indicates that respect for authority actually *is* declining in most advanced industrial societies. We suspect that this has contributed to the erosion of institutional authority. Performance still counts. But the tendency to idealize national leaders has been growing weaker, and their performance is being evaluated with a more critical eye.

Earlier in this book, we examined the curve depicting the relationship between subjective well-being and economic development. In the early phases of development, the curve rises steeply: additional income brings large increases not only in such things as life expectancy, but also in *subjective* well-being. After a certain point, however, the curve levels off, and additional economic growth is not associated with further increases in subjective well-being.

At this point, significant numbers of Postmaterialists begin to emerge. They take economic security for granted to such a degree that it has a relatively minor impact on their subjective well-being. Thus, despite the fact that Postmaterialists have higher levels of income, education, and occupational status than Materialists, they do *not* manifest higher levels of subjective well-being. They take their prosperity for granted and transfer their focus to other aspects of life, such as politics and the quality of the physical and social environment. These domains are subjectively more important to Postmaterialists than they are to Materialists, and they apply higher, more demanding standards to them. Thus, though Postmaterialists generally live in less noisy, less polluted neighborhoods than Materialists, they register lower levels of satisfaction with their environment.

They also evaluate politics by more demanding standards. Though they live in the same political systems as Materialists, and are more able to make these systems respond to their preferences (being more articulate and politically more active), they do not register higher levels of satisfaction with politics. The rise of Postmaterialist values is one symptom of a broader Postmodern shift that is transforming the standards by which the publics of advanced industrial societies evaluate governmental performance. It brings new, more demanding standards to the evaluation of political life and confronts political leaders with more active, articulate citizens. The position of elites has become more difficult in advanced industrial society. Mass publics are becoming increasingly critical of their political leaders and increasingly likely to engage in elite-challenging activities.

This leads to a paradoxical finding: the publics of prosperous, stable, and democratic advanced industrial societies do *not* show higher levels of satisfaction with their political systems than do the publics of poor, authoritarian countries; quite the contrary, astonishing as it may seem, they show significantly *less* confidence in their leaders and political institutions than do their counterparts in developing countries. In the short run, economic development tends to bring rising levels of political satisfaction; in the long run, however, it leads to the emergence of new and more demanding standards by which governmental performance is evaluated.

The Erosion of Institutional Authority

Let us now examine the shifts that took place in political values from 1981 to 1990, testing the same type of prediction as in the previous chapter: all orientations linked with Postmaterialist values should become more widespread. We find that pervasive changes are taking place in political, as well as social, values. There is evidence of a long-term shift in which the publics of advanced industrial societies are becoming more likely to act in autonomous, elite-challenging fashion. These changes make mass publics less respectful of elites and more likely to challenge them. Confidence in established political and societal institutions is declining; but the participant potential of most publics is rising. Thus, we find two related trends: the erosion of institutional authority, and the rise of citizen intervention in politics.

When governmental authority declined in given countries in the past, it was usually attributed to the fact that the specific government then in office was less effective, and instilled less confidence, than the previous government. This undoubtedly *is* part of the explanation: incompetent and corrupt governments tend to evoke less confidence than do competent, honest ones. But we believe that a long-term component is also involved here, in addition to fluctuations linked with specific officeholders.

This erosion of political authority can be traced to some of the same factors that were examined in the previous chapter. It has often been observed that in time of national danger the public tends to seek the security of strong leaders and strong institutions. Thus, during the traumatic insecurity of the Great Depression, a wave of upheavals took place in newly established democracies, from Italy to Germany to Hungary to Spain, which led to the rise of authoritarian leaders such as Mussolini, Hitler, Horthy, and Franco. Even in the United States, with its deep-rooted democratic tradition, the American people rallied behind Franklin Roosevelt, who exercised exceptionally sweeping powers and was elected for an unprecedented four terms.

Long-enduring security paves the way for the reverse phenomenon: the public gradually sees less need for the discipline and self-denial demanded by strong governments. A Postmaterialist emphasis on self-expression and self-realization becomes increasingly central.

Declining Confidence in Hierarchical Institutions

Evidence from the 1981 and 1990 surveys demonstrates the claims we have just laid out. Across nearly all of our societies, Materialists place more confidence in their country's hierarchical institutions—especially the armed forces, police, and church—than do Postmaterialists.

These findings are consistent with our argument that a sense of insecurity tends to motivate support for strong institutions and for strong political authority in particular. Having experienced a relatively high sense of economic and physical security throughout their formative years, Postmaterialists feel less need for strong authority than do Materialists. Moreover, Postmaterialists place relatively strong emphasis on self-expression—a value that inherently conflicts with the structure of hierarchical bureaucratic organizations.

The value-related differences point to the possibility of a shift over time, toward the outlook of the younger and more Postmaterialist respondents. Do we find it? The answer is yes. In most countries, we find lower levels of confidence in government institutions in 1990 than those that existed in 1981.

Our respondents were asked how much confidence they had in a dozen national institutions. Postmaterialists show lower levels of confidence in most established institutions than do Materialists, and in three cases the correlations were high enough to meet our criterion of "reasonably strong": Postmaterialist values are especially strongly linked with *low* levels of confidence in their country's police, armed forces, and church. Consequently, we predict that confidence in these institutions will decline.

As figure 10.3 demonstrates, from 1981 to 1990, confidence in the given society's police declined in 16 of the 20 countries for which we have data. Confidence rose only in Ireland and Iceland, and in Argentina and South Africa, two of the three societies in our sample that were undergoing regime changes (1981 data are not available for Hungary, the third such society).

Confidence in the country's armed forces shows a similar pattern (see figure 10.4). It declined in 17 of the 20 countries for which we have data—rising only in Northern Ireland and (again) in Argentina and South Africa. Confidence in one's country's church also moved on the predicted trajectory; as figure A.22 (in Appendix 3) demonstrates, it fell in 14 of the 20 cases where changes occurred; confidence in the churches rose only in the United States, Ireland, and Northern Ireland, and in Hungary, Argentina, and South Africa, the three countries undergoing regime changes.

Confidence in many other national institutions also showed a similar pattern of (1) being correlated with Materialist values and (2) declining over time. We

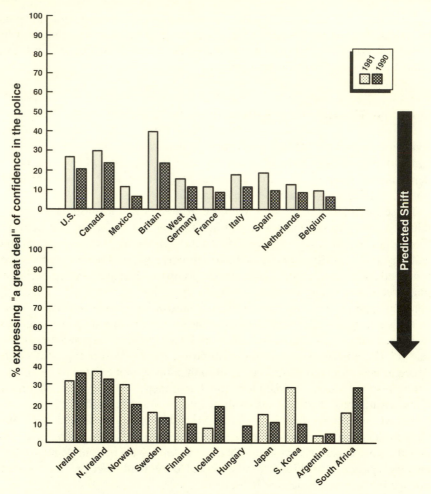

Figure 10.3. Percentages expressing "a great deal" of confidence in their country's police forces, in 1981 vs. 1990, in 20 countries. *Source*: 1981 and 1990 World Values surveys. 1981 data not available for Hungary.

do not analyze these attitudes here, however, since their correlation with Postmaterialist values falls below our .125 cutoff level.

Data from a number of other sources support the thesis that confidence in hierarchical institutions is declining. The National Opinion Center at the University of Chicago has been measuring confidence in U.S. national institutions every year since 1973. These institutions include Congress, the Executive Branch, the Press, the Military, Organized Labor, the Supreme Court, Television, Education, and Organized Religion. Nearly all of these institutions have suffered some decline since 1973. And in a number of cases, the 1993 levels of confidence were the lowest ever recorded during this 20-year period. This was true of the U.S. public's rating of Congress, the Press, Television, Educa-

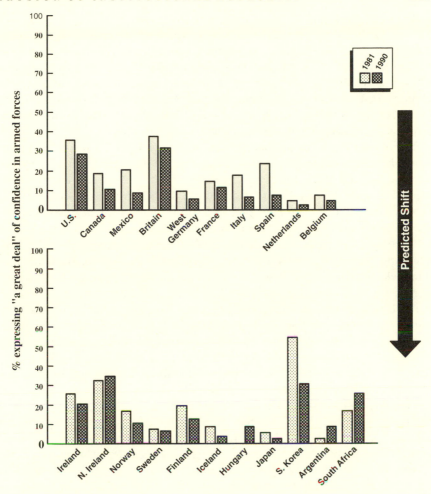

Figure 10.4. Percentages expressing "a great deal" of confidence in their country's armed forces, in 1981 vs. 1990, in 20 countries. *Source*: 1981 and 1990 World Values surveys.

tion, and Organized Religion. The decline in confidence was substantial. For example, in 1973 only 15 percent of the public said that they had "hardly any" confidence in Congress; in 1993, 41 percent said they had "hardly any" confidence. Similarly, though 1993 was not the low point of confidence in the Executive Branch (that was registered in 1974, when President Nixon resigned), there was an overall downward trend here too: in 1973, only 18 percent said they had "hardly any" confidence in the Executive Branch; in 1993, 32 percent said they had "hardly any" confidence (NORC surveys reported in *The American Enterprise*, November/December, 1993: 94–95).

Another manifestation of the collapse of public faith in politicians is the recent emergence of massive support for term limitations on elected representatives in Congress and, in some cases, in state legislatures as well. Although they probably are not constitutional, such proposals have been passed in every state where they have been on the ballot. Voters already have the right to limit the terms of their representatives by simply not reelecting them. But the mass mood seems to reflect a perception that, given the advantages incumbents have conferred on themselves, and given the fact that the voters have come to see them as a self-perpetuating privileged class, the only safe way to curtail their power is by placing formal limits on their tenure of power.

The old standards for evaluating elites no longer apply. A record that once would have ensured reelection is now insufficient. Thus, more than seven years after he had led allied forces to victory in World War II, a grateful nation elected Dwight Eisenhower president by a landslide margin. By contrast, shortly after the Cold War had come to a sudden and (from an American perspective) astonishingly successful conclusion, and immediately after a swift and (from an American perspective) almost bloodless victory in the Gulf War, and with an economy that was in relatively good shape, George Bush failed to win reelection in 1992. This was not just a failure of charisma on Bush's part. For within two years, his successor had become widely distrusted, and his party lost control of both houses of Congress. This happened though the economic indicators were doing even better than they were under Bush. It has become clear that the standard economic indicators no longer explain as much as they once did, in the realm of political behavior. Postmodern publics evaluate their leaders by different, and more demanding, standards than those applied throughout most of the modern era.

This phenomenon is not limited to the United States. Figure 10.5 shows changing responses to the question "Generally speaking, are you satisfied or dissatisfied with the way democracy is working in your country?" As we pointed out in chapter 4, this is not primarily a measure of whether the respondent supports democracy itself; it mainly taps his or her rating of how well the politicians currently in office are functioning. Although, as one would expect, these ratings tend to rise and fall with the economic cycle, they also show a long-term downward tendency. Thus, in the recessions of the early 1970s and the early 1980s, "dissatisfied" ratings became nearly as numerous as "satisfied" ratings among the combined European Community publics. But during the recession of the early 1990s, for the first time, negative ratings became more widespread than positive ratings. In 1993 dissatisfaction reached the highest level ever recorded. The economic downturn of the early 1990s seems to have contributed to this phenomenon, but it can't be the entire explanation: the recessions of the 1970s and 1980s were equally severe, but political dissatisfaction never rose to the heights it reached in 1993.

How deep does this dissatisfaction run? The respondents in the World Values surveys were asked how proud they were to be French, Mexican, Japanese, etc., answering on a scale that ran from "very proud" to "not at all proud" (see figure 10.6). In light of the evidence of a widespread decline of confidence in national institutions, one might reasonably expect pride in the nation itself

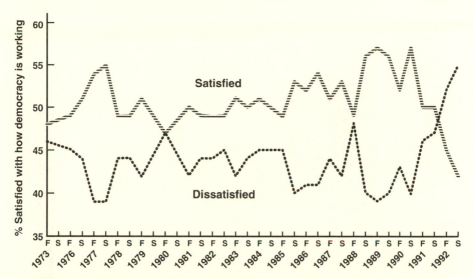

Figure 10.5. Satisfaction with the way democracy is working in the respondent's country, among the publics of the combined European Community countries, 1973–93. "S" indicates surveys carried out in the spring of the given year, "F" indicates surveys carried out in the fall. *Source*: European Community survey and Euro-Barometer surveys from 1976 through 1993.

to decline too—especially since national pride *is* strongly correlated with confidence in national institutions and with the strength of one's religious convictions. Furthermore, we find that Postmaterialists express lower levels of national pride than do Materialists (and the correlation is "reasonably strong"). Hence, we would predict a decline in feelings of national pride.

On the other hand, running counter to this expectation, there is widespread belief that this is "an era of rising nationalism." But is it? The reality is more complex. We believe that the traditional form of nationalism is rising in many countries, but not in most advanced industrial societies. There *has* been a rising tide of one form of "nationalism"—that is, of xenophobia linked with insecurity—in poorer and less secure societies: it has had dramatic and tragic consequences in India, Sri Lanka, Azerbaijia, Armenia, Sudan, Nigeria, Rwanda and the former Soviet Union and Yugoslavia.

But in advanced industrial societies, we are witnessing a quite different phenomenon: we find demands to transfer authority *away* from the existing nation-states to smaller, more immediate units having greater cultural coherence: from Spain to Catalonia, for example, or from Canada to Quebec. The partisans of such movements tend to be Postmaterialists, motivated by concerns for cultural autonomy and a sense of community. Very confusingly, this completely different phenomenon is *also* called "nationalism." The fact that the term "nationalism" is used to denote both hyperloyalty to the nation-state *and* withdrawing one's loyalty away from it to smaller units has given rise to a good

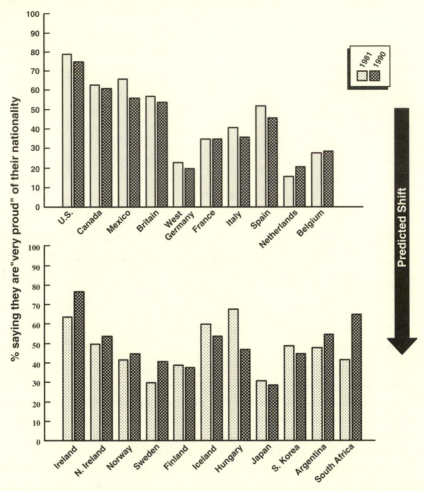

Figure 10.6. Percentages saying they are "very proud" of their nationality, in 1981 vs. 1990, in 21 countries. *Source*: 1981 and 1990 World Values surveys.

deal of confusion and misunderstanding; two quite different (indeed, almost opposite) things are lumped together as "rising nationalism." This usage equates contemporary Quebecois autonomists with the xenophobic nationalists of the nineteenth century. They are not at all the same thing. In advanced industrial societies, ethnic separatist movements generally do not involve an inward-looking parochialism. Instead, they represent a shift of focus away from the hierarchical nation-state in two directions: on one hand, a greater emphasis on community and local autonomy, and at the same time a growing openness to broader ties. Thus, the Quebecois separatists tend to be more favorable to North American free trade than are Canadians in general, and the Catalan "nationalists" tend to be partisans of European unification.

From 1981 to 1990, feelings of national pride tended to move on the same trajectory as did the other elements of this syndrome, but the results are mixed: in 12 out of 19 countries, we find a decline in the percentage expressing strong feelings of national pride, as figure 10.6 demonstrates. The results move in the predicted direction in 63 percent of the cases where change occurred. But there are a number of exceptions. In addition to the usual countertrends in Argentina and South Africa, national pride rose in Ireland, Northern Ireland, Norway, Sweden, the Netherlands, and Belgium. We do not find a simple split between secure and insecure societies.

Our predictions show a success rate of 63 percent; this is better than random, but it is not doing as well as with most political variables. It raises an interesting question: why is national pride not declining as much as we would expect in advanced industrial societies? We suspect that two major contemporary events are involved.

The first is a Western European reaction against massive non-European immigration. The immense disparity between living standards in Western Europe and developing countries, coupled with wide-bodied jet aircraft, has brought a large influx of visibly different immigrants into societies that never before had large numbers of them. Suddenly, most of these countries find themselves with large minorities of ethnically very distinct peoples, often coming from very far away. Interacting with the insecurity due to the recent recession, this has given rise to a wave of xenophobia—and the tendency to reemphasize one's own traditional ethnic identity. The other factor is the push toward European Union, which (like most major changes) has given rise to a traditionalist reaction in many countries.

An increase in feelings of national pride did not take place in North America during this period, despite the fact that the United States and Canada have had larger immigrant inflows than any Western European society. But more recently, the United States also has experienced strong pressures to limit further immigration.

The decline of confidence in established institutions and of trust in government does not represent a broad withdrawal of trust from the world in general: it is specifically a withdrawal of confidence from authoritarian institutions. National Election Study and General Social Survey data from the United States demonstrate that there was a significant downward movement in interpersonal trust from 1964 to 1994, but the United States seems to be exceptional in this respect. Interpersonal trust (as we have seen, a key element in pro-democratic political culture) is strongly linked with Postmaterialist values; consequently, we would predict rising, not falling, levels of interpersonal trust. As figure 10.7 demonstrates, this prediction is generally confirmed: interpersonal trust *rose* in 13 of the 19 countries in which change was observed. The exceptions include France, Northern Ireland, and South Korea, and the three societies undergoing regime change, Hungary, Argentina, and South Africa. Outside the United States, most publics are coming to trust people *more* but hierarchical institutions *less*.

Moreover, we find one striking exception to the decline of mass confidence

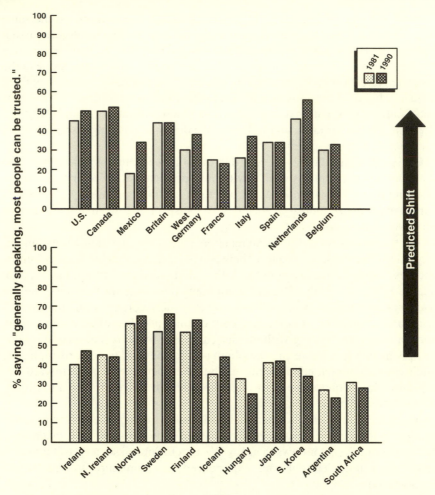

Figure 10.7. Percentage saying "generally speaking, most people can be trusted" in 1981 vs. 1990, in 21 societies. *Source*: 1981 and 1990 World Values surveys.

in established institutions: during the period 1981–90, confidence in "major corporations" did not decline. Though it started from relatively low levels in 1981, confidence in corporations showed a rising trend in most societies. This may have been linked with the collapse of state socialist economies, which made private enterprise look good by contrast. And in a sense, it is a logical reaction to the pronounced decline of trust in government: if the state is coming to be seen as the problem, rather than the solution, it becomes all the more important to have a strong countervailing force to offset the power of the state. In any case, it seems clear that one of the most pervasive defining tendencies of the modernization era—the tendency to look to the state as the solution to all problems—has reached its limits.

THE RISE OF CITIZEN INTERVENTION

Throughout advanced industrial democracies, voter turnout is stagnant or declining. In most countries, established political party machines are losing their grip on voters, and party membership has fallen to about half the level it had a few decades ago. And one frequently hears references to growing apathy on the part of the public. As we will demonstrate, these allegations of apathy are misleading: mass publics *are* deserting the old-line oligarchical political organizations that mobilized them in the modernization era—but, far from being apathetic, they are becoming more active than ever in a wide range of elite-challenging forms of political participation.

In contrast to widespread allegations of mass apathy, a more participant political role for mass publics has been predicted for some time. In 1977 it was suggested that Cognitive Mobilization (reflecting rising levels of formal education, political information, and cognitive skills) was making the publics of advanced industrial societies increasingly likely to engage in interventionist, elite-challenging politics (Inglehart, 1979: 291–321).

Throughout the world, the more educated tend to be more active in politics than the less educated (Milbrath and Goel, 1977; Verba, Nie, and Kim, 1978). And, throughout the world, younger birth cohorts are more educated than older ones. This implies that, as younger, more highly educated cohorts gradually replace the older, less educated ones in the adult population, we should witness a gradual rise in conventional political participation rates.

Moreover the *Political Action* study found a strong relationship between Postmaterialist values and "unconventional political behavior" (that is, elite-challenging action such as boycotts, unofficial strikes, and occupying buildings in order to press political demands), concluding "As relatively Postmaterialist younger age cohorts replace relatively Materialist ones in the adult electorate, we would anticipate a gradual rise in the public's propensity to employ 'unconventional' techniques of political protest (and, of course, a change in what is considered unconventional)" (Inglehart, 1979: 378–79).

Kaase and Barnes endorsed this prediction, in their conclusion to the same volume: "The dependence of unconventional political behavior on education, cognitive skills and Postmaterialism—well-documented in our analysis—displays too much of a structural component, and therefore permanence, to be considered just a fad of the young" (Barnes and Kaase, 1979: 524).

Because of changing values and skills levels, mass political participation was predicted to rise as intergenerational population replacement takes place. These predictions were published more than a decade before the data for the 1990 World Values Surveys were collected. They contradict the conventional wisdom that focuses on declining voting rates, concluding that citizens are losing interest in politics and the prevailing trend is toward mass apathy. But voting turnout largely reflects the parties' ability to mobilize their supporters and consequently is a misleading indicator of real mass interest and involvement. The World Values survey data show strong correlations between Material-

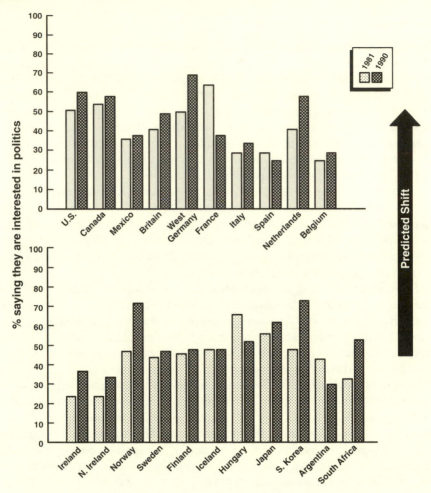

Figure 10.8. Percentages saying that they are interested in politics, in 1981 vs. 1990, in 21 countries. *Source*: 1981 and 1990 World Values surveys.

ist/Postmaterialist values and the more active forms of political participation (though not with voting). Accordingly, we predict that we will find rising, not falling, levels of mass political participation. Let us examine the evidence.

CONVENTIONAL POLITICAL PARTICIPATION

Evidence from the 21 countries surveyed in both 1981 and 1990 indicates that, though they may vote less regularly, most publics are *not* becoming apathetic; quite the contrary, they are becoming increasingly interested in politics. As figure 10.8 shows, political interest rates rose in 16 countries and fell in only four. The findings are unequivocal, and they contradict the conventional wisdom

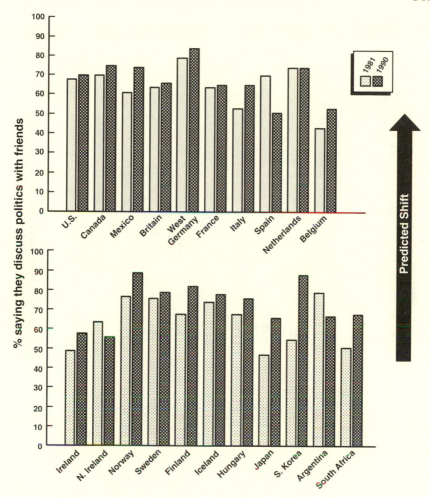

Figure 10.9. Percentages saying that they "often" or "sometimes" discuss politics with friends, in 1981 vs. 1990, in 21 countries. *Source*: 1981 and 1990 World Values surveys.

about mass apathy. Another good indicator of political interest is whether or not people discuss politics with others. Here, too, the predicted rise in conventional participation is taking place, as figure 10.9 indicates. The proportion of the population that discusses politics rose in 17 societies and fell in only three (with one country showing no change).

Another, more active form of conventional political participation also shows the predicted increase: as figure 10.10 demonstrates, from 1981 to 1990 the percentage reporting that they had signed a petition rose in 16 countries and fell in only four. When we examine trends over a still longer time period, the results are even more dramatic. Four of the countries that were included in both waves of the World Values survey were also surveyed for the 1974 Political

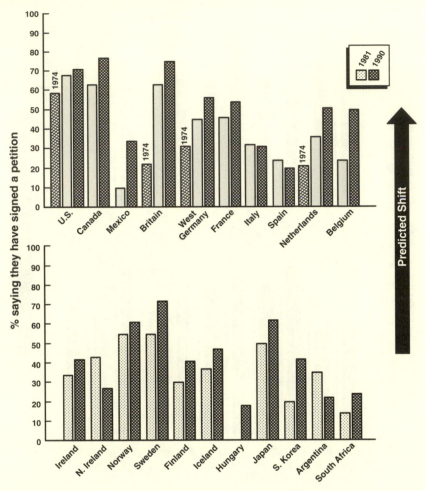

Figure 10.10. Percentages saying they have signed a petition, in 1981 vs. 1990, in 20 countries. *Source*: 1981 and 1990 World Values surveys. 1981 data not available for Hungary.

Action study (see Barnes et al., 1979: 548–49). The data for these countries (the United States, Britain, West Germany, and the Netherlands) are included in figure 10.10. In all four cases, we find even larger increases from 1974 to 1990 than we do from 1981 to 1990. In the United States, the percentage reporting that they had signed a petition rose from 58 percent in 1974, to 68 percent in 1981, to 71 percent in 1990; for Britain, they rose from 22 to 62 to 75 percent; for West Germany, the figures are 31, 43, and 56 percent; and in the Netherlands the percentage saying they had signed a petition rose from 21 percent in 1974 to 37 percent in 1981 to 50 percent in 1990.

This is dramatic evidence of rising mass political activism. How do we explain declining rates of voter turnout and falling political party membership, in light of these findings? The confusion over whether participation is rising or falling arises from the fact that we are dealing with two distinct processes: elite-directed participation is eroding, but more autonomous and active forms of participation are rising.

The decline in voter turnout reflects a long-term intergenerational decline in party loyalty. Although the younger, better-educated birth cohorts show higher rates of political interest, political discussion, and so forth than their elders, they have *lower* levels of party loyalty. Surveys from a number of Western European countries reveal that the postwar birth cohorts have considerably lower rates of political party loyalty than the older cohorts (Inglehart, 1990: 357–58). This finding parallels a pattern of intergenerational decline in party identification that has been found among the American electorate during the past two decades (Nie, Verba, and Petrocik, 1979; Abramson, 1979).

Although their higher levels of education and politicization predispose them to identify with *some* political party, the younger relatively Postmaterialist cohorts have less incentive to identify with any specific political party among the available choices. The established political parties were established in an era dominated by social class conflict and economic issues and tend to remain polarized along these lines. For the older cohorts, religion and social class still provide powerful cues in establishing one's political party loyalties. But the younger cohorts' loyalties are less strongly influenced by social class and religion. Moreover, in recent years, a new axis of polarization has arisen based on cultural and quality of life issues. Established parties have had difficulty in reorienting themselves in relation to this axis. Today, the established political party configurations in most countries do not yet adequately reflect the hottest contemporary issues; and those born in the postwar era have relatively little motivation to identify with the established political parties.

Even more important, however, is the fact that the younger birth cohorts are relatively Postmaterialist. This makes them less amenable to accepting the authority of hierarchical, oligarchical organizations like the old-line political parties. Accordingly, the last few decades have brought a decline of political party loyalties and membership in most advanced industrial societies.

But partisan loyalties and party organizations were the main reason for the high electoral turnout of earlier years. Hence, we find two divergent trends: on one hand, the bureaucratized and elite-directed forms of participation such as voting and party membership have declined, while on the other hand the individually motivated and elite-challenging forms of participation have risen.

The decline of partisanship need not continue indefinitely. A realignment of political party systems that made party polarization correspond more closely to issue polarization and less oligarchical forms of organization could stem the decline. Such a realignment seems to be under way with some Western parties, but it has not yet reversed the overall trend.

THE RISE OF UNCONVENTIONAL POLITICAL PARTICIPATION

Postmaterialists are much more likely to engage in unconventional political activities than are Materialists. Postmaterialists are those who have been raised under conditions of relative economic and physical security. Hence, they take survival for granted and devote more time and energy to relatively remote and abstract activities such as politics.

This has contributed to an international trend toward rising rates of unconventional, elite-challenging behavior. The World Values surveys included a battery of questions concerning one's readiness to take part in four forms of unconventional political action. The exact text of these questions asked, "I am going to read out some different form of political action that people can take and I'd like you to tell me, for each one, whether you have actually *done* any of these things, whether you might do it, or would never, under any circumstances, do it." The list includes (1) joining in boycotts, (2) attending lawful demonstrations, (3) joining unofficial strikes, and (4) occupying buildings or factories.

These questions are replicated from the *Political Action* study (Barnes et al., 1979). They were designed to test the hypothesis that intergenerational changes in values and skill levels are giving rise to a more activist public— one that is readier to intervene directly in political decision making, rather than limiting themselves to participation by voting, in which the public gives a blank check to a given set of elites, authorizing them to make all important political decisions for the next several years. In contrast with voting, unconventional participation is relatively disruptive and is designed to influence specific decisions.

Figure 10.11 shows the changes in the percentage saying that they actually have taken part in a boycott, or that they might do so. The former reports actual behavior, while the latter simply indicates a relative predisposition to do so. Both actual behavior and behavioral predispositions show clear upward trends from 1981 to 1990, but the numbers are larger and more reliable when we combine the two, as in this figure. Here again, we have 1974 data from four countries (the United States, Britain, West Germany, and the Netherlands) from the Political Action study, extending the time series over 16 years in these four cases. We predicted that we will observe an increase in this form of participation. And we find it: the percentage saying they have taken part in a boycott, or might do so, rose in 15 countries from 1981 (or from 1974) to 1990; it fell in five (we have no 1981 data from Hungary); the success rate for this prediction is 75 percent. Incidentally, the U.S. data in this figure constitute the sole anomaly in which the 1974 level was higher than the 1981 level (and even here, the overall trend is upward when continued to 1990). Generally, we find a steady upward trend, as this and the next two figures demonstrate. At the earliest time point, in 1974, such activities were still rare—which is why we used the label "unconventional political participation." Today, they have become so

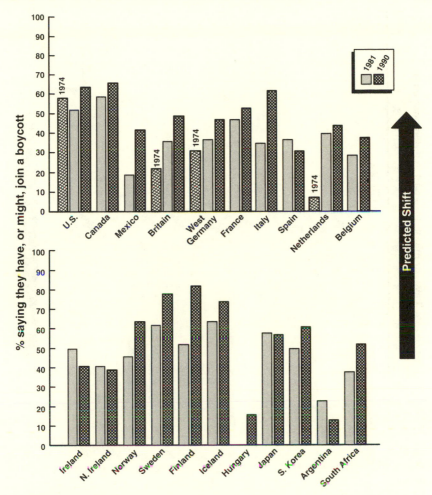

Figure 10.11. Percentages saying that they have taken part in a boycott, or might take part in one: 1981 vs. 1990, in 20 countries. *Source*: 1981 and 1990 World Values surveys. 1981 data not available for Hungary.

widespread that they are no longer unconventional. Another label such as "elite-challenging" participation seems appropriate.

Figure 10.12 shows the percentages that have taken part in demonstrations or are willing to do so. The percentage rises in 16 societies and declines in only one (three societies show no change, and 1981 data are lacking for Hungary). Here, and with both of the remaining "unconventional participation" variables, there is a perfectly monotonic rise from 1974 to 1990 in all four countries for which 1974 data are available.

Figures A.23 and A.24 (in Appendix 3) show the trends observed in the percentages saying they actually have taken part, or might take part, in an unoffi-

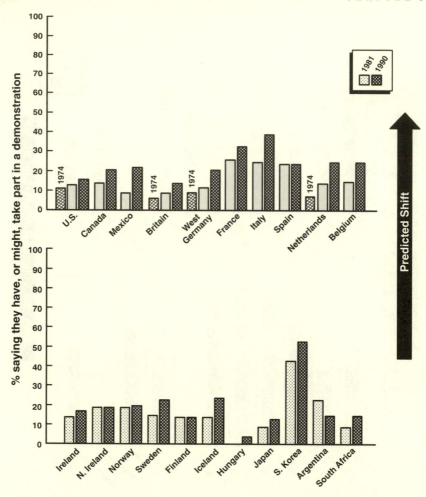

Figure 10.12. Percentages saying that they have taken part in a demonstration, or might do so, in 1981 vs. 1990, in 20 countries. *Source*: 1981 and 1990 World Values surveys. 1981 data not available for Hungary.

cial strike, and the percentage saying they actually have, or might, occupy a building. With unofficial strikes, the percentage rose in 14 societies and fell in four (with missing data for two countries and no change in one). And in regard to occupying buildings, the trend from 1981 (or from 1974) went up in 17 societies and declined in two (with 1981 missing data for one case and no change in another). The availability of a longer time series clearly improves our success rate with this variable, for both Britain and the Netherlands show slightly lower rates in 1990 than in 1981; but when we use 1974 as the base, the overall trend is markedly upward. This is in keeping with the principle that our predictions are uncertain for any given country over short time periods, but should hold up relatively well across many countries and over long periods. Across the four variables that measure changes in "unconventional" or elite-challenging political participation, the overall success rate for our predictions is 84 percent.

STATE CONTROL OF BUSINESS AND INDUSTRY, LEFT-RIGHT SELF-PLACEMENT AND CONFIDENCE IN AUTHORITARIAN INSTITUTIONS

We suggested earlier that since the industrial revolution, sociopolitical change has moved in two distinct phases. During the first (the Modernization phase), the dominant trend is a shift in salience and power from decentralized social institutions basing their legitimacy on the society's traditional culture heritage toward large centralized state institutions based on rational-legal authority. The leviathan state, of which the former USSR was the outstanding example, seemed to be the endpoint of this historical trend.

But this trend reverses itself in advanced industrial society. A Postmodern institutional and cultural shift takes place, in which there is increasing emphasis on individual autonomy, culturally, and a trend toward decentralization, marketization, and less hierarchical institutions.

We are witnessing a decline in the degree to which the individual is subordinated to society. We have seen evidence of the declining strength of traditional cultural norms that helped maintain the family and ensure the reproduction of society, and declining acceptance of the authority of hierarchical institutions, both political and nonpolitical. Related changes are taking place in the public's motivations to work and in their orientations toward the control of business and industry, as we will see. We find a pervasive trend toward weakening hierarchical controls over the individual.

But at the same time, we find indications of *rising* emphasis on society's responsibilities *to* the individual, and a tendency to blame society, rather than the individual, for social problems such as poverty. There has been rising emphasis on individual *rights* and entitlements, coupled with a declining emphasis on individual *responsibility*. The latter trend may be approaching its limits, however, in face of a growing awareness that giving the state responsibility for individual well-being may be beneficial in limited areas but tends to become oppressive and unworkable on a comprehensive scale. An awareness of these limits has emerged most acutely and most dramatically in the ex-communist societies of Central and Eastern Europe, but it has spread throughout industrial society.

Wildavsky (1987) and his associates (Thompson, Ellis, and Wildavsky, 1990) argue that the degree to which the individual is subordinated to the society is one of the two crucial dimensions on which cultures vary, and that there is a limited range of variation on this dimension because both extremes tend to be fatal: a viable society must maintain an equilibrium between the conflicting demands of individual freedom and conformity to societal norms.

But, we believe, in advanced industrial societies, the equilibrium point is significantly closer to the pole of individual freedom than it is in societies of scarcity. This is true because the emphasis can be skewed farther toward individual rights and entitlements when there are abundant resources; conversely, the need for tight social discipline is highest when the survival margin is narrow. Thus, one of the major concomitants of the rise of industrial society has been a long-term shift from social control toward individual freedom, and this shift is continuing. But there are limits to how far this or any other cultural change can move. Industrial society may currently be at an historical turning point where it is testing the limits to how much farther this trend can move.

The most important political event of the late twentieth century has been the withering away of communism. Although it was unexpected by most observers, it reflects underlying long-term forces that are common to all industrial societies.

One of these common factors has been a gradual decline in public support for state ownership and control of the economy. Already in 1981, this core element of the Marxist prescription for the good society had lost much of its mass appeal; by 1990, with the increasingly evident failure of Marxist societies, public support for state intervention fell still farther.

It would be a mistake to see the global movement away from communism as a move back to traditional capitalism, however. In most advanced industrial societies, though the trend in public preferences is away from Marxism, it is *not* back toward the laissez-faire capitalism that prevailed 60 to 90 years ago. Indeed, a key reason why capitalism is thriving today is the fact that it had already made a series of incremental but cumulatively massive reforms that brought about some much needed governmental regulation of the economy and society and developed extensive welfare state institutions through successive waves of change in the 1930s, the postwar era, the 1960s, and early 1970s. Today "Capitalism" is a misleading name for the welfare states of Western advanced industrial society, in which state expenditures range from a third to well over half of the given country's Gross National Product.

Clearly, the trend in these societies is not toward increasing the state hold on the economy; more often, it is toward privatization of functions carried out by a state that is now widely perceived as having grown too big. The idea that Small Is Beautiful was novel when it first emerged in the 1970s. It has gradually come to seem almost self-evident—and the beauty of smallness is being applied to government as well as to private organizations. Increasingly, big government is coming to be viewed with suspicion. Nevertheless, in some important ways, Western publics are still moving *away* from the traditional capitalist model, toward reducing the authority of owners. In other words, the wave of the future is *neither* communism nor traditional capitalism; instead, both types of societies are groping toward an optimal balance between state and society. Over time, it has become evident that neither laissez-faire capitalism nor a state-run society works well. At any given time, the optimal balance is uncertain, but a common model for industrial society is gradually emerging. This model cannot be defined a priori by some ideology; finding it is an empirical process, but it does seem to be emerging, and the tendency is toward convergence from both extremes. This global process can be seen throughout advanced industrial society.

The World Values surveys asked a question about who should own and manage business and industry. Four options were offered, ranging from the traditional capitalist position ("the owners should run their business or appoint the managers") to the classic Marxist position ("the state should be the owner and appoint the managers"), plus two other options, one giving employees a voice in selecting the managers, and the other giving employees full ownership and control.

First, let us examine changes in support for the Marxist alternative from 1981 to 1990. As figure 10.13 demonstrates, in 1981 public support for the Marxist option already was at extremely low levels in most countries. During the 1980s, its support eroded even further, approaching the vanishing point by 1990. Unfortunately, we do not have 1981 data from ex-socialist countries. At that time, one could not carry out this type of research in most state socialist countries, and even in Hungary, one of the most open societies, this question was not asked. But among publics of societies with market economies, support for state ownership was virtually a dead option in 1981. Iceland was an interesting exception, where 38 percent of the public favored state ownership in 1981, and the figure dropped only slightly in 1990. Mexico, Spain, Italy, and Argentina were the only other societies still having appreciable amounts of support for state ownership. In Mexico, for example, 9 percent of the public favored state ownership in 1981; but this fell to 3 percent in 1990. This was typical of the prevailing trend. In fact, Argentina was the *only* country of the 20 in which support for state ownership rose during this period.

For many years, the conventional wisdom was that youth naturally gravitated toward Marxism: "If my son were not a socialist at the age of 20, I would disown him; if he is still a socialist when he is 40, I will then disown him," as Clemenceau put it. This may have been true in the past, but our data indicate that it is not true today. The differences associated with age are extremely small in most countries.

We find a similar reversal of relationships when we cross-tabulate this attitude by Materialist/Postmaterialist values. Postmaterialists tend to support the conventional Left position on most social issues. They do *not* do so here. As we saw in chapter 8, in societies with market economies, there is practically no relationship between Materialist/Postmaterialist values and support for state ownership of business and industry. And in the formerly socialist countries the young, the better educated, and the Postmaterialists are *less* favorable to state ownership than are the old, the less educated, and the Materialists.

There is no reason why Postmaterialism should automatically be linked with support for state ownership. Traditionally, this was viewed as the Progressive or Leftist position; and probably for this reason, when Postmaterialists first appeared in significant numbers in Western Europe during the 1960s, they tended to think of themselves as Marxists. But this tendency weakened during the

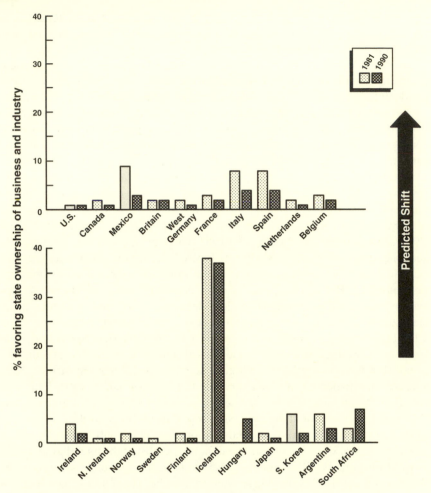

Figure 10.13. Percentages favoring state ownership of business and industry, in 1981 vs. 1990, in 20 countries. *Source*: 1981 and 1990 World Values surveys. 1981 data not available for Hungary.

1970s, and by the late 1980s it had all but vanished (Inglehart, 1990). In the Eastern European context, this relationship has actually reversed itself: their experience with the deadening repression of the socialist regimes under which they have grown up has led Postmaterialists to see state ownership and control as incompatible with the individual autonomy and self-expression that they value so highly (Inglehart and Siemienska, 1988). For them, expansion of state authority does not appear to be a progressive policy, but a repressive one.

This illustrates an important point: Postmaterialists do *not* automatically adopt whatever happens to be the conventional Left position. On many issues, they do gravitate toward the Left. But the rise of Postmaterialism has brought

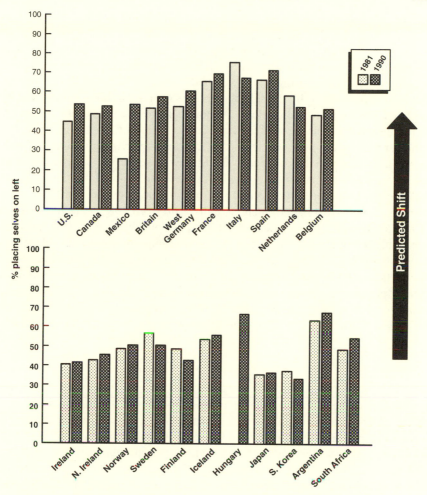

Figure 10.14. Percentages placing themselves on the Left half of a 10-point Left-Right ideological scale, in 1981 vs. 1990, in 20 countries. *Source*: 1981 and 1990 World Values surveys. 1981 data not available for Hungary.

a new perspective into play, one that sometimes runs against established political orthodoxy; it is reshaping the meaning of Left and Right.

Although Postmaterialists do not necessarily support state ownership of business and industry, they *do* tend to favor giving employees a say in the choice of managers. Materialists, conversely, are much more likely to support the owners' untrammeled right to run their enterprises. Hence, we would expect the former position to gain support and the latter to lose support over time. As figure A.25 shows (see Appendix 3), support for joint employee-owner choice of management did rise in 13 of the 18 countries in which changes were observed; conversely, as figure A.26 demonstrates (also in Appendix 3), support for the owners' right to determine management fell in 11 of the 19 countries in which changes were observed.

As we have seen, mass support for the classic Marxist prescription—state ownership of business and industry—had virtually disappeared by 1990. Especially to Marxist hard-liners, this seemed like the collapse of the Left itself. But is it? Not if we go by the self-perceptions of mass publics, rather than by outdated ideological formulations. Although Postmaterialists are no longer distinguished by their support for state ownership, they do—quite clearly—consider themselves to be located on the Left of the Left-Right political spectrum. Hence, despite the collapse of the Marxist alternative, we would predict rising levels of self-placement on the Left side of the scale. Figure 10.14 shows the changes observed in Left-Right self-placement from 1981 to 1990. As it demonstrates, Left self-placement actually rose from 1981 to 1990 in 14 out of the 20 countries for which we have data at both time points (the question was not asked in Hungary in 1981). As the foregoing findings make clear, this does *not* reflect an increase in support for the classic Marxist program. But it does reflect growing mass support for a variety of other issues, from environmental protection, to women's emancipation, to immigrants' rights, which today, to an increasing degree, constitute what people have in mind when they are asked whether they think of themselves as being on the Right or the Left.

CONCLUSIONS

Let us sum up the full array of changes observed across 21 nations. In the preceding chapter we found that with four types of items, the overwhelming majority of responses moved in the predicted direction from 1981 to 1990—that is, toward the pole that was correlated with Postmaterialist values. With one type of item, the overwhelming majority of responses moved in the opposite direction, defying our predictions and shifting in the direction preferred by the Materialists in 1981. This fifth category was by far the smallest category, however, based on only four questions.

In this chapter we have examined the changes found with several more types of variables. What is the overall success rate for all of our predictions? Table 10.1 shows the results for each category, including the Postmaterialist shift itself.

The results of this analysis reveal that in 72 percent of the 802 cases for which we have data, the values of the respective publics shifted in the direction specified by our deliberately oversimplified prediction.

But, as we have seen, the success rate of our predictions was highly differentiated cross-nationally. In most countries, the great majority of items moved in the predicted direction; but in both Argentina and South Africa, fully 78 percent of the items shifted in the *opposite* direction from that predicted by the intergenerational change model, bringing down the overall average considerably. But these deviant cases support our hypothesis that the shift is linked with

TABLE 10.1

Percentage of Shifts Moving in Predicted Direction, by Type of Variable

Category of Item	Number Moving in Predicted Direction	Total Number in Category	Percent Correctly Predicted
I. Authority, sexual, and civil norms	168	213	79
II. Religious Norms	143	199	72
III. Parent-Child Ties	25	76	33
IV. Political Behavior	114	137	83
V. State in Economy, Confidence in Institutions, Trust, Postmaterialism	129	177	73
Total	579	802	72

conditions of security. For both Argentina and South Africa experienced severe economic decline and political upheaval during the period 1981–90: powerful short-term influences offset the effects of intergenerational value change. One other country surveyed in both 1981 and 1990 (Hungary) experienced a nonviolent but wrenching transition from communism to democracy during the months before the 1990 survey, and here only half of the values items moved in the predicted direction. In the 18 remaining countries, almost 80 percent of the observed shifts were in the predicted direction.

As figure 10.15 shows, the cross-national differences in success rates for these predictions is systematic: in those that experienced rising prosperity during these years, the predicted Postmodern shift took place in the overwhelming majority of cases. In those countries that experienced economic stagnation or decline, this shift generally did not take place. In other words, predictable period effects were present. The linkage between economic growth rates and the percentage of values and norms shifting in the Postmodern direction is significant at the .01 level.

Our theory does *not* hold that, for some mysterious reason, there will always be a shift toward Postmodern values. It specifies that economic and physical security are conducive to these values and predicts that period effects will be present, in addition to the long-term effects of having experienced relatively secure conditions during one's formative years. Thus, we knew from the start that the prediction "everything correlated with Postmaterialism will move in that direction" was too simple. Even this oversimplified model correctly predicts 72 percent of the observed shifts. But this prediction is based on intergenerational population replacement effects alone; and we know that current conditions also matter. It is relatively easy to control for the effects of such economic factors as inflation and unemployment rates, for which quantitative indicators are readily available. It is more difficult to control for the effects of wars, civil unrest, the collapse of a regime,

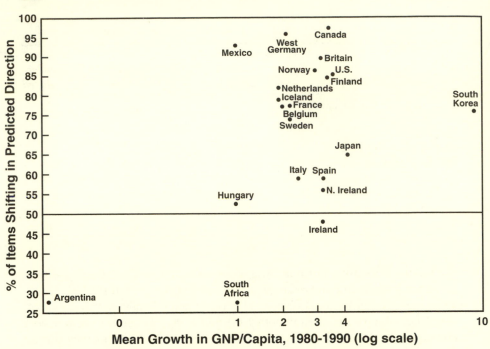

Figure 10.15. The impact of period effects on predicted value changes.
Proportion of items shifting in the predicted direction from 1981 to 1990, by rate of economic growth during that period. r = .47, significant at .01 level. *Source*: 1990 World Values Survey; economic growth data from World Bank, *World Development Report, 1993.*

and other types of political insecurity. Common sense suggests that political upheaval must have had a negative impact on the publics of Argentina, South Africa, and Hungary (all of which were experiencing regime transitions in 1990). We will not attempt to make a quantitative estimate of the impact of political upheaval here. We will simply note that when we exclude these three countries from our calculations (crudely controlling for societies undergoing massive political and economic upheaval), among the 18 societies that were *not* undergoing a change of regime, almost 80 percent of the observed shifts are in the predicted direction.

Political upheaval and regime change are part of reality. We do not, by any means, wish to exclude Argentina, South Africa, and Hungary from our broader analysis. Quite the contrary, they provide valuable clues concerning the kinds of changes that are probably taking place in Russia and much of Eastern Europe today. Our exercise in excluding them is not designed to pretend that they do not exist, but to provide a more differentiated view of cultural change. In the three societies that were undergoing major political and economic upheaval, the great majority of the observed changes moved *away* from Postmodern values; in the 18 societies that were experiencing relatively stable and prosperous conditions, about 80 percent of the changes moved *toward* Postmodernism.

The shift toward Postmodern values is based on a rising sense of mass security; accordingly, it takes place only in settings where countervailing period effects are not strong enough to reverse the effects of intergenerational population replacement. In societies that were enjoying reasonably secure circumstances (18 out of the 21 cases examined here), the predicted shift toward Postmodern orientations clearly *is* the prevailing trend.

These processes have both alarming and encouraging implications. On one hand, established institutions that have shaped industrial society for generations seem to be losing their authority over the average citizen. Public confidence is declining, not only in key governmental institutions such as parliament, police, civil service, and armed forces, but also in political parties, churches, educational systems, and the press. We even find a weakening sense of attachment to that most basic of all Western institutions, the nation-state itself.

There are potential dangers in this evolution. Societal institutions could become too atrophied to cope with a national emergency if one arose. But there are positive aspects as well. In societies characterized by too much respect for authority, it is conducive to democratization. For the erosion of state authority has been accompanied by a rising potential for citizen intervention in politics. Partly this is due to a shift in values, with a weakening emphasis on the goals of economic and physical security that favor strong authority; but another factor that favors rising citizen intervention is the long-term rise in educational levels and in mass political skills that have characterized all industrial societies. In the long run, industrialized societies of both East and West must cope with long-term changes that are making their publics less amenable to doing as they are told, and more adept at telling their governments what to do.

CHAPTER 11

Trajectories of Social Change

MODERNIZATION WAS ONCE an immensely influential concept, but it went out of fashion in the 1970s. A revised concept of Modernization still has an important role to play. But it is becoming increasingly clear that the phenomenon that Marx and Weber and Lerner and Deutsch wrote about is not the final stage of history. Socioeconomic change has begun to move in a new direction.

This book has examined changes in political and economic goals, religious norms, and family values—and how these changes affect economic growth rates, political party strategies, and the prospects for democratic institutions. A survey of the belief systems of most of the world's population reveals coherent cultural patterns that are closely linked with the economic levels of given societies. Economic development, cultural change, and political change go together in coherent and roughly predictable patterns: some trajectories of socioeconomic change are far more likely than others.

But change is not linear. In advanced industrial societies the prevailing direction of development is shifting from Modernization to Postmodernization. This new trajectory brings declining emphasis on the functional rationality that characterized industrial society, and increasing emphasis on self-expression and the quality of life. As Postmodern values become more widespread, various societal changes from equal rights for women to democratic political institutions and the decline of state socialist regimes become increasingly likely. With Postmodernization, a new worldview is gradually replacing the paradigm that has dominated industrializing societies since the Industrial Revolution. It reflects a shift in what people want out of life. It is transforming basic norms governing politics, work, religion, family, and sexual behavior.

Distinctive belief systems are linked with both the Modernization and Postmodernization trajectories. These belief systems are not mere consequences of economic or social changes, but integral parts of a broad syndrome in which culture shapes socioeconomic conditions and is also shaped by them, in reciprocal fashion. Let us sum up our findings.

The shift from the Modernization phase into the Postmodernization phase reflects the principle of diminishing marginal utility. Industrialization and Modernization required breaking the cultural constraints on accumulation that are found in any steady-state economy. In Western history, this break with traditional constraints was what Weber described as the rise of the Protestant Ethic. Eventually, when Western societies had become rich, diminishing returns from economic growth lead to a Postmodern shift, which in some ways is the decline of the Protestant Ethic.

The spread of materialistic motivations was one of the central characteristics of Modernization. In Postmodern society, emphasis on economic security and economic growth is giving way to an increasing emphasis on the quality of life. The disciplined, self-denying, and achievement-oriented norms of industrial society are yielding to an increasingly broad latitude for individual choice of lifestyles.

We are also reaching limits to the development of the hierarchical bureaucratic organizations that helped create modern society. The bureaucratic state, the disciplined, oligarchic political party, the mass-production assembly line, the old-line labor union, and the hierarchical corporation made the industrial revolution and the modern state possible. But the trend toward bureaucratization, centralization, and government ownership and control is now reversing itself, both because it is reaching limits to its effectiveness and because of changing priorities among the publics of advanced industrial societies. Public confidence in hierarchical institutions is eroding throughout these societies.

THE CULTURAL CHANGES OF POSTMODERNIZATION

Having attained high levels of economic security, the populations of the first nations to industrialize have gradually come to emphasize Postmaterialist values; these groups give higher priority to the quality of life than to economic growth. This transformation has been taking place throughout advanced industrial society during the past few decades and is only one component of a broader cultural shift toward Postmodern values. This cultural change is bringing changes at the societal level, such as the shift away from the politics of class conflict, to political conflict based on such issues as environmental protection and the status of women and sexual minorities.

In the analysis of intergenerational cultural change, there is no substitute for long-term time series data. Although replication is not as exciting as asking new questions, it is crucial for the analysis of change. We have been extremely fortunate in having colleagues from many countries who were sufficiently interested in long-term social change to replicate and analyze key survey questions in exactly the same form over a period of many years. These colleagues are thanked at the beginning of this book, and this acknowledgment is far more than an empty formality. This many-sided effort has produced an unprecedentedly rich body of evidence concerning how mass values and motivations change and has led to cumulative progress in which some findings about social change are now rather clear.

In our first article on value change in 1971, we argued that a shift from Materialist to Postmaterialist values was taking place in advanced industrial societies, as a result of a process of intergenerational value change. This claim was highly controversial at the time; literally scores of articles and books attacked the thesis. The most widespread counterinterpretation argued that the observed age differences were not a permanent part of the outlook of given birth cohorts, but simply a life-cycle difference that would fade away as the younger cohorts aged. The intergenerational change thesis implied that a long-term shift in prevailing values would occur as the young replaced the older cohorts in industrial societies; the life-cycle interpretation implied that no societal change was taking place. In subsequent years, a large body of empirical evidence has emerged that demonstrates rather conclusively that the predicted shift has, indeed, taken place.

In 1995 a monumental five-volume analysis of the role of mass attitudes in politics was published. Sponsored by the European Science Foundation, it brings together the results of analyses by more than 50 social scientists from a dozen European countries. The evidence is now so strong that, although the volume on the political impact of values (Van Deth and Scarbrough, 1995) contains contributions by some of my most prominent earlier critics, one of its main conclusions is that the shift toward Postmaterialists values is, indeed, taking place. Thus, though highly critical of my theory, Scarbrough's evaluation of the empirical evidence concludes, "Indisputably, across much of Western Europe, value orientations are shifting. . . . The potency of Postmaterialist theory lies in providing us with one of the few explicated accounts of value change in contemporary West European societies" (Scarbrough, 1995: 157). A leading American critic comes to the same conclusion (Duch, 1996: 666). The debate has changed; the question no longer is, "Is an intergenerational shift to Postmaterialist values taking place?" but rather *"Why* is this intergenerational value shift taking place?"

Subsequent analyses in this massive work explore the impact of Postmaterialist values on political behavior. Summing up the findings from the entire five volumes, the project's coordinators, Kaase and Newton, conclude, "We find substantial support for the model which traces social changes to value changes, and value changes into changes in political attitudes and behavior, especially through the process of intergenerational replacement. . . . It is clear that the decline of religious values and the rise of Postmaterialist values have transformed the cultural composition of Western democracies in recent decades" (Kaase and Newton, 1995:63).

This book has examined the relevant time series evidence concerning this broad cultural transformation of advanced industrial society. We find that (in more than 800 tests) most variables moved in the predicted direction in most countries. Although this test is based on surveys from only two time points, 1981 and 1990, we also have a much more broader database indicating that the theoretically related Materialist/Postmaterialist shift is an enduring intergenerational change; this supports the interpretation that this may also hold true for the 40 variables examined in this book.

New societal goals are gradually replacing those that dominated Western society since the Industrial Revolution. This shift in motivations springs from the fact that there is a fundamental difference between growing up with the feeling that survival is precarious and growing up with the assumption that one's physical survival can be taken for granted. The difference between feeling secure or insecure about survival is so basic that it has led to a shift from the modern values that characterized industrial society, to the postmodern values that characterize advanced industrial society. This change is eroding many of the key institutions of industrial society.

Postmodern values bring declining confidence in religious, political, and even scientific authority; they also bring a growing mass desire for participation and self-expression. The two trends combine to make the task of political elites more difficult. What might have been a satisfactory performance by the old criteria is not considered satisfactory today. Especially in the political realm, respect for authority is weakening. Mass support for a bigger government role in society and confidence in government are both diminishing. In political participation, the emphasis is shifting from voting to more active and issue-specific forms of mass participation. Mass loyalties to long-established hierarchical political parties are eroding. No longer content to be disciplined troops, the public has become increasingly autonomous and elite-challenging. Consequently, though voting turnout is stagnant or declining, people are participating in politics in increasingly active and more issue-specific ways. Moreover, a growing segment of the population is coming to value freedom of expression and political participation as things that are good in themselves, rather than simply as a possible means to attain economic security. Overall, these changes are conducive to the expansion of democracy.

But these changes have had a traumatic impact on the old-line political machines of industrial society, which are in disarray almost everywhere. Until recently, it seemed to be almost a law of nature that government control of economy and society would continue to expand. That development has now reached its natural limits—both for functional reasons and because of declining mass confidence in government and a growing resistance to government intrusion.

In economic behavior, we find a gradual shift in what motivates people to work: emphasis is shifting from maximizing one's income and job security, toward a growing insistence on interesting and meaningful work. On one hand, we find a growing emphasis on more collegial and participatory styles of management. But simultaneously, there is a reversal of the tendency to look to government for solutions, and a growing acceptance of capitalism and market principles. Both trends are linked with a growing rejection of hierarchical authority patterns and increasing emphasis on individual autonomy. Ever since the rise of capitalism, people have almost automatically turned to government to offset the power of private business. Today there is a widespread feeling that the growth of government is reaching a point where it becomes ineffective and an even greater threat to individual autonomy than that presented by private corporations.

In sexual norms and gender roles, we find a continued movement away from the rigid norms that were a functional necessity in agrarian society, where children born outside a traditional two-parent family were likely to starve, and where sexual abstinence was a key means of population control. The development of effective birth control technology, together with unprecedented prosperity and the welfare state, have eroded the functional basis of traditional norms in this area; this has led to greater flexibility for individual choice in sexual behavior, with a particularly dramatic increase in the acceptance of sexual behavior outside marriage and of homosexuality. These changes reflect enduring long-term trends. But we also find one striking reversal: a trend toward reemphasizing the importance of the traditional two-parent family in child-rearing. Throughout advanced industrial society, there was a *growing* emphasis on the importance of parent-child ties during the period from 1981 to 1990. Many of the economic and social functions of the family have eroded, but society has not yet come up with a satisfactory substitute for the psychological role of the family in providing love, self-esteem, and socialization. Teachers and social workers play important roles, but they cannot provide the intense love and individual attention over a lifetime that parents usually give a child.

In the realm of ultimate values, we find both continuity and change. Secularization was one of the key trends associated with Modernization, and the publics of most advanced industrial societies show declining confidence in churches and falling rates of church attendance and are placing less emphasis on organized religion. But spiritual concerns are not vanishing: on the contrary, we find a consistent cross-national tendency for people to spend *more* time thinking about the meaning and purpose of life.

All of these trends are linked with the emergence of greater economic security. In the highly uncertain world of subsistence societies, the need for absolute standards and a sense that an infallible higher power will ensure that things ultimately turn out well filled a major psychological need. Today, the spiritual emphasis among mass publics is turning from security to significance: from a search for reassurance in the face of existential insecurity to a search for the significance of life.

Cultural Change Is Coherent, Not Random

This book has demonstrated that there are powerful linkages between belief systems and political and socioeconomic variables such as democracy or economic growth rates. It also demonstrated coherent and to some extent predictable patterns of change in values and belief systems.

Throughout the past century, a wide variety of social analysts have argued that a society's culture—that is, the basic values, beliefs, and skills of its people—are closely linked with its economic and political system. Although there has been continuing debate over the direction of causality, the concept that values are linked with economic and political behavior has gained widespread acceptance.

Although it has long been believed that given cultural patterns tend to go with given economic and political systems, in the past this belief has rested mainly on impressionistic evidence: it was difficult to demonstrate empirically because cross-culturally comparable measures of belief systems on a global scale were not available. This study has shown that cross-culturally similar syndromes of beliefs and values exist—and that they show astonishingly strong linkages with key economic and political variables. A given society's cultural system and its economic and political systems are opposite sides of the same coin.

CULTURAL CHANGE HAS IMPORTANT CONSEQUENCES

Cultural Factors in Economic Growth

We find strong evidence that cultural factors help shape the economic growth rates of given societies. This idea has been resisted in the past, partly because culture has generally been perceived as a diffuse and permanent feature of given societies: if culture determines economic growth, then the outlook for economic development would seem hopeless.

With the realization that culture is something that can be measured on a quantitative empirical basis, this illusion of diffuseness and permanence disappears. We no longer need deal with gross stereotypes. For the empirical evidence demonstrates that, though they change gradually, central elements of culture can and do change over time.

Our analysis suggests that two aspects of a given society's culture are particularly relevant to economic growth: the values emphasized in socializing children—with an Achievement Motivation cluster being especially significant—and the degree to which a society's people emphasize Materialist or Postmaterialist values.

The question "Is economic growth due to cultural factors or to economic factors?" misses the point. Cultural factors are intimately linked with economic factors; and the two sets of variables interact to provide a strong explanation of why, over the long term, some societies have shown much higher rates of economic growth than others. A model that includes both cultural factors and economic factors has a significantly better fit and explains more of the variance than does a model that relies on economic variables alone. Motivational factors seem to have a strong impact on economic growth, as Weber argued long ago.

Culture and Democracy

An analysis of empirical linkages between culture and democracy demonstrates that democracies have strikingly different political cultures from authoritarian societies. Almost without exception, stable democracies rank high on subjective well-being and interpersonal trust, and authoritarian societies rank low on them. These linkages persist when we control for economic level and social structure. Moreover, these cross-national differences are relatively stable over time. Economic development is conducive to democracy because it brings cultural changes and changes in social structure, and cultural factors seem to be even more important than occupational structure, educational levels, or income equality.

The evidence suggests that the remarkably strong linkage found between political culture and democracy is more a matter of culture contributing to democracy, than of democracy determining culture. With rising levels of economic development, cultural patterns tend to emerge that are increasingly supportive of democracy.

This transformation does not come easily or automatically. Determined elites, in control of the army and police, can resist pressures for democratization. But with economic development, mass publics tend to give an increasingly high priority to autonomy and self-expression. And as they mature, industrial societies develop increasingly specialized and educated labor forces, a culture of trust and well-being emerges, and Postmaterialist values begin to spread among the public. It becomes increasingly difficult and costly to repress demands for political liberalization.

In short, economic development leads to cultural changes that make mass publics more likely to *want* democracy and more skillful at *getting* it.

Changing Values and a Changing Political Agenda

The goals of both individuals and societies are changing as a result of the diminishing marginal utility of economic growth. In this respect, cultural change behaves as if it were a rational response to the changing socioeconomic environment. These shifts at both individual and societal levels are transforming the political agenda of advanced industrial societies, giving rise to new issues, new political movements, and new political parties.

The rise of Postmodern values changed the political agenda throughout advanced industrial society, moving it away from an emphasis on economic growth at any price, toward increasing concern for its environmental costs. It has also brought a shift from political cleavages based on social class conflict, toward cleavages based on cultural issues and quality of life concerns. Economic conflicts remain important. But in the past they dominated the scene to such a degree that many observers thought that economics was virtually the whole story. Today, this view seems less plausible. Economic conflicts are increasingly sharing the stage with new issues that were almost invisible a generation ago: environmental protection, abortion, ethnic conflicts, women's rights, and gay and lesbian rights are heated issues today. Conversely, the core of the Marxist program, state ownership and management of industry, has become virtually a forgotten cause.

A new dimension of political conflict has become increasingly salient: it reflects a polarization between Modern and Postmodern worldviews. This new dimension cuts across the traditional Left-Right conflict over ownership of the means of production and distribution of income. Its growing salience is transforming the meaning of Left and Right and changing the social bases of Left and Right. Historically, support for the Left was based on the working class, while the Right drew primarily on the middle and upper classes. Today, increasingly, support for the Left comes from middle-class Postmaterialists, while a new Right draws support from less secure segments of the working class. The new cleavage pits culturally conservative and xenophobic forces, disproportionately supported by Materialists, against change-oriented movements and parties, emphasizing gender and cultural issues and environmental protection, and disproportionately supported by Postmaterialists.

The role of cultural changes in the rise of new political cleavages is complex. The forces that gave rise to the Ecologists (on one hand) and the National Front (on the other) in France, or the Greens and the Republikaner in Germany, cannot give rise to similar parties in a society like the United States, because of institutional constraints that make it difficult for new parties to emerge here— even though the same forces clearly are present. And even in societies with proportional representation, the success of such parties partly depends on the strategies adopted by their leaders. But a less obvious change *has* taken place: the issues underlying U.S. politics have changed profoundly, with the old parties adopting the same new agenda as in other advanced industrial societies.

PREDICTABLE PATTERNS OF CHANGE

Changing cultural emphases on economic growth, global democratization, and the rise of new issues all reflect the fact that both Modernization and Postmodernization bring broad clusters of changes that are, to some extent, *predictable*. This predictability has three aspects:

1. We find predictable syndromes of economic, cultural, and political change: they are predictable in the sense that a broad range of characteristics are *linked*: if you know one component, you can predict the other components with far better than random success.

2. If the foregoing is true it follows that, when specific economic changes are known to be taking place, one can make predictions about future cultural and political changes. For example, if educational levels or income levels are rising, they may have predictable cultural consequences. And, as we have seen, rising levels of existential security also have predictable cultural consequences. These are probabilistic predictions. They will not come true in every case, because the predictions are based on only one component of reality, and reality is influenced by many factors. Nevertheless, over many societies, in the long run, certain outcomes tend to emerge with far greater likelihood than others.

3. When intergenerational population replacement processes are involved, they provide another element of predictability. Because important elements of culture, such as basic values and educational levels, tend to change through intergenerational population replacement, when intergenerational differences are observed one can predict the changes that will result from intergenerational population replacement. Furthermore, using a technique developed by Abram-

son, one can calculate not only the direction but the *amount* of change that intergenerational population replacement should produce—and the amount observed since 1970 is very near this predicted value.

Population replacement is not the only factor involved, but in the long run, a knowledge of intergenerational differences in basic values enables one to predict, with far better than random success, the direction of change, and even the amount of change, that will take place per year as a result of this process.

A broad cultural shift is occurring, involving orientations toward politics, work, religion, leisure, and norms governing childbearing, childrearing, and sexual behavior. The shift is not universal: it reflects the degree to which given birth cohorts have experienced security or insecurity during their preadult years. Intergenerational value differences are small or nonexistent in societies that have not experienced economic growth during the past three or four decades. But most societies around the world *have* experienced rising standards of living, and in them one finds significant intergenerational differences in many basic values. Thus, in 18 of the 21 societies for which we have data from both the 1981 and 1990 World Values surveys, most of these values shifted in the predicted direction during this period.

We are dealing with a coherent syndrome of changes which share a common cause: relative security during one's formative years. In the 1981 data, a number of variables showed a pattern that suggested intergenerational change: (1) young and old showed contrasting values, and (2) these variables were strongly correlated with Materialist/Postmaterialist values, with the young differing from the old in the same way as Postmaterialists differed from Materialists. When this pattern was present, we interpreted it as indicating a cultural shift, in which the values of the young and the Postmaterialists would become more widespread as time went by (Inglehart, 1988, 1990).

Intergenerational population replacement is not the only factor involved: period effects, reflecting current conditions, also have an impact—but the direction of their impact is predictable. Since our theory holds that these changes are driven by rising levels of security, we would expect the period effects to move accordingly: a major decline in the economic and physical security experienced by a given society would tend to retard or reverse the effects of intergenerational population replacement, and periods of exceptional prosperity would tend to magnify the effects of generational change.

A total of 40 variables in our 1981 survey showed strong correlations with Materialist/Postmaterialist values. These 40 variables ranged from values concerning work, to attitudes concerning gender roles, homosexuality, and political participation; though diverse, they all are influenced by the degree to which a sense of basic security or insecurity has shaped one's outlook. Our expectation was that intergenerational population replacement would tend to bring a shift toward whatever values were held by the younger, more Postmaterialist cohorts. On the whole these expectations were confirmed. We put our predictions to several hundred tests, examining the changes that took place from 1981 to 1990 in 21 countries. Our predictions were borne out most of the

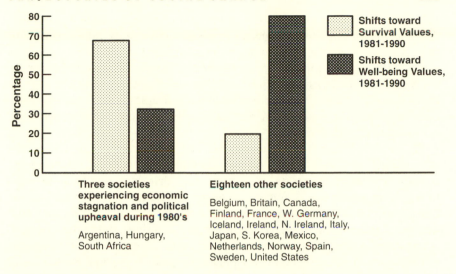

Figure 11.1. Security/Insecurity and cultural change. *Source*: 1981 and 1990 World Values surveys.

time. Economic, political, and cultural change seem to go together in coherent and broadly predictable patterns.

Nevertheless, the results of the World Values surveys show one major finding that runs counter to our predictions: four items dealing with the importance of parent-child ties were strongly correlated Postmaterialist values but did *not* move in the predicted direction from 1981 to 1990. This finding was not an isolated fluke: it appeared in society after society. It seems to reflect a reversal of trends, in which mass publics are now coming to attach more, not less, importance to parent-child ties. This may reflect a growing public awareness that the decline of the two-parent family has been linked with a wide range of social pathologies, from academic failure to drug abuse, poor health, and high crime rates.

Despite this anomaly, in most countries most items moved in the predicted direction. But in two countries, an overwhelming majority of variables moved in the other direction: in both Argentina and South Africa, fully 78 percent of the items shifted in the *opposite* direction from that predicted by the intergenerational change model. And in Hungary, only half of the values items moved in the predicted direction. These deviant cases support the hypothesis that the shift is connected with conditions of security. For all three of these countries experienced severe economic decline and political upheaval during 1981–90: powerful short-term influences offset the effects of intergenerational value change. In the 18 remaining countries, almost 80 percent of the observed shifts moved in the predicted direction.

Figure 11.1 illustrates our overall findings concerning cultural change. As it indicates, in the three societies that experienced economic stagnation and political upheaval during the 1980s, most of these variables shifted *away* from the Postmodern pole, toward greater emphasis on survival values. But these three societies were exceptional. In the 18 societies that experienced more or less normal conditions during the 1980s, these same variables overwhelmingly shifted toward the Postmodern pole. In other words, under conditions of insecurity we find a consistent and predictable cultural shift in one direction; under conditions of rising security, we find an equally coherent and overwhelming shift in the opposite direction.

This is an exciting finding: it suggests that social science can sometimes have predictive power. When dealing with relatively enduring aspects of the outlook of given birth cohorts, we can anticipate that change will tend to move in a specific direction, as intergenerational population replacement occurs. Other factors such as the rise and fall of the economic cycle and war or peace also shape the outlook of a given society at a given time. But in the long run, across many societies, such situational factors tend to cancel each other out: the influence of intergenerational population replacement, on the other hand, tends to work in a specific direction for many decades, and its cumulative impact can be decisive.

To sum up our findings about cultural change in cross-national perspective, let us turn to figure 11.2. This figure maps each of our more than 40 societies on the Modernization and Postmodernization dimensions, respectively. This map is similar to figure 3.5. But we go beyond this earlier figure here, presenting a dynamic perspective: with every society for which we have valid data from both 1981 and 1990, we show its position at both time points. Thus, figure 11.2 shows two dots for Sweden, labeled Sweden 81 and Sweden 90, showing the position of the Swedish public as measured in the 1981 and 1990 surveys, respectively.

This graph is based on a factor analysis that utilizes only about half as many variables as the one underlying figure 3.5, since we used only those indicators of the Modernization and Postmodernization dimensions that were included in both surveys. Figure A.27 (in Appendix 3) shows the variables we used in this analysis and their loadings on the two main axes. Although it uses 22 more surveys and 20 fewer variables than the corresponding analysis based on the 1990 data only, the resulting factor structure is a close approximation of the one shown in chapter 3 (see figure 3.2). And on the whole, the positions of the given societies are similar to those they had in 1990.

The massive database underlying figure 11.2 (based on 65 surveys, carried out in 44 societies) indicates that we are dealing with coherent and stable cross-cultural differences. Although we are particularly interested in the *changes* that occur from 1981 to 1990, let us emphasize the fact that the position of each society in 1981 is relatively close to its position in 1990: the societies' locations are anything but random. Thus, Sweden 81 is located relatively near to Sweden 90; and USA 81 is relatively close to USA 90; as are South Korea 81 and South Korea 90, Spain 81 and Spain 90, and so on. This reflects the fact that the basic cultural values of given societies are relatively stable.

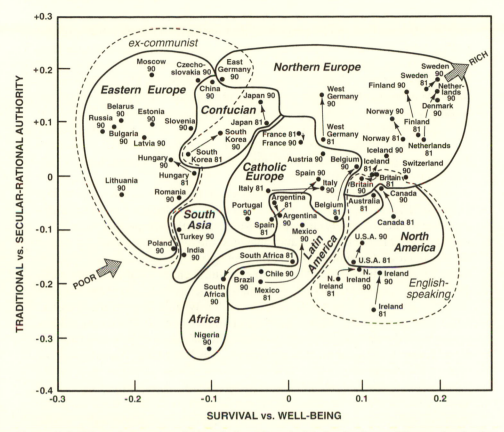

Figure 11.2. Where the peoples of 44 societies fall on the Modernization and Postmodernization dimensions in 1981 and 1990.
Positions are based on the mean scores of the respective publics on each of the two dimensions.
Source: 1981–93 World Values surveys.

Moreover, these societies fall into coherent clusters. Although we are dealing with 22 additional surveys, the same basic pattern emerges as the one we saw earlier, in figure 3.5. This pattern reflects a variety of influences: the broadest generalization is that the locations of these societies tends to reflect their levels of economic development, with the poorer societies located toward the lower left-hand corner and the richer ones near the upper right-hand corner of figure 11.2. But a society's religious heritage, language, geographic location, and whether or not it experienced communist domination all seem to influence the cultural locations of these societies. Thus the Nordic societies constitute a coherent cluster near the upper right; and they form part of a broader (historically Protestant) Northern European cluster. The countries of Catholic Europe form another coherent cluster, as do the Confucian-influenced societies of East Asia. Eastern Europe forms another cluster; and it falls into a broader ex-communist zone that incorporates Eastern Europe, plus culturally adjacent portions of Northern Europe and East Asia. The United States and Canada form a compact North American cluster into which all four surveys fall; but this in turn is part of a broader English-speaking zone that includes Great Britain (at both time points) and the Republic of Ireland and Northern Ireland (in both 1981 and 1990). Australia 81 also falls into this English-speaking zone, adding one more element of coherence: Australia was not included in the 1990 survey, so it did not appear in our previous analyses—but it was surveyed in 1981, and the basic values of the Australian public fall neatly into the English-speaking cluster. Despite its great geographical distance, culturally speaking Australia is a close neighbor of Britain and Canada. We find a stable and coherent pattern of cross-cultural differences.

But significant cultural changes have been taking place, and they are visible in figure 11.2. And though this analysis is based on a different set of variables from the 40 items closely linked with Materialist/Postmaterialist values that were analyzed in the two preceding chapters, the overall pattern of changes is fairly similar to that summarized in figure 11.1.

The most striking aspect of this map of cultural change is the fact that most of the arrows point upward or to the right: this means that most of the changes are moving away from the Traditional authority pole toward the Secular-rational authority pole; or from Survival values toward the Well-being values. In other words, the main shift is from the cultural values linked with *low* levels of economic development, toward the values linked with *higher* levels of economic development.

But some of these shifts move in the opposite direction, toward traditional values and survival values, and the pattern is far from random. All three of the societies that were undergoing economic stagnation and political collapse show shifts that are mainly downward or to the left. In the case of Argentina, the movement is minimal. In the case of Hungary, it is more substantial, with the main component of change being toward stronger emphasis on survival values, and a secondary component of secularization. The South African public shows the largest changes of all, with a sizable shift toward survival values and a lesser movement toward traditional religious authority.

The 18 remaining societies for which we have data on cultural change experienced relatively normal conditions. In 16 of these 18 cases the main shift is upward or to the right (or both)—that is, in the direction linked with economic development. Social change is influenced by many factors, and this generalization has some exceptions: Great Britain showed a net shift toward emphasis on survival values from 1981 to 1990; and the French public showed a slight movement toward emphasis on traditional religious authority (though the shift is so small that it may simply reflect sampling error). But in South Korea, Japan, Western Germany, Norway, Iceland, Finland, Sweden, the Netherlands, Ireland, Northern Ireland, Belgium, Italy, Spain, Canada, the United States, and Mexico, the main shift is either upward or to the right or both. Some of these shifts are minimal, but some are rather large. And to a considerably greater than random degree, cultural change has been moving in the direction of Modernization and Postmodernization: though it is far from perfect, there is some degree of predictability to cultural change.

Let us emphasize that this pattern of predominant shifts does not apply to the entire world. The subset of societies for which we have data from both 1981 and 1990 overrepresents the more prosperous and stable societies (it is generally difficult to carry out survey research in impoverished and unstable societies). Hungary and South Africa exemplify a trend that is underrepresented here: we would *not* expect to find a movement toward the secular and well-being values in societies undergoing traumatic changes. This is an important point. Much of the world, including most of the former Soviet Union, is currently in turmoil. We would *not* expect to find a shift toward Postmodern values in these societies; instead, we would expect to find a shift toward greater emphasis on traditional authority and survival values under these conditions.

On the other hand, after a difficult transition, Poland currently is enjoying the highest rate of economic growth in Europe; Eastern Germany (with massive aid from the West) is also rapidly rebuilding its economy; and the Czech Republic, Slovenia, and Estonia are in relatively good economic shape. Eastern Germany in 1990 was already relatively near to being a part of Northern Europe; we would expect it to move closer to Western Germany, and these other societies to gradually become part of Europe during the next decade. Future waves of the World Values survey will reveal whether these expectations are fulfilled.

WHY DID THE POSTMODERN SHIFT OCCUR? DIMINISHING MARGINAL RETURNS FROM ECONOMIC DEVELOPMENT

The shift from Modernization to Postmodernization reflects the diminishing marginal utility of economic determinism: economic factors tend to play a decisive role under conditions of economic scarcity, but as scarcity diminishes, other factors shape society to an increasing degree.

From a rational actor's perspective, economic development should eventually bring a shift in survival strategies. At low levels of economic development, even modest economic gains bring a high return in terms of caloric intake, clothing, shelter, medical care, and life expectancy itself. Under these conditions, giving top priority to economic growth is a highly effective survival strategy. Societies are not rational actors, but they behave as if they were—in the long run. Once a society has reached a certain threshold of development, further economic growth brings only minimal gains in both life expectancy and in subjective well-being. Noneconomic aspects of life become increasingly important influences on how long and how well a people live. Beyond this point, a rational strategy would be to place increasing emphasis on quality of life concerns, rather than to continue the inflexible pursuit of economic growth as if it were a good in itself.

Once industrialization became possible, modernizing societies focused on rapid economic growth as the best way of maximizing survival and well-being. But no strategy is optimal for all circumstances. Modernization was dramatically successful in raising life expectancies, but it has begun to produce diminishing returns in advanced industrial societies. Postmodernization is a shift in survival strategies, moving from maximizing economic growth to maximizing survival and well-being, through lifestyle changes.

BEYOND POSTMODERNISM?

Every stable culture is linked with a congruent authority system. But the Postmodern shift is a move away from both traditional authority and state authority. We find declining confidence in hierarchical institutions throughout advanced industrial society. By the early 1990s, political leaders around the world were experiencing some of the lowest levels of support ever recorded. This was not just because they were less competent than their predecessors: it reflects a systematic decline in the basis of mass support for established political institutions.

Such trends cannot continue forever. Political systems either adapt in ways that generate internalized support, or they collapse and are replaced by new political systems. Ultimately, the systems that emerge and survive will be systems that have found some effective legitimating formula. This formula, whatever it is, may mark the emergence of Post-Postmodern politics.

Similarly, the role of the family has been diminishing for many decades. The logical endpoint once seemed to be its complete disappearance, with reproduction and childrearing being taken over by the state as envisioned in *Brave New World* (Huxley, 1932). In the decade from 1981 to 1990, this trend seems to have reached its natural limits.

All societies that survive for long have social norms limiting reproduction and violence, based on a moral order that makes it possible to govern societies without depending solely on external coercion. Growing permissiveness and increasing room for individual autonomy from societal constraints have been the dominant trend in the evolution of social norms throughout the past century. The apparent reversal of this trend in the area of family values raises the question "Is the Postmodern trend approaching natural limits in other areas as well?" We do not yet find evidence that advanced industrial societies have reached a Post-Postmodern threshold in other domains. During the period from 1981 to 1990, the great majority of changes moved in the Postmodern direction. But no trend goes on in the same direction forever. Just as Modernization eventually gave way to Postmodernization, we can safely assume that Postmodernization is not the final stage of history. The past few decades have seen massive cultural change, and most of the innovation has come from the Postmodern side, which has largely controlled the agenda for change. But all trends eventually reach limits. The question is simply *when* this will happen with Postmodernism.

Postmodernism is many sided, and some components might continue while others taper off. One aspect of Postmodernism that seems likely to have a limited life span is the rejection of rationality itself. Since the species emerged, reason has been the key instrument for human coping with the environment. It will not be discarded. What is likely to happen, instead, is a shift away from the overemphasis on instrumental rationality that characterized industrial society, toward a more balanced synthesis of functional rationality and a renewed concern for ultimate ends, in which the pursuit of human well-being and self-expression is a major component.

Postmodern societies emerged as a consequence of Modernization, which eventually gave rise to such a high level of existential security that survival came to be taken for granted by growing segments of those societies. The application of reason through science and technology solved the problems of subsistence to such an extent that instrumental rationality eventually became less crucial. But the Postmodern worldview would ultimately collapse without the economic and technological base that it increasingly takes for granted. Some Postmodern thinkers may see themselves as antimodern, but they are, in fact, profoundly *post*modern: they reflect a worldview that could only come after the successful attainment of modernity.

Postmodern discourse sometimes claims that there is a radical discontinuity between modernity and postmodernity. Postmodernity does reflect a major change, but it grows out of modernity. Postmodern values would be difficult to sustain without a thriving industrial and technological infrastructure. Even in terms of Postmodern values, the rejection of modernity would be unattractive if it meant going back to a life expectancy of 35 years, coupled with the need for sexual abstinence before marriage and for women to spend their entire adult lives in childbearing and childrearing. Postmodernity must necessarily coexist with modernity.

Postmodernity reflects a rejection of instrumental rationality and an increased concern for ultimate ends, but, ironically, many Postmodern thinkers have given up on the quest for any universal moral consensus: moral rules are held to be merely conventions that simply reflect the interests of the dominant elite. All that is left for philosophers to do is to debunk whatever moral systems do appear.

Habermas has not given up: he believes that a valid moral consensus can be reached, provided that it is arrived at through communication free from domination—a goal that is difficult but not impossible. Evidence presented above indicates that, although belief systems generally do support a given political and economic order, value systems are not simply elite-dominated myths: the worldviews that eventually prevail also reflect the life experience of ordinary people, and official doctrine is not credible in the long run unless it also corresponds to this life experience. Thus, the ability of elites to manipulate the masses is limited. Elites are, by definition, people who have more influence than most people; but ordinary people are not always gullible. As Abraham Lincoln put it, "You may fool all the people some of the time; and you can even fool some of the people all the time; but you can't fool all of the people all the time." Moreover, evidence presented here suggests that, as ordinary people obtain greater resources, going from being illiterate peasants to become relatively secure, well-educated people, the balance between elites and masses shifts in favor of the masses. It is not as easy to manipulate highly educated publics, who have access to a wide variety of ideas, as it is an illiterate public who may be unaware of any alternative to the official truth. The goal of a consensus on ultimate goals, freely arrived at, is not totally unrealistic.

Habermas's quest for a new moral consensus, reached through free rational debate, is not an impossible goal. But it may be too intellectual an approach. There are two competing alternatives, both of which have the advantage of appealing to standards that are already present.

The ideologues of the ecology movement present nature as an objective standard that is a given, as natural law was claimed to be. Nature has a major asset: like tradition, it is not merely conventional but given to us from outside. Traditional belief systems held that "Whatever is, is Right" (either because it was ordained by God, or because it reflected the collective wisdom of the ages). High ecology holds that "Whatever is natural is Right," because it reflects the result of evolutionary and ecological equilibria. Ecology also has the advantage of universality—it transcends the cultural heritages of different societies: there is one Mother Earth for all of us.

The chief remaining alternative is the revival of tradition—including traditional religions. Tradition has the asset of hallowed age; for many people, its norms have been familiar since youth and were familiar to their parents and grandparents. But it also has a major disadvantage: the mythology of traditional religion is clothed in archaic symbols that emerged in pastoral or agrarian societies. The image of God as "the Good Shepherd" is less compelling in an era when most people have far more daily contact with computers than with sheep. Moreover, traditional religions can be dangerously divisive in an increasingly global society: they present the traditional normative system of a specific culture as absolute and universal values. The rigidity of any absolute belief system can give rise to fanatic intolerance, as the historical struggles between Christianity and Islam or between Protestant and Catholic demonstrate.

To function in Postmodern societies, religion would need to take on a universal perspective and become integrated with the intellectual heritage of natural science, which is an important part of most people's consciousness in these societies. Some thinkers have been moving in this direction. Teilhard de Chardin (1959), for example, views the universe as incomplete, with both human society and God still being constructed. Humanity is not a helpless puppet but plays a decisive role as the story unfolds. From this perspective, the account of creation in the book of Genesis could be seen as a first approximation, in pastoral imagery, of the more recent account provided by the Big Bang theory—which is also no more than a rough approximation of the ultimate account. Both traditional religion and modern science provide successive approximations of a truth that is vast beyond human comprehension: a thousand years from now humanity will probably know a great deal more than now, but still have an ant's view of the universe. Humans are rational beings that need both material sustenance and a moral orientation in order to function well. The search for meaning and purpose in life will continue.

At this point in time, the publics of advanced industrial societies are moving toward Postmodern values and placing increasing emphasis on the quality of life. Empirical evidence from around the world shows that cultural patterns are closely linked with the economic and political characteristics of given societies. The Modernization syndrome is linked with a shift from traditional to rational-legal values; but the emergence of advanced industrial society gives rise to a shift from survival values to postmodern values, in which a variety of changes, from equal rights for women to the emergence of democratic political institutions, become increasingly likely.

Economic, cultural, and political change go together in coherent patterns, and they are changing the world in broadly predictable ways.

A NOTE ON SAMPLING; FIGURES A.1 AND A.2

THE WORLD VALUES SURVEYS provide a broader range of variation than has ever before been available for analyzing the values and attitudes of mass publics. The 1990–93 surveys were carried out in 43 societies representing almost 70 percent of the world's population and covering the full range of variation, from societies with per capita incomes as low as $300 per year to societies with per capita incomes as high as $30,000 per year, and from long-established democracies with market economies to ex-socialist states and authoritarian states. The 1981–84 surveys provide time series data for 22 of these societies, enabling us to analyze the changes in values and attitudes that took place during the years between the two sets of surveys.

The World Values surveys grew out of a study launched by the European Values Systems Study Group (EVSSG) under the leadership of Jan Kerkhofs and Ruud de Moor, with an advisory committee consisting of Gordon Heald, Juan Linz, Elisabeth Noelle-Neumann, Jacques Rabier, and Helene Riffault. In 1981 the EVSSG carried out surveys in 10 West European societies; it evoked such widespread interest that it was replicated in 14 additional countries.

Findings from these surveys suggested that predictable cultural changes were taking place: many variables showing large intergenerational differences were strongly correlated with Postmaterialist values. To monitor possible changes, a new wave of surveys was designed and pretested and went into the field in 1990. This second wave of surveys built on findings from the 1981 European Values Survey but was designed to be carried out globally. It was designed and coordinated by Karel Dobbelaere, Loek Halman, Stephen Harding, Felix Heunks, Ronald Inglehart, Jan Kerkhofs, Renate Koecher, Jacques Rabier, and Noel Timms, with Ruud de Moor serving as chair. Inglehart organized the surveys in the non-European countries and in several East European countries.

Most of the first-wave World Values surveys were carried out in spring 1981, but fieldwork for the South Korean survey took place in 1982, and fieldwork for the Argentine survey was in 1984. Similarly, most of the second-wave surveys were carried out in 1990, but two (the Swiss and Polish surveys) completed their fieldwork in 1989, and two surveys (those in Russia and Turkey) were completed in early 1991, while another (in Slovenia) was carried out in early 1992, and still another (in Romania) was carried out in spring 1993.

SAMPLING, FIELDWORK, AND PRINCIPAL INVESTIGATORS FOR THE 1990 SURVEYS

Survey organizations, sample sizes, fieldwork period, and the principal investigators for each country are shown below. If not otherwise noted, the investigator is affiliated with the institution that carried out fieldwork:

ARGENTINA—Instituto Gallup de la Argentina (Buenos Aires) N = 1,001; February–April 1991. Principal investigator, Marita Carballo de Cilley, Catholic University of Argentina.

AUSTRIA—Fessel + GFK Institut (Vienna) N = 1,460; June–July 1990. Principal investigators, Paul Zulehner and Christian Friesl, University of Vienna.

BELARUS—Institute of Sociology, Belarus Academy of Sciences (Minsk) N = 1,015; October–November 1990. Principal investigator, Andrei Vardomatski.

BELGIUM—Dimaraso-Gallup, Belgium (Brussels) N = 2,792; June 1990. Principal investigators, Jan Kerkhofs and Karel Dobbelaere, University of Leuven, and Jacques-Rene Rabier, formerly of the Commission of the European Communities.

BRAZIL—Instituto Gallup de Opiniao Publica (São Paolo) N = 1,782; October 1991–January 1992. Principal investigator, Carlos Eduardo Meirelles Matheus.

BRITAIN—Gallup (London) N = 1,484; June–September 1990. Principal investigators, David Barker, Stephen Harding, Gordon Heald, and Noel Timms, University of Leicester.

BULGARIA—National Public Opinion Center (Sofia) N = 1,034; August 1990. Principal investigators, Andrei Raichev and Kancho Stoichev.

CANADA—Gallup-Canada (Toronto) N = 1,730; May–June 1990. Principal investigators, Neil Nevitte, University of Calgary, and Ronald Inglehart, University of Michigan.

CHILE—Centro de Estudios de la Realidad Contemporanea (Santiago) N = 1,500; May 1990. Principal investigators, Carlos Huneeus and Marta Lagos, Academia de Humanismo Cristiano.

CHINA—China Statistical Information Center (Beijing), N = 1,000; July–December 1990. Principal investigators, Jiang Xingrong, Xiang Zongde, and Ronald Inglehart.

CZECHOSLOVAKIA—Association for Independent Social Analysis (Prague) N = 1,396; September 1990. Principal investigators, Vladimir Rak, Marek Boguszak, and Ivan Gabal, Association for Independent Social Analysis, Blanka Filipcova, Institute of Sociology, Czechoslovak Academy of Sciences, and Hans Dieter Klingemann, Berlin Science Center for Social Research.

DENMARK—Socialforskningsinstituttet [Danish National Institute of Social Research] (Copenhagen) N = 1,030; April–May 1990. Principal investigators, Ole Riis and Peter Gundelach, University of Aarhus.

ESTONIA—Mass Communication Research and Information Center (Tallinn) N = 1,008; June–August 1990. Principal investigators, Mikk Titma, Andrus Saar, and Hans-Dieter Klingemann.

FINLAND—Suomen Gallup [Gallup-Finland] (Helsinki) N = 588; April 1990. Principal investigators, Leila Lotti and Juhani Pehkonen.

FRANCE—Faits et Opinions (Paris) N = 1,002; June–July 1990. Principal investigator, Helene Riffault.

(EAST) GERMANY—Institut für Demoskopie (Allensbach) N = 1,336; fall 1990. Principal investigators, Renate Köcher and Elisabeth Noelle-Neumann.

(WEST) GERMANY—Institut für Demoskopie (Allensbach) N = 2,201; June–July 1990. Principal investigators, Renate Koecher and Elisabeth Noelle-Neumann.

HUNGARY—Gallup, Hungary (Budapest) N = 999; May–June 1990. Principal investigators, Elemer Hankiss and Robert Manchin, Center for Value Sociology, Hungarian Academy of Sciences.

ICELAND—University of Iceland, Social Science Research Institute, N = 702; April 1990. Principal investigators, Stefan Olafsson and Fridrik Jonsson.

INDIA—Indian Institute of Public Opinion (New Delhi) N = 2,500; July–December 1990. Principal investigators, Eric de Costa, V. P. Madhok, and Ronald Inglehart.

IRELAND—Economic and Social Research Institute (Dublin) N = 1,000; July–October 1990. Principal investigator, Michael Fogarty.

NORTHERN IRELAND—N = 304; July–September 1990. Principal investigators, David Barker, Stephen Harding, Gordon Heald, and Noel Timms.

ITALY—Centro internazionale di ricerche sociali sulle aree montane (Trento) N = 2,010; October–November 1990. Principal investigator, Renzo Gubert, University of Trento.

JAPAN—Nippon Research Center Ltd. [Gallup-Japan] (Tokyo) N = 1,011; September 1990. Principal investigator, Kenji Iijima, Nippon Research Center, and Yuji Fukuda and Seiko Yamazaki, Dentsu Institute for Human Studies.

SOUTH KOREA—Ewha University (Seoul) N = 1,251; June–July 1990. Principal investigator, Soo Young Auh, Ewha University.

LATVIA—Public Opinion Research Group, Latvian Sociological Association (Riga) N = 903; June–August 1990. Principal investigators, Brigita Zepa and Hans-Dieter Klingemann.

LITHUANIA—Vilnius State University Sociological Laboratory (Vilnius) N = 1,000; June–August 1990. Principal investigators, Rasa Alishauskiene and Hans-Dieter Klingemann.

MEXICO—Market and Opinion Research International [MORI de Mexico] (Mexico City) N = 1,531; May 1990. Principal investigators, Miguel Basanez, Instituto Tecnologico Autonomo de Mexico, and Ronald Inglehart.

MOSCOW—Institute of Sociology, Soviet Academy of Sciences (Moscow) N = 1,012; October–November 1990. Principal investigators, Elena Bashkirova and Vladimir Yadov.

NETHERLANDS—Institut voor Sociaal-Wetenschappelijk Onderzoek (Tilburg) N = 1,017; June–August 1990. Principal investigators, Ruud de Moor, Felix Heunks, and Loek Halman, University of Tilburg.

NIGERIA—Research and Marketing Services, Ltd. [Gallup-Nigeria] (Lagos) N = 939; May–June 1990. Principal investigators, Kareem Tejumola and Ronald Inglehart.

NORWAY—Survey division of Norwegian Central Bureau of Statistics (Oslo) N = 1,239; April–June 1990. Principal investigator, Ola Listhaug, University of Trondheim

POLAND—Osrodek Badania Opinii Publicznej [survey unit of Polish Radio-Television] (Warsaw) N = 938; November–December 1989. Principal investigator, Renata Siemienska, University of Warsaw.

PORTUGAL—EuroExpansao, S.A. (Lisbon) N = 1,185; May–July 1990. Principal investigators, Luis de Franca, Jorge Vala, and J. C. Jesumo, Instituto de Estudios para o Desenvolvimento.

RUSSIA—Institute for Social and Political Research, Soviet Academy of Sciences (Moscow) N = 1,961; January 1991. Principal investigator, Vladimir Andreyenkov.

ROMANIA—Institute for Research on Quality of Life, Romanian Academy of Sciences (Bucharest) N = 1,103; spring 1993. Principal Investigators, Catalin Zamfir, Nicolae Lotreanu, and Mattei Dogan.

SLOVENIA—Center for Public Opinion Research, University of Ljubljana N = 1,035; February 1992. Principal investigator, Niko Tos.

SOUTH AFRICA—Markinor (Johannesburg) N = 2,736; October–November 1990. Principal investigator, Christine Woessner.

SPAIN—DATA, Madrid N = 2,637; April–May 1990. Principal investigators, Francisco Andres Orizo and Javier Elzo, Deusto University.

SPAIN—Analisis Sociologicas, Economicos y Politicos (ASEP) (Madrid) N = 1,510; May 1990. Principal investigator, Juan Diez Nicolas, Complutense University, Madrid.

SWEDEN—Svenska Institutet for Opinionsundersokingar (SIFO)[Gallup-Sweden] (Stockholm) N = 1,047; April–May 1990. Principal investigator, Thorleif Petterson, University of Uppsala

SWITZERLAND—ISOPUBLIC, Institut Suisse d'Opinion Publique (Zurich) N = 1,400; November 1988–February 1989. Principal investigator, Anna Melich, University of Geneva and Commission, European Community.

TURKEY—Bogazici University, Department of Political Science (Istanbul) N = 1,030; November 1990–January 1991. Principal investigators, Ustun Erguder, Yilmaz Esmer, and Ersin Kalaycioglu.

U.S.A.—The Gallup Organization (Princeton) N = 1,839; May–June 1990. Principal investigators, George Gallup, Alec Gallup, and Max Larsen, the Gallup Organization, and Ronald Inglehart, University of Michigan.

Representative national samples were interviewed in all cases except for subnational surveys in Northern Ireland and the greater Moscow region (which was surveyed in addition to the entire Russian Republic); and in 1981 a survey was carried out in the Tambov region of the Russian Republic. The quality of the samples varies from country to country. Surveys in Western countries were carried out by professional survey organizations with a great deal of experience, most of them members of the Gallup chain. In other countries they were carried out by the respective national academies of sciences or university-based institutes, some of which had carried out few previous surveys.

All of these surveys were carried out through face-to-face interviews, with a sampling universe consisting of all adult citizens aged 18 and older. Apart from the regional samples mentioned above, national samples were targeted except in the following cases: In Chile, the sample covers the central portion of the country, which contains 63 percent of the total population; the income level of this region is about 40 percent higher than the national average. In Argentina, sampling was limited to the urbanized central portion of the country, where about 70 percent of the population is concentrated, and which also has above-average incomes. In India, the sample was stratified to allocate 90 percent of the interviews to urban areas and 10 percent to rural areas, and to have 90 percent of the respondents with literate respondents (who are slightly less than 50 percent of the population). In Nigeria, the fieldwork was limited to urban areas plus a sample of rural areas within 100 kilometers of an urban center. In China the sample is 90 percent urban. The samples have been weighted accordingly to make the samples replicate the national population parameters more closely. Similarly, the 1981 surveys in Western Europe, the United States, Canada, and Mexico oversampled the youngest group aged 16–24 (by approximately 50 percent). These respondents receive proportionately less weight in the weight variable. The samples from China, India, and Nigeria undersample the illiterate and rural portions of the public and oversample the more educated and urban portions; the weight variable is designed to correct for this problem by giving greater weight to the less educated. Both the 1981 and 1990 samples from both the United States and South Africa were stratified by race; the weight variable corrects for this. The Swiss survey is stratified by language group, producing a sample that overrepresents the French- and Italian-speaking groups; it is weighted to obtain a nationally representative sample. The weight variable also corrects for obvious deviations from national population parameters in age and education in other countries. In most cases, the more highly educated are oversampled and are accordingly weighted less heavily than the less educated. In the 1990 Italian sample, however, the more educated are substantially undersampled and are weighted more heavily to compensate for it.

The surveys from low-income countries tend to have larger error margins than those from other countries. The samples from India, Nigeria, and China by design under-sampled the illiterate portion of the public and oversampled the urban areas and the more educated strata. Since the oversampled groups tend to have orientations relatively similar to those found in industrial societies, our data probably underestimate the size of cross-national differences involving these countries; nevertheless, these three countries frequently show very distinctive orientations. The present dataset is weighted to correct for these (and other) features of sampling; but it would be unrealistic to view the samples from these three countries as fully comparable to those from advanced industrial societies. We considered these societies extremely important, from both substantive and theoretic perspectives; though obtaining random probability samples from them would require far more funding than was available for this project, we accorded a high priority to including them and were willing to accept a higher error margin than is present elsewhere in order to do so.

Fieldwork was carried out by professional survey research organizations in all countries except South Korea and Turkey, where sampling was designed by faculty and interviewing was executed by students from Ewha University and Bogazici University, respectively. In most cases, stratified multistage random sampling was used, with the samples being selected in two stages. First, a random selection of sampling locations was made; this ensured that all types of locations were represented in proportion to their population. Next, a random selection of individuals was drawn up. In Great Britain, Northern Ireland, Italy, and the Republic of Ireland, individuals were selected from electoral rolls; in Slovenia they were selected from a central registry of citizens. In Norway, Sweden, and Denmark, stratified random samples were interviewed, with response rates averaging 71 percent. The United States and Canada used stratified random samples, with three callbacks. The Japanese used a stratified multistage random sample, drawing names from records maintained by local government agencies; completed interviews were obtained with 62 percent of the individuals drawn. In some other countries, the final selection was made by quota sampling with quotas assigned on the basis of sex, age, occupation, and region, using census data as a guide to the distribution of each group in the population. The Chinese survey used stratified multistage random sampling, first stratifying the provinces according to three levels of economic development, with several provinces being randomly selected within each of these strata. Within each province, approximately 20 sampling points were selected randomly, with five individuals being interviewed at each point. The population was stratified according to rural-urban residence, sex, age, occupation, and education, and within these sampling points, each stratum was sampled by quota, with a 10 percent subsample of illiterate persons. The Indian survey was stratified to cover 14 states representing different geographic and socioeconomic regions of the country, with 2,500 interviews distributed among these states in proportion to their population. Within these 14 states, about 10 percent of the Parliamentary Constituencies were selected and 50 interviews allocated to each one. The interviews were then stratified according to town size, allocating 90 percent to urban areas, but stratifying according to population within the urban sample. A quota sample was then designed that is representative in terms of age and sex, but not education, since the sample design called for 90 percent of the interviews to be carried out with the literate part of the public. Within this segment, interviews were stratified according to education. Interviews were carried out in the eight most widely spoken languages of India, but the rural 10 percent of the sample was confined to the five Hindi-speaking states in the sample. The Nigerian sample was stratified in a similar fashion, with 90 percent of the interviews being carried out with the urban and

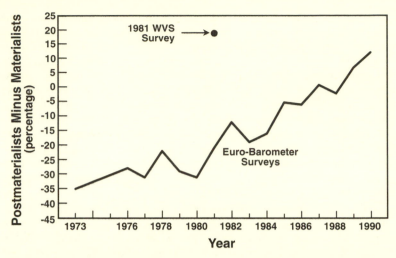

Figure A.1. Discrepancy between results from the 1981 Danish World Values Survey and the 30 Euro-Barometer surveys carried out in Denmark from 1973 to 1990.

literate segments of the population. It was then stratified by age, sex, and education within 17 provinces representing the major ethnic groups in the country. Most surveys in these countries undersample rural and illiterate respondents, who tend to give large numbers of "don't know" responses. Our samples from all three low-income countries underrepresent the rural and illiterate segments of the population; though the samples have been weighted accordingly, this compensates imperfectly. These samples do provide representative coverage of the various regions, cultural groups, and age and gender groups.

This project was a confederation of equal partners. It was carried out with very little central funding and hence with minimal central control. In most countries, funding for fieldwork and analysis was obtained from local sources. Inevitably, the quality of fieldwork varies cross-nationally; the problems are not restricted to low-income societies. The 1981 Danish survey heavily overrepresented the more educated strata; in this case, it was possible to compare certain key variables with results from other surveys, since Denmark is included in the Euro-Barometer surveys carried out each spring and fall. As figure A.1 illustrates, the results concerning Postmaterialist values from the 1981 Danish sample show major deviations from all of the other surveys carried out in that period. Hence, although the 1990 Danish sample (carried out by another institute) seems to be of excellent quality, we do not use the 1981 sample for cross-time comparisons.

Although, as we have just indicated, these data have numerous imperfections, our experience in analyzing them suggests that the results from most societies are in the right ballpark in global perspective. A variety of indications point to this conclusion. Figure A.2 provides one piece of evidence. It shows how the responses of the publics from these 43 societies compare with each other on the two major dimensions of cross-cultural variation (based on responses to scores of items) discussed in chapter 2. If there were a great deal of error in measurement, one might expect to find the various soci-

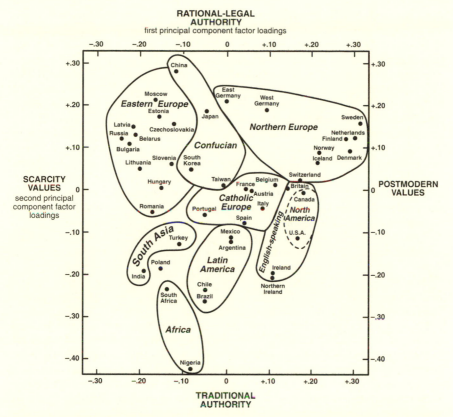

Figure A.2. Where given societies fall on two cultural dimensions: adding Taiwan to the picture. *Source*: 1990–93 World Values Survey. Positions are based on the mean scores of the publics of the given nation on each of the two dimensions.

eties scattered more or less randomly across these two key dimensions of cross-cultural variation. But the actual results show a remarkably clear and coherent pattern, as is immediately evident from inspection of figure A.2.

The four Latin American societies all fall into one coherent cluster. Though surveyed independently, they produce relatively similar results. The same is true of the United States and Canada, and of the two African societies. Their peoples' values were measured separately, by different organizations and by people who had no idea what the others were finding; nevertheless, the results from the four Latin American societies, the two African societies, or the United States and Canada are much more similar to each other than they are to other societies. They are not identical: excellent books have been written about the cultural differences between the United States and Canada, for example. But virtually all informed observers (including the authors of those books) would consider Canada to be culturally more similar to the United States than to almost any other country except, perhaps, Britain or Australia. If the Canadian public had instead shown values similar to those of China or Chile, or if Switzerland's nearest neighbor had been India, it would have given rise to understandable skepticism among informed observers. But the empirical findings are remarkably coherent.

Similarly, the Northern European societies form another cluster, with the five Nordic societies concentrated at one end and East and West Germany at the other; Catholic Europe constitutes another cluster, adjacent to Northern Europe but distinct from it. The four English-speaking societies form another cluster, with Britain next to the Northern European cluster but also proximate to Canada (which is adjacent to the United States). The three East Asian societies are also relatively close to each other. After this book had been completed, we received data from a survey carried out in Taiwan in 1994 in preparation for the 1995 World Values Survey. The results from Taiwan have been added to this figure. We find that Taiwan falls into the East Asian cluster: like the other three East Asian societies, it occupies a position on the cultural map between the Western European societies and most of the Eastern European societies. As we have seen, 10 of the 12 Eastern European societies fall into a common cluster. East Germany might seem to be an anomaly, since it falls just outside the Eastern European cluster, but its anomalous location fits historical reality perfectly: though a member of the Eastern bloc for several decades, it maintained exceptionally close ties with West Germany and is now again a part of Germany. East Germany's location on our cultural map of the world reflects this heritage, falling on the fringe of the East European cluster, and adjacent to West Germany.

Poland clearly is an outlier: though geographically and historically located in Eastern Europe, it is an intensely Catholic society, and the worldview of the Polish people emphasizes traditional cultural norms to a far greater extent than is true of other Eastern European societies, or other industrial societies more broadly. The other predominantly Roman Catholic societies of the Eastern European group (Lithuania, Hungary, and Slovenia) deviate in the same direction, but not to the same degree. We believe that Poland's deviant position reflects a genuine distinctiveness of that society; but even if we are wrong on this point, Poland is the only striking anomaly in a remarkably coherent overall pattern. The face validity of the cross-national pattern is high. With very few exceptions, 43 independently executed surveys produce results in which societies that informed observers would consider relatively similar show similar orientations.

There are a number of additional indications that the findings from these surveys are in the right ballpark. For the most part, when we can check our results against findings from other sources, they are reasonably consistent. Moreover, the pattern of internal correlations shows an excellent fit with theoretical expectations. For example, Postmaterialist values are more prevalent among the young than among the old in nearly all societies; but the strength of this relationship varies a good deal cross-culturally, being strong in those societies that have experienced rapid economic growth during the past several decades, and weak or nonexistent in those that have experienced little or no growth. This is true more broadly: the findings show remarkably coherent patterns in cross-level analyses. With a wide variety of variables, the values and attitudes of the respective publics show strong relationships with logically related macrosocietal characteristics, from economic development level to political institutions. The overall pattern of cross-national differences is remarkably coherent.

APPENDIX 2

PARTIAL 1990 WVS QUESTIONNAIRE, WITH SHORT LABELS

FOR ITEMS USED IN FIGURE 3.2

(The short labels shown on Figure 3.2 appear in bold italics)

Please say, for each of the following, how important it is in your life:

		Very Important	Quite Important	Not Very Important	Not at All Important
Work Important	A) Work	1	2	3	4
Family Important	B) Family	1	2	3	4
Friends Important	C) Friends, acquaintances	1	2	3	4
Leisure Important	D) Leisure time	1	2	3	4
Politics Important	E) Politics	1	2	3	4
Religion Important	F) Religion	1	2	3	4

Discuss Politics
When you get together with your friends, would you say you discuss political matters frequently, occasionally or never?

1 Frequently
2 Occasionally
3 Never

Not Happy
Taking all things together, would you say you are

1 Very happy
2 Quite happy
3 Not very happy
4 Not at all happy

Reject Outgroups *[Scores on this index range from 0 to 3, depending on how many of the following groups are mentioned]*
On this list are various groups of people. Could you please sort out any that you would not like to have as neighbors?

	Mentioned	Not Mentioned
I) Immigrants/foreign workers	1	2
J) People who have AIDS	1	2
L) Homosexuals	1	2

In Good Health

All in all, how would you describe your state of health these days? Would you say it is

1 Very good
2 Good
3 Fair
4 Poor
5 Very poor

Affect Balance [Scores on the Bradburn Affect Balance Scale are the number of mentions of items A, C, E, G, and I minus the sum of items B, D, F, H, and J: in short, the number of positive feelings reported minus the number of negative feelings reported]

We are interested in the way people are feeling these days. During the past few weeks, did you ever feel

	YES	NO
A) Particularly excited or interested in something	1	2
B) So restless you couldn't sit long in a chair	1	2
C) Proud because someone had complimented you on something you had done	1	2
D) Very lonely or remote from other people	1	2
E) Pleased about having accomplished something	1	2
F) Bored	1	2
G) On top of the world/feeling that life is wonderful	1	2
H) Depressed or very unhappy	1	2
I) That things were going your way	1	2
J) Upset because somebody criticized you	1	2

Trust People

Generally speaking, would you say that most people can be trusted or that you can't be too careful in dealing with people?

1 Most people can be trusted
2 Can't be too careful

Have Free Choice

Some people feel they have completely free choice and control over their lives, and other people feel that what they do has no real effect on what happens to them. Please use the scale to indicate how much freedom of choice and control you feel you have over the way your life turns out.

1	2	3	4	5	6	7	8	9	10
None at all								A great deal	

Life Satisfaction

All things considered, how satisfied are you with your life as a whole these days? Please use this card to help with your answer.

1	2	3	4	5	6	7	8	9	10
Dissatisfied								Satisfied	

State/Employee Management

There is a lot of discussion about how business and industry should be managed. Which of these four statements comes closest to your opinion?

1 The owners should run their business or appoint the managers
2 The owners and the employees should participate in the selection of managers
3 The government should be the owner and appoint the managers
4 The employees should own the business and should elect the managers

Jobs to Own Nationality

Do you agree or disagree with the following?

	Agree	Disagree	Neither
When jobs are scarce, employers should give priority to [American] people over immigrants [*countries other than U.S.: substitute own nationality*]	1	2	3

Good and Evil Are Clear

Here are two statements which people sometimes make when discussing good and evil. Which one comes closest to your own point of view?

A. There are absolutely clear guidelines about what is good and evil. These always apply to everyone, whatever the circumstances.
B. There can never be absolutely clear guidelines about what is good and evil. What is good and evil depends entirely upon the circumstances at the time.

1 Agree with statement A
2 Disagree with both
3 Agree with statement B

God Is Important

And how important is God in your life? Please use this card to indicate—10 means very important and 1 means not at all important.

1	2	3	4	5	6	7	8	9	10
Not at all									Very

Want Many Children

What do you think is the ideal size of the family—how many children, if any?

0 None
1 1 child
2 2 children
3 3 children
4 4 children
5 5 children
6 6 children
7 7 children
8 8 children
9 9 children
10 10 or more

Child Needs Both Parents
If someone says a child needs a home with both a father and a mother to grow up happily, would you tend to agree or disagree?

  1 Tend to agree
  2 Tend to disagree

Woman Needs Children
Do you think that a woman has to have children in order to be fulfilled or is this not necessary?

  1 Needs children
  2 Not necessary

Respect Parents
With which of these two statements do you tend to agree?

  A. Regardless of what the qualities and faults of one's parents are,
      one must always love and respect them
  B. One does not have the duty to respect and love parents who have not
      earned it by their behavior and attitudes

  1 Tend to agree with statement A
  2 Tend to agree with statement B

Here is a list of qualities which children can be encouraged to learn at home. Which, if any, do you consider to be especially important?

		IMPORTANT
Hard Work	C) Hard work	1
Responsibility	D) Feeling of responsibility	1
Imagination	E) Imagination	1
Tolerance	F) Tolerance and respect for other people	1
Thrift	G) Thrift, saving money and things	1
Determination	H) Determination, perseverance	1
Religious Faith	I) Religious faith	1
Obedience	K) Obedience	1

Interested in Politics
How interested would you say you are in politics?

  1 Very interested
  2 Somewhat interested
  3 Not very interested
  4 Not at all interested

Now I'd like you to tell me your views on various issues. How would you place your views on this scale? 1 means you agree completely with the statement on the left, 10 means you agree completely with the statement on the right, or you can choose any number in between.

State Responsible

Individuals should take more responsibility for providing for themselves						The state should take more responsibility to ensure that everyone is provided for			
1	2	3	4	5	6	7	8	9	10

Postmaterialist Values *[scores on this index range from 0 to 5, depending on how many of items C, F, H, J, and K are chosen as either first or second priority in their group]*

There is a lot of talk these days about what the aims of this country should be for the next 10 years. On this card are listed some of the goals which different people would give top priority. Would you please say which one of these you, yourself, consider the most important?

And which would be the next most important?

	First Choice	Second Choice
A Maintaining a high level of economic growth	1	1
B Making sure this country has strong defense forces	2	2
C Seeing that people have more to say about how things are done at their jobs and in their communities	3	3
D Trying to make our cities and countryside more beautiful	4	4

If you had to choose, which one of the things on this card would you say is most important?

And which would be the next most important?

	First Choice	Second Choice
E Maintaining order in the nation	1	1
F Giving people more say in important government decisions	2	2
G Fighting rising prices	3	3
H Protecting freedom of speech	4	4

Here is another list. In your opinion, which one of these is most important?

And what would be the next most important?

	First Choice	Second Choice
I A stable economy	1	1
J Progress toward a less impersonal and more humane society	2	2
K Progress toward a society in which ideas count more than money	3	3
L The fight against crime	4	4

Here is a list of various changes in our way of life that might take place in the near future. Please tell me for each one, if it were to happen, whether you think it would be a good thing, a bad thing, or don't you mind?

		Good	Don't Care	Bad
Money	A Less emphasis on money and material possessions	1	2	3
Technology	C More emphasis on the development of technology	1	2	3
Respect Authority	E Greater respect for authority	1	2	3

Trust Science

In the long run, do you think the scientific advances we are making will help or harm mankind?

1 Will help
2 Some of each
3 Will harm

There are a number of groups and movements looking for public support. For each of the following movements, which I read out, can you tell me whether you approve or disapprove of this movement?

		Approve		Disapprove	
		Strongly	Somewhat	Somewhat	Strongly
Ecology	A Ecology movement or nature protection	1	2	3	4
Women's Movement	E Women's movement	1	2	3	4

Please tell me for each of the following statements whether you think it can always be justified, never be justified, or something in between, using this card.

		Never Justified			In Between					Always Justified	
Homosexual OK	L Homosexuality	1	2	3	4	5	6	7	8	9	10
Abortion OK	N Abortion	1	2	3	4	5	6	7	8	9	10
Divorce OK	O Divorce	1	2	3	4	5	6	7	8	9	10

National Pride

How proud are you to be [French]? [*Countries other than France: substitute own nationality*]

1 Very proud
2 Quite proud
3 Not very proud
4 Not at all proud

DATA ON DEMOCRATIZATION

Scores on democracy, cultural, macroeconomic, and social structure variables are reported in tables A.1, A.2, A.3, and A.4 for the 43 countries of this study. The countries are listed in alphabetical order. The scores on democracy are given in table A.1. The measures include (1) the number of years of continuous democracy since 1920 (as of 1995), with a maximum score of 75 years, (2) the level of democracy in 1990 and 1995, based on the Freedom House scores, which range from 2 (low) to 14 (high), and (3) the change in the level of democracy from 1990 to 1995, computed as the 1990 level subtracted from the 1995 level. For 1990, the scores are from Freedom House, *Freedom in the World 1990*. The 1995 political rights and civil liberties rankings are from *Freedom Review* 26, no. 1 (1995): 15–16. The scores for cultural variables in table A.2 include several measures based on the 1990–91 World Values Survey. The Postmaterialist values score is the mean percentage of respondents giving first choice (out of a group of four goals) to each of the five Postmaterialist goals. It ranges from 7 percent in China to 33 percent in Finland, with a mean of 19.6 percent. While each of the four goals would be given top priority by 25 percent of the sample on a random basis, the Postmaterialist goals get top priority only 20 percent of the time. The subjective well-being index is the mean of two differences—the percent of respondents answering happy minus the percent unhappy, and the percent satisfied minus the percent dissatisfied. The interpersonal trust score is the percentage of respondents saying "most people can be trusted." Another measure from the 1990–91 World Values Survey is the percentage of respondents favoring revolutionary change, as determined by the answer to the question "The entire way our society is organized must be changed by revolutionary action." The percentage of respondents favoring gradual reform is determined by the answer to the question "Our society must be gradually improved by reforms."

The macroeconomic variables in table A.3 include GNP per capita in 1957, 1970, 1980, and 1990. GNP per capita for 1957 is from *World Handbook of Political and Social Indicators* (Russett et al., 1964, 155–57). The values for 1970, 1980, and 1990 are from *World Bank World Development Report 1993* and earlier editions. Income inequality is measured by the size of the income share received by the upper quintile of households, from studies in the 1970s and 1980s. Income inequality measures are missing for 10 countries, and all former Soviet cases are scored as the mean of the other ex-socialist countries of Eastern Europe (34 percent). The first social structure variable in table A.4 is the percentage of the nation's GDP produced by the service sector in 1988. In the second column, the percentage of the college-age population enrolled in higher education in 1988 is from the World Bank, *World Development Report 1993*, 294–95. The cumulative percentage of citizens belonging to 16 types of voluntary associations is from the 1990–91 World Values Survey. The index of ethnolinguistic fractionalization, an indicator of subcultural pluralism, is from the *World Handbook of Political and Social Indicators* (Taylor and Jodice, 1983). Expressed as a fraction between 0 and 1, it is the probability that two randomly selected persons from one country will not speak the same language.

TABLE A.1
Scores on Democracy

Country	Years of Continuous Democracy	Level of Democracy, 1990	Level of Democracy, 1995	Change, 1990–95
Argentina	10	13	11	−2
Austria	49	14	14	0
Belarus	0	5	8	3
Belgium	75	14	14	0
Brazil	9	12	10	−2
Britain	75	14	13	−1
Bulgaria	3	2	12	10
Canada	75	14	14	0
Chile	4	9	12	3
China	0	2	2	0
Czechoslovakia	4	4	13	9
Denmark	75	14	14	0
E. Germany	4	4	13	9
Estonia	3	5	11	6
Finland	75	14	14	0
France	37	13	13	0
Hungary	4	9	13	4
Iceland	75	14	14	0
India	17	11	8	−3
Ireland	75	14	13	−1
Italy	49	14	13	−1
Japan	49	14	12	−2
Latvia	3	5	11	6
Lithuania	3	5	12	7
Mexico	0	9	8	−1
Moscow	MD	5	9	4
Netherlands	75	14	14	0
Nigeria	0	5	3	−2
N. Ireland	MD	9	9	0
Norway	75	14	14	0
Poland	4	9	12	3
Portugal	18	13	14	1
Romania	0	2	9	7
Russia	0	5	9	4
Slovenia	3	2	13	11
South Africa	1	5	11	6
South Korea	3	11	12	1
Spain	17	14	13	−1
Sweden	75	14	14	0
Switzerland	75	14	14	0
Turkey	0	10	6	−4
United States	75	14	14	0
W. Germany	46	14	13	−1

TABLE A.2
Scores on Cultural Variables

Country	Post-materialist Values	Subjective Well-being	Interpersonal Trust	Percent Support Revolution	Percent Support Reform
Argentina	19	59	23	8	81
Austria	22	59	32	2	78
Belarus	14	−2	26	26	46
Belgium	27	77	33	3	76
Brazil	19	55	7	16	74
Britain	24	75	44	5	81
Bulgaria	13	4	30	22	59
Canada	25	69	52	5	82
Chile	19	53	23	5	72
China	7	42	60	7	68
Czechoslovakia	16	32	28	42	42
Denmark	23	85	58	2	76
E. Germany	19	57	26	13	84
Estonia	13	25	28	22	61
Finland	33	76	63	3	88
France	27	67	23	4	74
Hungary	12	28	25	6	77
Iceland	21	89	44	3	82
India	13	28	34	11	72
Ireland	22	80	47	4	76
Italy	27	66	37	8	84
Japan	25	54	42	2	77
Latvia	12	10	19	31	59
Lithuania	16	13	31	32	59
Mexico	21	51	33	17	71
Moscow	15	6	34	33	41
Netherlands	32	85	56	2	75
Nigeria	13	33	23	26	62
N. Ireland	20	82	44	5	75
Norway	20	81	65	2	66
Poland	13	58	35	23	65
Portugal	17	51	21	4	85
Romania	12	20	16	MD	MD
Russia	11	−1	38	15	50
Slovenia	16	23	17	14	73
South Africa	18	30	28	19	60
South Korea	18	51	34	7	83
Spain	25	65	34	4	90
Sweden	25	86	66	6	86
Switzerland	30	86	43	MD	MD
Turkey	22	47	10	14	61
United States	22	77	50	7	76
W. Germany	25	70	38	2	66

TABLE A.3
Scores on Macroeconomic Variables

Country	GNP/ Capita 1957	GNP/ Capita 1970	GNP/ Capita 1980	GNP/ Capita 1990	Income Inequality
Argentina	490	770	2,390	2,380	MD
Austria	670	1,287	10,230	19,000	MD
Belarus	600	1,234	4,140	3,110	34
Belgium	1,198	1,804	12,180	17,580	MD
Brazil	293	267	2,050	2,920	MD
Britain	1,189	1,818	7,920	16,080	39
Bulgaria	380	829	4,150	1,840	32
Canada	1,947	2,473	10,130	20,380	40
Chile	379	565	2,150	1,950	MD
China	73	109	290	370	34
Czechoslovakia	680	1,561	5,820	3,190	33
Denmark	1,057	2,120	12,950	22,440	40
E. Germany	600	1,260	7,180	12,000	MD
Estonia	600	1,628	5,531	4,170	34
Finland	794	1,749	9,720	24,540	44
France	943	1,924	11,730	19,590	46
Hungary	490	1,094	4,180	2,780	34
Iceland	572	2,469	11,330	22,090	MD
India	73	101	240	360	45
Ireland	550	980	4,880	10,370	39
Italy	516	1,104	6,480	16,882	41
Japan	306	861	9,890	25,840	41
Latvia	650	1,425	4,778	3,590	34
Lithuania	650	1,234	4,140	3,110	34
Mexico	262	455	2,090	2,490	57
Moscow	650	MD	MD	MD	34
Netherlands	836	1,554	11,470	17,570	40
Nigeria	78	84	505	290	42
N. Ireland	600	1,273	5,544	1,125	MD
Norway	1,130	1,890	12,650	22,830	39
Poland	475	978	3,900	1,690	36
Portugal	224	406	2,370	4,950	56
Romania	360	778	2,340	1,620	MD
Russia	600	1,357	4,550	3,430	34
Slovenia	400	451	2,600	3,000	MD
South Africa	395	611	2,300	2,530	62
South Korea	144	105	1,520	5,450	40
Spain	293	561	5,400	11,010	41
Sweden	1,380	2,549	13,520	23,780	37
Switzerland	1,428	2,333	16,440	32,250	45
Turkey	220	292	1,470	1,640	57
United States	2,577	3,575	11,360	21,810	41
W. Germany	927	1,901	13,590	22,360	47

TABLE A.4
Scores on Social Structure Variables

Country	Percent in Service Sector	Percent in Higher Education	Organizational Membership (Cumulative Percent)	Ethno-linguistic Fractionization
Argentina	44	22	3	.307
Austria	51	33	112	.126
Belarus	41	20	MD	MD
Belgium	64	37	145	.551
Brazil	49	12	85	.071
Britain	56	25	116	.325
Bulgaria	37	31	70	.220
Canada	56	70	170	.755
Chile	56	19	81	.140
China	21	2	83	.118
Czechoslovakia	38	18	MD	.490
Denmark	58	32	175	.049
E. Germany	39	30	168	.017
Estonia	35	20	120	MD
Finland	50	47	175	.159
France	59	40	75	.261
Hungary	49	15	72	.098
Iceland	55	32	235	.054
India	38	6	MD	.886
Ireland	52	26	93	.045
Italy	56	20	77	.038
Japan	57	31	20	.015
Latvia	35	20	118	MD
Lithuania	35	20	87	MD
Mexico	56	14	93	.305
Moscow	50	MD	MD	MD
Netherlands	58	34	242	.102
Nigeria	29	3	MD	.733
N. Ireland	56	25	115	MD
Norway	51	43	188	.039
Poland	43	22	MD	.028
Portugal	54	18	68	.006
Romania	33	9	45	.252
Russia	41	20	105	MD
Slovenia	40	18	62	MD
South Africa	49	3	MD	.877
South Korea	46	39	145	MD
Spain	57	34	15	.436
Sweden	54	33	205	.083
Switzerland	56	26	95	.504
Turkey	46	14	MD	.255
United States	65	75	185	.505
W. Germany	47	32	135	.026

TABLE A.5
Data Used in Economic Growth Regressions

Country	Growth[a]	GDP[b]	Primary[c]	Secondary[d]	Investment[e]	Four-Item[f]	Postmaterialism[g]
Austria	3.141	3.908	1.05	0.5	0.24373	0.46	2.11
Belgium	3.0639	4.379	1.09	0.69	0.19595	0.22	2.02
Brazil	3.2383	1.313	0.95	0.11	0.20599	−0.32	1.67
Canada	3.0608	6.069	1.04	0.52	0.201	0	2.14
China	5.5	0.567	0.75	0.41	0.20163	0.9	1.36
Denmark	2.4935	5.49	1.03	0.65	0.21627	0.2	1.99
Finland	3.5184	4.073	0.97	0.74	0.25217	0.38	2.23
France	2.9729	4.473	1.44	0.46	0.2224	0.09	2.04
Germany	2.7082	5.217	1.33	0.53	0.20923	0.52	2.14
India	1.9398	0.533	0.61	0.2	0.19982	−0.46	1.58
Ireland	2.9652	2.545	1.1	0.35	0.22252	−0.44	1.96
Italy	3.5253	3.233	1.11	0.34	0.22909	−0.1	2.07
Japan	5.5539	2.239	1.03	0.74	0.31723	0.82	1.81
Korea	6.6378	0.69	0.94	0.27	0.2493	0.47	1.66
Mexico	2.26	2.157	0.8	0.11	0.20675	−0.15	1.86
Netherlands	2.3531	4.69	1.05	0.58	0.19853	0.13	2.26
Nigeria	0.7517	0.552	0.36	0.03	0.147	−1.24	1.67
Norway	3.551	5.001	1.18	0.53	0.29782	0.1	1.81
South Africa	1.428	2.627	0.89	0.15	0.2555	−0.46	1.73
Spain	3.6954	2.425	1.1	0.23	0.22484	−0.24	1.94

	Growth[a]	GDP[b]	Primary[c]	Secondary[d]	Investment[e]	Four-Item[f]	Postmaterialism[g]
Sweden	2.542	5.149	0.98	0.55	0.21237	0.5	2.09
Switzerland	1.9991	6.834	1.18	0.26	0.25747	−0.03	2.1
Turkey	2.8506	1.255	0.75	0.14	0.19792	−0.19	1.95
United Kingdom	2.1637	4.97	0.95	0.67	0.15317	−0.01	2
United States	2.0976	7.38	1.18	0.86	0.13906	−0.28	2.06

[a]Growth: Growth rate of real per capita GDP from 1960 to 1989. *Source:* Levine and Renelt (1992).

[b]GDP: The 1960 value of real per capita GDP (1980 base year). *Source:* Levine and Renelt (1992).

[c]Primary: The number of students enrolled in primary school grade level relative to the total population of that age group in 1960. *Source:* Levine and Renelt (1992).

[d]Secondary: The number of students enrolled in secondary school grade level relative to the total population of that age group in 1960. *Source:* Levine and Renelt (1992).

[e]Investment: Average from 1960 to 1989 of the ratio of real domestic investment (private plus public) to real GDP. *Source:* Levine and Renelt (1992).

[f]Four-Item: Four-Item Achievement Motivation Index comprised of (Thrift + Determination) − (Obedience + Religious Faith). *Source:* 1990 World Values Survey.

[g]Postmaterialism: Mean score of Postmaterialism. Source: 1990 World Values Survey.

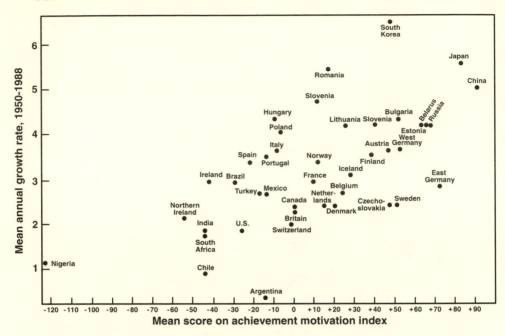

Figure A.3. Achievement motivation and economic growth (ex-socialist societies included). Mean annual economic growth rate, 1950–88, by achievement motivation index. r = .64, N = 42, significant at .0000 level. *Source*: 1981 and 1990 World Values surveys.

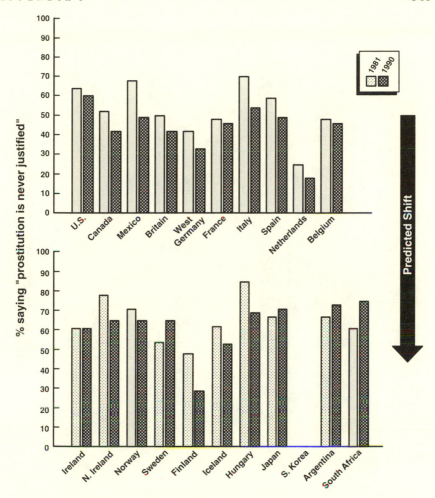

Figure A.4. Percentages saying that "Prostitution is *never* justified" in 1981 vs. 1990, in 20 countries. *Source*: 1981 and 1990 World Values surveys. Comparable data not available for South Korea.

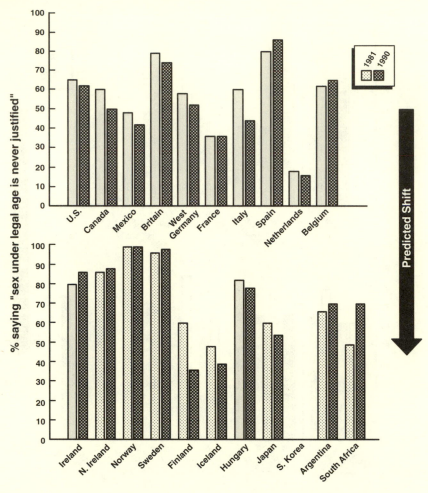

Figure A.5. Percentages saying that "Sex under the legal age is *never* justified" in 1981 vs. 1990, in 20 countries. *Source*: 1981 and 1990 World Values surveys.

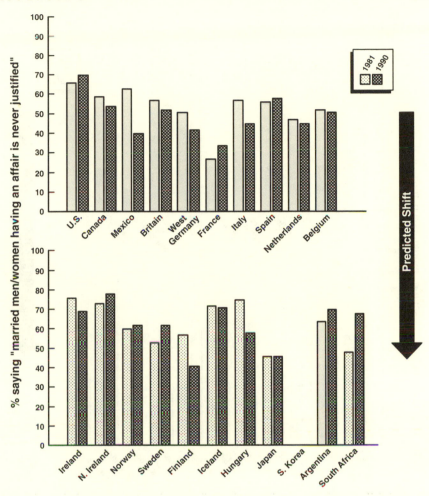

Figure A.6. Percentages saying that "Married men/women having an affair is *never* justified" in 1981 vs. 1990, in 20 countries. *Source*: 1981 and 1990 World Values surveys.

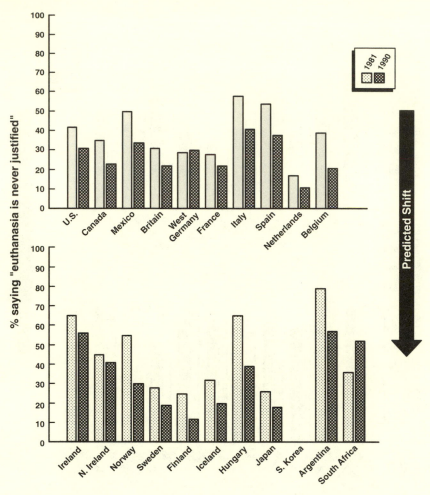

Figure A.7. Percentages saying that "Euthanasia is *never* justified" in 1981 vs. 1990, in 20 countries. *Source*: 1981 and 1990 World Values surveys.

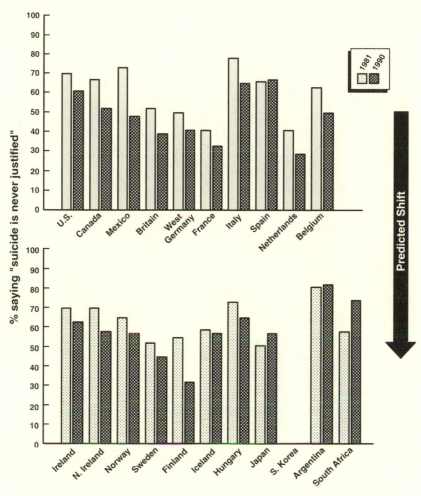

Figure A.8. Percentages saying that "Suicide is *never* justified" in 1981 vs. 1990, in 20 countries. *Source*: 1981 and 1990 World Values surveys.

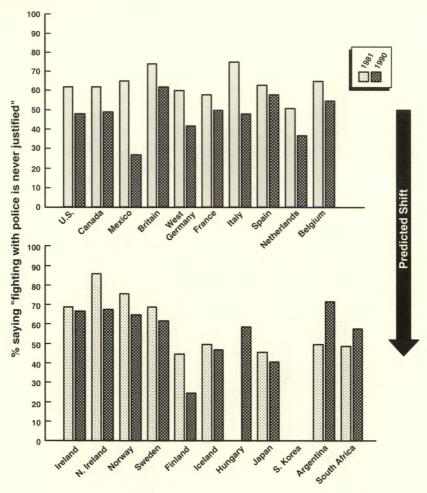

Figure A.9. Percentages saying that "Fighting with the police is *never* justified" in 1981 vs. 1990, in 20 countries. *Source*: 1981 and 1990 World Values surveys.

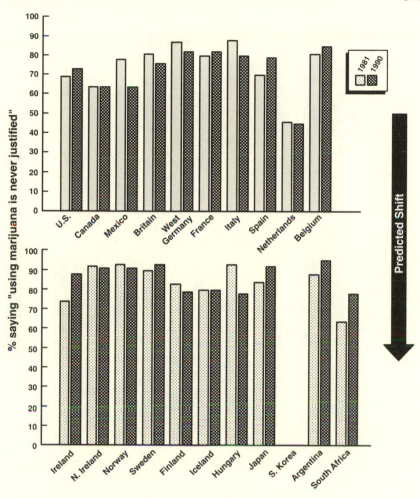

Figure A.10. Percentages saying that "Using marijuana is *never* justified" in 1981 vs. 1990, in 20 countries. *Source*: 1981 and 1990 World Values surveys.

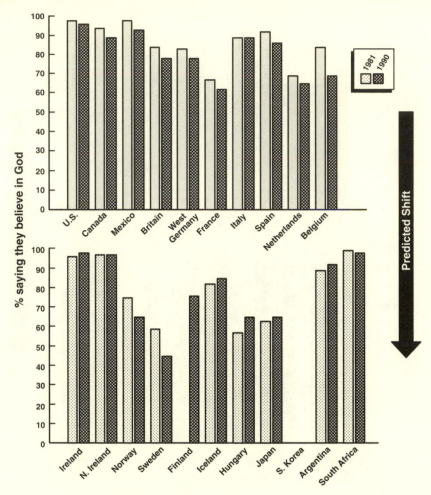

Figure A.11. Percentages saying they believe in God, in 1981 vs. 1990, in 20 countries. *Source*: 1981 and 1990 World Values surveys.

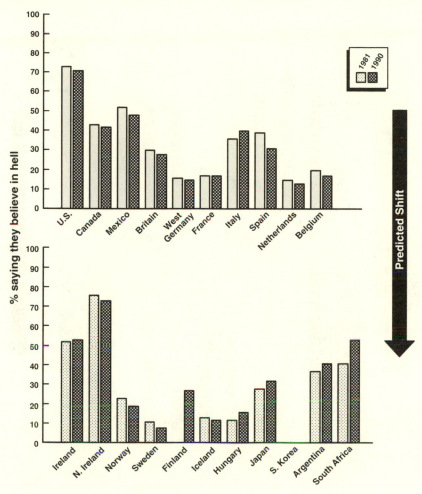

Figure A.12. Percentages saying they believe in hell, in 1981 vs. 1990, in 20 countries. *Source*: 1981 and 1990 World Values surveys.

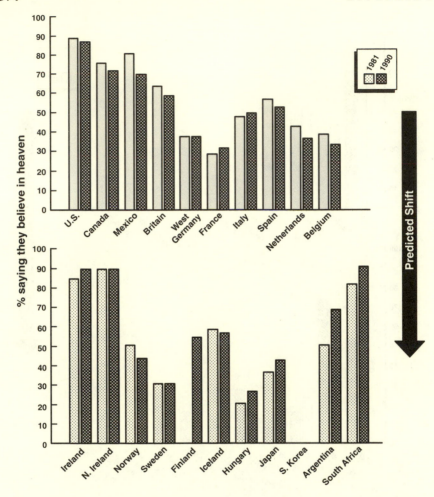

Figure A.13. Percentages saying they believe in heaven, in 1981 vs. 1990, in 20 countries. *Source*: 1981 and 1990 World Values surveys.

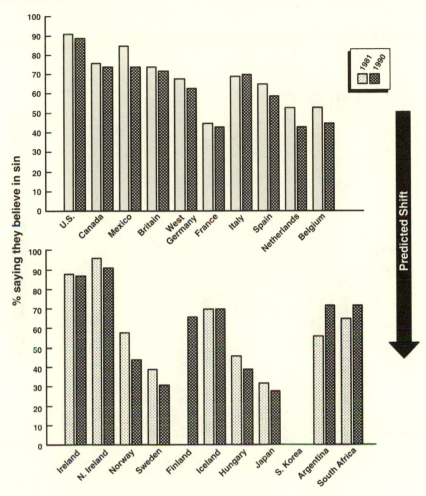

Figure A.14. Percentages saying they believe in sin, in 1981 vs. 1990, in 20 countries. *Source*: 1981 and 1990 World Values surveys.

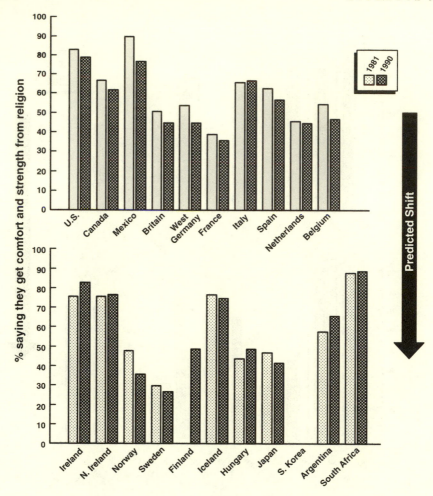

Figure A.15. Percentages saying they get comfort and strength from religion, in 1981 vs. 1990, in 20 countries. *Source*: 1981 and 1990 World Values surveys.

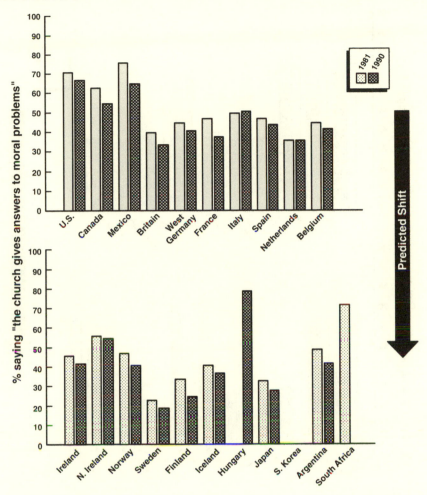

Figure A.16. Percentages saying that the church in their country is giving adequate answers to moral problems, in 1981 vs. 1990, in 20 countries. *Source*: 1981 and 1990 World Values surveys.

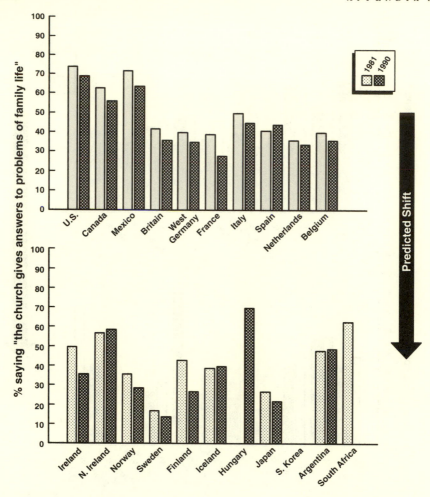

Figure A.17. Percentages saying that the church in their country is giving adequate answers to problems of family life, in 1981 vs. 1990, in 20 countries. *Source*: 1981 and 1990 World Values surveys.

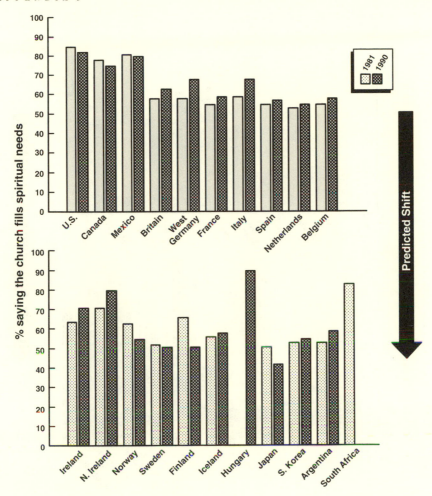

Figure A.18. Percentages saying that the church in their country is giving adequate answers to people's spiritual needs, in 1981 vs. 1990, in 20 countries. *Source*: 1981 and 1990 World Values surveys.

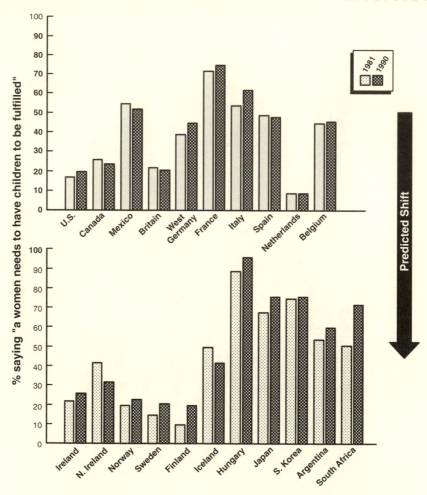

Figure A.19. Percentages saying "A woman has to have children in order to be fulfilled," in 1981 vs. 1990, in 21 countries. *Source*: 1981 and 1990 World Values surveys.

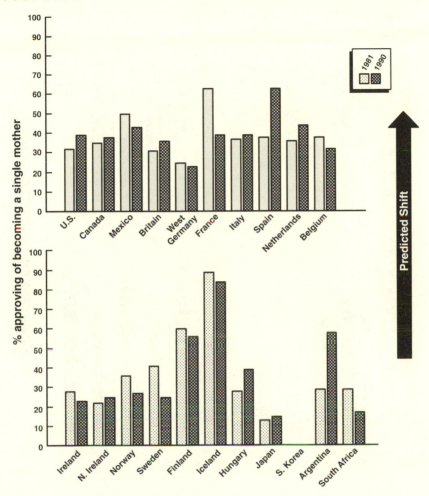

Figure A.20. Percentages approving of a woman having a child as a single parent, in 1981 vs. 1990, in 20 countries. *Source*: 1981 and 1990 World Values surveys. Not asked in South Korea.

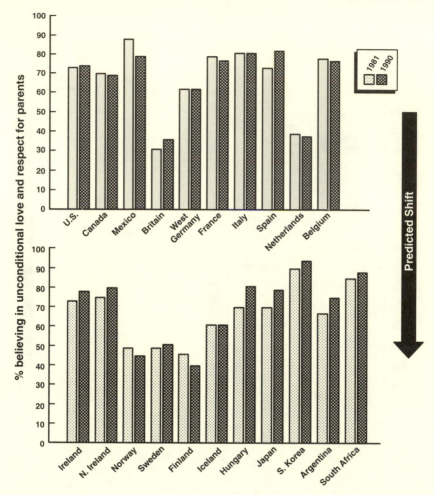

Figure A.21. Percentages believing one has a duty to love and respect one's parents, regardless of their faults, in 1981 vs. 1990, in 21 countries. *Source*: 1981 and 1990 World Values surveys.

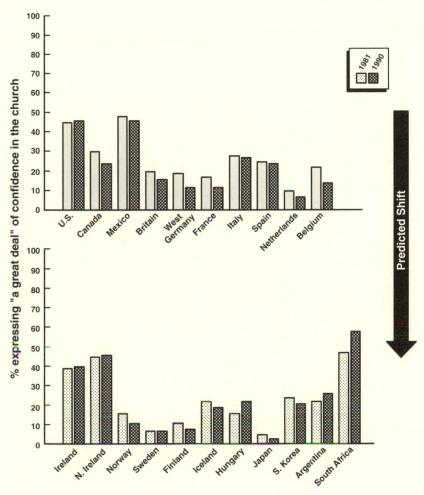

Figure A.22. Percentages expressing "a great deal" of confidence in the church in their country, in 1981 vs. 1990, in 21 countries. *Source*: 1981 and 1990 World Values surveys.

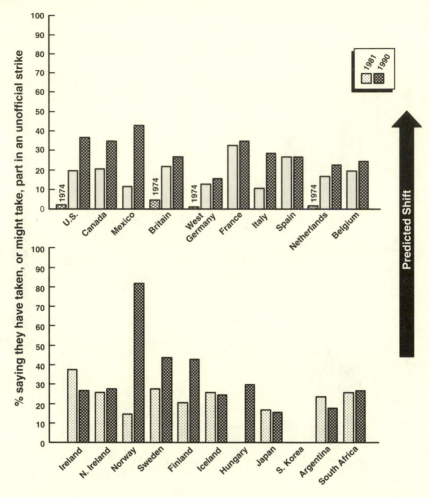

Figure A.23. Percentages saying that they have taken part in an unofficial strike, or might do so, in 1981 vs. 1990, in 20 countries. *Source*: 1981 and 1990 World Values surveys. 1981 data not available for Hungary.

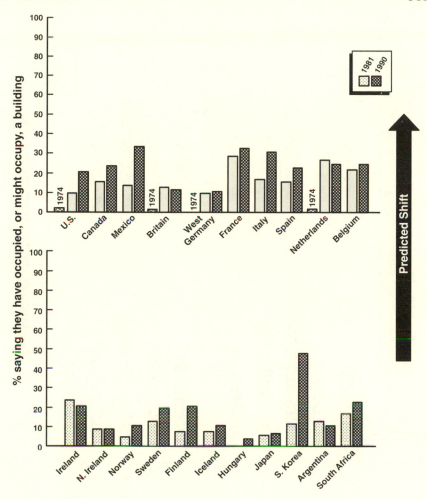

Figure A.24. Percentages saying that they have occupied a building, or might do so, in 1981 vs. 1990, in 20 countries. *Source*: 1981 and 1990 World Values surveys. 1981 data not available for Hungary.

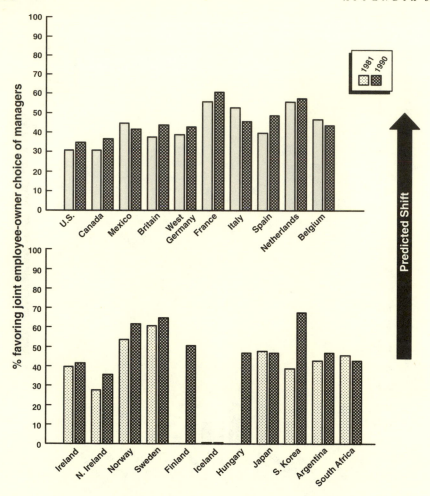

Figure A.25. Percentages favoring joint employee-owner participation in choosing managers in business and industry, in 1981 vs. 1990, in 20 countries. *Source*: 1981 and 1990 World Values surveys. 1981 data not available for Hungary.

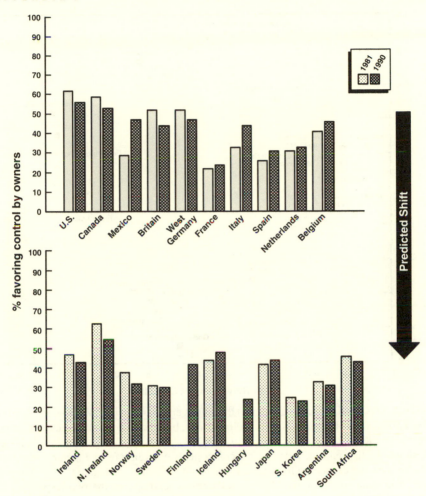

Figure A.26. Percentages favoring owner's right to choose managers in business and industry, in 1981 vs. 1990, in 20 countries. *Source*: 1981 and 1990 World Values surveys. 1981 data not available for Hungary.

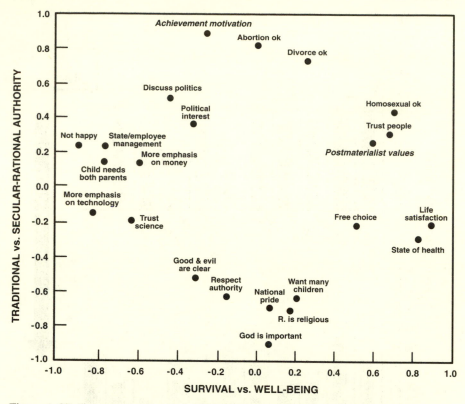

Figure A.27. Cross-national variation in the values emphasized in different societies: the Modernization and Postmodernization dimensions, based on the combined data from the 1981 and 1990 World Values surveys. *Source*: 1981–93 World Values surveys. This figure shows the first and second principal components emerging from a factor analysis of data from 65 representative national surveys of 44 societies, aggregated to the national level. The scales on the margins show each item's loadings on the two respective dimensions. The items in italics ("achievement motivation" and "Postmaterialist values") are multi-item indices.

APPENDIX 4

CONSTRUCTION OF KEY INDICES USED IN THIS BOOK

THE FOLLOWING SPSS INSTRUCTIONS show how key indices used in this book were created.

1. MATERIALIST/POSTMATERIALIST VALUES (FOUR-ITEM INDEX): [V1000]

COMPUTE V1000 = 2
IF ((V259 = 1 AND V260 = 3) OR (V259 = 3 AND V260 = 1)) V1000 = 1
IF ((V259 = 2) AND (V260 = 4)) OR ((V259 = 4) AND (V260 = 2)) V1000 = 3
(range = 1–3; missing data = 9)

This index is based on the respondent's first and second choices in the original four-item Materialist/Postmaterialist values battery. If both Materialist items are given high priority, the score is "1"; if both Postmaterialist items are given high priority, the score is "3"; if one Materialist item and one Postmaterialist item are given high priority, the score is "2." If the respondent makes only one or no choices, the result is missing data.

2. MATERIALIST/POSTMATERIALIST VALUES (12-ITEM INDEX): [V1010]

IF (V257 = 3 OR V258 = 3) V1001 = 1
IF (V259 = 2 OR V259 = 4) V1002 = 1
IF (V260 = 2 OR V260 = 4) V1003 = 1
IF (V261 = 2 OR V261 = 3) V1004 = 1
IF (V262 = 2 OR V262 = 3) V1005 = 1
COMPUTE V1010 = V1001 + V1002 + V1003 + V1004 + V1005

This index is based on all 12 items in the Materialist/Postmaterialist values battery; it simply sums up the total number of Postmaterialist items that were given high priority (i.e., ranked as either first or second most important in its group of four items). Accordingly, scores range from zero (none of the five Postmaterialist items was given high priority) to five (all five of the Postmaterialist items were given high priority).
(range = 0–5; missing data = 9)

3. BRADBURN AFFECT BALANCE SCALE: [V1032]

IF (V84 = 1) V1020 = 1
IF (V86 = 1) V1021 = 1
IF (V88 = 1) V1022 = 1
IF (V90 = 1) V1023 = 1
IF (V92 = 1) V1024 = 1

COMPUTE V1025 = V1020 + V1021 + V1022 + V1023 + V1024

IF (V85 = 1) V1026 = 1

IF (V87 = 1) V1027 = 1

IF (V89 = 1) V1028 = 1

IF (V91 = 1) V1029 = 1

IF (V93 = 1) V1030 = 1

COMPUTE V1031 = V1026 + V1027 + V1028 + V1029 + V1030

COMPUTE V1032 = V1025 − V1031

This index sums up the number of positive affect items that are chosen, and the number of negative affect items that are chosen, and then subtracts the negative affect score from the positive affect score.
(range = −5 to +5)

4. ACHIEVEMENT MOTIVATION SCALE (FOUR-ITEM INDEX): [V1046]

IF (V228 = 1) V1040 = 1

IF (V233 = 1) V1041 = 1

COMPUTE V1042 = V1040 + V1041

IF (V234 = 1) V1043 = 1

IF (V236 = 1) V1044 = 1

COMPUTE V1045 = V1043 + V1044

COMPUTE V1046 = V1042 − V1045

Respondents were asked, "Here is a list of qualities which children can be encouraged to learn at home. Which, if any, do you consider to be especially important?" Among the options were "Thrift" and "Determination," on one hand, and "Obedience" and "Religious faith," on the other hand. Each individual's score on this index represents the number of choices emphasizing the former two items, minus the number of choices emphasizing the latter two items.
(range = −2 to +2; missing data = 9)

5. ETHNOCENTRISM ("REJECT OUTGROUPS") [V1053]

IF (V77 = 1) V1050 = 1

IF (V78 = 1) V1051 = 1

IF (V80 = 1) V1052 = 1

COMPUTE V1053 = V1050 + V1051 + V1052

Respondents were asked, "On this list are various groups of people. Could you please sort out any that you would not like to have as neighbors?" The list included (among others) "Immigrants/foreign workers," "People who have AIDS," and "Homosexuals." Scores on this index range from 0 to 3, depending on how many of these three groups are mentioned.
(range = 0–3; missing data = 9)

6. Subjective Well-being Index

(This index is created at the national level, based on overall percentages scoring above given levels in the given nation. No SPSS instructions are provided, since this index is not created at the individual level.)

1. For each nation, calculate the percentage scoring HIGH on V18 (*"How happy are you these days?"*) minus the percentage scoring LOW on V18:

codes 1–2 = "high" ("very happy" + "quite happy");

codes 3–4 = "low" ("not very happy" + "not at all happy").

2. For each nation, calculate the percentage scoring HIGH on V95 minus the percentage scoring LOW on V95 ("How satisfied are you with your life as a whole these days? Please use this scale to answer: 1 = very dissatisfied . . . 10 = very satisfied"):

codes 1–4 = "low";

codes 7–10 = "high."

3. Sum the two figures obtained in (1) and (2) above.

4. Divide this result by 2.

On this index, a score of "0" indicates that as many people consider themselves unhappy or dissatisfied with their lives as a whole, as consider themselves happy or satisfied. A score of −100 would result if everyone in the given society considered themselves happy and satisfied with their lives as a whole; a score of +100 would mean that everyone considered themselves unhappy and dissatisfied with their lives as a whole. Range = −100 to +100.

All of these indices either measure priorities (rather than levels); or subtract the percentage high from the percentage low to control for the fact that respondents in some cultures have a tendency to give extreme scores, while those in others have a tendency to give moderate scores. This minimizes the impact of response set which, as chapter 4 demonstrates, is likely to be a particularly serious source of measurement error in cross-cultural research.

A P P E N D I X   5

COMPLETE 1990 WVS QUESTIONNAIRE, WITH VARIABLE NUMBERS

IN ICPSR DATASET

Country Codes and Number of Interviews in 1981 and 1990

Code	1990-91 Surveys Country	N	Code	1981 Surveys Country	N
1	France	1,002	42	Austria	1,460
2	Britain	1,484	44	Turkey	1,030
3	W. Germany	2,101	45	Moscow	1,012
4	Italy	2,018	46	Lithuania	1,000
5	Netherlands	1,017	47	Latvia	903
6	Denmark	1,030	48	Estonia	1,008
7	Belgium	2,792	50	Russia	1,961
8	Spain	4,147	51	France81	1,200
9	Ireland	1,000	52	Britain81	1,231
10	N. Ireland	304	53	W. Germany81	1,305
11	U.S.	1,839	54	Italy81	1,348
12	Canada	1,730	55	Netherlands81	1,221
13	Japan	1,011	56	Denmark81	1,182
14	Mexico	1,531	57	Belgium81	1,145
15	S. Africa	2,736	58	Spain81	2,303
16	Hungary	999	59	Ireland81	1,217
18	Norway	1,239	60	N. Ireland81	312
19	Sweden	1,047	61	U.S. 81	2,325
21	Iceland	702	62	Canada81	1,254
22	Argentina	1,002	63	Japan81	1,204
23	Finland	588	64	Mexico81	1,837
24	S. Korea	1,251	65	S. Africa81	1,596
25	Poland	938	66	Hungary81	1,464
26	Switzerland	1,400	67	Australia81	1,228
28	Brazil	1,782	68	Norway81	1,246
29	Nigeria	1,001	69	Sweden81	954
30	Chile	1,500	70	Tambov81	1,262
31	Belarus	1,015	71	Iceland81	927
32	India	2,500	72	Argentina81	1,005
33	Czechoslovakia	1,396	73	Finland81	1,003
34	E. Germany	1,336	74	South Korea81	970
35	Slovenia	1,035			
36	Bulgaria	1,034			
37	Romania	1,103		V1 = Study number	
39	China	1,000		V25 = Country code	
41	Portugal	1,185		V35 = Interview number	

WORLD VALUES SURVEY
1990 QUESTIONNAIRE

SHOW CARD A

Please say, for each of the following, how important it is in your life.

	Very Important	*Quite Important*	*Not Very Important*	*Not at All Important*	*DK*
V 4 A) Work	1	2	3	4	9
V 5 B) Family	1	2	3	4	9
V 6 C) Friends, acquaintances	1	2	3	4	9
V 7 D) Leisure time	1	2	3	4	9
V 8 E) Politics	1	2	3	4	9
V 9 F) Religion	1	2	3	4	9

Note: Throughout these surveys, "0" is used as a Not Ascertained (N.A.) code. With single-digit variables, "9" is also occasionally used as a N.A. code. An asterisk indicates items asked in both the 1981 and 1990 surveys.

V 10* When you get together with your friends, would you say you discuss political matters frequently, occasionally, or never?

  1 Frequently
  2 Occasionally
  3 Never
  9 Don't know

V 11 When you yourself hold a strong opinion, do you ever find yourself persuading your friends, relatives, or fellow workers to share your views? IF SO, does it happen often, from time to time, or rarely?

  1 Often
  2 From time to time
  3 Rarely
  4 Never
  9 Don't know

SHOW CARD B
I am now going to read out some statements about the environment. For each one I read out, can you tell me whether you agree strongly, agree, disagree, or strongly disagree? (READ OUT EACH STATEMENT AND CODE AN ANSWER FOR EACH)

	Strongly Agree	*Agree*	*Disagree*	*Strongly Disagree*	*DK*
V 12 I would give part of my income if I were certain that the money would be used to prevent environmental pollution	1	2	3	4	9
V 13 I would agree to an increase in taxes if the extra money is used to prevent environmental pollution	1	2	3	4	9
V 14 The government has to reduce environmental pollution but it should not cost me any money	1	2	3	4	9
V 15 All the talk about pollution makes people too anxious	1	2	3	4	9
V 16 If we want to combat unemployment in this country, we shall just have to accept environmental problems	1	2	3	4	9
V 17 Protecting the environment and fighting pollution is less urgent than often suggested	1	2	3	4	9

V 18* Taking all things together, would you say you are (READ OUT, REVERSING ORDER FOR ALTERNATE CONTACTS)

1 Very happy
2 Quite happy
3 Not very happy
4 Not at all happy
9 Don't know

SHOW CARD C*

Please look carefully at the following list of voluntary organizations and activities
and say

(a) which, if any, do you belong to?
(CODE ALL 'YES' ANSWERS UNDER [a])
(b) which, if any, are you currently doing
unpaid voluntary work for?
(CODE ALL 'YES' ANSWERS UNDER [b])

		(a) *Belong to*	(b) *Do Unpaid Work for*
V 19 A)	Social welfare services for elderly, handicapped, or deprived people	1	V 37 1
V 20 B)	Religious or church organizations	1	V 38 1
V 21 C)	Education, arts, music, or cultural activities	1	V 39 1
V 22 D)	Trade unions	1	V 40 1
V 23 E)	Political parties or groups	1	V 41 1
V 24 F)	Local community action on issues like poverty, employment, housing, racial equality	1	V 42 1
V 25 G)	Third world development or human rights	1	V 43 1
V 26 H)	Conservation, the environment, ecology	1	V 44 1
V 27 I)	Professional associations	1	V 45 1
V 28 J)	Youth work (e.g., scouts, guides, youth clubs, etc.)	1	V 46 1
V 29 K)	Sports or recreation	1	V 47 1
V 30 L)	Women's groups	1	V 48 1
V 31 M)	Peace movement	1	V 49 1
V 32 N)	Animal rights	1	V 50 1
V 33 O)	Voluntary organizations concerned with health	1	V 51 1
V 34 P)	Other groups	1	V 52 1
V 35	None	1	V 53 -
V 36	Don't know	9	V 54 -

*For V 19 to V 54, "1" indicates "mentioned," "2" indicates "not mentioned." The
Chinese questionnaire translated "Trade unions" (V 22 and V 40) as "Trading associations," which was chosen by very few people. "Professional associations" was
translated as "Occupational organizations," which evokes the (government-
sponsored) labor unions; thus, for China, V 27 is functionally equivalent to V 22.
The Swiss survey used the phrase "charitable organization" for "social welfare services" in V 19 and V 37.*

SHOW CARD D

Thinking about your reasons for doing voluntary work, please use the following five-point scale to indicate how important each of the reasons below have been *in your own case*. (WHERE 1 IS UNIMPORTANT AND 5 IS VERY IMPORTANT)

		Unimportant				*Very Important*	*DK*
V 55 A)	A sense of solidarity with the poor and disadvantaged	1	2	3	4	5	9
V 56 B)	Compassion for those in need	1	2	3	4	5	9
V 57 C)	An opportunity to repay something, give something back	1	2	3	4	5	9
V 58 D)	A sense of duty, moral obligation	1	2	3	4	5	9
V 59 E)	Identifying with people who were suffering	1	2	3	4	5	9
V 60 F)	Time on my hands, wanted something worthwhile to do	1	2	3	4	5	9
V 61 G)	Purely for personal satisfaction	1	2	3	4	5	9
V 62 H)	Religious beliefs	1	2	3	4	5	9
V 63 I)	To help give disadvantaged people hope and dignity	1	2	3	4	5	9
V 64 J)	To make a contribution to my local community	1	2	3	4	5	9
V 65 K)	To bring about social or political change	1	2	3	4	5	9
V 66 L)	For social reasons, to meet people	1	2	3	4	5	9
V 67 M)	To gain new skills and useful experience	1	2	3	4	5	9
V 68 N)	I did not want to, but could not refuse	1	2	3	4	5	9

SHOW CARD E*
On this list are various groups of people. Could you please sort out any that you
would not like to have as neighbors? (CODE AN ANSWER FOR EACH)

		Mentioned	*Not Mentioned*
V 69 A)	People with a criminal record	1	2
V 70 B)	People of a different race	1	2
V 71 C)	Left-wing extremists	1	2
V 72 D)	Heavy drinkers	1	2
V 73 E)	Right-wing extremists	1	2
V 74 F)	People with large families	1	2
V 75 G)	Emotionally unstable people	1	2
V 76 H)	Muslims	1	2
V 77 I)	Immigrants/foreign workers	1	2
V 78 J)	People who have AIDS	1	2
V 79 K)	Drug addicts	1	2
V 80 L)	Homosexuals	1	2
V 81 M)	Jews	1	2
V 82 N)	Hindus	1	2

The Slovenian survey and the Lithuanian, Latvian, and Estonian surveys asked about
"Gypsies," rather than "Hindus," in V 82.
The surveys in the Baltic countries asked about "extremists" (not "left-wing extrem-
ists") in V 71, and about "people of other nationalities" in V 73.

V 83* All in all, how would you describe your state of health these days? Would you
say it is (READ OUT, REVERSING ORDER FOR ALTERNATE CONTACTS)

  1 Very good
  2 Good
  3 Fair
  4 Poor
  5 Very poor
  9 Don't know

We are interested in the way people are feeling these days. During the past few
weeks, did you ever feel (READ OUT AND MARK ONE CODE FOR EACH
STATEMENT)*

		YES	NO
V 84 A)	Particularly excited or interested in something	1	2
V 85 B)	So restless you couldn't sit long in a chair	1	2
V 86 C)	Proud because someone had complimented you on something you had done	1	2
V 87 D)	Very lonely or remote from other people	1	2
V 88 E)	Pleased about having accomplished something	1	2
V 89 F)	Bored	1	2

V 90 G)	On top of the world/feeling that life is		
	wonderful	1	2
V 91 H)	Depressed or very unhappy	1	2
V 92 I)	That things were going your way	1	2
V 93 J)	Upset because somebody criticized you	1	2

V 94* Generally speaking, would you say that most people can be trusted or that you can't be too careful in dealing with people?

1 Most people can be trusted
2 Can't be too careful
9 Don't know

SHOW CARD F
V 95* Some people feel they have completely free choice and control over their lives, and other people feel that what they do has no real effect on what happens to them. Please use the scale to indicate how much freedom of choice and control you feel you have over the way your life turns out.

1   2   3   4   5   6   7   8   9   10
None at all   A great deal
                                           DK = 99

SHOW CARD G
V 96* All things considered, how satisfied are you with your life as a whole these days? Please use this card to help with your answer.

1   2   3   4   5   6   7   8   9   10
Dissatisfied   Satisfied
                                           DK = 99

SHOW CARD H
V 97 Why are there people in this country who live in need? Here are four possible reasons. Which one reason do you consider to be most important? (CODE ONE UNDER [a] BEL0W) And which reason do you consider to be the second most important? (CODE ONE UNDER [b] BELOW)

	V 97 (a) Most Important	V 98 (b) Second Most Important
Because they are unlucky	1	1
Because of laziness and lack of willpower	2	2
Because there is injustice in our society	3	3
It's an inevitable part of modern progress	4	4
None of these	5	5
Don't know	9	9

India only: additional codes 6 and 8 refer to ascetic and religious motivations.

SHOW CARD I*

Here are some aspects of a job that people say are important. Please look at them and tell me which ones you personally think are important in a job? (CODE ALL MENTIONED)

		Mentioned	Not Mentioned
V 99 A)	Good pay	1	2
V 100 B)	Pleasant people to work with	1	2
V 101 C)	Not too much pressure	1	2
V 102 D)	Good job security	1	2
V 103 E)	Good chances for promotion	1	2
V 104 F)	A job respected by people in general	1	2
V 105 G)	Good hours	1	2
V 106 H)	An opportunity to use initiative	1	2
V 107 I)	A useful job for society	1	2
V 108 J)	Generous holidays	1	2
V 109 K)	Meeting people	1	2
V 110 L)	A job in which you feel you can achieve something	1	2
V 111 M)	A responsible job	1	2
V 112 N)	A job that is interesting	1	2
V 113 O)	A job that meets one's abilities	1	2
V 114	None of these	1	2

ASK ALL WORKING; OTHERS SKIP TO V 118

How much pride, if any, do you take in the work that you do? (READ OUT)

V 115* 1 A great deal
        2 Some
        3 Little
        4 None
        9 Don't know

SHOW CARD J

Overall, how satisfied or dissatisfied are you with your job?

V 116* 1   2   3   4   5   6   7   8   9   10
         Dissatisfied   Satisfied
                                    DK = 99

SHOW CARD K
How free are you to make decisions in your job? Please use this card to indicate how much decision-making freedom you feel you have.

V 117*   1   2   3   4   5   6   7   8   9   10
          None at all   A great deal
                                      DK = 99

ASK ALL
SHOW CARD L
Here are some statements about why people work. Irrespective of whether you have a job, or not, which of them comes closest to what you think?

		Not	
	Mentioned	*Mentioned*	
V 118	1	2	Work is like a business transaction. The more I get paid, the more I do; the less I get paid, the less I do
V 119	1	2	I will always do the best I can, regardless of pay
V 120	1	2	Working for a living is a necessity; I wouldn't work if I didn't have to
V 121	1	2	I enjoy working, but I don't let it interfere with the rest of my life
V 122	1	2	I enjoy my work; it's the most important thing in my life
V 123	1	2	I never had a paid job
V 124	1	2	Don't know

Imagine two secretaries, of the same age, doing practically the same job. One finds out that the other earns $50 a week more than she does. The better-paid secretary, however, is quicker, more efficient, and more reliable at her job. In your opinion, is it fair or not fair that one secretary is paid more than the other? (**Countries other than U.S.: Please use own currency**)

V 125* 1 Fair
         2 Unfair
         9 Don't know

SHOW CARD M

There is a lot of discussion about how business and industry should be managed. Which of these four statements comes closest to your opinion? (CODE ONE ONLY)

V 126* 1 The owners should run their business or appoint the managers
      2 The owners and the employees should participate in the selection of managers
      3 The government should be the owner and appoint the managers
      4 The employees should own the business and should elect the managers
      9 Don't know

SHOW CARD N

People have different ideas about following instructions at work. Some say that one should follow instructions of one's superiors even when one does not fully agree with them. Others say that one should follow one's superior's instructions only when one is convinced that they are right. With which of these two opinions do you agree?

V 127* 1 Should follow instructions
      2 Depends
      3 Must be convinced first
      9 Don't know

Do you agree or disagree with the following statements?

	Agree	Neither	Disagree	DK
V 128 A) When jobs are scarce, men have more right to a job than women	1	2	3	9
V 129 B) When jobs are scarce, people should be forced to retire early	1	2	3	9
V 130 C) When jobs are scarce, employers should give priority to British people over immigrants (**countries other than U.K.: please substitute your nationality**)	1	2	3	9
V 131 D) It is unfair to give work to handicapped people when able-bodied people can't find jobs	1	2	3	9

SHOW CARD O

How satisfied are you with the financial situation of your household?

V 132*   1   2   3   4   5   6   7   8   9   10
          Dissatisfied   Satisfied
                                      DK = 99

How often, if at all, do you think about the meaning and purpose of life? (READ OUT IN REVERSE ORDER FOR ALTERNATE CONTACTS)

V 133* 1 Often
       2 Sometimes
       3 Rarely
       4 Never
       9 Don't know

Do you ever think about death? Would you say

V 134 1 Often
      2 Sometimes
      3 Rarely
      4 Never
      9 Don't know

I am going to read out a list of statements about the meaning of life. Please indicate whether you agree or disagree with each of them. (READ OUT IN REVERSE ORDER FOR ALTERNATE CONTACTS)

	Agree	*Disagree*	*Neither*	*DK*
V 135 A) Life is meaningful only because God exists	1	2	3	9
V 136 B) The meaning of life is that you try to get the best out of it	1	2	3	9
V 137 C) Death is inevitable; it is pointless to worry about it	1	2	3	9
V 138 D) Death has a meaning only if you believe in God	1	2	3	9
V 139 E) If you have lived your life, death is a natural resting point	1	2	3	9
V 140 F) In my opinion, sorrow and suffering only have meaning if you believe in God	1	2	3	9
V 141 G) Life has no meaning	1	2	3	9

SHOW CARD P

Here are two statements which people sometimes make when discussing good and
evil. Which one comes closest to your own point of view?

V 142* A. There are absolutely clear guidelines about what is good and evil.
These always apply to everyone, whatever the circumstances.

B. There can never be absolutely clear guidelines about what is
good and evil. What is good and evil depends entirely upon the
circumstances at the time.

1 Agree with statement A
2 Disagree with both
3 Agree with statement B
9 Don't know

V 143* (a) Do you belong to a religious denomination?

1 Yes—GO TO (b)
2 No—GO TO (c)

(b) (IF YES) Which one? (CODE UNDER [b] BELOW)
(c) (IF NO) Were you ever a member of a religious denomination?
Which one? (CODE UNDER [c] BELOW)

	V 144 (b) *Religious Denomination*	V 145 (c) *Before*
Roman Catholic	1	1
Mainline Protestant	2	2
Fundamentalist Protestant	3	3
Jew	4	4
Muslim	5	5
Hindu	6	6
Buddhist	7	7
Other	8	8
Never	—	0
No answer	9	9

*NOTE: Japan, South Korea, and many Eastern European countries used different
codes from these. For these and other deviations from the above, see V 144 and V
145 in the section on Nation-Specific Codes.*

ASK ALL

V 146 Were you brought up religiously at home?

1 Yes
2 No

SHOW CARD Q

V 147* Apart from weddings, funerals, and christenings, about how often do you attend religious services these days?

1 More than once a week
2 Once a week
3 Once a month
4 Christmas/Easter day
5 Other specific holy days
6 Once a year
7 Less often
8 Never, practically never

Do you personally think it is important to hold a religious service for any of the
following events?

		Yes	No	DK
V 148 A)	Birth	1	2	9
V 149 B)	Marriage	1	2	9
V 150 C)	Death	1	2	9

Independently of whether you go to church or not, would you say you are (READ
OUT REVERSING ORDER)

V 151* 1 A religious person
       2 Not a religious person
       3 A convinced atheist
       9 Don't know

Generally speaking, do you think that your church is giving, in your country, adequate answers to (READ OUT AND CODE ONE ANSWER FOR EACH)*

		YES	NO	DK
V 152 A)	The moral problems and needs of the individual	1	2	9
V 153 B)	The problems of family life	1	2	9
V 154 C)	People's spiritual needs	1	2	9
V 155 D)	The social problems facing our country today	1	2	9

Do you think it is proper for churches to speak out on

	YES	NO	DK
V 156 A) Disarmament	1	2	9
V 157 B) Abortion	1	2	9
V 158 C) Third world problems	1	2	9
V 159 D) Extramarital affairs	1	2	9
V 160 E) Unemployment	1	2	9
V 161 F) Racial discrimination	1	2	9
V 162 G) Euthanasia	1	2	9
V 163 H) Homosexuality	1	2	9
V 164 I) Ecology and environmental issues	1	2	9
V 165 J) Government policy	1	2	9

Which, if any, of the following do you believe in? (READ OUT AND CODE ONE ANSWER FOR EACH)*

	YES	NO	DK
V 166 A) God	1	2	9
V 167 B) Life after death	1	2	9
V 168 C) A soul	1	2	9
V 169 D) The Devil	1	2	9
V 170 E) Hell	1	2	9
V 171 F) Heaven	1	2	9
V 172 G) Sin	1	2	9
V 173 H) Resurrection of the dead	1	2	9
V 174 I) Reincarnation	1	2	9

SHOW CARD R

Which of these statements comes closest to your beliefs? (CODE ONE ANSWER ONLY)

V 175*

    1 There is a personal God
    2 There is some sort of spirit or life force
    3 I don't really know what to think
    4 I don't really think there is any sort of spirit, God, or life force
    9 Not answered

SHOW CARD S

And how important is God in your life? Please use this card to indicate—10 means very important and 1 means not at all important.

V 176*   1   2   3   4   5   6   7   8   9   10
        Not at all   Very
                                   DK = 99

Do you find that you get comfort and strength from religion?

V 177* 1 Yes
        2 No
        9 Don't know

Do you take some moments of prayer, meditation or contemplation or something like that?

V 178* 1 Yes
        2 No
        9 Don't know

How often do you pray to God outside of religious services? Would you say

V 179 1 Often
       2 Sometimes
       3 Hardly ever
       4 Only in times of crisis
       5 Never
       9 Don't know

SHOW CARD T
Overall, how satisfied or dissatisfied are you with your home life?

V 180* 1   2   3   4   5   6   7   8   9   10
　　　　Dissatisfied　　　　　　　　　　　Satisfied
　　　　　　　　　　　　　　　　　　　　DK = 99

Are you currently (READ OUT AND CODE ONE ONLY)

V 181* 1 Married
　　　　2 Living as married
　　　　3 Divorced
　　　　4 Separated
　　　　5 Widowed
　　　　6 Single

Have you been married before?

V 182 1 Yes—more than once
　　　　2 Yes—only once
　　　　3 No—never

NOTE: In the 1990 Dutch survey, V 182 was worded as "How often have you been married?" 1 = once, 2 = more than once, 3 = more than twice. This question gave rise to confusion in many countries; it was not clear whether being married before meant "have you ever been married?" or "have you ever been married before your present marriage?"

ASK ALL EXCEPT SINGLES
Do (did) you and your partner share any of the following? (READ OUT AND CODE ALL MENTIONED)*

V 183　　1　　Attitudes toward religion
V 184　　1　　Moral attitudes
V 185　　1　　Social attitudes
V 186　　1　　Political attitudes
V 187　　1　　Sexual attitudes
V 188　　1　　None of these
V 189　　1　　Don't know

For V 183–V 196, code "2" indicates "not mentioned."

ASK ALL
And how about your parents? Do (did) you and your parents share any of the following? (READ OUT AND CODE ALL MENTIONED)*

V 190　　1　　Attitudes toward religion
V 191　　1　　Moral attitudes
V 192　　1　　Social attitudes
V 193　　1　　Political attitudes
V 194　　1　　Sexual attitudes
V 195　　1　　None of these
V 196　　1　　Don't know

If someone said that individuals should have the chance to enjoy complete sexual freedom without being restricted, would you tend to agree or disagree?

V 197* 1 Tend to agree
      2 Neither/it depends
      3 Tend to disagree
      9 Don't know

SHOW CARD U

Here is a list of things which some people think make for a successful marriage. Please tell me, for each one, whether you think it is very important, rather important or not very important for a successful marriage:*

		Very Important	*Rather Important*	*Not Very Important*
V 198 A)	Faithfulness	1	2	3
V 199 B)	An adequate income	1	2	3
V 200 C)	Being of the same social background	1	2	3
V 201 D)	Mutual respect and appreciation	1	2	3
V 202 E)	Shared religious beliefs	1	2	3
V 203 F)	Good housing	1	2	3
V 204 G)	Agreement on politics	1	2	3
V 205 H)	Understanding and tolerance	1	2	3
V 206 I)	Living apart from your in-laws	1	2	3
V 207 J)	Happy sexual relationship	1	2	3
V 208 K)	Sharing household chores	1	2	3
V 209 L)	Children	1	2	3
V 210 M)	Tastes and interests in common	1	2	3

Have you had any children? IF YES, how many?

V 211* 0 No child—skip to V 213
      1 1 child
      2 2 children
      3 3 children
      4 4 children
      5 5 children
      6 6 children or more
      9 No answer

How many of them are still living at home?

V 212 0 No child
      1 1 child
      2 2 children
      3 3 children
      4 4 children
      5 5 children
      6 6 children or more
      9 No answer

ASK ALL

What do you think is the ideal size of the family—how many children, if any?

V 213* 0 None
        1 1 child
        2 2 children
        3 3 children
        4 4 children
        5 5 children
        6 6 children
        7 7 children
        8 8 children
        9 9 children
       10 10 or more
       99 Don't know

If someone says a child needs a home with both a father and a mother to grow up happily, would you tend to agree or disagree?

V 214* 1 Tend to agree
        2 Tend to disagree
        9 Don't know

(*South Korean 1981 survey contains one undocumented code "4"*)

Do you think that a woman has to have children in order to be fulfilled, or is this not necessary?

V 215 1 Needs children
       2 Not necessary
       3 Don't know (in some countries)
       9 Don't know (in other countries)

Do you agree or disagree with the following statement? (READ OUT)

	YES	NO	DK
V 216* Marriage is an outdated institution	1	2	9

If a woman wants to have a child as a single parent but she doesn't want to have a stable relationship with a man, do you approve or disapprove?

V 217* 1 Approve
        2 Depends
        3 Disapprove
        9 Don't know

SHOW CARD V
People talk about the changing roles of men and women today. For each of the following statements I read out, can you tell me how much you agree with each. Please use the responses on this card.

		Strongly Agree	Agree	Dis-agree	Strongly Disagree	DK
V 218 A)	A working mother can establish just as warm and secure a relationship with her children as a mother who does not work	1	2	3	4	9
V 219 B)	A preschool child is likely to suffer if his or her mother works	1	2	3	4	9
V 220 C)	A job is all right, but what most women really want is a home and children	1	2	3	4	9
V 221 D)	Being a housewife is just as fulfilling as working for pay	1	2	3	4	9
V 222 E)	Having a job is the best way for a woman to be an independent person	1	2	3	4	9
V 223 F)	Both the husband and wife should contribute to household income	1	2	3	4	9

SHOW CARD W
With which of these two statements do you tend to agree? (CODE ONE ANSWER ONLY)

V 224*
A.   Regardless of what the qualities and faults of one's parents are, one must always love and respect them
B.   One does not have the duty to respect and love parents who have not earned it by their behavior and attitudes
1   Tend to agree with statement A
2   Tend to agree with statement B
9   Don't know

SHOW CARD X
Which of the following statements best describes your views about parents' responsibilities to their children? (CODE ONE ONLY)

V 225*

1 Parents' duty is to do their best for their children even at the expense of their own well-being
2 Neither
3 Parents have a life of their own and should not be asked to sacrifice their own well-being for the sake of their children
9 Don't know

SHOW CARD Y

Here is a list of qualities which children can be encouraged to learn at home. Which, if any, do you consider to be especially important? Please choose up to five. (CODE FIVE ONLY)*

		IMPORTANT
V 226 A)	Good manners	1
V 227 B)	Independence	1
V 228 C)	Hard work	1
V 229 D)	Feeling of responsibility	1
V 230 E)	Imagination	1
V 231 F)	Tolerance and respect for other people	1
V 232 G)	Thrift, saving money, and things	1
V 233 H)	Determination, perseverance	1
V 234 I)	Religious faith	1
V 235 J)	Unselfishness	1
V 236 K)	Obedience	1

(*V 226–V 236: code "2" indicates items that were not chosen*)

SHOW CARD Z

Do you approve or disapprove of abortion under the following circumstances?*

		Approve	Disapprove
V 237 A)	Where the mother's health is at risk by the pregnancy	1	2
V 238 B)	Where it is likely that the child would be born physically handicapped	1	2
V 239 C)	Where the woman is not married	1	2
V 240 D)	Where a married couple do not want to have any more children	1	2

How interested would you say you are in politics?

V 241 1 Very interested
　　　2 Somewhat interested
　　　3 Not very interested
　　　4 Not at all interested
　　　9 Don't know

The Swiss survey asked about interest in international politics, national politics, regional politics, and community politics. Responses to the question about community politics (which showed the highest levels of interest) were used here.

SHOW CARD AA

Now I'd like you to look at this card. I'm going to read out some different forms of political action that people can take, and I'd like you to tell me, for each one, whether you have actually done any of these things, whether you might do it or would never, under any circumstances, do it.*

	Have Done	Might Do	Would Never Do	DK
V 242 A) Signing a petition	1	2	3	9
V 243 B) Joining in boycotts	1	2	3	9
V 244 C) Attending lawful demonstrations	1	2	3	9
V 245 D) Joining unofficial strikes	1	2	3	9
V 246 E) Occupying buildings or factories	1	2	3	9

(For V 242, the normal N.A. code is "0," but "8" was used in some countries)

SHOW CARD BB

V 247*   Which of these two statements comes closest to your own opinion?

   A. I find that both freedom and equality are important. But if I were to choose one or the other, I would consider personal freedom more important, that is, everyone can live in freedom and develop without hindrance.

   B. Certainly both freedom and equality are important. But if I were to choose one or the other, I would consider equality more important, that is, that nobody is underprivileged and that social class differences are not so strong.

   1   Agree with statement A
   2   Agree with neither/depends
   3   Agree with statement B
   9   Don't know

SHOW CARD CC

V 248 In political matters, people talk of "the Left" and "the Right." How would you place your views on this scale, generally speaking?*

1   2   3   4   5   6   7   8   9   10
Left   Right
                                  DK 5 99
                   Not answered 5 98

SHOW CARD DD

V 249* On this card are three basic kinds of attitudes concerning the society we live in. Please choose the one which best describes your own opinion. (CODE ONE ONLY)

   1   The entire way our society is organized must be radically changed by revolutionary action
   2   Our society must be gradually improved by reforms
   3   Our present society must be valiantly defended against all subversive forces
   9   Don't know

SHOW CARD EE

Now I'd like you to tell me your views on various issues. How would you place your views on this scale? 1 means you agree completely with the statement on the left, 10 means you agree completely with the statement on the right, or you can choose any number in between.

V 250

1	2	3	4	5	6	7	8	9	10

DK = 99

A) Incomes should be made more equal

There should be greater incentives for individual effort

V 251

1	2	3	4	5	6	7	8	9	10

DK = 99

B) Private ownership of business and industry should be increased

Government ownership of business and industry should be increased

V 252

1	2	3	4	5	6	7	8	9	10

DK = 99

C) Individuals should take more responsibility for providing for themselves

The state should take more responsibility to ensure that everyone is provided for

V 253

1	2	3	4	5	6	7	8	9	10

DK = 99

D) People who are unemployed should have to take any job available or lose their unemployment benefits

People who are unemployed should have the right to refuse a job they do not want

V 254

1	2	3	4	5	6	7	8	9	10

DK = 99

E) Competition is good. It stimulates people to work hard and develop new ideas

Competition is harmful. It brings out the worst in people

V 255

1	2	3	4	5	6	7	8	9	10

DK = 99

F) In the long run, hard work usually brings a better life

Hard work doesn't generally bring success—it's more a matter of luck and connections

V 256

1	2	3	4	5	6	7	8	9	10

DK = 99

G) People can only accumulate wealth at the expense of others

Wealth can grow so there's enough for everyone

SHOW CARD FF
There is a lot of talk these days about what the aims of this country should be for the
next 10 years. On this card are listed some of the goals which different people would
give top priority. Would you please say which one of these you, yourself, consider
the most important? (CODE ONE ANSWER ONLY UNDER [a] BELOW)

And which would be the next most important? (CODE ONE ANSWER ONLY
UNDER [b] BELOW)

	V 257 (a) First Choice	V 258 (b) Second Choice
Maintaining a high level of economic growth	1	1
Making sure this country has strong defense forces	2	2
Seeing that people have more to say about how things are done at their jobs and in their communities	3	3
Trying to make our cities and countryside more beautiful	4	4
Don't know	9	9

SHOW CARD GG*
a) If you had to choose, which one of the things on this card would you say is most
important? (CODE ONE ANSWER ONLY)

b) And which would be the next most important? (CODE ONE ANSWER ONLY)

	V 259 (a) First Choice	V 260 (b) Second Choice
Maintaining order in the nation	1	1
Giving people more to say in important government decisions	2	2
Fighting rising prices	3	3
Protecting freedom of speech	4	4
Don't know	9	9

SHOW CARD HH*

a) Here is another list. In your opinion, which one of these is most important?
(CODE ONE ANSWER ONLY)

b) And what would be the next most important? (CODE ONE ANSWER ONLY)

	V 261 (a) First Choice	V 262 (b) Second Choice
A stable economy	1	1
Progress toward a less impersonal and more humane society	2	2
Progress toward a society in which ideas count more than money	3	3
The fight against crime	4	4
Don't know	9	9

V 263 * Of course, we all hope that there will not be another war, but if it were to come to that, would you be willing to fight for your country?

   1 Yes
   2 No
   9 Don't know

SHOW CARD II*

Here is a list of various changes in our way of life that might take place in the near future. Please tell me for each one, if it were to happen whether you think it would be a good thing, a bad thing, or don't you mind?

	Good	Don't Mind	Bad
V 264 A) Less emphasis on money and material possessions	1	2	3
V 265 B) Decrease in the importance of work in our lives	1	2	3
V 266 C) More emphasis on the development of technology	1	2	3
V 267 D) Greater emphasis on the development of the individual	1	2	3
V 268 E) Greater respect for authority	1	2	3
V 269 F) More emphasis on family life	1	2	3
V 270 G) A simple and more natural lifestyle	1	2	3

V 271 * In the long run, do you think the scientific advances we are making will help or harm mankind?

1 Will help
2 Some of each
3 Will harm
9 Don't know

SHOW CARD JJ*

Please look at this card and tell me, for each item listed, how much confidence you have in them: is it a great deal, quite a lot, not very much, or none at all? (CODE ONE ANSWER FOR EACH ITEM—READ OUT REVERSING ORDER FOR ALTERNATE CONTACTS)

	A Great Deal	*Quite a Lot*	*Not Very Much*	*None at All*
V 272 A) The church	1	2	3	4
V 273 B) The armed forces	1	2	3	4
V 274 C) The education system	1	2	3	4
V 275 D) The legal system	1	2	3	4
V 276 E) The press	1	2	3	4
V 277 F) Trade unions	1	2	3	4
V 278 G) The police	1	2	3	4
V 279 H) Parliament	1	2	3	4
V 280 I) Civil service	1	2	3	4
V 281 J) Major companies	1	2	3	4
V 282 K) The social security system	1	2	3	4
V 283 L) TV/European Community	1	2	3	4

V 284 M) NATO	1	2	3	4
V 285 N) The [American]* political system	1	2	3	4

In Western European countries and China, V 283 refers to the European Community; elsewhere, it refers to TV newscasters.

The item concerning NATO (V 284) was not asked in some countries.

In Slovenia, V 280 ("Civil service") was worded as "Local administration" to distinguish it from Yugoslav authority.

In Lithuania, Latvia, and Estonia, the following changes were made: V 276 = this republic's (Lithuanian, etc.) mass media, V 279 = this republic's parliament, V 281 = cooperatives, V 283 the People's Front (Baltic independence movement), V 284 = this republic's government, V 285 = government of the USSR.

In Russia, substitutions were made for V 279–V 285: V 279 Parliament (USSR), V 281 = Government (USSR), V 282 = Parliament (Russia), V 283 = TV, V 284 = Government (Russia), V 285 = Soviet political system.

On this card are listed some things people have said make them proud of the [U.S.]*
Do any of these things make you proud of this country?
Is there anything else?
And is there anything else? (CODE UP TO TWO MENTIONS)

	V 286 First Choice	V 287 Second Choice
[American]* scientific achievements	1	1
The American political system	2	2
American sporting achievements	3	3
American culture and arts	4	4
American economic achievements	5	5
American health and welfare system	6	6
None of these things make me proud	7	7
DK	9	9

In Spain (ASEP survey) only, the codes for V 286–V 287 were: 0 = scientific achievements, 1 = the political system, 2 = sporting achievements, 3 = culture and arts, 4 = economic achievements, 5 = health and welfare system, 6 = Spain's history, 7 = the language, 8 = none, 9 = don't know.

In China, the above codes were used, with the addition of code 8 = "the long, long Chinese history."

V 288 Generally speaking, would you say that this country is run by a few big interests looking out for themselves, or that it is run for the benefit of all the people?

1 Run by a few big interests
2 Run for all the people
9 Don't know

V 289 How much do you trust the government in [Washington]* to do what is right? Do you trust it almost always, most of the time, only some of the time, or almost never?

1 Almost always
2 Most of the time
3 Only some of the time
4 Almost never

Substitute your nation for "U.S." or "American" or "Washington"

SHOW CARD KK
There are a number of groups and movements looking for public support. For each of the following movements, which I read out, can you tell me whether you approve or disapprove of this movement? (READ OUT AND CODE ONE ANSWER FOR EACH) Please use the responses on this card!

	Approve		Disapprove		
	Strongly	*Somewhat*	*Somewhat*	*Strongly*	*DK*
V 290 A) Ecology movement or nature protection	1	2	3	4	9
V 291 B) Anti-nuclear energy movement	1	2	3	4	9
V 292 C) Disarmament movement	1	2	3	4	9
V 293 D) Human rights movement at home or abroad	1	2	3	4	9
V 294 E) Women's movement	1	2	3	4	9
V 295 F) Anti-apartheid movement	1	2	3	4	9

SHOW CARD LL*

Please tell me for each of the following statements whether you think it can always
be justified, never be justified, or something in between, using this card. (READ
OUT STATEMENTS REVERSING ORDER FOR ALTERNATE CONTACTS.
CODE ONE ANSWER FOR EACH STATEMENT)

V 296 A) Claiming government benefits
which you are not entitled to   1 2 3 4 5 6 7 8 9 10
Never   Always
DK = 99

V 297 B) Avoiding a fare on public
transport   1 2 3 4 5 6 7 8 9 10
DK = 99

V 298 C) Cheating on tax if you have
the chance   1 2 3 4 5 6 7 8 9 10
DK = 99

V 299 D) Buying something you knew
was stolen   1 2 3 4 5 6 7 8 9 10
DK = 99

V 300 E) Taking and driving away a car belonging
to someone else (joyriding)   1 2 3 4 5 6 7 8 9 10
DK = 99

V 301 F) Taking the drug marijuana or
hashish   1 2 3 4 5 6 7 8 9 10
DK = 99

V 302 G) Keeping money that you
have found   1 2 3 4 5 6 7 8 9 10
DK = 99

V 303 H) Lying in your own interest   1 2 3 4 5 6 7 8 9 10
DK = 99

V 304 I) Married men/women having
an affair   1 2 3 4 5 6 7 8 9 10
DK = 99

V 305 J) Sex under the legal age of
consent   1 2 3 4 5 6 7 8 9 10
DK = 99

V 306 K) Someone accepting a bribe in
the course of their duties   1 2 3 4 5 6 7 8 9 10
DK = 99

V 307 L) Homosexuality   1 2 3 4 5 6 7 8 9 10
DK = 99

V 308 M) Prostitution   1 2 3 4 5 6 7 8 9 10
DK = 99

V 309 N) Abortion   1 2 3 4 5 6 7 8 9 10
DK = 99

V 310 O) Divorce   1 2 3 4 5 6 7 8 9 10
                                                                    DK = 99

V 311 P) Fighting with the police   1 2 3 4 5 6 7 8 9 10
                                                                    DK = 99

V 312 Q) Euthanasia, terminating the
          life of the incurably sick   1 2 3 4 5 6 7 8 9 10
                                                                    DK = 99

V 313 R) Suicide   1 2 3 4 5 6 7 8 9 10
                                                                    DK = 99

V 314 S) Failing to report damage you've done
          accidentally to a parked vehicle   1 2 3 4 5 6 7 8 9 10
                                                                    DK = 99

V 315 T) Threatening workers who refuse to
          join a strike   1 2 3 4 5 6 7 8 9 10
                                                                    DK = 99

V 316 U) Killing in self-defense   1 2 3 4 5 6 7 8 9 10
                                                                    DK = 99

V 317 V) Political assassinations   1 2 3 4 5 6 7 8 9 10
                                                                    DK = 99

V 318 W) Throwing litter in a public
          place   1 2 3 4 5 6 7 8 9 10
                                                                    DK = 99

V 319 X) Driving under the influence
          of alcohol   1 2 3 4 5 6 7 8 9 10
                                                 Never   Always
                                                                    DK = 99

SHOW CARD MM

(a) Which of these geographical groups would you say you belong to first of all?

(b) And the next?

	V 320 (a) First	V 321 (b) Next
Locality or town where you live	1	1
State or region of country where you live	2	2
The U.S. as a whole	3	3
North America	4	4
The world as a whole	5	5
(*see nation-specific codes*)	6	6
Don't know	9	9

V 322 How proud are you to be British?*
[*substitute your own nationality for British*]

1 Very proud
2 Quite proud
3 Not very proud
4 Not at all proud
9 Don't know

SHOW CARD NN

Now I want to ask you some questions about your outlook on life. Each card I show you has two contrasting statements on it. Using the scale listed, could you tell me where you would place your own view? 1 means you agree completely with the statement on the left, 10 means you agree completely with the statement on the right, or you can choose any number in between.

V 323   1 2 3 4 5 6 7 8 9 10   DK = 99
      A) One should be cautious about   You will never achieve much
         making major changes in life   unless you act boldly

V 324   1 2 3 4 5 6 7 8 9 10   DK = 99
      B) Ideas that have stood the test   New ideas are generally
         of time are generally best   better than old ones

V 325   1 2 3 4 5 6 7 8 9 10   DK = 99
      C) When changes occur in my life,   When changes occur in my life,
         I worry about the difficulties   I welcome the possibility that
         they may cause   something new is beginning

SHOW CARD OO

A variety of characteristics are listed here. Could you take a look at them and select those which apply to you?

V 326 A) I usually count on being successful in everything I do	1
V 327 B) I enjoy convincing others of my opinion	1
V 328 C) I often notice that I serve as a model for others	1
V 329 D) I am good at getting what I want	1
V 330 E) I own many things others envy me for	1
V 331 F) I like to assume responsibility	1
V 332 G) I am rarely unsure about how I should behave	1
V 333 H) I often give others advice	1
V 334 None of the above	1

(For V 327-V 334, code "2" indicates "not mentioned")

SHOW CARD PP

I am going to read out some statements about the government and the economy. For each one, could you tell me how much you agree or disagree? Please use the responses on this card.

		Agree Completely	Agree Somewhat	Neither Agree nor Disagree	Disagree Somewhat	Disagree Completely	Don't Know
V 335 A)	This country's economic system needs fundamental changes	1	2	3	4	5	6
V 336 B)	Our government should be made much more open to the public	1	2	3	4	5	6
V 337 C)	We are more likely to have a healthy economy if the government allows more freedom for individuals to do as they wish	1	2	3	4	5	6
V 338 D)	If an unjust law were passed by the government I could do nothing at all about it	1	2	3	4	5	6
V 339 E)	Political reform in this country is moving too rapidly	1	2	3	4	5	6

SHOW CARD QQ
I now want to ask you how much you trust various groups of people: Using the responses on this card, could you tell me how much you trust: (READ OUT EACH AND CODE AN ANSWER FOR EACH)

	Trust Them Completely	Trust Them a Little	Neither Trust nor Distrust Them	Do Not Trust Them Very Much	Do Not Trust Them at All	Don't Know
V 340 A) Your family	1	2	3	4	5	9
V 341 B) The British in general *(substitute your nationality for British)*	1	2	3	4	5	9
V 342 C) Black Americans	1	2	3	4	5	9
V 343 D) Hispanic Americans	1	2	3	4	5	9
V 344 E) Canadians	1	2	3	4	5	9
V 345 F) Mexicans	1	2	3	4	5	9
V 346 G) Russians	1	2	3	4	5	9
V 347 H) Chinese	1	2	3	4	5	9

Here, as elsewhere, "0" indicates N.A.

Items C through H were asked in 15 of the 43 countries surveyed in 1990. The nationalities referred to in these items vary from country to country: items C and D indicate some important ethnic group within the given country; E and F indicate some neighboring nationality; G and H refer to the Americans, the Chinese, or the Russians. See Nation-Specific Variables section in ICPSR codebook for details.

V 348 Were you born in the United States [this country]?

1 Yes
No (If no): Where were you born?
2 Latin America
3 North America
4 Asia
5 Europe
6 Africa
7 Other

V 349 (If no) In what year did you come to the United States [to this country]?

1 Within past 2 years
2 Within past 3–5 years
3 6–10 years ago
4 11–15 years ago
5 More than 15 years ago

V 350 To which of the following groups do you belong above all? Just call out one of the letters on this card. SHOW CARD

1 [A] Above all, I am an Hispanic American
2 [B] Above all, I am a black American
3 [C] Above all, I am a white American
4 [D] Above all, I am an Asian American
5 [E] I am an American first and a member of some ethnic group second

(the groups coded in V350 vary from country to country; see the section on Nation-Specific Codes in ICPSR codebook for codes used in countries other than the U.S.)

V 351 If there were a general election tomorrow, which party would you vote for? If DON'T KNOW: Which party appeals to you most?
(see Nation-Specific Codes in ICPSR codebook for codes used in given countries)

V 352 And which party would be your second choice?
(see Nation-Specific Codes in ICPSR codebook for codes used in given countries)

DEMOGRAPHICS

V 353* Sex of respondent

1 Male
2 Female

V 354* (a) Can you tell me your date of birth, please? _____
V 355* (b) This means you are ____ years old.

NOTE: The surveys carried out in Sweden, South Africa, and the Baltic countries did not ascertain the respondent's exact age, but did provide a collapsed six-category age variable; see V 404 in ICPSR codebook.

V 356* At what age did you or will you complete your full-time education, either at school, or at an institution of higher education? Please exclude apprenticeships. (WRITE IN AGE)

Except as noted, the following categories were used in all surveys *(see Nation-Specific Codes in ICPSR codebook for exceptions)*

0   N.A.
1   Completed formal education at 12 years of age or earlier
2   Completed education at 13 years of age
3   Completed education at 14
4   Completed education at 15
5   Completed education at 16
6   Completed education at 17
7   Completed education at 18
8   Completed education at 19
9   Completed education at 20
10 Completed education at 21 years of age or older
99 N.A., don't know

V 357* Do you live with your parents?

1 Yes
2 No

Are you yourself employed now or not?*
IF YES:
About how many hours a week? If more than one job: only for the main job
V358*

Has paid employment
30 hours a week or more   1
Less than 30 hours a week   2
Self-employed   3

If no paid employment
Retired/pensioned   4
Housewife not otherwise employed   5
Student   6
Unemployed   7
Other (PLEASE SPECIFY)   8

In which profession/industry do you or did you work? If more than one job, the main job (WRITE IN)*

_____

_____

What is/was your job there? (WRITE IN AND CODE BELOW)*

The following codes were used in most countries (see Nation-Specific Codes in ICPSR codebook for exceptions):

V 359
  1 Employer/manager of establishment with 10 or more employees
  2 Employer/manager of establishment with less than 10 employees
  3 Professional worker lawyer, accountant, teacher, etc.
  4 Middle level non-manual—office worker, etc.
  5 Junior level non-manual—office worker, etc.
  6 Foreman and supervisor
  7 Skilled manual worker
  8 Semiskilled manual worker
  9 Unskilled manual worker
  10 Farmer: employer, manager on own account
  11 Agricultural worker
  12 Member of armed forces
  13 Never had a job

V 360*   Are you the chief wage earner?

1 Yes—GO TO V 363

2 No—GO TO V 361

3 Equal wage earner (treated as "Yes")—(GO TO V 363)

V 361

(a) Is the chief wage earner employed now or not?

1 Yes
2 No

(b) In which profession/industry does/did he or she work? (WRITE IN)

_____

V 362 (c) What is/was his/her job? (WRITE IN AND CODE BELOW)

Most countries used the following codes (see Nation-Specific Codes in ICPSR codebook for exceptions):

1 Employer/manager of establishment with 10 or more employees
2 Employer/manager of establishment with less than 10 employees
3 Professional worker lawyer, accountant, teacher, etc.
4 Middle level non-manual—office worker, etc.
5 Junior level non-manual—office worker, etc.
6 Foreman and supervisor
7 Skilled manual worker
8 Semiskilled manual worker
9 Unskilled manual worker
10 Farmer: employer, manager on own account
11 Agricultural worker
12 Member of armed forces
13 Never had a job

ASK ALL
SHOW INCOME CARD
V 363 Here is a scale of incomes and we would like to know in what group your household is, counting all wages, salaries, pensions, and other incomes that come in. Just give the letter of the group your household falls into, before taxes and other deductions.
(see Nation-Specific Codes in ICPSR codebook for categories):

1	2	3	4	5	6	7	8	9	10
C	D	E	F	G	H	I	J	K	L

No answer = 98

V 364* *INTERVIEWER CODE BY YOURSELF*
    Socioeconomic status of respondent
Most countries used the following codes (see Nation-Specific Codes in ICPSR codebook for exceptions):

1 AB Upper, upper-middle class
2 C1 Middle, non-manual workers
3 C2 Manual workers—skilled, semiskilled
4 DE Manual workers—unskilled, unemployed

V 365 (a) Time at the end of the interview: _____

V 366 (b) Total length of interview: Hours   Minutes

V 367 During the interview the respondent was

1 Very interested
2 Somewhat interested
3 Not very interested

(a) Town where interview was conducted: _____

V 368 (b) Size of town:
Most countries used the following codes (see Nation-Specific Codes in ICPSR code-book for exceptions):

1 Under 2,000
2 2,000–5,000
3 5–10,000
4 10–20,000
5 20–50,000
6 50–100,000
7 100–500,000
8 500,000 and more

V 369 Ethnic group (CODE BY OBSERVATION):
Unless otherwise noted, all countries used the following coding scheme:

1 Caucasian/white
2 Negro/Black
3 South Asian Indian, Pakistani, etc.
4 East Asian Chinese, Japanese, etc.
5 Arabic
6 Other
9 N.A.

V 370 Region where the interview was conducted:
(see Nation-Specific Codes section in the ICPSR codebook) The following is the U.S. example:

1 New England
2 Middle Atlantic states
3 South Atlantic
4 East South Central
5 West South Central
6 East North Central
7 West North Central
8 Rocky Mountain states
9 Northwest
10 California

V 371 Citizenship
(see Nation-Specific Codes in ICPSR codebook)

V 372 Urban/Rural
(see Nation-Specific Codes in ICPSR codebook)

V 373 Language spoken by respondent
(see Nation-Specific Codes in ICPSR codebook)
(Canada, India, Switzerland, and Baltic nations only)

V 374 European Integration Scale
(This question was asked in Western Europe only)

There is much talk about what the individual member states of the European Community have in common and what makes each one distinct. [INTERVIEWER SHOWS CARD WITH SEVEN-POINT SCALE. STATEMENT A IS AT ONE END; STATEMENT B IS AT OPPOSITE END]

Statement A:
Some people say: If the European member states were truly to be united, this would mean the end of their national, historical, and cultural identities. Their national economic interests would also be sacrificed.

Statement B:
Others say: Only a truly united Europe can protect its states' national, historical, and cultural identities and their national economic interests from the challenges of the superpowers.

Which statement is closest to your own opinion, the first or the second? Please use the scale listed. "1" would mean that you agree completely with A, and "7" would mean that you agree completely with B. The numbers in between allow you to show where your own opinion falls, if you would place yourself somewhere in between.

1 Agree completely with statement A
2
3
4
5
6
7 Agree completely with statement B
9 Don't know, N.A.

V 375   Educational Level
(see Nation-Specific Codes in ICPSR codebook)

CONSTRUCTED VARIABLES

V 376   Weight Variable

This weight factor compensates for various features of sampling in given countries to make the samples replicate the national population parameters more closely. For example, the 1981 surveys in Western Europe, the United States, Canada, and Mexico oversampled (by approximately 50 percent) the youngest group aged 16–24. These respondents receive proportionately less weight in this variable. The samples from China, India, and Nigeria undersample the illiterate and rural portions of the public and oversample the more educated and urban portions; the weight variable is designed to correct for this problem by giving greater weight to the less educated. Both the 1981 and 1990 South African samples were stratified by race, interviewing approximately as many whites as Blacks; the weight variable corrects for this. This variable also corrects for obvious deviations from national population parameters in age and education in other countries. In most cases, the more highly educated are oversampled and are accordingly weighted less heavily than the less educated. In the 1990 Italian sample, however, the more educated are substantially undersampled and are weighted more heavily to compensate for it.

Finally, the 1990 Spanish sample has a much larger N than most other samples, which would give it disproportionate importance in any analysis involving pooled samples; it is down-weighted. Similarly, this study includes many small countries, and their combined Ns would far outweigh the results from the larger countries: unweighted, the Nordic countries plus the Baltic countries would outweigh India, China, the United States, and Russia. This weight factor gives greater weight to the more populous countries than to the less populous ones, so that pooled analyses (which are often convenient) more closely approximate global reality. The weighted N of the combined 67 surveys assembled here is 89,672, as compared with the unweighted N of 89,909.

REFERENCES

Aberbach, Joel D., Robert D. Putnam, and Bert A. Rockman. 1981. *Bureaucrats and Politicians in Western Democracies*. Cambridge, Mass.: Harvard University Press.

Abrams, Mark, et al. 1985. *Values and Social Change in Britain*. London: Macmillan.

Abramson, Paul R. 1979. "Developing Party Identification: A Further Examination of Life-cycle, Generational and Period Effects." *American Journal of Political Science* 23:78–96.

Abramson, Paul R., John H. Aldrich, and David W. Rohde. 1986. *Change and Continuity in the 1984 Elections*. Washington, D.C.: C. Q. Press.

———. 1994. *Change and Continuity in the 1992 Elections*. Washington: C. Q. Press.

Abramson, Paul R., and Ronald Inglehart. 1986. "Generational Replacement and Value Change in Six West European Societies." *American Journal of Political Science* 30:1–25.

———. 1987. "Generational Replacement and the Future of Post-Materialist Values." *Journal of Politics* 49:231–41.

———. 1992. "Generational Replacement and Value Change in Eight West European Societies." *British Journal of Political Science* 22:183–228.

———. 1994. "Education, Security, and Postmaterialism." *American Journal of Political Science* 38 (3): 797–814.

———. 1995. *Value Change in Global Perspective*. Ann Arbor: University of Michigan Press.

Achen, Christopher. 1985. "Proxy Variables and Incorrect Signs on Regression Coefficients." *Political Methodology* 11:299–316.

Adorno, Theodor W., et al. 1950. *The Authoritarian Personality*. New York: Harper.

Ajzen, Icek, and Martin Fishbein. 1974. "Factors Influencing Intentions and the Intention-behavior Relation." *Human Relations* 27:1–15.

Albala-Bertrand, Luis. 1992. *Democratic Culture and Governance: Latin America on the Threshold of the Third Millennium*. Paris: UNESCO/Hispanamerica.

Alford, Robert R. 1963. *Party and Society: The Anglo-American Democracies*. Chicago: Rand McNally.

Almond, Gabriel. 1983. "Communism and Political Culture Theory." *Comparative Politics* 13 (1): 127–38.

Almond, Gabriel, and Sidney Verba. 1963. *The Civic Culture: Political Attitudes and Democracy in Five Nations*. Princeton: Princeton University Press.

Almond, Gabriel, and Sidney Verba (eds.). 1990. *The Civic Culture Revisited*. Boston: Little, Brown.

Altemeyer, Bob. 1981. *Right-Wing Authoritarianism*. Winnepeg: University of Manitoba Press.

———. 1988. *Enemies of Freedom*. San Francisco: Jossey-Bass.

Alwin, Duane F. 1986. "Religion and Parental Child-Rearing Orientations: Evidence of A Catholic-Protestant Convergence." *American Journal of Sociology* 92:412–40.

Andrews, Frank (ed.). 1986. *Research on the Quality of Life*. Ann Arbor: ISR.

Andrews, Frank, and Stephen Withey. 1976. *Social Indicators of Well-Being in America*. New York: Plenum.

Arat, Zehra F. 1988. "Democracy and Economic Development: Modernization Theory Revisited." *Comparative Politics* 21:21–36.

Ashford, Sheena, and Noel Timms. 1992. *What Europe Thinks: A Study of Western European Values*. Aldershot: Dartmouth.

Auletta, Ken. 1982. *The Underclass*. New York: Random House.

Axelrod, Robert. 1984. *The Evolution of Cooperation*. New York: Basic Books.

Bahry, Donna. 1987. "Politics, Generations and Change in the USSR." In James R. Millar (ed.), *Politics, Work and Daily Life in the USSR*. Cambridge: Cambridge University Press.

Baker, Kendall L., Russell Dalton, and Kai Hildebrandt. 1981. *Germany Transformed*. Cambridge: Harvard University Press.

Banfield, Edward. 1958. *The Moral Basis of a Backward Society*. Chicago: Free Press.

Barnes, Samuel, et al. 1979. *Political Action*. Beverly Hills: Sage.

Barro, Robert. 1990. "Government Spending in a Simple Model of Endogenous Growth." *Journal of Political Economy*. 98:103–25.

———. 1991. "Economic Growth in a Cross Section of Countries." *Quarterly Journal of Economic Growth* 106:407–44.

Barton, Paul E. 1992. *America's Smallest School: The Family*. Princeton: Educational Testing Service.

Basanez, Miguel. 1993. "Protestant and Catholic Ethics: An Empirical Comparison." Paper presented at conference on "Changing Social and Political Values: A Global Perspective," Complutense University, Madrid, September 27–October 1.

Basanez, Miguel, Ronald Inglehart, and Alejandro Moreno. 1997. *Human Beliefs and Values: A Cross-Cultural Sourcebook*. Ann Arbor: University of Michigan Press.

Baudrillard, Jean. 1973. *Le miroir de la production*. Tournai: Castermans.

———. 1974. *La société de consommation: ses mythes, ses structures*. Paris: Gallimard.

———. 1983. *Simulations*. New York: Semiotext.

Bean, Clive, and Elim Papadakis. 1994. "Polarized Priorities or Flexible Alternatives? Dimensionality in Inglehart's Materialism-Postmaterialism Scale." *International Journal of Public Opinion Research* 6 (9): 264–88.

Beardsley, Richard K., John W. Hall, and Robert E. Ward. 1959. *Village Japan*. Chicago: University of Chicago Press.

Beck, Ulrich. 1992. *Risk Society: Towards a New Modernity*. London: Sage.

Beck, E. M., James L. Massey, and Stewart E. Tolnay. 1989. "Black Lynchings: The Power Threat Hypothesis." *Social Forces* 67:605–23.

Bell, Daniel. 1973. *The Coming of Postindustrial Society*. New York: Basic Books.

———. 1976. *The Cultural Contradictions of Capitalism*. New York: Basic Books.

Bennulf, Martin, and Soren Holmberg. 1990. "The Green Breakthrough in Sweden." *Scandinavian Political Studies* 13 (2): 165–84.

Bentler, Peter M. 1990. "Comparative Fit Indices in Structural Models." *Psychological Bulletin* 107:238–46.

Betz, Hans-Georg. 1990. "Value Change in Postmaterialist Politics: The Case of West Germany." *Comparative Political Studies* 23:239–56.

Block, J. 1981. "Some Enduring and Consequential Structures of Personality." In Albert I. Rabin et al. (eds.), *Further Explorations in Personality*, pp. 27–43. New York: Wiley-Interscience.

Böltken, Ferdinand, and Wolfgang Jagodzinski. 1985. "In an Environment of Insecurity: Postmaterialism in the European Community, 1970 to 1980." *Comparative Political Studies* 17:453–84.

Bollen, Kenneth A. 1979. "Political Democracy and the Timing of Development." *American Sociological Review* 44:572–87.

———. 1980. "Issues in the Comparative Measurement of Political Democracy." *American Sociological Review* 45:370–90.

———. 1993. "Liberal Democracy: Validity and Source Biases in Cross-National Measures." *American Journal of Political Science* 37:1207–30.

Bollen, Kenneth A., and Robert Jackman. 1985. "Political Democracy and the Size Distribution of Income." *American Sociological Review* 48:468–79.

Boudon, Raymond. 1973. *Education, Opportunity, and Social Inequality: Changing Prospects in Western Society*. New York: Wiley.

Boynton, Robert, and Gerhard Loewenberg. 1973. "The Development of Public Support for Parliament in Germany." *British Journal of Political Science* 3:169–89.

Brim, Orville G., and Jerome Kagan (eds.). 1980. *Constancy and Change in Human Development*. Cambridge, Mass.: Harvard University Press.

Brunk, Gregory G., Gregory A. Caldeira, and Michael S. Lewis-Beck. 1987. "Capitalism, Socialism and Democracy: An Empirical Inquiry." *European Journal of Political Research* 15:459–70.

Brzezinski, Zbigniew. 1989. *The Grand Failure: The Birth and Death of Communism in the Twentieth Century*. New York: Scribner's.

Bürklin, Wilhelm, Markus Klein, and Achim Russ, 1994. "Dimensionen des Wertewandels: Eine empirische Längsschnittanalyse zur Dimensionalität und der Wandlungsdynamik gesellschaftlicher Wertorientierungen." *Politische Vierteljahresschrift* 35 (4): 579–606.

Burkhart, Ross E., and Michael S. Lewis-Beck. 1994. "Comparative Democracy: The Economic Development Thesis." *American Political Science Review* 88:903–10.

Campbell, Angus, Phillip E. Converse, and Willard Rodgers. 1976. *The Quality of Life*. New York: Russell Sage.

Cardoso, Fernando Henrique, and Enzo Faletto. 1971 (English translation, 1979). *Dependency and Development in Latin America*. Berkeley: University of California Press.

Carkoglu, Ali, and Sean Blinn. 1994. "Issue Dimension Volatility in Election Manifestoes: The Post-Materialist Revolution, Party Competition and Electoral Change in Post-war Democracies." Paper presented at the 1994 annual meeting of the Midwest Political Science Association, Chicago.

Cernea, Michael M. 1993. "Culture and Organization: The Social Sustainability of Induced Development." *Sustainable Development* 1 (2): 18–29.

Chatfield, C. 1989. *The Analysis of Time Series: An Introduction*. London: Chapman and Hall.

Chen, E. Y. K. 1979. *Hyper-growth in Asian Economies*. New York: Holmes and Meier.

Clark, Terry N. 1995. "Who Cares if Social Class Is Dying or Not?" Paper presented at conference on social class at Nuffield College, Oxford, February 1995. Research report no. 353.

Clark, Terry N., Seymour M. Lipset, and Mike Rempel. 1993. "The Declining Political Significance of Social Class." *International Sociology* 8 (3): 293–316.

Clarke, Harold D., and Nitish Dutt. 1991. "Measuring Value Change in Western Industrialized Societies: The Impact of Unemployment." *American Political Science Review* 85:905–20.

Cole, Harold, George Malaith, and Andrew Postlewaite. 1992. "Social Norms, Saving Behavior and Growth." *Journal of Political Economy* 100:1092–1125.

Conradt, David P. 1993. *The German Polity.* 5th ed. New York: Longmans.

Costa, Paul T., Jr., and Robert McCrae. 1980. "Still Stable after All These Years: Personality as a Key to Some Issues in Adulthood and Old Age." In Paul B. Baltes and Orville G. Brim (eds.), *Life-Span Development and Behavior*, vol. 3, pp. 65–102. New York: Academic Press.

Crepaz, Markus. 1990. "The Impact of Party Polarization and Postmaterialism on Voter Turnout—A Comparative Study of 16 Industrial Democracies." *European Journal of Political Research* 18:183–205.

Cusack, Thomas. 1991. "The Changing Contours of Government." Discussion paper, Berlin Science Center.

Dahl, Robert A. 1971. *Polyarchy: Participation and Opposition.* New Haven: Yale University Press.

Dalton, Russell J. 1977. "Was There a Revolution? A Note on Generational versus Life Cycle Explanations of Value Differences." *Comparative Political Studies* 9:459–75.

———. 1991a. "The Dynamics of Party System Change." In Karlheinz Reif and Ronald Inglehart(eds.), *Eurobarometer: The Dynamics of European Public Opinion*, pp. 215–52. New York: St. Martin's.

———. 1991b. "Responsiveness of Parties and Party Systems to the New Politics." In Hans-Dieter Klingemann, Richard Stöss, and Bernhard Wessels (eds.), *Politische Klasse und politische Institutionen*, pp. 145–71. Opladen/Wiesbaden: Westdeutscher Verlag.

———. 1993. *Politics in Germany.* 2d ed. New York: Harper Collins.

Dalton, Russell J., Scott C. Flanagan, and Paul Allen Beck (eds). 1984. *Electoral Change in Advanced Industrial Democracies: Realignment or Dealignment?* Princeton: Princeton University Press.

Davis, James A. 1996. Review essay on Paul R. Abramson and Ronald Inglehart, *Value Change in Global Perspective. Public Opinion Quarterly* 60 (summer): 322–31.

Dawkins, Richard. 1989. *The Selfish Gene.* Revised edition. Oxford: Oxford University Press.

De Graaf, Nan Dirk. 1988. *Postmaterialism and the Stratification Process.* Utrecht: Interdisplinair Sociaal wetenschappelijk Onderzoeksinstitut.

Derrida, Jacques. 1976. *Of Grammatology.* Baltimore: Johns Hopkins University Press.

———. 1979. *Spurs: Nietzsche's Styles.* Chicago: University of Chicago Press.

———. 1981. *Positions.* Chicago: University of Chicago Press.

Deutsch, Karl W. 1964. "Social Mobilization and Political Development." *American Political Science Review* 55:493–514.

Diamond, Jared. 1993. "The Diffusion of Language Groups in Africa." *Discover* 14:53–62.

Diamond, Larry, Juan J. Linz, and Seymour M. Lipset (eds.). 1989. *Democracy in Developing Countries*: vol. 2, *Africa*, vol. 3, *Asia*, vol. 4, *Latin America*. Boulder, Colo.: Lynne Rienner.

Diez Nicolas, Juan. 1994. "Postmaterialismo y desarollo economico en Espana." In Juan Diez-Nicolas and Ronald Inglehart (eds.), *Tendencias Mundiales de Cambio en los Valores Sociales y Politicos: Una Perspectiva Global*, pp. 125–56. Madrid: Fundesco.

Di Palma, Giuseppe. 1990. *To Craft Democracies: An Essay on Democratic Transitions.* Berkeley: University of California Press.

Dollar, David. 1992. "Outward-oriented Developing Economies Really Do Grow More

Rapidly: Evidence from 95 LDCs, 1976–1985." *Economic Development and Cultural Change*. 13 (79): 523–44.

Duch, Raymond M. 1996. Review of Paul R. Abramson and Ronald Inglehart, *Value Change in Global Perspective*. *American Political Science Review* 90:665–67.

Duch, Raymond M., and Michael A. Taylor. 1993. "Postmaterialism and the Economic Condition." *American Journal of Political Science* 37:747–89.

Duncan, Otis Dudley. 1968. "Social Stratification and Mobility: Problems in the Measurement of a Trend." In Eleanor B. Sheldon and Wilbert E. Moore (eds.), *Indicators of Social Change: Concepts and Measurement*, pp. 341–73. New York: Russell Sage.

Duvall, Raymond, Steven Jackson, Bruce M. Russett, Duncan Snidal, and David Sylvan. 1981. "A Formal Model of 'Dependencia Theory:' Structure and Measurement." In Richard L. Merritt and Bruce M. Russett (eds.), *From National Development to Global Community*, pp. 215–61. London: Allen and Unwin.

Easton, David. 1963. *The Political System*. New York: Wiley.

Eckstein, Harry. 1961. *A Theory of Stable Democracy*. Princeton: Princeton University Press.

———. 1988. "A Culturalist Theory of Political Change." *American Political Science Review* 82:789–804.

Elster, Jon. 1982. "Marxism, Functionalism and Game Theory: The Case for Methodological Individualism." *Theory and Society* 11:453–82.

Erikson, Erik H. 1982. *The Life Cycle Completed: A Review*. New York: Norton.

Esman, Milton J., and Norman T. Uphoff. 1984. *Local Organizations: Intermediaries in Rural Development*. Ithaca: Cornell University Press.

Ester, Peter, Loek Halman, and Ruud de Moor. 1993. *The Individualizing Society: Value Change in Europe and North America*. Tilburg: Tilburg University Press.

Fershtman, Chaim, and Yoram Weiss. 1993. "Social Status, Culture and Economic Performance." *Economic Journal* 103:946–59.

Fishbein, Martin, and Icek Ajzen. 1975. *Belief, Attitude, Intention and Behavior*. Reading, Mass.: Addison-Wesley.

Flanagan, Scott. 1982. "Changing Values in Advanced Industrial Societies." *Comparative Political Studies* 14:403–44.

———. 1987. "Changing Values in Advanced Industrial Society Revisited: Towards a Resolution of the Values Debate." *American Political Science Review* 81:1303–19.

Foucault, Michel. 1965 [1961]. *Madness and Civilization*. Translated by Richard Howard. New York: Pantheon.

———. 1972. *The Archaeology of Knowledge*. Translated by A. M. Sheridan Smith. New York: Pantheon.

———. 1977 [1975]. *Discipline and Punish*. Translated by Alan Sheridan. New York: Vintage.

———. 1978. *The History of Sexuality*. Translated by Robert Hurley. New York: Pantheon.

Ganzeboom, Harry B. G., and Henk Flap (eds.). 1989. *New Social Movements and Value Change: Theoretical Developments and Empirical Analyses*. Amsterdam: SISWO.

Gibson, James L., and Raymond M. Duch. 1992. "The Origins of a Democratic Culture in the Soviet Union: The Acquisition of Democratic Values." Paper presented at the 1992 annual meeting of the Midwest Political Science Association, Chicago.

————. 1994. "Postmaterialism and the Emerging Soviet Democracy." *Political Research Quarterly* 47 (1): 5–39.

Glenn, Norval D. 1976. "Cohort Analysis' Futile Quest: Statistical Attempts to Separate Age, Period and Cohort Effects." *American Sociological Review* 41:900–904.

————. 1977. *Cohort Analysis*. Beverly Hills, Calif.: Sage.

————. 1987. "Social Trends in the United States: Evidence from Sample Surveys." *Public Opinion Quarterly* 51:109–26.

Gonick, Lev S., and Robert M. Rosh. 1988. "The Structural Constraints of the World-Economy on National Political Development." *Comparative Political Studies* 21:171–99.

Gouldner, Alvin. 1979. *The Future of the Intellectuals and the Rise of the New Class*. New York: Seabury.

Granato, James, Ronald Inglehart, and David Leblang. 1996a. "The Effect of Cultural Values on Economic Development: Theory, Hypotheses and Some Empirical Tests." *American Journal of Political Science* 40 (3): 607–31.

————. 1996b. "Cultural Values, Stable Democracy and Economic Development: A Reply." *American Journal of Political Science* 40 (3): 680–96.

Granato, James, and Motoshi Suzuki. 1995. "The Use of the Encompassing Principle to Resolve Empirical Controversies in Voting Behavior: An Application to Voter Rationality in Congressional Elections." Typescript.

Greenstein, Fred I. 1969. *Personality and Politics*. Chicago: Markham.

Gubert, Renzo (ed.). 1992. *Persitenze e mutamenti dei Valori degli Italinan nel Contesto Europea*. Trento: Reverdito Edizioni.

Habermas, Jürgen. 1975. *Legitimation Crisis*. Boston: Beacon Press.

————. 1979. Einleitung. In *Stichworte zur "Geistigen Situation der Zeit,"* edited by Jürgen Habermas. Frankfurt: Suhrkamp.

————. 1980. "The Hermeneutic Claim to Universality." In Josef Bleicher (ed.), *Contemporary Hermeneutics*, pp. 114–53. London: Routledge and Kegan Paul.

————. 1984. *The Theory of Communicative Action*. Vol. 1. Boston: Beacon Press.

————. 1987a. *The Philosophical Discourse of Modernity*. Cambridge, Mass.: MIT Press.

————. 1987b. *The Theory of Communicative Action*. Vol. 2. Boston: Beacon Press.

Halman, Loek, Felix Heunk, Rund de Moor, and Harry Zanders. 1987. *Traditie, Secularisatie en Individualisering*. Tilburg: University of Tilburg Press.

Hamilton, David L. 1981. "Stereotyping and Intergroup Behavior: Some Thoughts on the Intergroup Approach." In David L. Hamilton (ed.), *Cognitive Processes in Stereotyping and Intergroup Behavior*, pp. 333–54. Hillsdale, N.J.: Erlbaum.

Harrison, Lawrence E. 1992. *Who Prospers? How Cultural Values Shape Economic and Political Success*. New York: Basic Books.

Heidegger, Martin. 1949. "Über den Humanismus." Frankfurt: Klostermann.

Hein, Simon. 1992. "Trade Strategy and the Dependency Hypothesis: A Comparison of Policy, Foreign Investment and Economic Growth in Latin America and East Asia." *Economic Development and Cultural Change* 13 (79): 495–521.

Hellevik, Ottar. 1993. "Postmaterialism as a Dimension of Cultural Change." *International Journal of Public Opinion Research* 5:211–33.

————. 1994. "Measuring Cultural Orientation: Ranking vs. Rating." *International Journal of Public Opinion Research* 6 (9): 292–95.

Helliwell, John F. 1994. "Empirical Linkages between Democracy and Economic Growth." *British Journal of Political Science* 24:175–98.

Hendry, David, and Jean-François Richard. 1989. "Recent Developments in the Theory of Encompassing." In Bernard Cornet and Henry Tulkens (eds.), *Contributions to Operations Research and Econometrics*, pp. 329–50. Cambridge, Mass.: MIT Press.

Herz. Thomas. 1979. "Der Wandel von Wertvorstellungen in westlichen Industriegesellschaften." *Kölner Zeitschrift für Soziologie und Sozialpsycholoie* 31:282–302.

Hibbs, Douglas A., Douglas Rivers, and Nicholas Vasilatos. 1982. "The Dynamics of Political Support for American Presidents among Occupational and Partisan Groups." *American Journal of Political Science* 26:312–32.

Hirsch, Robert. 1976. *The Social Limits to Growth*. Cambridge, Mass.: Harvard University Press.

Hoffmann-Martinot, Vincent. 1991. "Gruene and Verts: Two Faces of European Ecologism." *West European Politics* 14 (4): 70–95.

Horkheimer, Max, and Theodor W. Adorno. 1972 [1947]. *Dialectic of Enlightenment*. Translated by John Cumming. New York: Seabury.

Hout, Michael, Clem Brooks, and Jeff Manza. 1993. "The Persistence of Classes in Post-Industrial Societies." *International Sociology* 8 (3): 259–77.

Hout, Michael, and Andrew M. Greeley. 1987. "The Center Doesn't Hold: Church Attendance in the United States, 1940–1984." *American Sociology Review* 52 (June): 325–45.

Huber, John. 1989. "Values and Partisanship in Left-Right Orientations: Measuring Ideology." *European Journal of Political Research* 17:599–621.

Huber, John, and Ronald Inglehart. 1995. "Expert Interpretations of Party Space and Party Locations in 42 Societies." *Party Politics* 1 (1): 73–112.

Huntington, Samuel P. 1984. "Will More Countries Become Democratic?" *Political Science Quarterly* 99:193–218.

———. 1991. *The Third Wave: Democratization in the Twentieth Century*. Norman, Okla.: University of Oklahoma Press.

———. 1994. "The Clash of Civilizations?" *Foreign Affairs* 72 (3): 22–49.

Huxley, Aldous L. 1932. *Brave New World*. London.

Hyman, Herbert H. 1972. *Secondary Analysis of Sample Surveys: Principles, Procedures, and Potentialities*. New York: Wiley.

Hyman, Herbert H., and Paul B. Sheatsley. 1954. "'The Authoritarian Personality': A Methodological Critique." In Richard Christie and Marie Jahoda (eds.), *Studies in the Scope and Method of the Authoritarian Personality*, pp. 50–122. Glencoe: Free Press.

Inglehart, Marita R. 1991. *Reactions to Critical Life Events: A Social Psychological Analysis*. New York: Praeger.

Inglehart, Ronald. 1970. "The New Europeans: Inward or Outward Looking?" *International Organization* 24 (1): 129–39.

———. 1971. "The Silent Revolution in Europe." *American Political Science Review* 4:991–1017.

———. 1976. "Changing Values and Attitudes toward Military Service among the American Public." In Nancy Goldman and David Segal (eds.), *The Social Psychology of Military Service*. Beverly Hills: Sage.

———. 1977. *The Silent Revolution: Changing Values and Political Styles*. Princeton: Princeton University Press.

———. 1979. "Value Priorities and Socioeconomic Change." In Samuel Barnes et al. (eds.), *Political Action: Mass Participation in Five Western Democracies*, pp. 305–42. Beverly Hills: Sage.

————. 1981. "Post-Materialism in an Environment of Insecurity." *American Political Science Review* 75:880–900.

————. 1985a. "Aggregate Stability and Individual-Level Flux in Mass Belief Systems: The Level of Analysis Paradox." *American Political Science Review* 79:97–116.

————. 1985b. "New Perspectives on Value Change." *Comparative Political Studies* 17:485–532.

————. 1988. "The Renaissance of Political Culture." *American Political Science Review* 82 (4): 1203–30.

————. 1990. *Culture Shift in Advanced Industrial Society*. Princeton: Princeton University Press.

————. 1994. "Polarized Priorities or Flexible Alternatives? A Comment." *International Journal of Public Opinion Research* 6 (9): 289–92.

————. 1995. "Public Support for Environmental Protection: The Impact of Objective Problems and Subjective Values in 43 Societies." *PS: Political Science and Politics* (March): 57–71.

Inglehart, Ronald, and Paul Abramson. 1992a. "Generational Replacement and Value Change in Eight West European Societies." *British Journal of Political Science* (April): 183–228.

————. 1992b. "Value Change in Advanced Industrial Society: Problems in Conceptualization and Measurement." Paper presented at the annual meeting of the Western Political Science Association, San Francisco.

————. 1993. "Values and Value Change on Five Continents." Paper presented at 1993 annual meeting of the American Political Science Association, Washington, D.C.

————. 1994. "Economic Security and Value Change." *American Political Science Review* 88:336–54.

Inglehart, Ronald, and Hans-Dieter Klingemann. 1996. "Dimensionen des Wertewandels: Eine Replik." *Politische Vierteljahresschrift* 33 (June): 319–40.

Inglehart, Ronald, Neil Nevitte, and Miguel Basanez. 1996. *The North American Trajectory: Social Institutions and Social Change*. Hawthorne, N.Y: Aldine de Gruyter.

Inglehart, Ronald, and Renata Siemienska. 1988. "Political Values and Dissatisfaction in Poland and the West: A Comparative Analysis." *Government and Opposition* 23 (2): 440–57.

Inkeles, Alex, and Raymond Bauer. 1968. *The Soviet Citizen: Daily Life in a Totalitarian Society*. New York: Atheneum.

Inkeles, Alex, and Larry Diamond. 1980. "Personal Qualities as a Reflection of National Development." In Frank Andrews and Alexander Szalai (eds.), *Comparative Studies in Quality of Life*, pp. 91–109. London: Sage.

Inkeles, Alex, and David Smith. 1974. *Becoming Modern: Individual Change in Six Developing Countries*. Cambridge, Mass.: Harvard University Press.

Jackman, Robert W. 1973. "On the Relationship of Economic Development to Political Performance." *American Journal of Political Science* 36:611–21.

————. 1987. "The Politics of Economic Growth in Industrial Democracies, 1974–1980." *Journal of Politics* 49:242–56.

Jackman, Robert W., and Ross A. Miller. 1996a. "The Poverty of Political Culture." *American Journal of Political Science* 40 (3): 697–716.

————. 1996b. "A Renaissance of Political Culture?" *American Journal of Political Science* 40 (3): 632–59.

Jackson, David, and Duane Alwin. 1980. "The Factor Analysis of Ipsative Measures." *Sociological Methods and Research* 9:218–38.

Jackson, James S., and Marita R. Inglehart. 1996. "Reverberation Theory: Stress and Racism in Hierarchically Structured Communities." In S. E. Hobfoll and M. de Vries (eds.), *Stress in Communities: Moving beyond the Individual*. Norwell, Mass.: Kluwer (forthcoming).

Jaeggi, Urs. 1979. "Drinnen und Draussen." In Jürgen Habermas (ed.), *Stichworte zur "Geistigen Situation der Zeit,"* pp. 443–73. Frankfurt: Suhrkamp.

Jennings, M. Kent, and Gregory Markus. 1984. "Partisan Orientations over the Long Haul: Results from the Three-wave Socialization Panel." *American Political Science Review* 78:1000–1018.

Jennings, M. Kent, and Richard G. Niemi. 1981. *Generations and Politics*. Princeton: Princeton University Press.

Kaase, Max, and Kenneth Newton. 1995. *Beliefs in Government*. Oxford: Oxford University Press.

Kesselman, Mark. 1979. Review of Ronald Inglehart, *The Silent Revolution*. *American Political Science Review* 73:284–86.

Kinder, Donald, and D. Roderick Kiewiet. 1979. "Sociotropic Politics: The American Case." *British Journal of Political Science* 11:129–61.

Kitschelt, Herbert. 1994. *The Transformation of European Social Democracy*. New York: Cambridge University Press.

———. 1995. *The Radical Right in Western Europe: A Comparative Analysis*. Ann Arbor: University of Michigan Press.

Kitschelt, Herbert, and Staf Hellemans. 1990. "The Left-Right Semantics and the New Politics Cleavage." *Comparative Political Studies* 23 (2): 210–38.

Klages, Helmut. 1988. *Wertdynamik: Über die Wandelbarkeit des Selbstverständlichen*. Osnabrück (Texte und Thesen: 212).

———. 1992. "Die gegenwärtige Situation der Wert- und Wertwandelforschung—Probleme und Perspektiven." In Helmut Klages, Hans Jürgen Hippler, and Willi Herbert (eds.), *Werte und Wandel: Ergebnisse und Methoden eniner Forschungstradition*, pp. 5–39. Frankfurt: Campus Verlag.

Klandermans, P. Bert. 1990. "Linking the 'Old' and 'New': Movement Networks in the Netherlands." In Russell J. Dalton and Manfred Kuechler (eds.), *Challenging the Political Order: New Social and Political Movements in Western Democracies*. New York: Oxford University Press.

Klingemann, Hans-Dieter, Richard Hofferbert, and Ian Budge. 1994. *Parties, Policies and Democracy*. Boulder: Westview Press.

Knutsen, Oddbjorn. 1989. "Cleavage Dimensions in Ten West European Countries: A Comparative Empirical Analysis." *Comparative Political Studies* 21 (4): 495–534.

———. 1995. "Party Choice." In Jan W. van Deth and Elinor Scarbrough (eds.), *The Impact of Values*, pp. 461–91. Oxford: Oxford University Press.

Kolb, Eberhard. 1988. *The Weimar Republic*. Trans. P. S. Falla. London: Unwin Hyman.

Kramer, Gerald H. 1971. "Short-Term Fluctuations in U.S. Voting Behavior, 1896–1964." *American Political Science Review* 65:131–43.

Kraus, Stephen J. 1995. "Attitudes and the Prediction of Behavior: A Meta-Analysis of the Empirical Literature." *Personality and Social Psychology Bulletin* 21 (1): 58–75.

Kriesi, Hanspeter. 1989. "New Social Movements and the New Class in the Netherlands." *American Journal of Sociology* 94 (5): 1078–1116.

Kuhn, Thomas. 1962. *The Structure of Scientific Revolutions*. Chicago: University of Chicago Press.

Ladd, Everett C., Jr. 1978. "The New Lines Are Drawn: Class and Ideology in America." *Public Opinion* 1:48–53.

Landell-Mills, Pierre. 1992. "Governance, Cultural Change and Empowerment." *Journal of Modern African Studies* 30 (4): 543–67.

Lane, Robert. 1965. "The Politics of Consensus in an Age of Affluence." *American Political Science Review* 59 (4): 874–95.

LaPiere, R. T. 1934. "Attitudes versus Actions." *Social Forces* 13:230–37.

Leamer, Edward. 1983. "Let's Take the 'Con' out of Econometrics." *American Economic Review* 73:31–43.

Lenski, Gerhard. 1963. *The Religious Factor*. New York: Anchor-Doubleday.

Lerner, Daniel. 1958. *The Passing of Traditional Society: Modernizing the Middle East*. New York: Free Press.

Lesthaeghe, Ron, and Dominique Meekers. 1986. "Value Changes and the Dimensions of Familism in the European Community." *European Journal of Population* 2:225–68.

Levine, Ross, and David Renelt. 1992. "A Sensitivity Analysis of Cross-Country Growth Regressions." *American Economic Review* 82 (4): 942–63.

Levinson, Daniel J., et al. 1979. *The Seasons of a Man's Life*. New York: Knopf.

Lewis-Beck, Michael. 1986. "Comparative Economic Voting: Britain, France, Germany and Italy." *American Journal of Political Science* 30:315–46.

Lijphart, Arend. 1979. "Religious vs. Linguistic vs. Class Voting." *American Political Science Review* 73:4442–58.

———. 1991. "Political Parties." In David Butler (ed.), *Democracy at the Polls*, pp. 214–47. Washington, D.C.: American Enterprise Institute.

Lindblom, Charles. 1977. *Politics and Markets: The World's Political-Economic Systems*. New York: Basic Books.

Lipset, Seymour Martin. 1959. "Social Requisites of Democracy: Economic Development and Political Legitimacy." *American Political Science Review* 53:69–105.

———. 1960. *Political Man*. New York: Doubleday.

———. 1979. "The New Class and the Professoriate." In B. Bruce-Briggs (ed.), *The New Class?* pp. 67–68. New Brunswick: Transaction Books.

———. 1981. *Political Man: The Social Bases of Politics*. Expanded ed. Baltimore: Johns Hopkins University Press.

Lipset, Seymour Martin, Martin Trow, and James S. Coleman. 1956. *Union Democracy*. Glencoe, Ill.: Free Press.

Lucas, Robert. 1988. "On the Mechanics of Economic Development." *Journal of Monetary Economics* 21:3–32.

Lyon, David. 1994. *Postmodernity*. Minneapolis: University of Minnesota Press.

Lyotard, Jean-François. 1984 [1979]. *The Postmodern Condition: A Report on Knowledge*. Translated by Geoff Bennington and Brian Massumi. Minneapolis: University of Minnesota Press.

Manabe, Kazufumi. 1995. "People's Attitudes toward Technology and Environment in China." (In Japanese). *Kwansei Gakuin University Annual Studies* (forthcoming).

Mankiw, Gregory, David Romer, and David Weil. 1992. "A Contribution to the Empirics of Economic Growth." *Quarterly Journal of Economics* 152:407–37.

Markus, Gregory B. 1988. "The Impact of Personal and National Conditions on the Presidential Vote: A Pooled Cross-Sectional Analysis." *American Journal of Political Science* 32:137–54.

Maslow, Abraham K. 1954. *Motivation and Personality*. New York: Harper and Row.

McLanahan, Sara, and Irwin Garfinkel. 1986. *Single Mothers and Their Chidren: A New American Dilemma*. Washington, D.C.: Urban Institute Press.

McLanahan, Sara, and Gary Sandefur. 1994. *Growing up with a Single Parent: What Hurts, What Helps*. Cambridge, Mass.: Harvard University Press.

McClelland, David. 1961. *The Achieving Society*. Princeton: Van Nostrand.

McClelland, David C., et al. 1953. *The Achievement Motive*. New York: Appleton-Century-Crofts.

Meadows, Donella H., Dennis L. Meadows, Jorgen Randers, and William W. Behrens. 1972. *The Limits to Growth*. New York: Universe.

Melich, Anna (ed.). 1991. *Les Valeurs des Suisses*. Berne: Lange.

Michels, Roberto. 1962. *Political Parties: A Sociological Study of the Oligarchical Tendencies of Modern Democracy*. New York: Collier Books.

Milbrath, Lester W., and M. Goel. 1977. *Political Participation*. 2d edition. Chicago: Rand McNally.

Miller, Arthur H. 1974. "Political Issues and Trust in Government: 1964–1970." *American Political Science Review* 68 (3): 951–72.

Minkenberg, Michael. 1990. *Neokonservatismus und Neue Rechte in den USA*. Baden-Baden: Nomos Verlagsgesellschaft.

Mizon, Grayham, and Jean-François Richard. 1986. "The Encompassing Principle and Its Application to Non-nested Hypothesis Tests." *Econometrica* 54:657–78.

Moore, Barrington. 1966. *The Social Origins of Dictatorship and Democracy*. Boston: Beacon Press.

Muller, Edward N. 1988. "Democracy, Economic Development and Income Inequality." *American Sociological Review* 53:50–68.

Muller, Edward N., and Mitchell A. Seligson. 1994. "Civic Culture and Democracy: The Question of Causal Relationships." *American Political Science Review* 88 (3): 635–52.

Müller-Rommel, Ferdinand (ed.). 1990. *New Politics in Western Europe: The Rise and the Success of Green Parties and Alternative Lists*. Boulder: Westview Press.

Nie, Norman, Sidney Verba, and John Petrocik. 1979. *The Changing American Voter*. Cambridge, Mass.: Harvard University Press.

Nieuwbeerta, Paul, and Nan Dirk De Graaf. 1997. "Class Voting and the Influence of Varying Class Structures in 16 Western Countries: 1956–1990." In Geoffrey Evans (ed.), *The End of Class Politics: Class Voting in Comparative Perspective*. Oxford: Oxford University Press (forthcoming).

O'Donnell, Guillermo. 1978. "Reflections on the Pattern of Change in the Bureaucratic Authoritarian State." *Latin American Research Review* 13 (1): 3–38.

O'Donnell, Guillermo, Philippe C. Schmitter, and Laurence Whitehead (eds.). 1986. *Transitions from Authoritarian Rule: Prospects for Democracy*. Baltimore: Johns Hopkins University Press.

Offe, Claus. 1990. "Reflections on the Institutional Self-transformation of Movement Politics: A Tentative Stage Model." In Russell J. Dalton and Manfred Kuechler (eds.), *Challenging the Political Order: New Social and Political Movements in Western Democracies*, pp. 232–50. New York: Oxford University Press.

Olson, Mancur. 1982. *The Rise and Decline of Nations*. New Haven: Yale University Press.

Orizo, Francisco Andres, and Alejandro Sanchez Fernandez. *El Sistema de Valors dels Catalans*. Barcelona: Institut Catala d'Estudis Mediterranis.

Orwell, George. 1949. *1984*. Boston: Harcourt-Brace.

Ostrom, Charles W., Jr. 1990. *Time Series Analysis: Regression Techniques*. 2d edition. Newbury Park, Calif.: Sage.

Powell, G. Bingham. 1982. *Contemporary Democracies: Participation, Stability and Violence*. Cambridge, Mass.: Harvard University Press.

Przeworski, Adam, and Fernando Limongi. 1993. "Political Regimes and Economic Growth." *Journal of Economic Perspectives* 7 (3): 51–69.

Putnam, Robert D., with Robert Leonardi and Rafaella Nanetti. 1993. *Making Democracy Work: Civic Traditions in Modern Italy*. Princeton: Princeton University Press.

Pye, Lucian W. 1990. "Political Science and the Crisis of Authoritarianism." *American Political Science Review* 84 (1): 3–19.

Riffault, Helene (ed.). 1994. *Les Valeurs des Francais*. Paris: Presses Universitaires de France.

Rohrschneider, Robert. 1988. "Citizens' Attitudes toward Environmental Issues: Selfish or Selfless?" *Comparative Political Studies* 21:347–67.

———. 1990. "The Roots of Public Opinion toward New Social Movements: An Empirical Test of Competing Explanations." *American Journal of Political Science* 34 (1): 1–30.

———. 1993. "Environmental Belief Systems in Western Europe: A Hierarchical Model of Constraint." *Comparative Political Studies* 26:3–29.

Rokeach, Milton. 1968. *Beliefs, Attitudes and Values*. San Francisco: Jossey-Bass.

———. 1973. *The Nature of Human Values*. New York: Free Press.

Romer, Paul. 1986. "Increasing Returns and Long-run Growth." *Journal of Political Economy* 94:1002–37.

———. 1990. "Endogenous Technical Change." *Journal of Political Economy* 98:71–102.

Rostow, W. W. 1961. *The Stages of Economic Growth*. Cambridge: Cambridge University Press.

Rotter, Julian B. 1966. "Generalized Expectancies for Internal vs. External Control of Reinforcement." *Psychological Monographs: General and Applied* 80:591–609.

Russett, Bruce, et al. 1964. *World Handbook of Political and Social Indicators*. New Haven: Yale University Press.

Samuelson, Robert J. 1995. *The Good Life and Its Discontents*. New York: Random House.

Scarbrough, Elinor. 1995. "Materialist-Postmaterialist Value Orientations." In Jan W. van Deth and Elinor Scarbrough (eds.), *The Impact of Values*, pp. 123–59. Oxford: Oxford University Press.

Schumacher, E. F. 1973. *Small Is Beautiful: Economics as if People Mattered*. New York: Harper and Row.

Schumpeter, Joseph. 1947. *Capitalism, Socialism and Democracy*. 2d ed. New York: Harper and Brothers.

Shively, W. Phillips. 1991. Feature Review of *Culture Shift in Advanced Industrial Society*. *Journal of Politics* 53:235–38.

Silver, Brian D. 1987. "Political Beliefs of the Soviet Citizen: Sources of Support for Regime Norms." In James R. Millar (ed.), *Politics, Work, and Daily Life in the USSR:*

A Survey of Former Soviet Citizens, pp. 207–35. Cambridge: Cambridge University Press.

Skocpol, Theda. 1982. "Bringing the State Back In." *Items* 36 (1/2): 1–8. Reprinted in Roy Macridis and Bernard Brown (eds.), *Comparative Politics: Notes and Readings* (8th ed., 1996), pp. 57–65. Belmont: Wadsworth.

Sokal, Alan D. 1996. "Transgressing the Boundaries: Toward a Transformative Hermeneutics of Quantam Gravity." *Social Text* 46–47 (summer): 217–52.

Solow, Robert. 1956. "A Contribution to the Theory of Economic Growth." *Quarterly Journal of Economics* 70 (1): 65–94.

Sombart, Werner. 1913. *The Jews and Modern Capitalism*. London: Fisher, Unwin.

Statistiches Bundesamt. 1994. *Datenreport, 1994*. Bonn: Bundeszentrale für politische Bildung.

Swan, Trevor. 1956. "Economic Growth and Capital Accumulation." *Economic Record* 22:334–61.

Szekelyi, Maria, and Robert Tardos. 1993. "Attitudes That Make a Difference: Expectancies and Economic Progress." Discussion papers of the Institute for Research on Poverty, University of Wisconsin.

Tajfel, Henri. 1978. *Differentiation between Social Groups: Studies in the Social Psychology of Intergroup Relations*. London: Academic Press.

Tajfel, Henri, and J. C. Turner. 1979. "An Integrative Theory of Intergroup Conflict." In W. G. Austin and S. Worchel (eds.), *The Social Psychology of Intergroup Relations*, pp. 33–47. Monterey, Calif.: Brooks/Cole.

Tanzi, Vito, and Ludger Schuknecht. 1995 (December). "The Growth of Government and the Reform of the State in Industrial Countries." Washington, D.C.: IMF working paper.

Tawney, Richard Henry. 1955. [1922]. *The Acquisitive Society*. New York: Harcourt, Brace.

———. 1926. *Religion and the Rise of Capitalism: A History*. Gloucester, Mass.: P. Smith.

Taylor, Charles L., and David A. Jodice. 1983. *World Handbook of Political and Social Indicators*. 3d ed. New Haven: Yale University Press.

Teilhard de Chardin, Pierre. 1959. *The Phenomenon of Man*. Translated by Bernard Wall. New York: Harper and Brothers.

Thomassen, Jacques A., and Jan van Deth. 1989. "How New Is Dutch Politics?" *West European Politics* 12:61–78.

Thompson, Michael, Richard Ellis, and Aaron Wildavsky. 1990. *Cultural Theory*. Boulder: Westview Press.

Trump, Thomas M. 1991. "Value Formation and Postmaterialism: Inglehart's Theory of Value Change Reconsidered." *Comparative Political Studies* 24:365–90.

Tufte, Edward R. 1978. *Political Control of the Economy*. Princeton: Princeton University Press.

van Deth, Jan W. 1983a. "The Persistence of Materialist and Post-Materialist Value Orientations." *European Journal of Political Science* 9:407–31.

———. 1983b. "Ranking the Ratings: The Case of Materialist and Postmaterialist Value Orientations." *Political Methodology* 11: 63–79.

———. 1984. *Politieke Waarden*. Amsterdam: CT Press.

———. 1989. "Fighting a Trojan Horse: The Persistence and Change of Political Orientations." In Harry Ganzeboom and Hendrik Flap (eds.), *New Social Movements and Value Change*, pp. 89–112. Amsterdam: SISWO.

Van Deth, Jan W., and Elinor Scarbrough (eds.). 1995. *The Impact of Values*. Oxford: Oxford University Press.

Verba, Sidney, Norman H. Nie, and Jae-On Kim. 1978. *Participation and Political Equality*. Cambridge: Cambridge University Press.

Voye, Liliane, Bernadette Bawin-Legros, Jan Kerkhofs, and Karel Dobbelaere. 1992. *Belges, Hereux et Satisfaits*. Brussels: De Boeck-Wesmael.

Wallerstein, Judith, and Sanrda Blakeslee. 1989. *Second Chances: Men, Women and Children a Decade after Divorce*. New York: Ticknor and Fields.

Watanuki, Joji. 1977. *Politics in Postwar Japanese Society*. Tokyo: Tokyo University Press.

Whitehead, Barbara D. 1993. "Dan Quayle Was Right." *Atlantic Monthly* (April): 47–84.

———. 1946 [1925]. "Politics as a Vocation." In Hans H. Gerth and C. Wright Mills (eds.), *From Max Weber: Essays in Sociology*, pp. 77–128. New York: Oxford University Press.

Weber, Max. 1958 [1904–5]. *The Protestant Ethic and the Spirit of Capitalism*. New York: Scribner's.

Whitehead, Barbara Dafoe. 1993. "Dan Quayle Was Right." *Atlantic Monthly* (April): 47–84.

Wicker, Allan W. 1969. "Attitudes versus Actions: The Relationship of Verbal and Overt Behavioral Responses to Attitudinal Objects." *Journal of Social Issues* 25:41–78.

Wildavsky, Aaron. 1987. "Choosing Preferences by Constructing Institutions: A Cultural Theory of Preference Formation." *American Political Science Review* 81:3–21.

Wiley, Lawrence. 1957. *Village in the Vaucluse*. Cambridge, Mass.: Harvard University Press.

Wilson, Richard W. 1992. *Compliance Ideology: Rethinking Political Culture*. Cambridge: Cambridge University Press.

World Bank. 1993. *World Development Report, 1993*. New York: Oxford University Press.

Zaller, John, and Stanley Feldman. 1992. "A Simple Theory of the Survey Response." *American Journal of Political Science* 36:579–616.

Zulehner, Paul, and Herman Denz. 1993. *Wie Europe lebt und glaubt*. Düsseldorf: Patmos.

About the Author

RONALD INGLEHART is Professor of Political Science and Program Director at the Institute for Social Research at the University of Michigan. Among his books are *The Silent Revolution: Changing Values and Political Styles among Western Publics* and *Culture Shift in Advanced Industrial Society,* both published by Princeton University Press.